An Introduction to Macroeconomics

An Introduction to Macroeconomics

A HETERODOX APPROACH TO ECONOMIC ANALYSIS

Edited by

Louis-Philippe Rochon
Full Professor of Economics and Director, International Economic Policy Institute, Laurentian University, Sudbury, Canada

Sergio Rossi
Full Professor of Economics and Chair of Macroeconomics and Monetary Economics, University of Fribourg, Switzerland

Cheltenham, UK • Northampton, MA, USA

Published by
Edward Elgar Publishing Limited
The Lypiatts
15 Lansdown Road
Cheltenham
Glos GL50 2JA
UK

Edward Elgar Publishing, Inc.
William Pratt House
9 Dewey Court
Northampton
Massachusetts 01060
USA

A catalogue record for this book
is available from the British Library

Library of Congress Control Number: 2016931788

Printed on elemental chlorine free (ECF)
recycled paper containing 30% Post-Consumer Waste

ISBN 978 1 78254 936 9 (cased)
ISBN 978 1 78254 937 6 (paperback)
ISBN 978 1 78254 938 3 (eBook)

Typeset by Servis Filmsetting Ltd, Stockport, Cheshire
Printed and bound in the USA

Contents in brief

List of contributors   xiii

Acknowledgements   xiv

Introduction: the need for a heterodox approach to economic
analysis   1
Louis-Philippe Rochon and Sergio Rossi

**PART I   ECONOMICS, ECONOMIC ANALYSIS AND
           ECONOMIC SYSTEMS**

1   What is economics?   21
    Louis-Philippe Rochon and Sergio Rossi

2   The history of economic theories   42
    Heinrich Bortis

3   Monetary economies of production   76
    Louis-Philippe Rochon

PART II   MONEY, BANKS AND FINANCIAL ACTIVITIES

4   Money and banking   97
    Marc Lavoie and Mario Seccareccia

5   The financial system   117
    Jan Toporowski

6   The central bank and monetary policy   134
    Louis-Philippe Rochon and Sergio Rossi

**PART III   THE MACROECONOMICS OF THE SHORT AND
             LONG RUN**

7   Aggregate demand   151
    Jesper Jespersen

8   Inflation and unemployment   172
    Alvaro Cencini and Sergio Rossi

9   The role of fiscal policy   193
    Malcolm Sawyer

10 Economic growth and development   211
    Mark Setterfield

11 Wealth distribution   233
    Omar Hamouda

PART IV   INTERNATIONAL ECONOMY

12 International trade and development   259
    Robert A. Blecker

13 Balance-of-payments-constrained growth   282
    John McCombie and Nat Tharnpanich

14 European monetary union   300
    Sergio Rossi

PART V   RECENT TRENDS

15 Financialization   319
    Gerald A. Epstein

16 Imbalances and crises   336
    Robert Guttmann

17 Sustainable development   359
    Richard P.F. Holt

    Conclusion: do we need microfoundations for macroeconomics?   381
    John King

Index   399

Full contents

List of contributors   xiii

Acknowledgements   xiv

Introduction: the need for a heterodox approach to
economic analysis   1
Louis-Philippe Rochon and Sergio Rossi

PART I   ECONOMICS, ECONOMIC ANALYSIS AND
ECONOMIC SYSTEMS

1   What is economics?   21
Louis-Philippe Rochon and Sergio Rossi
    Introduction   21
    The role of ideology in economics   25
    Is economics a science?   28
    The use of models and of mathematics   30
    Economics and the social sciences   33
    What then is economics?   36
    Micro- versus macroeconomics   38
    A portrait of Adam Smith (1723–90)   41

2   The history of economic theories   42
Heinrich Bortis
    Why are these topics important?   44
    Two broad groups of economic theories   44
    The history of economics   46
    The history of political economy   54
    Neoclassical–Walrasian economics and classical–Keynesian
    political economy assessed   72
    A portrait of David Ricardo (1772–1823)   75

3   Monetary economies of production   76
Louis-Philippe Rochon
    Why are these topics important?   77
    The neoclassical/mainstream view   77

The heterodox view 80
Conclusion 90
A portrait of John Maynard Keynes (1883–1946) 93

PART II   MONEY, BANKS AND FINANCIAL ACTIVITIES

4   Money and banking 97
Marc Lavoie and Mario Seccareccia
Why are these topics important? 98
Money, banks, and their origins 98
Understanding the heterodox approach to banks
and the modern payment system from a simple
balance-sheet perspective 107
Concluding remarks 114
A portrait of Alain Parguez (1940–) 116

5   The financial system 117
Jan Toporowski
Why are these topics important? 118
Mainstream economic theory 119
What is wrong with the textbook approach? 123
The financing needs of modern capitalism 126
The economic consequences of long-term finance 128
Finance in Keynes's analysis 130
A portrait of Hyman Philip Minsky (1919–96) 133

6   The central bank and monetary policy 134
Louis-Philippe Rochon and Sergio Rossi
Why are these topics important? 135
The mainstream perspective 136
The heterodox perspective 141
A portrait of Alfred S. Eichner (1937–88) 148

PART III   THE MACROECONOMICS OF THE SHORT AND LONG RUN

7   Aggregate demand 151
Jesper Jespersen
Why are these topics important? 152
The National Accounting System: some principles
and definitions 152
From statistical concepts to macroeconomic theory 154

The neoclassical theory of aggregate demand 156

The Keynesian theory of aggregate demand and
output 159

The income multiplier 164

Expected aggregate demand and supply: effective demand 166

Demand management policies 168

A portrait of Richard Kahn (1905–89) 171

8 Inflation and unemployment 172
Alvaro Cencini and Sergio Rossi

Why are these topics important? 173

Inflation 174

Unemployment 180

Towards a monetary macroeconomic analysis of
inflation and unemployment 183

A portrait of Bernard Schmitt (1929–2014) 192

9 The role of fiscal policy 193
Malcolm Sawyer

Why are these topics important? 194

Is there a need for fiscal policy? 194

The role of automatic stabilizers 200

Functional finance and the post-Keynesian
approach to fiscal policy 201

Conclusion 207

Appendix A 208

Appendix B 209

A portrait of Michał Kalecki (1899–1970) 210

10 Economic growth and development 211
Mark Setterfield

Why are these topics important? 212

Economic growth: the statistical record 213

Supply versus demand in the determination of
long-run growth 218

What forces shape demand formation and growth
in the long run? 220

Keynesian growth theory 222

Properties of Keynesian growth theory 225

A portrait of Nicholas Kaldor (1908–86) 232

11   Wealth distribution   233
Omar Hamouda
    Why are these topics important?   234
    Some introductory remarks   235
    Mainstream economic theory of wealth distribution   236
    States of income distribution: a description   241
    Heterodox perspectives   246
    A new macroeconomics approach: stock of wealth
    and social well-being   250
    Some concluding remarks   254
    A portrait of Karl Marx (1818–83)   256

PART IV   INTERNATIONAL ECONOMY

12   International trade and development   259
Robert A. Blecker
    Why are these topics important?   260
    The orthodox approach: the theory of comparative
    advantage   261
    The heterodox alternative: imbalanced trade,
    unemployment, and absolute competitive
    advantages   267
    Long-run development and infant-industry
    protection   271
    Trade liberalization and trade agreements   273
    Manufactured exports and the fallacy of
    composition   276
    Conclusions   278
    A portrait of Joan Robinson (1903–83)   281

13   Balance-of-payments-constrained growth   282
John McCombie and Nat Tharnpanich
    Why are these topics important?   283
    The determination of the balance-of-payments
    equilibrium growth rate   284
    The Harrod foreign trade multiplier and the Hicks
    supermultiplier   286
    Price and non-price competitiveness in
    international trade   288
    The role of the growth of capital flows   290
    Resource-constrained, policy-constrained and
    balance-of-payments-constrained growth   292

Structural change and the multi-sectoral Thirlwall's Law 294
Tests of the model and empirical evidence 294
A portrait of Paul Davidson (1930–) 299

14 European monetary union 300
Sergio Rossi
Why are these topics important? 301
The mainstream perspective 301
The heterodox perspective 306
A portrait of Robert Triffin (1911–93) 315

PART V   RECENT TRENDS

15 Financialization 319
Gerald A. Epstein
Why are these topics important? 320
What is financialization? 320
How old is financialization? 322
Dimensions of financialization 322
Impacts of financialization 327
Conclusion 331
A portrait of Karl Paul Polanyi (1886–1964) 334

16 Imbalances and crises 336
Robert Guttmann
Why are these topics important? 337
The mainstream view of a self-adjusting economy 337
Overproduction versus underconsumption 338
Growth and distribution 342
Cyclical growth dynamics 343
External imbalances and adjustments 349
Concluding remarks 354
A portrait of Mikhail Tugan-Baranovsky (1865–1919) 358

17 Sustainable development 359
Richard P.F. Holt
Why are these topics important? 360
The neoclassical model of economic growth and development 361
The debate over 'strong' and 'weak' sustainability 362

Growth versus development   365
Heterodox economics and true economic
development   367
Investments for sustainable development   371
Measuring a new standard of living for sustainable
development   374
Conclusion   376
A portrait of Amartya Sen (1933–)   380

**Conclusion: do we need microfoundations for
macroeconomics?**   381
John King
Why are these topics important?   382
The mainstream perspective   383
A heterodox critique   388
Why it all matters   395
A portrait of Robert Skidelsky (1939–)   398

Index   399

Contributors

Robert A. Blecker, American University, Washington, DC, United States

Heinrich Bortis, University of Fribourg, Switzerland

Alvaro Cencini, University of Lugano, Switzerland

Gerald A. Epstein, University of Massachusetts Amherst, United States

Robert Guttmann, Hofstra University, New York, United States and CEPN–Université Paris XIII, France

Omar Hamouda, York University, Canada

Richard P.F. Holt, Southern Oregon University, Ashland, United States

Jesper Jespersen, University of Roskilde, Denmark

John King, La Trobe University, Melbourne, Australia and Federation University Australia

Marc Lavoie, University of Ottawa, Canada

John McCombie, University of Cambridge, United Kingdom

Louis-Philippe Rochon, Laurentian University, Sudbury, Canada

Sergio Rossi, University of Fribourg, Switzerland

Malcolm Sawyer, University of Leeds, United Kingdom

Mario Seccareccia, University of Ottawa, Canada

Mark Setterfield, New School for Social Research, New York and Trinity College, Connecticut, United States

Nat Tharnpanich, Trade Policy and Strategy Office, Ministry of Commerce, Thailand

Jan Toporowski, School of Oriental and African Studies, University of London, United Kingdom

Acknowledgements

The editors would like to thank all the contributors to this book for their collaboration in preparing this volume to enhance the understanding of economic analysis in a pluralistic perspective. They also wish to express their gratitude to Edward Elgar Publishing for their enthusiastic and professional support during the development of the book. Finally, they are most grateful to Amos Pesenti for his excellent research assistance, to Denise Converso–Grangier for her contribution in preparing the full typescript for the publication process, and to Dee Compson for her professional efficiency in copy-editing the whole book.

Louis-Philippe Rochon and Sergio Rossi

Introduction: the need for a heterodox approach to economic analysis

Louis-Philippe Rochon and Sergio Rossi

This textbook explains that there is an urgent need to consider a heterodox approach to economic analysis, as regards macroeconomic theory as well as policy. To be sure, the global financial and economic crisis that erupted in 2007–08 illustrates this need; this crisis is eventually a crisis of economics, since it originates in an essentially wrong approach to the working of our economic systems. Hence, it does not come as a surprise that the majority of economic policy actions taken in the aftermath of this crisis do not work as expected by their proponents. In fact, neither 'fiscal consolidation' (that is, austerity) measures nor 'quantitative easing' policies can live up to their promises, which amount to wishful thinking (to jump-start the economic engine dramatically hit by the crisis). A fundamentally different approach to economic analysis is actually necessary in order to understand and eventually solve this crisis for good.

In this introduction we provide a detailed overview of the contents of this volume, and point out its distinguishing features with respect to orthodox thinking. We thereby show that another, largely different perspective is required to avoid the fundamental flaws of orthodox economic analyses. This allows us also to point out the need for pluralism in economic research and education, because the lack of it led the economics profession astray under the neoliberal regime that has been increasingly dominating the global economy since the demise of the Bretton Woods system in the early 1970s.

The first chapter, written by the co-editors of this textbook, explains the meaning and purpose of economic analysis. In the first section, the authors present and criticize the mainstream definition of economics, which aims at the 'efficient allocation of scarce resources'. This definition includes three main concepts, each with very specific and powerful meanings in economics, namely, efficiency, allocation and scarcity. In this view, the main issue to address thereby is how to allocate a given supply of resources. The first section also briefly discusses the differences between microeconomics and macroeconomics, emphasizing how mainstream macroeconomics is crucially built on the key assumption of aggregating individuals' behaviour, that is, on microeconomic foundations. Rochon and Rossi also point out that there is no need for money to exist in mainstream models. Indeed, orthodox models explaining consumption, investment, and economic growth contain no money essentially. Money is introduced much later, as part of a discussion about the banking system, as an afterthought, or as an attempt to make these economic models appear more realistic. This is the reason why the first chapter offers an alternative interpretation of the scope and contents of economics.

First, the authors argue that macroeconomics should not be a simple aggregation of individual behaviour and microeconomic magnitudes, that there are characteristics special to macroeconomics, and that social classes (or macro-groups) play an important role in determining economic outcomes. Based on macro-groups, economic dynamics become very important in explaining consumption, investment, prices and economic growth. Further, by emphasizing groups, one can ask a different set of questions and cast these questions within the framework of political economy rather than economics, as clearly explained in Chapter 2. The first chapter shows thereby that markets are not free, but governed by laws and institutions that play a central role in any economic activity. Moreover, in casting this view with regard to social groups, the importance of power becomes paramount, notably, the power over the determination of wages, the power over access to credit, and the power of the state. Ultimately, we live in a money-using economy, so, as Schumpeter argued, money should be introduced at the beginning of the discussion of economics (Chapter 3 delves into this subject matter in more detail). That is why this textbook, in contrast to all other macroeconomics textbooks, begins with an explanation of money (Chapter 3) and the banking system and finance (Chapters 4, 5 and 6) after a survey chapter on the history of economic theories, which is required in order to understand the general framework of any economic analysis, be it theoretical or policy oriented.

Chapter 2, contributed by Heinrich Bortis, therefore presents the bigger picture within which economic theories have developed, ranging between two camps, namely, economics and political economy. The first section of this chapter provides the essential reason for studying the history of economic thought – dealing with differing or even contradictory theories of value, distribution, employment and money induces one to independent and open-minded thinking, that is, what John Maynard Keynes (1926) called the 'emancipation of the mind'. This should enable students of the history of economic thought to distil the most plausible theoretical principles, which are the grounds on which policy proposals may be eventually made. Indeed, economic theorizing must be based on the history of economic thinking to have an informed broader picture of the state of the art. In light of this, the second section presents two broad groups of theories – economics and political economy – to bring into the open the fundamental differences in economic theorizing. In economics, the great problems (value and price, distribution and employment) are market issues essentially, and money is neutral. By contrast, the starting point of political economy is the social and circular process of production: the fundamental prices are the prices of production, not market prices; income and wealth distribution are governed by social forces, and employment by effective demand; money and finance play an essential role. The third and fourth sections sketch the historical development of economics and political economy respectively. Economics starts with Adam Smith, who conceived of the economy and society as a self-regulating system. Jean-Baptiste Say (a follower of Adam Smith) claimed therefore that there can be no unemployment. The great systems of economics were then created in the course of the Marginalist Revolution (1870–90). Léon Walras worked out the general equilibrium model; Alfred Marshall the partial equilibrium approach. Both became constitutive of contemporary mainstream economics. By contrast, the French surgeon François Quesnay is at the origin of the political economy line. He considered the flows of goods and money within the social and circular process of production to produce the net output at the free disposal of society. As regards production, David Ricardo worked out the labour value principle and the surplus principle of distribution. Piero Sraffa revived the classical (Ricardian–Marxian) approach, which had been submerged by the Marginalist Revolution. John Maynard Keynes elaborated the principle of effective demand, represented by the multiplier relation, implying the existence of involuntary unemployment. At the time of writing, the post-Keynesian and classical–Keynesian followers of Sraffa and Keynes form, together with Marxists, the core of modern political economy, representing an alternative to the neoclassical mainstream. The last section of Chapter 2 discusses the plausibility of these two approaches. The capital-theory debate emerges thereby as the theoretical watershed between economics and political economy.

The third chapter focuses on monetary economies of production. Everybody knows the old song, 'Money makes the world go round'. In reality, this is a good approximation of how our economic system operates. Indeed, as Louis-Philippe Rochon explains in this chapter, we live in a monetary economy. This means that we cannot purchase goods without money; we cannot invest without money; we cannot hire workers without paying them a wage in money. Money is indeed at the core of our economic system. While this may be quite apparent to many, money does not feature in neoclassical economics, or if it does, it is merely there to give some semblance of reality to an otherwise unrealistic view of the world. This chapter first discusses the barter view of money in neoclassical analysis, and how in this view what serves as 'money' has evolved through time. In this framework money is introduced to facilitate trade and has no other purposes. In this sense, there is no need for money in discussing employment, wages, supply and demand, investment, and economic growth. In fact, there is no need for money even to discuss prices in neoclassical analysis. This chapter offers a criticism and an alternative view, which is focused on the creation and circulation of money, and its relationship with debt, which characterizes a 'revolutionary' approach. To be sure, money is necessary to explain production, employment as well as economic growth.

Chapter 4, written by Marc Lavoie and Mario Seccareccia, elaborates on this. It provides a brief analysis of the historical evolution of money and recalls some debates about it. Since money, in its essence, is merely the outcome of a balance-sheet operation, banks play a key role in any monetary economy. The purpose of this chapter is to describe why all aspects of macroeconomic analysis in a modern economy must necessarily involve the monetary system. Monetary relations result from the existence of a group of key institutions in a monetary economy, namely banks, which, together with the central bank, are crucial in the modern payment system and are the purveyors of liquidity to the whole economy. This chapter starts therefore with an explanation of how banks are the principal creators of money in nearly all modern economies, and why, by their very nature, they are private–public partnerships, especially evident at times of crisis when the public 'trust' that is so critical to their existence is broken, therefore requiring a regulatory framework within which the activity of creators of money is severely circumscribed. Lavoie and Seccareccia consider the composition of this creation of money by the banking system, including the central bank, and show why it varies with the performance of the economic system. This is followed by an investigation of the logic of money creation in the traditional analysis of the monetary circuit and how this has been transformed somewhat under the so-called regime of financialization (which is discussed in Chapter 15), especially with the perverse incentives generated by off-balance-sheet operations via securitization. As in most first-year textbooks, Lavoie and Seccareccia begin by discussing the specifics of bank balance-sheet operations and how bank money is created endogenously either to finance productive activity, as in the traditional circuit model of financing production, or more recently through the financing of household consumption spending. They thus consider how different forms of spending behaviour by either the private or public sector lead to the creation or destruction of money. They thereby comment on the role that the public sector plays on the asset side of banks' balance sheets, which is also critical to how the banking sector's net worth is usually re-established after recessions. Finally, this chapter provides a discussion of payment and settlement systems and of the role played by the interbank market, where the central bank can set the overnight rate of interest and thus largely control interest rates in the economy. The interbank rate of interest is a critical instrument for the conduct of monetary policy. This discussion establishes a bridge with Chapters 5 and 6 (on the financial system and monetary policy respectively).

Chapter 5, by Jan Toporowski, explains notably that the financial system emerges out of the financing needs of production and exchange in a capitalist economy. A special role is played by the financing needs of the state, for which are created the institutional foundations of the long-term debt markets that characterize the modern capitalist economy (that is, stock markets, insurance, and investment funds). These markets develop further with financial innovations that provide new scope for financial operations alongside production and exchange. Financial operations are a distinguishing feature of Marxist political economy – in the case of Hilferding's *Finanzkapital* (Hilferding, [1910] 1981) and the financial theories of Kalecki and Steindl derived from Hilferding's work – as well as Keynes's macroeconomics and post-Keynesian theories. By way of contrast, consistently with the irrelevance of money in neoclassical economics as explained in Chapter 3, mainstream macroeconomics and portfolio theory do not integrate the financial sector within a theory of how a capitalist economy operates with a complex financial system. The mainstream view also confuses saving with credit, exemplified in the theory of interest. The financial approach to macroeconomic theory is developed, by way of contrast, in the 'financial instability hypothesis' of Hyman Minsky, considering how debt changes over a business cycle. Minsky's view is distinguished from post-Keynesian theories by Minsky's denial of Keynes's interest rate theory of investment, but has contributed the notion of usury (due to excessive debt) common in post-Keynesian theories of financialization, as explained in Chapter 15.

Chapter 6, written by Louis-Philippe Rochon and Sergio Rossi, points out the specific role of the central bank in domestic payment and settlement systems – as money and credit provider. It focuses on the emission of central bank money as the means of final payment for every transaction on the interbank market. It thereby distinguishes between the monetary intermediation carried out by the central bank as a matter of routine – and necessity – and the financial intermediation that it carries out, as a lender of last resort, when its counterparties are not in a position to obtain enough credit on the interbank market. The authors show thereby that the central bank is crucial for financial stability, thus introducing the reader to the need to go much beyond price stability (particularly as measured on the goods market) for monetary policy-making. This chapter then focuses on monetary policy strategies, instruments and transmission mechanisms. Two major strategies (monetary targeting and inflation targeting) are discussed, criticizing their conceptual framework, and observing their macroeconomic costs as measured by so-called 'sacrifice ratios' with respect to output and employment losses. As the authors explain, monetary policy must contribute to macroeconomic stabilization and not just worry about price stability on the goods market. This discussion is elaborated on to present traditional as well as 'unconventional' monetary policy tools, critically considering their consequences on the whole economy. This framework is further expanded to present the 'transmission channels' of monetary policy, considering also the ongoing discussion about regulatory capital and financial reforms as well as banking supervision at national and international levels that aim to influence aggregate demand and thus achieve the relevant monetary policy goals.

Chapter 7, contributed by Jesper Jespersen, explains that aggregate demand comprises private consumption, private investment, government expenditure and net exports. Connected with this, it points out that neoclassical economists consider aggregate demand as rather unimportant. They argue that output (gross domestic product – GDP) is determined mainly by the supply of labour and capital, quite independently of demand. They consider the market system as self-adjusting, which leads them to conclude that, in the long run, 'the supply of goods creates their demand'. By contrast, according to heterodox economists and Keynesian macroeconomic theory, aggregate demand is an important analytical concept: it is the major driving force behind the level of output and employment in the short and longer run. This consideration makes demand management policies instrumental for creating macroeconomic stability and economic growth. Richard Kahn was notably one of the first Keynesian economists who contributed to the theory of aggregate demand: he invented the analytical concept of the investment multiplier as a short-run dynamic phenomenon. This chapter expands on this, presenting Keynesian demand management policies, notably in periods where aggregate demand is lower than potential GDP: fiscal policy, monetary policy, and exchange rate policy should be expansionary in recessions, and might be restrictive in boom periods. Demand management policies can thus close output gaps and make the macroeconomic system more stable. Against this background, neoclassical scepticism builds on the assumption that the macroeconomic system is self-adjusting: if wages are fully flexible, then the labour market will adjust by itself to full employment. In such cases aggregate demand, also by itself, adjusts to potential output (GDP) via changes in real wealth and/or changes in net foreign trade. Hence, demand management policies are at best superfluous in the orthodox view. As shown by this chapter, these different analytical outcomes depend on the theoretical macroeconomic framework: Keynesian aggregate demand analysis leaves the future open, which creates room for demand management policy; by way of contrast, the neoclassical assumption of automatic market adjustment makes aggregate demand equal to potential supply of output – thereby excluding both inflation and unemployment over the long run, unless the state intervenes, disturbing this 'free market equilibrium'.

Chapter 8, written by Alvaro Cencini and Sergio Rossi, focuses therefore on inflation and unemployment. It starts with an overview of both pathologies, explaining several basic concepts like the consumer price index, the purchasing power of money, inflation, deflation, unemployment and stagflation. It then points out their relevance and effects: income redistribution and monetary instability caused by inflation; social and economic disruptions caused by unemployment. The next stage is devoted to a critical analysis of the way mainstream economics has attempted to explain inflation and unemployment. In particular this chapter shows that inflation should not be confused with a rise in the cost of living and that neither demand–pull nor supply–push price variations cause a loss in the purchasing power of money, as only the agents' purchasing power is affected by a price variation originating in either demand or supply on the market for produced goods and services. It also shows that agents' forms of behaviour cannot reduce total demand and thereby be at the origin of an excess in total supply leading to unemployment. In the last section of this chapter the authors explain that inflation and unemployment are the twin outcomes of one single macroeconomic cause, that is, a pathological process of capital accumulation and overaccumulation. Their analysis is entirely macroeconomic and rests on Keynes's identities between total supply and total demand, and between savings and investment at the macroeconomic level. These two identities necessitate an analysis capable of reconciling them with the numerical disequilibria defining inflation and deflation. With regard to this, the authors argue that from a macroeconomic point of view only pathological unemployment matters and that involuntary unemployment, in Keynes's terms, is the consequence of an excess in total supply, that is to say, deflation. By investigating the process of capital accumulation the authors reveal the mechanisms leading to both inflation and deflation and so make sense of the global economic crisis that erupted after the bursting of the financial bubble in 2007–08.

Chapter 9, by Malcolm Sawyer, explains the role of fiscal policy. It explains that fiscal policy relates to the balance between government expenditures and tax revenues, which is important for the level of employment and economic activity. In doing so, the chapter points out that the need for fiscal policy arises from the perspective, generally denied by mainstream economists, that the capitalist economy is subject to cyclical fluctuations as well as to unemployment arising from inadequacy of aggregate demand, as discussed in Chapter 7. As a matter of fact, the private sector exhibits instabilities and suffers from insufficient aggregate demand to underpin full employment and capacity utilization. Fiscal policy is one instrument (amongst a number) to address these features, through public budget positions that offset inadequate private demand and through automatic stabilizers and discretionary fiscal policy to offset variations in demand. This chapter sets up the arguments relating to fiscal policy in the framework of a closed economy (for simplicity). It explains the equilibrium condition that (in *ex ante* terms) injections equals leakages: $I + G = S + T$ (with I private investment, G government expenditure, S private savings and T tax revenues). If $S > I$, then $G > T$ is required. The chapter explains the implications of that in terms of realization of savings and for budget deficits. As regards the mainstream view, the latter argues that at equilibrium $S = I$, and the mechanisms by which this is said to occur refer to the ('natural') interest rate. Further, in this view, the so-called 'Ricardian equivalence' between agents' taxation and public debt to finance government spending leads to the 'crowding out' effect of expansionary fiscal policies, as explained in Chapter 7. By contrast, the heterodox view that I and S tend not to be equal explains that budget deficits can be funded when $S > I$. Indeed, appropriate budget deficits do not put pressure on interest rates, particularly in a recession, because there are excessive savings with respect to desired investment by the business sector of the economic system. This chapter also briefly discusses the so-called 'functional finance' approach, thus pointing out that the objective of fiscal policy should be high levels of employment and not balanced budgets *per se*.

In Chapter 10, Mark Setterfield focuses on economic growth and development. He first provides a definition of economic growth, followed by an overview of its statistical record. Three salient features of the growth record are thus emphasized: the extent and unevenness of economic growth (resulting in the processes of 'catching up' and – for most – 'falling behind'); the unbalanced nature of economic growth (resulting in structural change, as exemplified by deindustrialization); and fluctuations in the pace of economic growth over time (which can be interpreted either as growth cycles or discrete and historically specific episodes of growth). This chapter then considers whether economic growth is a supply-led or demand-led process, contrasting mainstream neoclassical (supply-led) and alternative post-Keynesian (demand-led) views. Simple analytics (such as shifting production possibility frontiers, with economies operating either on these shifting frontiers – neoclassical case – or within their interiors – post-Keynesian case) are used to illustrate the differences between views. Next, the chapter invites further consideration of the post-Keynesian (demand-led) view of economic growth. Both Kaleckian and Kaldorian growth theories are thus sketched using simple analytics (on a par with multiplier analysis), drawing attention to the different sources of autonomous demand that each theory considers to be the key 'driver' of long-run growth. Various properties of economic growth (inspired by the post-Keynesian view of the growth process) are then considered. These include the paradox of thrift (an increase in the saving rate is harmful to economic growth); income distribution and economic growth, including discussion of the fact that raising the profit share of income may be harmful to GDP growth; technical progress ('Verdoorn's Law'); and interaction of supply and demand in long-run growth (endogeneity of potential output to actual output; the two-way interaction of actual and potential output, resulting in self-reinforcing virtuous and vicious circles of growth). This last topic invites further consideration of the role of supply factors in demand-led growth theory, as taken up in Chapter 17 (on sustainable development).

Chapter 11, by Omar Hamouda, expands on income and wealth distribution. Whether from the micro- or macroeconomic perspective, the purpose of studying economics has always been and will continue to be to focus on two fundamental questions: (1) How and what to produce in terms of goods and services? (2) Who receives what from the ongoing creation of wealth? Whether the economic aspects of these two questions are interrelated and uniquely determined, as the neoclassical approach maintains, or are determined separately by different sets of forces, as held by many other schools of thought, the implication – in terms of understanding what is meant by income distribution – is subject to controversial interpretations. The object of this chapter is to expose and elucidate various perspectives on the concepts of income share, and income distribution and redistribution in relation to the distribution of contribution and effort. In this chapter, income distribution is understood as the share that the remunerating factors of production get for their contribution to the creation of wealth. Income redistribution refers to income reallocation among members of a community regardless of whether they participate or not in the creation of wealth. In different eras in history, stages of economic development, political structures as well as the type of moral guidance dictated how, when, and who gets what from the proceeds derived from the common effort in producing what is required to satisfy human needs. This chapter is thus devoted first to exploring the general conception of shared income derived from the wealth of a nation. This wealth is referent to more than just economic criteria, especially in pre-industrial economies or those that do not adhere to market forces. The focus of this chapter then turns to how income is distributed under purely economic considerations, as explained and justified in the classical and the neoclassical schools of thought. Finally, the chapter reviews how the post-World War II 'welfare state' has slowly shaped and created a system of income redistribution decided by economic policies and regulation.

In Chapter 12, Robert A. Blecker focuses on trade and development. He begins this chapter with a brief review of the conventional arguments for free trade in general, and for a policy of economic openness as the best route to long-run growth and development. In fact, exports can be an important part of a development strategy, especially when they grow as part of a 'virtuous circle' of industrialization and rising incomes at home, but policies of pure free trade have not historically been the most successful. The most successful developing nations since the late nineteenth century have been those that have combined a significant role for the public sector in economic management with active promotion of exports and selective reliance on markets (but not complete state domination of markets). In addition, the comparative advantage model rests on the twin assumptions of full employment and balanced trade, which do not generally hold in reality, and without which the global trading system does not necessarily work in the mutually beneficial ways implied by standard theories. In the real world, some countries use mercantilist policies (which this chapter defines) to foster absolute competitive advantages and to increase national employment at the expense of their trading 'partners'. As a result, mercantilist strategies have generally outperformed neoliberal strategies based on open markets with little state direction. The chapter also includes a brief discussion and update of Joan Robinson's view of 'new mercantilism', for example as regards currency undervaluation (more recently dubbed 'currency war'). Multinational corporations and global financial investors can profit from free access to foreign markets and foreign mercantilist practices (like undervalued currencies and repressed wages), leading to a world in which 'outsourcing' or 'offshoring' undermines distributional equity and the social fabric in the advanced economies without guaranteeing equitable development in the Global South.

These issues are further elaborated upon in Chapter 13 by John McCombie and Nat Tharnpanich, who focus on balance-of-payments-constrained growth. Neoclassical growth theory explains differences in economic growth from the supply side within the framework of a closed economy. Economic growth is thus modelled with respect to an aggregate production function, with either exogenous or endogenous technical change, and the economy is assumed to be at full employment. However, it is clear that in many cases the economic growth rates of countries are interlinked through trade flows and the balance of payments. The concept of a balance-of-payments equilibrium growth rate is that it is the growth rate consistent with equilibrium on the current account, or where there is a sustainable growth of net capital inflows. If this growth rate is below the growth of productive potential, the country is said to be balance-of-payments constrained. In these circumstances, it will have a lower rate of induced technical change, a lower rate of capital accumulation, increasing inefficiency, and greater disguised unemployment. This chapter outlines this approach. It shows that, in the long run, the economic growth of a country is determined by the growth rate of its exports (operating through both the Harrod foreign trade multiplier and the Hicks supermultiplier). The key to the growth of exports is primarily a country's degree of non-price competitiveness, which is determined by the value of its income elasticity of demand for exports and imports relative to that of other countries. In this model, unlike the neoclassical growth model, economic growth is demand driven. This chapter shows how the economic performance of one country, or group of countries, can constrain the economic performance of another country or group. It also shows how economic growth of a country (y) may be explained by the simple rule $y = x/\pi = \varepsilon z/\pi$, where x is the growth rate of exports, π is the domestic income elasticity of demand, ε is the income elasticity of demand for exports, and z is the growth rate of the country's export markets. While the full model is more complicated than this, this simple rule, known as 'Thirlwall's Law', provides a good empirical explanation as to why economic growth rates differ around the world.

Sergio Rossi, in Chapter 14, focuses on European monetary union, presenting its own history and the workings of its main institutions since the 1960s. He also explains the euro-area crisis, pointing out its monetary and structural factors. He thereby shows the fundamental flaws of the single-currency area as well as of its anti-crisis policies at both national and European levels. The discussion is expanded to present an alternative path to European monetary integration, in the spirit of Keynes's International Clearing Union based on a supranational currency unit, which in fact can be issued without the need for its member countries to dispose of their monetary sovereignty and thereby preserves national interest rate policies as a relevant instrument to steer economic performance at the euro-area level. The first section sets off from the original proposals for European monetary union, as put to the fore in the Werner Plans of the early 1970s – as a halfway station between so-called 'economists' and 'monetarists', the former (led notably by Germany) being in favour of a convergence of macroeconomic magnitudes before European countries may actually enter into a fixed exchange rate regime, and the latter (including France and Italy) favouring an early fixing of exchange rates, which they considered as a factor of economic convergence for the countries involved. The section focuses then on the Delors Plan, which led to the 1992 Maastricht Treaty and the adoption of the European single currency in 1999. It further explains the institution and workings of the European Central Bank, including its governance and lack of accountability with regard to its (single) monetary policy goal. The second section expands on this, to explain that the euro-area crisis does not really originate in 'excessive public deficits' and debt as a percentage of GDP in the Maastricht sense. As a matter of fact, it is a monetary–structural crisis originating in the institutional design and workings of the European single-currency area. Beyond increasing intra-euro-area trade imbalances and speculative capital flows, the European single currency has given rise to payment imbalances – as captured by the TARGET2 payment system – which need a symmetric rebalancing to avoid the depressionary spiral induced by a widespread fiscal austerity and monetary inactivity by the European Central Bank. The third section therefore presents an alternative path to European monetary integration, which is akin to 'Keynes's Plan' presented at the 1944 Bretton Woods conference, since it reintroduces national currencies while making sure that all intra-euro-area international payments are finalized between the relevant national central banks through the emission of a scriptural means of final payment by an international settlement institution resident at the European Central Bank, the Bank for International Settlements, or the International Monetary Fund. The discussion of this alternative refers also to Robert Triffin, notably to his own critiques of a single-currency area for Europe and to his alternative proposal in that regard.

Chapter 15, by Gerald A. Epstein, addresses financialization, that is, the growing and excessive importance of financial motives, markets and institutions in the working of today's capitalist economies. According to standard macroeconomic analysis, finance in a capitalist economy serves households, non-financial businesses and governments in several ways (as explained in Chapter 5): by providing households with safe places to store their savings, and by channelling these savings to productive and profitable uses by non-financial corporations; by providing opportunities for households to save for their retirement; by allowing corporations to mobilize large sums of capital for investment in productive enterprises; and by providing ways for households and firms to insure against risks. According to this idealized view of the world, there is a clear separation between the financial sector and the 'real sector', and finance prospers when it serves the 'real economy'. In contrast to this idealized vision, modern capitalist economies seem to be structured in a starkly different way. As shown by the global financial crisis that erupted in 2007, the financial sector in many advanced capitalist economies has been operating in a rather closed loop in which it enriches itself, often at the expense of households and non-financial corporations, rather then serving the 'real economy'. Further, the CEOs and boards of directors of non-financial corporations manage many of these corporations as if they were simply portfolios of financial assets to be manipulated to maximize the short-term income of small groups of corporate executives, rather than the long-run growth and profitability of corporations. In short, there is increasing evidence that many modern capitalist economies have become 'financialized' and this 'financialization' has contributed to significant economic and social ills, including huge financial crises, increased inequality between the top managers of corporations and everyone else, and to stunted investment in long-term productivity growth. Epstein presents the most important theories of financialization, gives a brief historical description of the evolution of financialization in contemporary economies, and surveys the key empirical evidence on the impacts of financialization on instability, inequality and economic growth. The author explores many dimensions of financialization, namely its impact on financial instability, its impact on investment and employment decisions by non-financial corporations, its impact on public finance and public deficits, the role of financialization in generating inequality, and public policies for confronting the problems associated with financialization, such as financial transactions taxes, restrictions on stock options, and industrial policy.

In Chapter 16, Robert Guttmann expands on this to explain economic imbalances and crises. There is overpowering evidence that our capitalist system is subject to endemic imbalances, which, if large and/or persistent enough, lead to crisis. This is a recurrent pattern in which underlying imbalances and crises enter into a dialectical relationship, with crises serving as adjustment processes that may (or may not) resolve the imbalances triggering them in the first place. Whereas orthodox economic theory tends to treat crises as exogenous shocks intruding from the outside to upset our supposedly self-balancing system, we need to understand this phenomenon instead as intrinsic to capitalist economies. The key to this reinterpretation effort is to pinpoint the imbalances that such a system gives rise to as a matter of its normal *modus operandi*. For a long time economists of all stripes have analysed imbalances between demand and supply at the micro-level of individual actors or sectoral level of markets and industries, primarily to show that affected parties respond to any disequilibria in such a way as to eliminate any excess of demand or supply. Their argument, crystallized in the famous Marshallian cross of intersecting demand and supply schedules, works with appropriate changes in the price level, sending corresponding signals for both sides of the marketplace to respond to. But when structural changes in our economic system led to increasingly pre-set prices that resisted falling in situations of excess supply, the standard market equilibrium argument broke down. In the face of growing downward price rigidity, suppliers would end up slashing output and employment rather than prices. It was up to John Maynard Keynes to identify, in the midst of the Great Depression, the horrifying fallacy of composition, where what was good for individual actors was disastrous for the system as a whole, as expenditure cutbacks of some would impose income losses on others and so trigger additional cuts in spending. Keynes's solution, namely to bring in the government as an extra-market actor not bound by private-sector budget constraints and profit motives to boost total demand in the economy, gave rise to a revolution in economic thinking and transformed our system into a mixed (private–public) economy subject to active crisis management by the state. Keynes's emphasis on inadequate demand generated by the private sector represents only one side in an age-old debate among that minority of economists seeking to explain the cyclical fluctuations of our economy's growth pattern. Juxtaposing Keynes's underconsumption argument has been Marx's emphasis on overproduction according to whom the capitalists' incessant chase for greater profits ('surplus value'), motivated by their competition with each other, would inherently drive supplies beyond the system's limited absorption capacity. The underconsumption versus overproduction argument is given added weight when one links (cyclical) economic growth patterns to (functional) income distribution, as has been attempted by Kalecki. The Kaleckian link between economic growth and income distribution integrates micro-level actions (mark-up pricing, investment function) and macro-level determinants (wage and profit shares) to yield a more profound insight into capitalism's inherent demand–supply imbalance. It points directly to what unites all three of these heterodox masters (Marx, Keynes and Kalecki), which is grounded in the relationship between wages and productivity. As crystallized in Keynes's notion of 'efficiency wages', the balanced growth of our economic system depends on both of these variables growing at pretty much the same rate. Some sort of crisis will occur when productivity levels outgrow wages or vice versa. Business cycle theory has also focused on the role of credit, a major factor in the destabilization of our economy's growth pattern as recognized by Mikhail Tugan-Baranovsky, the Austrians (such as Friedrich von Hayek), and above all Hyman Minsky, whose 'financial instability hypothesis' has made it irrefutably clear that business cycles are to a significant extent driven by parallel credit cycles. In the Minskian world, the inevitable accumulation of excessive debt renders economic actors increasingly vulnerable and eventually forced to deleverage when acute incidences of financial instability arise to trigger recessionary adjustments. His emphasis on the relationship between debt servicing charges and income levels identifies, besides demand–supply and wage–productivity imbalances, a third crucial imbalance capable of triggering a crisis. Minsky highlighted another aspect of crucial importance – the presence of long waves around which our (relatively short-term) business cycles are woven. While he stressed the financial factors underpinning such long waves (implying a 'financial supercycle' of leverage-enhancing financial innovations and growing propensity for risk), others have approached the subject of these longer-term phases of rapid and slow growth as a matter of commodity price movements (Nikolai Kondratiev), bursts of technological change (Joseph Alois Schumpeter), or institutional transformations (the French Regulation School). One major insight from long-wave theory is that some crises, especially those occurring either in the beginning or towards the end of the wave's downward phase, are more serious – both in depth and length – than normal cyclical downturns. Such 'structural' crises deserve special attention. Their imbalances typically engulf the entire system, cannot be resolved by crisis as adjustment process, and need reform. In today's globalized economy, and as sharply confirmed by the unfolding of the latest structural crisis from late 2007 onward, we have a new source of crisis-prone imbalance to consider: in the absence of corrective adjustment mechanisms, a major flaw in how globalization has played out, the interaction dynamics of chronic deficit and surplus countries creates tensions within the world economy that threaten to explode in new types of crisis – currency crises, sovereign debt crises, ecological crises, or resource supply crises. The story of capitalism is one of transformational imbalances and many-faceted crises – a fact that economists yet need to acknowledge.

In Chapter 17, focusing on sustainable development, Richard P.F. Holt lays the foundations for a sustainable approach to economic development, which incorporates quality of life and sustainability in ways that the neoclassical model does not, by looking at different capital stocks and distinguishing between development and economic growth. The traditional assumption that more economic growth means higher quality of life is being questioned around the world. Economic development as defined in this chapter means a broad-based increase in the standard of living, which includes quality of life and sustainability, while economic growth is described as any increase in undifferentiated output or income. Economists and policy-makers have often used the terms interchangeably. This chapter makes a clear distinction. Besides scholarly work that makes this distinction, there are also popular and political groups advocating for such a distinction. For example, efforts by the United Nations through the United Nations Human Development Index and alternative domestic measures such as the 'genuine progress indicator' (GPI) are based on capabilities and sustainability of development that improves quality of life and sustainability that go beyond traditional definitions and measurements of economic growth. Many communities in both industrialized and developing countries are developing locally based indicators of sustainability or quality of life to supplement traditional economic measures. All of these measures show an increasing recognition that economic development depends on more than raising national income. This is based in part on the reality that economic prosperity depends on environmental and social sustainability in ways that the neoclassical model has not addressed adequately. It also reflects a desire for balancing economic well-being with other aspects of well-being such as health and human relationships. The discussion in this chapter goes beyond traditional views. It focuses on both positive and negative impacts of economic growth on quality of life, sustainability, and how the fruits of this growth are shared among income groups important for economic prosperity. The term 'sustainability' is used most often in discussions of natural resource depletion or carrying capacity of the environment. This chapter uses it in its broader framework to include all inputs necessary to maintain a given standard of living or quality of life. This includes what economists call 'human capital', such as skills and health of a population, and the 'social capital' of viable private and public institutions. This chapter also argues that thinking and acting locally as well as globally must address concerns about economic development. This is not to argue that national and international policy or economic performance have no effect on local conditions. They have important consequences for communities and the individuals who live in them. But economic, geographic and social realities cause substantial regional variation in growth and development in all countries.

The last chapter, by John King, offers a conclusion to this textbook, raising the question of the need of microfoundations to macroeconomics. The chapter begins by asking why we might need a separate (sub)discipline of macroeconomics, relatively autonomous from microeconomics. The author uses the example of unemployment: excess supply cannot be eliminated by reducing price in a macroeconomic context, as Keynes (1936) rightly explained in Chapter 19 of his *General Theory*. This is a fallacy of composition. Yet, as King notes, supporters rarely set out the mainstream case for microfoundations, as it is simply taken for granted. As King explains, microfoundations are an example of question begging or persuasive language, which is often found in economics. Consider, for example, 'free-market economics' (in its Australian translation, 'economic rationalism'). Who would ever want to be *un*free (or *ir*rational)? 'Microfoundations' is also a metaphor. King notably provides examples of other metaphors that are used in economics, and discusses thereby the criteria for identifying good (and bad) metaphors. He thus suggests that 'microfoundations' is a bad metaphor, which would have the consequence – if generally accepted – of destroying macroeconomics as a separate, relatively autonomous (sub-)discipline. Insistence on providing microfoundations can also be seen as part of the 'economics imperialism' project, since if it were applied to the other social sciences it would also destroy their autonomy. Further, the case against microfoundations can be reinforced by considering a number of additional fallacies of composition, which are sometimes described as 'paradoxes'. The most familiar is the 'paradox of thrift'. The global financial crisis has brought to prominence the 'paradox of liquidity' (or deleveraging). These are considered in some detail in the last chapter, where the author also devotes some space to the (Kaleckian) 'paradox of costs', and the potential for wage-led economic growth to restore prosperity, for instance in the euro area as a whole and in a number of its member countries in particular. This takes us back to John Maynard Keynes and the absence of any unambiguous macroeconomic connection between wages and unemployment. Further, what Paul Davidson (2003–04) criticized as 'imperfectionism' is certainly wrong; our paradoxes would still apply, even if all markets were perfectly competitive and all prices (and wages) were perfectly flexible downwards. Hence removing market imperfections would not eliminate the fallacy of composition or reduce the importance of downward causation. To conclude: language matters in economics. So does methodology. Students of economics should be prepared to learn from other social sciences, and from the philosophy of science. And so should their teachers.

 REFERENCES

Davidson, P. (2003–04), 'Setting the record straight on *A History of Post Keynesian Economics*', *Journal of Post Keynesian Economics*, **26** (2), 245–72.

Hilferding, K. ([1910] 1981), *Das Finanzkapital. Eine Studie über die jüngste Entwicklung des Kapitalismus* [Finance Capital. A Study of the Latest Phase of Capitalist Development], London: Routledge and Kegan Paul.

Keynes, J.M. (1926), *The End of Laissez-Faire*, London: Hogarth Press.

Keynes, J.M. (1936), *The General Theory of Employment, Interest and Money*, London: Macmillan.

Part I

Economics, economic analysis and economic systems

1

What is economics?

Louis-Philippe Rochon and Sergio Rossi

 OVERVIEW

This chapter:

- critically discusses the mainstream definition of economics, based on the 'efficient allocation of scarce resources';

- explains the differences between microeconomics and macroeconomics, and emphasizes how mainstream macroeconomics is built on the assumption of aggregating individuals' behaviour, that is, on microeconomic foundations;

- shows that neoclassical models explaining consumption, investment and economic growth contain no money essentially, thereby being fundamentally inappropriate to understand the real world;

- argues that macroeconomics should not be a simple aggregation of individual behaviour and microeconomic magnitudes, and that social classes play an important role in determining economic outcomes.

This analysis explains thereby that markets are not really free, but governed by laws and institutions, which play a central role in any economic activity. Further, in casting this view in terms of social groups, the importance of power becomes paramount: power over the determination of wages, power over access to credit, and the power of the state – all elements that have been missing and cannot be introduced in orthodox economics.

Introduction

In his 1924 tribute to Alfred Marshall, his former teacher, British economist John Maynard Keynes (1924, p. 322) noted that:

> the master-economist must possess a rare combination of gifts. He must be mathematician, historian, statesman, philosopher – in some degree. He must

understand symbols and speak in words. He must contemplate the particular in terms of the general and touch abstract and concrete in the same flight of thought. He must study the present in the light of the past for the purposes of the future.

Keynes's insights were profound, and they put a considerable burden of knowledge on economists. This is no surprise, as the stakes are very high. After all, there are a number of economic issues that need to be addressed and explained, and economists play a central role in explaining them, from the wages we get paid, to the jobs we have or the jobs so many of us would like to have, to the interest rates we pay on our credit cards, bank loans and mortgages, to taxes and the prices of goods and services.

Economic policy also plays an important role. Should governments involve themselves in the workings of markets and if so, what should this involvement be? What role should central banks play? And while people are happy when the economy is growing soundly, many lose their jobs and even their homes when the economy goes bad. Economics impacts us all.

An economist must therefore be able to understand the world around him or her and to propose solutions to the problems we face. The list of problems is a long one: unemployment, inflation, income inequality between the rich and the poor, pollution of the environment, economic growth and recessions, and many more.

To understand the world, the economist must possess knowledge that goes well beyond the strict confines of 'economics'. What Keynes was suggesting in the above quote is that economics is not a science that can be studied in isolation, at the same level as physics or chemistry, but it borrows many elements from other disciplines, especially from other social sciences. Indeed, to be a good economist, and this has never been truer than today, economists must recognize that political science, history, psychology, sociology, mathematics, logic, ecology and philosophy, to name but a few, provide indispensable inputs in forming the economist's mind. In other words, if the goal of the economist is to better understand the world we live in, or what we call the 'real world', rather than some hypothetical world, he or she must keep an open mind and build bridges with other disciplines. To ignore these other influences is bad economics, and can only result in bad economic policies.

But not all economists in the profession share this pluralist approach. Indeed, the majority of them argue that there is no need to understand political science or sociology, or even to study history. Many economists will even tell you that there is no need to read anything published more than a decade ago. According to this view, economics is about markets governed by natural laws that are immutable through time and independent of social conditions and institutions. In this view, economics is about studying individual behaviour and finding optimal solutions that are independent of history and time. Indeed, for most of the economics profession, the same economic theory should be able to explain problems in the United States in 2014 as in Sub-Saharan Africa in 1814. According to this view, the laws of economics are immutable and apply to all places at all times.

The chapters in this book take a different approach. They propose an alternative approach to economic theory and therefore to economic policy as well, taking into account socioeconomic conditions and institutions as they evolve through time: the problems in Brazil today are not the same as in the United States; the institutions in Europe are not the same as in North America. To think otherwise can only be dangerous, if we apply these policies to the real world. So, contrary to what Margaret Thatcher once said, that 'there is no alternative' (TINA), this book offers you not only a credible alternative, but also one that provides a realistic view of how the real world actually works.

While we discuss this more fully below, the mantra of TINA sends a dangerous message, and those who believe in its wisdom are doomed to repeat the mistakes of the past. A striking example of this flawed logic is the economic and financial crisis that began in 2007, which bears many similarities to the 1929 Great Depression – hence why many have nicknamed it the Great Recession or the Lesser Depression. The similarities are striking not only in the statistics, like the unemployment rate or the rate of economic growth, but also in the response that many governments gave at the beginning of the crisis. As in the Great Depression, in 2009 governments initially responded by increasing public spending, which had the immediate success of stopping the downward economic spiral. The problem is that many policy-makers and economists interpreted this as the end of the Great Recession, and proclaimed that economic growth was thus right around the corner. They quickly advised governments to begin cutting back on expenditures otherwise their policy would prove inflationary or destabilizing.

Indeed, once the economy appeared stabilized in 2010, several governments, under pressure to rein in their expenses, quickly abandoned their expansionary policies and started to cut expenses, and in some countries in very drastic ways. This was the case for many countries in Europe that adopted so-called 'fiscal consolidation', such as Greece, Italy, Spain, Portugal and Ireland, among others.

This is what we call 'austerity policies' – the idea that economies can grow from cutting government expenditures. Some have also called this approach 'expansionary fiscal contraction'. Yet, seven years after the official end of the crisis (2009), we are still barely in the recovery phase of the expansion, and many parts of the world are slipping back into recession. For instance, Europe is gripped with a severe crisis of its own, and, in the United States and Canada, economies are growing at very low rates, prompting many to ask whether we are in a situation of 'secular stagnation', which can be described as permanent low economic growth. Once again, there is doubt about the conventional wisdom.

In fact, history teaches us many things, and if economists and governments had studied the Great Depression and its aftermath, perhaps we would not, almost a decade after the 2007 crash, still be underperforming, for the reaction governments had in the recent past is not dissimilar to how governments reacted in the aftermath of the 1929 Great Depression.

Yet, the pluralist message is being heard more and more, and while it is a slow uphill battle, it is nonetheless the right path to follow for the common good. The economists contributing to this book have studied the real world long and hard, and arrived at the conclusion that we must rethink the old ways. US economist Alfred Eichner (1983, p. 238) once wrote that:

> [t]his situation in which economists find themselves is therefore not unlike that of many natural scientists who, when faced with mounting evidence in support of first, the Copernican theory of the universe and then, later, the Darwinian theory of evolution, had to decide whether undermining the revelatory basis of Judeo-Christian ethics was not too great a price to pay for being able to reveal the truth.

Yet economics seems to be in denial, and refusing to recognize the limitations of conventional thinking.

A growing number of economists, however, are recognizing the limits of the old ways – as are students. For instance, there is currently a growing movement among students around the world called 'Rethinking Economics', the purpose of which is precisely to introduce more pluralism within the teaching of economics. In France, 'Les Economistes Atterrés' ('The Appalled Economists') is a group of faculty and students who are leading the fight to introduce more pluralism within economics. Other movements exist elsewhere as well. And at Harvard University, in November 2011, students walked out of Gregory Mankiw's economics class, over what they interpreted as a 'conservative bias' in his economics. Indeed, many claim that the economic theories and policies advocated, among many others, by Professor Mankiw were at the root of the 2007–08 crisis. The students at Harvard University were aware of this, and they left the class, demanding changes.

Keynes had warned us about such wrong policies. As he tells us in the single-paragraph first chapter of his most famous book, *The General Theory of Employment, Interest and Money*, published in 1936, 'the characteristics of the special case assumed by the [neo]classical theory happen not to be those of the economic society in which we actually live, with the result that its teaching is misleading and disastrous if we attempt to apply it to the facts of experience'. This book is largely based on that warning.

The role of ideology in economics

Understanding the world around us requires us to interpret what is going on, and that is not an easy task because it is always obfuscated by ideology. As we discuss below as well as in the next chapter, there are two overall visions about how the economy works, or two ideologies, and whichever one you adhere to will taint the way you see the world around you. These ideologies are in direct opposition to one another, and there are tremendous social forces and vested interests that seek to ensure the continued dominance of one over the other.

In essence, do you see markets being better off left to themselves and without any interference from the government? This is the 'laissez-faire' approach or the (neo)classical approach to which Keynes referred to above: leave markets alone, minimize or even eliminate all government 'interference', which can only make things worse. Markets have some built-in stabilizers that ensure markets on their own are able to return to equilibrium.

We can illustrate this view using the analogy of a bowl and a marble. Once you drop the marble in the bowl, after moving around the marble will eventually gravitate toward the bottom of the bowl and then will come to a stop or a position of rest, that is, in equilibrium at the bottom. In this sense, this equilibrium can be defined as a position of gravitation. What we must not do, therefore, is to put anything in the path of the marble. On its own, without help, the marble will eventually return to its position of equilibrium.

As such, according to this approach, governments and government legislation often become obstacles that prevent markets from reaching their equilibrium. In other words, governments become the cause of economic recessions and depressions when imposing regulations, high taxes, tariffs, or by spending too much. Unions are also to blame, since they demand higher wages for their workers than what markets dictate and support. The end result is that resources are misallocated or misused and wasted, and that leads to unemployment, inflation, and slow economic growth or recessions.

From this philosophy are derived economic policies aimed at eliminating public deficits (balanced budgets legislation, for instance) as well as policies aimed at lowering taxes, and making it more difficult to join labour unions. The overall aim is to reduce the influence of institutions, including the state, in the workings of markets.

The second approach is completely different, opposite in many respects, and sees markets, when left to themselves, as prone to instability, excesses and even crises. This contrasting approach argues that there are no inherent forces within markets that would enable economies to grow on their own for prolonged periods of time, or to push the economy back to an 'equilibrium' position.

The difference between these two approaches largely comes down to how we see the role of the state – as a force for good or evil? As stated above, if one sees governments as intrusive, then naturally any involvement of the public sector will be seen as an assault on the wisdom of free markets. But others see governments in a positive light, as a way of helping markets overcome some of their excesses and problematic behaviour. In this sense, the role of government is paramount.

In fact, without governments, markets are prone to periods of great instability. One of the reasons for this is that we live in a world of uncertainty, a central theme of John Maynard Keynes's thinking – we cannot predict the future. As he writes, 'we simply do not know' the future. Uncertainty has important consequences on how individuals and firms behave. Indeed, the 'extreme precariousness' of our knowledge of the future but also of our understanding of how markets work can have undesired consequences. Despite this, we somehow take decisions everyday. Keynes called that little voice that somehow guides us in making these decisions in a framework of uncertainty 'animal spirits'.

In light of this climate of uncertainty, pessimism and optimism regarding the future are key in understanding what drives individuals and firms to act. For instance, when there is too much pessimism about the future, firms may not want to invest or seek funding from banks, which themselves may not want to lend. Consumers may not want to spend but instead wish to accumulate savings. All these forms of behaviour contribute to depressing total demand on the market for produced goods and services.

This is where the government comes in. In times of great uncertainty, when aggregate demand is weak, governments can have a stabilizing influence on markets. When we are in a recession, and there is great uncertainty about the future of the economy, the government can enhance economic activity by means of an expansionary fiscal policy, that is, increase public spending. By purchasing goods and services from the private sector, or by transferring money to consumers, governments contribute to increasing total demand on the product market. In turn, this helps to create an atmosphere of confidence or optimism (or less pessimism), which then will allow firms to want to invest again and banks to lend (see Chapter 3 for a description of the monetary circuit). Hence, economic agents act according to 'sudden bursts of optimism and pessimism' as Keynes tells us.

In most universities, the first approach is taught and free market economics is presented as the only credible approach. Students are never asked to question this approach. They learn it, and then are quizzed on it, and eventually must accept it in order to graduate, at which time they go off in the private or public sector to work as economists, where they apply the lessons learned. If they become graduate students, they must write a thesis using this world view, or risk not receiving their degree. And once they become an economics professor, since they know nothing else, they also teach it. This is how the circle perpetuates itself. Yet, as Nobel Laureate Joseph Stiglitz (2002) wrote, economics as taught 'in America's graduate schools. . .bears testimony to a triumph of ideology over science'.

This is a fundamental argument of this book. You will be introduced in fact to two overall approaches to economics, which we can label orthodox (or neo-classical or mainstream) and heterodox. Each approach has its own assumptions and hypotheses, each is rooted in a given ideology, and each offers not only a very different interpretation of the real world but also vastly different theories and sets of policies to adopt in order to solve a number of economic problems. Each approach asks very different questions and hence provides very different answers.

Before we explore these two distinct approaches in detail, let us first discuss an argument that is of considerable importance: is economics a science?

Is economics a science?

In the sciences, knowledge is gained through observations and experimentation. For instance, we can test hypotheses in a laboratory, under specific conditions. We can recreate the conditions of space, or test the effects of the lack of gravity on humans who are preparing to go in outer space – all within a laboratory. We can run computer simulations on how a new plane engine may perform, and test how changes in its design can affect performance.

Also, we know that there are immutable laws: the law of gravity, Newton's three laws of motion, the laws of thermodynamics, or Einstein's law of relativity. And these laws do not change through time. For instance, gravity was the same 1000 years ago as it is today. Gravity may be different on Earth than it is on Jupiter, but the laws that govern gravity are specific. The same applies to the laws of motion: the planets, for instance, move in the same way today as billions of years ago. Light travels as fast today as it did in the past. Moreover, in the world of hard sciences, if the real world is complicated, we can always hold certain variables constant and isolate the effect of one variable on another. And if one experiment fails, we can repeat it as many times as needed until we obtain the desired results.

In economics, however, little or none of this can be done. For instance, we cannot recreate the conditions of the real world in a laboratory, such as the labour market or the banking system, and carry out tests to verify a hypothesis; nor can we simply hold certain real-world variables constant, or measure the specific effect of a single variable on the economy – what economists call the *ceteris paribus* condition, which translates into 'all other things being equal'. The real world is far too complicated; it is a place where everything is happening at once.

Of course, this does not mean that we cannot carry out tests or use models to advance our knowledge of how economic systems work, but these must be done properly and on a series of explicit (rather than largely implicit) hypotheses. Further, these hypotheses must be rooted in reality and not simply *ad hoc* to satisfy the conclusions of the model.

In economics, however, societies and markets change all the time. The way cars are built today has nothing to do with how they were built in the days of Henry Ford; while government spending accounted for very little of overall GDP a century ago, today it accounts for far more. Today's institutions, like governments but also trade unions and corporations, do not resemble their former selves. Indeed, corporations today are more complex and intricate than they were a century ago; a bank today performs very differently than in the past, not to mention the existence of shadow banks. As institutions change, they impact the way markets operate and perform, so a policy that may have been relevant at a time when agriculture accounted for an important part of the economy cannot surely be as relevant today where agriculture accounts for a relatively small part of overall economic output.

These observations are important in deciding the use of models. Obviously, models must reflect how markets evolve and change over time. In using models, we must consider carefully the assumptions and hypotheses that are made: how much do they reflect the real world? And just as crucial, how important are the variables we exclude? Would their inclusion change the conclusions and if so, how and why?

Regarding the changing nature of institutions, the question we need to ask is whether institutions today are the same as in the past, and if not, can this be a sufficient reason to rethink economics? After all, does it really matter that institutions change? Could we not simply ignore these changes and go on analysing markets as if everything remained the same through time?

Change is therefore a central theme of our economies, and therefore there can be no universal laws in economics, like the law of gravity or the laws of motion. As a result, economics is not a hard science. Given these changes, among many others, we cannot expect the same theories of economics from a century ago to still be relevant today. As a result, economic policies that may have been successful in the past may simply be wrong today.

This does not mean that economists cannot behave like scientists and observe the world around them. In this sense, economics is scientific, and is based, as Keynes tells us, on a 'vigorous observation of the real world'. The scientific method goes from observations to theorizing, going, however, much beyond surface phenomena. So there is a definite scientific approach within economics, as in other social sciences.

While this discussion may appear sensible to the vast majority of us, in reality, it is shared today by only a very small percentage of economists and policy-makers. As stated above, at the time of writing the vast majority of the profession believes in a very narrow definition of economics, one that we hope to show you in this book is wrong. Economists who believe in that approach believe in the laws of economic theory, that is, in the idea that economic theories are immutable – they can be applied anywhere and anytime. But what happens when the real world does not behave like the theories predict? What is wrong? In physics, when the real world does not live up to the theory, the theory is judged to be wrong and is eventually replaced. This is what happened, for instance, with the notion that the Earth is flat, or that the Sun rotated around the Earth.

As such, in economics, mainstream economists do not accept the scientific approach: despite the failure of many of their theories and policies, they still believe their theories are correct. They lay blame rather with institutions like the state and unions for interfering with the laws of markets. The idea that their theories may be wrong is simply not a possibility in their minds. Two wonderful quotes by Keynes illustrate this picture well. First, in the *General Theory*, Keynes (1936, p. 16) compared this approach to 'Euclidean geometers in a non-Euclidean world who, discovering that in experience straight lines apparently parallel often meet, rebuke the lines for not keeping straight'. This is what mainstream economists do: they blame the real world for not behaving like their theory predicts. If only they followed Keynes's wise words: 'When the facts change, I change my mind. What do you do, sir?'

The use of models and of mathematics

Let us discuss the role models play in economics a bit more.

Economists will often use tables and graphs to interpret and explain the world around them, or use sophisticated mathematics and statistical analysis. This is part of the economist's bag of devices. This does not negate the above discussion. In using models and mathematics, however, one must be careful to use them properly. Also, the absence of mathematics or sophisticated models does not render a theory useless. Economists must first be able to tell the story and explain the real world, and only after should they rely on models and mathematics to support their conclusions, if the case warrants it.

Models are a simplification of reality, and as such they do not have to be complicated, but they must be realistic in the sense that they are meant to be a simplification of the real world, not a simplification of some fictitious world. Models are rooted in assumptions, and it is these assumptions that must be a satisfactory reflection of the real world. If the assumptions are wrong, the model becomes useless. Imagine trying to explain the rotation of the Earth or the movement of planets based on the hypothesis that the Earth is flat, and that all celestial objects rotate around it.

For instance, our economies grow through increases in the demand for goods and services. As such, demand plays a central role. Any model that does not give demand such a role cannot be taken seriously. As another example, we live in a money-using economy where wages are paid in money, bank loans are made in terms of money, and money is what we use to buy goods. Hence, money must be at the very core of our economic models, and if this is not the case, the model must be cast aside in favour of one that integrates money in its analysis.

Some other common assumptions we find in the most celebrated models are that full employment always prevails, unemployment is only temporary, money does not exist at all, economies evolved from barter, time is finite in the sense that models work only over a few periods, there is no accumulation of capital (that is, no investment), there exists only one good, and so on. Now, you tell us if these are realistic assumptions. Economist John Kay (2011) remarked quite appropriately that '[s]uch models are akin to Tolkien's Middle Earth, or a computer game like Grand Theft Auto'. Strangely enough, mainstream economists will admit that their assumptions are not realistic, but for them this is of no importance in so far as their models are internally consistent.

A perfect example of the dangers of using bad economic models is the total failure of mainstream economics in predicting the financial crisis that erupted in 2007–08. Indeed, not a single (or very few) mainstream economist saw it coming. In fact, a few months before the crisis began in August 2007, the then Chairman of the US Federal Reserve, Ben Bernanke (2007), stated in his Congressional testimony in March 2007 that, '[a]t this juncture, the impact on the broader economy and financial markets of the problems in the subprime market seems likely to be contained'. Less than a year later, on 10 January 2008, he boldly claimed that '[t]he Federal Reserve is not currently forecasting a recession' (Bernanke, 2008).

The crisis was a proof of the complete collapse of mainstream economics. This prompted even the Queen of England, on 5 November 2008, to ask the question: 'Why did nobody notice it developing?' (Davidson, 2015, p. 1).

The answer is quite simple: nobody noticed the crisis because most economists are working with models that are simply wrong, and based on a series of flawed assumptions. In fact, in mainstream models, crises cannot occur, because markets are thought to be efficient. These models may acknowledge problems in one market or another, but not a systemic failure of the whole system at once. Yet, as 2007–08 has showed us, this can happen and happens from time to time.

With respect to mathematics, like models, it plays an important role, but one that should be subservient to the story. In other words, economics is about telling a story of the world around us. This story must first be told, and once told mathematics may be used to support that story.

The problem, however, is that today models and mathematics have taken over the economics, and economists rely too much on mathematics. As a result, the economic story gets lost. The increasingly more sophisticated models and statistical techniques become the focus of research, rather than economics. In a sweeping rebuke of the profession, economist Deirdre McCloskey (2005, p. 85), referring to the increasing mathematical nature of economics, wrote that '[i]f I am right in my criticism of economics – I pray that I am not – then much of what economists do nowadays is a waste of time'. This is precisely what we were pointing out above: the story of economics has been lost and replaced with mathematical sophistication. We need to go back to telling the story, which is what this book does.

Indeed, this is not only a recent story. In fact, Keynes, while recognizing the importance of mathematics in a supportive role, also warned us about the dangers of placing too much faith in mathematics. In *The General Theory* he wrote that:

> [t]oo large a proportion of recent 'mathematical' economics are mere concoctions, as imprecise as the initial assumptions they rest on, which allow the author to lose sight of the complexities and interdependencies of the real world in a maze of pretentious and unhelpful symbols. (Keynes, 1936, p. 272)

Note that Keynes is precisely referring to the notion that many economists are more interested in making more sophisticated models than in explaining the real world. In terms of models, as Keynes (1973, p. 296) wrote in 1938 in a letter to his friend and colleague Roy Harrod:

> [e]conomics is a science of thinking in terms of models joined to the art of choosing models which are relevant to the contemporary world. It is compelled to be this, because, unlike the typical natural science, the material to which it is applied is, in too many respects, not homogeneous through time.

Joan Robinson (1962, p. 21), a colleague of Keynes at Cambridge University, explains that 'it is the business of economists, not to tell us what to do, but show why what we are doing anyway is in accord with proper principles'.

Economics is indeed the art of choosing models that are relevant to the world we live in, which is changing constantly. It must respect 'proper principles'.

The task is not an easy one, of course, but that is the challenge economists set themselves and that too many simply ignore.

Hence, better modelling (meaning more mathematical sophistication) is not the same as better economics. Today, there is a lot of energy being invested into making better and more sophisticated models, with an increasingly degree of complexity, which is somehow supposed to help the economist in his or her task of evaluating the economy and predict the future. Yet, the complexity of the model is irrelevant if its assumptions are flawed or wrong. Models must respect these 'proper principles'.

Economics and the social sciences

Where does economics fit then? It is, as Keynes (1973, p. 296) tells us, 'essentially a moral science and not a natural science'.

Before looking at how economics is actually related to other social sciences, we must first understand the world that economics is trying to analyse. In other words, what is this real world we live in? This should make clear why economics is right at home in the social sciences.

The approach or vision of economics in this book can be traced back a few hundred years to what is called the 'classical' period. This is the time of such great economists like Adam Smith, David Ricardo and Karl Marx – a time when agriculture was a dominant component of economic activity. While it is often the tradition to see vast differences between these three economists, and undoubtedly there were important differences, they all shared a similar approach to economics – they all saw mid-eighteenth-century society in terms of a struggle between social classes. Indeed, society was divided into the capitalists, that is, those who owned the means of production and in particular owned the tools to till the land and grow crops; the rentiers or those who rented the land to the capitalists; and the workers, that is, those who worked in the fields.

This way of seeing society as comprising social classes or macro-groups leads inevitably to the possibility of conflict – the potential conflict between classes as to the division of wealth. If you grow a sufficient amount of corn to guarantee crops the following year, what do you do with what is left over, or what is called the surplus? In other words, what do you do with the surplus corn over and above what is needed for planting the crops next season? Who gets what? How is it divided between capitalists, rentiers and workers?

After all, rentiers own the land on which the crops grew. So are they not entitled to the surplus? Without their land, there would not have been any crops to begin with. Yet, capitalists are the ones who own the machines needed to ensure the crops are planted and harvested, so surely they should get the surplus? But what about workers? After all, they are the ones who do the actual, physical work. Without workers to do the hard work, there would be no corn. As you can see, everyone claims a part of the surplus, and in this distribution of the surplus lies a potential conflict.

This way of seeing society is still relevant today. We still have capitalists who own factories and companies; the rentiers, or what we often call financial capitalists; and of course, we still have a large class of workers. Inevitably, there is still the great potential for conflict. Workers and their unions are again under attack and increasingly so. Corporations are making record profits, yet workers' wages are stagnating.

Related to this whole discussion is the debate over the increased polarization of wealth: the growing discrepancy between the very rich and the poor. This is the great conflict over the distribution of income and wealth. This has been made strikingly clear in recent years with social movements like 'Occupy Wall Street', which drew attention over what has become known as the '1 per cent'. At the core of this anger is the fact that the wealth is becoming increasingly concentrated at the top, among the 1 per cent and even among the 0.1 per cent of the population, while the rest struggles to make ends meet.

As this book will show, the distribution of income is an important component of overall economic growth. If the distribution of income or wealth is skewed, then this will affect economic growth in a negative way. There are many questions regarding this problem. What causes inequality? How is it precisely related to economic activity and growth? How do we solve the problem? Indeed, there is perhaps no more pressing matter today than the question over the inequality of income and wealth distribution within, as well as between, countries.

These are not easy questions to answer. But one thing is clear – to answer them, we must understand how economic policy is made, and how social dynamics come into play. This requires understanding what goes on beyond the confines of a narrowly defined notion of economics. As Keynes argued, we need to understand a bit of everything. So how then is economics related to other social sciences, and what can they teach the economist?

Political science can teach us many things about how economic policies are actually formulated and adopted. Economists can only recommend policies: politicians are the ones who implement them, so an understanding of how political parties and governments operate, and how policies are ultimately adopted, is paramount. Why is one policy adopted rather than another? Sometimes it has less to do with what is right for the country than what is the right thing to do for a political party to get re-elected. This will often have to do with the ideological leanings of the political party in power, and whether its representatives believe in free markets. As far as political science can help us understand power relationships between individuals and groups, the economist must be able to understand these relationships when he or she provides policy advice.

Psychology is another of the social sciences that has much to do with economics. For instance, economists are very interested in why and how consumers spend their income, and why firms decide to invest. Keynes famously referred to investment decisions by firms as being influenced by 'animal spirits'. According to Keynes (1936, pp. 161–2):

> Even apart from the instability due to speculation, there is the instability due to
> the characteristic of human nature that a large proportion of our positive activities
> depend on spontaneous optimism rather than mathematical expectations, whether
> moral or hedonistic or economic. Most, probably, of our decisions to do something
> positive, the full consequences of which will be drawn out over many days to come,
> can only be taken as the result of animal spirits – a spontaneous urge to action
> rather than inaction, and not as the outcome of a weighted average of quantitative
> benefits multiplied by quantitative probabilities.

Hence, understanding 'human nature', as Keynes puts it, is an important aspect of the economist's work. But what governs these animal spirits and these bursts of optimism? If not based on mathematical calculations, we must understand the motivations of the mind, which may require us to know the psychology behind such motivations.

Also, psychology helps us to understand motivations, the difference between needs and wants, full rationality versus bounded rationality, the impact of cognitive dissonance on decision-making, and more. It is a growing area of interest for economists looking to understand how decisions are made in an uncertain and complex world.

There is much to learn from sociology as well, especially with respect to the behaviour of social classes and movements, the exercise of power, the role of institutions, and the evolution of capitalism. In his famous book, *The Great*

Transformation, Karl Polanyi (1944) discusses the concept of 'embedded-ness', that is, the notion that individuals and firms are part of a greater existing social structure, and the actions between them must be analysed within these social networks.

Finally, history has probably the most important influence on economists. For instance, the economic and financial crisis that began in 2007–08 shares many characteristics with the Great Depression of the 1930s. Indeed, when the crisis erupted in 1929, income inequality, that is, the difference between the rich and the poor, was strikingly similar to the inequality that existed in 2007, thereby suggesting that in both cases inequality had an important role to play. Moreover, like in 1929, in the aftermath of the current crisis, governments adopted expansionary fiscal policies in the hope of turning fortunes around and leading us to a path of recovery. Yet, like in the Great Depression, when the governments stopped their fiscal largesse the economies slowed down and threatened to bring about another round of recession. Studying history should lead policy-makers to avoid repeating the mistakes of the past – mistakes that are unfortunately repeated today owing to the short-sightedness of most of the economics profession.

What then is economics?

In the previous sections we explored how economics is influenced by ideology, and what it shares with other social sciences. But we have not yet discussed what economics is. What then is economics?

This is not an easy question to answer. It depends on who you ask. As has become clear by now, there are two very different approaches or visions in economic analysis, and these two very broad schools of thought adopt very different methodologies – they ask very different questions and provide very different answers.

We can call these two approaches by two very general names – 'orthodox' and 'heterodox' – although there may also be other names. For instance, orthodox economics is often referred to as neoclassical economics or mainstream economics. Today, the large majority of the economics profession shares this approach. Heterodox economics is an approach that not only rejects orthodox economics and its presuppositions, but also proposes a clear alternative. It can also be labelled post-Keynesian or even post-classical economics.

If you ask an orthodox economist to define economics, you will get a very different answer than if you ask a heterodox economist. This should not be a surprise to you by now. After all, as we tried to make clear, different visions entail a different definition of economics.

In the next chapter we will develop the peculiarities of each school of thought, but let us focus here on a definition of what economics is, or rather, what does the economist do?

According to orthodox economists, the usual answer is that economics is about the 'efficient allocation of scarce resources'. There are three important words here: efficient, allocation and scarce.

According to this approach, scarcity plays a central role: when economists say resources are scarce, they mean their supply is limited. All resources or goods are scarce, irrespective of whether you are discussing labour, capital goods, water, or money.

Since the supply is scarce, it must therefore be allocated carefully among the various demands for the good. Hence, the supply must be rationed. We cannot allocate too much of one resource to a particular market, because then there will be too little in other markets.

This brings us finally to the efficient component of the above definition. It is assumed that markets are the best way to allocate the scarce resources among the competing demands for them. The laws of the market, which are deemed supreme, are entrusted with this allocation. It is assumed that markets do not harm – on their own they will achieve this efficient allocation. In this sense, there should be no interference with the laws of markets, and any institution, say the state or trade unions, but also price boards and more, that intervene with markets must be eliminated or their influence seriously curtailed.

Heterodox economists, however, consider economics in a very different way. First of all, rationing existing supplies of resources implies that markets are always operating at full employment. Yet, this is not the case, as economies typically do not perform at full capacity. In the real world, there is always some slack such that an efficient allocation is not required. For instance, the labour market usually has a 'reserve army of unemployed'. There is therefore no need to allocate labour efficiently between one sector and another.

Economists must therefore try to explain why markets do not function at full employment, and propose policies that will resolve these problems. Neoclassical economists usually attribute these problems to 'market failures', as if correcting for these failures will automatically bring economies to full employment. Such market failures are usually attributed to the intervention and interference of governments and other institutions.

In contrast, heterodox economists see these problems as inherent in the way markets operate: markets are complex and how they operate must be properly and adequately explained. Heterodox economists must therefore explain how production occurs, how labour is integrated into the process of production and accumulation, how wages are determined, and how profits are generated. What are the requirements for economic growth?

In this sense, economics becomes the study of the dynamic process of production, accumulation and distribution within the context of existing social and institutional relations, and the requirements for economic growth, while keeping in mind that these processes are subject to periods of instability, the forces of which must be explained.

Micro- versus macroeconomics

Before we end this introductory chapter, let us discuss briefly the differences between microeconomics and macroeconomics.

Simply put, microeconomics (from the Greek meaning 'that which is small') is about the behaviour of individual agents, households, firms and markets or industries. Government policies are also analysed for their impact on individual agents.

Macroeconomics, on the other hand, is about the economy as a whole, and how economic policies impact the overall economy – more specifically, growth, unemployment, distribution and inflation.

Neoclassical or mainstream economics believes that macroeconomics is simply an aggregation of individual behaviour. In other words, the roots of macroeconomics are to be found in microeconomics, that is, what economists call microfoundations (see the Conclusion of this volume for a full discussion). In this sense, there is no need for macroeconomics. After all, if we can understand the economy as a whole based on the study of a 'representative agent', then why bother with macroeconomics? Hence, by studying the behaviour of one agent we can extrapolate and understand the whole economy.

Yet, macroeconomics is subject to laws of its own that are unrelated to microeconomics. There are a number of fallacies of composition, or paradoxes, according to which what may be good for an individual or a firm may be harmful for the economy as a whole. A few examples will shed some light on this.

Take, for instance, savings. It makes sense for individuals to save a fraction of their income for a rainy day. After all, increased savings gives us security in case something unexpected happens. Yet, when we save, we are obviously not consuming. So, assume that everyone saves, then firms would be unable to sell many of their goods or services, and the economy would suffer. Increased savings for all may result in unemployment. This is the paradox of thrift.

Macroeconomics is more than just the study of the economy as a whole, as it also analyses the laws of production and distribution that govern it. By focusing on social groups rather than individuals, macroeconomics is about the dynamics of power relationships and the hierarchy of these groups relative to others, and the place of institutions. These questions cannot be treated by microeconomics, such that a field of its own, macroeconomics, is required to do justice to the complexity of these relations.

Finally, we live in a money-using economy, so, as Schumpeter argued, money should be introduced at the very beginning of economics (Chapter 4 discusses this argument in more detail). That is why this book, in contrast to all other macroeconomics textbooks, begins with an explanation of money (Chapter 4), the banking system and finance (Chapters 5 and 6), rather than considering them later on, which is typical of mainstream textbooks.

 REFERENCES

Bernanke, B.S. (2007), 'The economic outlook', Testimony Before the Joint Economic Committee of the US Congress, Board of Governors of the Federal Reserve System, 28 March, accessed 22 October 2015 at www.federalreserve.gov/newsevents/testimony/bernanke20070328a. htm.

Bernanke, B.S. (2008), 'The economic outlook', Testimony Before the Committee on the Budget of the US House of Representatives, Board of Governors of the Federal Reserve System, 17 January, accessed 22 October 2015 at www.federalreserve.gov/newsevents/testimony/ bernanke20080117a.htm#fn1.

Davidson, P. (2015), *Post Keynesian Theory and Policy: A Realistic Analysis of the Market Oriented Capitalist Economy*, Cheltenham, UK and Northampton, MA, USA: Edward Elgar Publishing.

Eichner, A. (1983), *Why Economics is Not Yet a Science*, Armonk, NY: M.E. Sharpe.

Kay, J. (2011), 'The map is not the territory: an essay on the state of economics', *John Kay: Accessible and Relevant Economics* [website], 4 October, accessed 24 August 2015 at www. johnkay.com/2011/10/04/the-map-is-not-the-territory-an-essay-on-the-state-of-economics.

Keynes, J.M. (1924), 'Alfred Marshall, 1842–1924', *Economic Journal*, **24** (135), 311–72.

Keynes, J.M. (1936), *The General Theory of Employment, Interest and Money*, London: Macmillan.

Keynes, J.M. (1973), *The Collected Writings of John Maynard Keynes. Volume XIV: The General*

Theory and After, Defence and Development, London: Macmillan and Cambridge University Press.

McCloskey, D. (2005), 'The trouble with mathematics and statistics in economics', *History of Economic Ideas*, **13** (3), 85–102.

Polanyi, K. (1944), *The Great Transformation. The Political and Economic Origins of Our Time*, New York: Farrar & Rinehart.

Robinson, J. (1962), *Economic Philosophy*, Harmondsworth, UK: Penguin Books.

Smith, A. (1759), *The Theory of Moral Sentiments*, London: A. Millar.

Smith, A. (1776), *An Inquiry into the Nature and Causes of the Wealth of Nations*, 2 vols, London: W. Strahan and T. Cadell.

Stiglitz, J.E. (2002), 'There is no invisible hand', *The Guardian*, 20 December, accessed 24 August 2015 at www.theguardian.com/education/2002/dec/20/highereducation.uk1.

A PORTRAIT OF ADAM SMITH (1723–90)

Adam Smith, born in Kirkcaldy, Scotland, is considered, along with David Ricardo and Karl Marx, as one of the fathers of classical political economy, a period that is also known as the birth of economics.

Among his vast contribution to economic analysis, Smith is known in particular for two important books, *The Theory of Moral Sentiments* (1759) and *An Inquiry into the Nature and Causes of the Wealth of Nations* (1776), more commonly referred to simply as *The Wealth of Nations*. Smith was a leading member of the Scottish Enlightenment movement.

Smith began his studies in social philosophy at the age of 14 at the University of Glasgow, and in 1740 entered Oxford University. Through a series of public lectures at the University of Edinburgh in 1748, Smith befriended in 1750 colleague and philosopher David Hume, himself an accomplished writer. This friendship resulted in Smith returning to the University of Glasgow to accept a professorship in Logic in 1751, and then in Moral Philosophy in 1752. He would eventually become rector of that university in 1787, although it was more an honorary position.

Smith wrote *The Theory of Moral Sentiments* in 1759, the premise of which is based on the notion that morality was influenced by the sympathy between individuals in society. The book was very successful and gave Smith great notoriety. He received a Doctorate in Law in 1762 from the University of Glasgow.

From 1764 to 1766, Smith left academia to tutor the future Duke of Buccleuch. This enabled him to travel widely through Europe, especially in France, where he befriended a number of intellectuals, notably François Quesnay, a leader of the Physiocrats. He retired in 1766 to his native Kirkcaldy, where he would eventually write *The Wealth of Nations*, a book that would take him more than nine years to write.

To this day *The Wealth of Nations* remains one of the most important books written in economics. The book is subject to different interpretations. Neoclassical economists tend to place the notion of the invisible hand at the heart of the book, emphasizing the virtues of free markets. For heterodox economists, by contrast, the book is more about the creation of wealth. Following the views of Quesnay and the Physiocrats, to generate wealth in the next period, the economy must produce an output that is capable of reproducing itself in the current period. Any surplus production must be divided among the various social classes, and this can generate conflict.

2

The history of economic theories

Heinrich Bortis

 OVERVIEW

This chapter presents the historical development of two fundamentally important strands of thought in the history of economic theories, namely economics and political economy:

- It deals with the basic properties of economics: the rational behaviour of economic agents on the marketplace is supposed to be coordinated by markets such that all the resources, labour most importantly, are fully employed.

- It puts to the fore the essential features of political economy, which aims at understanding the functioning of the socioeconomic system, representing a monetary production economy.

- It emphasizes the political economy strand. François Quesnay's fundamental *tableau économique*, the theoretical founding piece of political economy, is carefully presented and its link with modern classical–Keynesian political economy established. Here the macroeconomic price equation rests on the classical labour value and surplus principles. The quantity equation (the supermultiplier) embodies Keynes's principle of effective demand. A macroeconomic equilibrium with permanent involuntary unemployment is thus possible.

- The chapter also asks which of the two approaches – economics or political economy – is more plausible. It suggests that, for both theoretical and historical reasons, modern classical–Keynesian political economy picturing a monetary production economy is definitely superior to neoclassical economics, dealing with a market economy.

⊙→ KEYWORDS

• **Labour value principle:** Elaborated by David Ricardo, this states that the value of a product is, in principle, governed by the direct and indirect labour time socially necessary to produce it. Direct labour time is expended on producing the final product (say shoes), indirect labour on producing the means of production (used up fixed capital [machinery], intermediate products [leather] and basic products [electricity]).

• **Marginal principle:** Of fundamental importance in economics, this concept definitely came into being in the course of the Marginalist Revolution. The marginal principle appears in various shapes, namely marginal utility, marginal costs and marginal productivity. Marginal utility represents the additional utility occurring in response to an extra unit of some good consumed. Marginal costs are the supplementary costs arising if an additional unit of some good is produced. Marginal productivity indicates the output increase in response to employing an extra unit of some factor of production (labour, land, or capital).

• **Principle of effective demand:** Established by John Maynard Keynes in his *General Theory* (1936), this principle is based on the macroeconomic equilibrium condition 'saving = investment' and is expressed through the investment multiplier. This principle states that economic activity is, basically, not governed by supply factors (available resources) but by demand factors – public and private consumption and investment most importantly. A lack of effective demand will result in an underemployment equilibrium, implying involuntary unemployment.

• **Say's Law:** The French economist Jean Baptiste Say (1767–1832) claimed that supply creates its own demand. To produce leads to selling goods against money, which is, in turn, used to buy other goods. Hence, general overproduction and involuntary unemployment are both impossible. This supply-sided vision characterizes neoclassical mainstream economics until now.

• **Supermultiplier:** This is an elaborated form of Keynes's investment multiplier. The economy is set into motion by autonomous variables (government expenditures and exports). This brings about a cumulative process of production of both consumption and investment goods. The level of consumption is governed by the spending power of the population, depending, in turn, on the distribution of income. A more equitable distribution of income enhances the spending power of the population and is, as such, positively linked to the level of employment.

• **Surplus principle:** It was David Ricardo who neatly defined the social surplus over socially necessary (natural) wages within the framework of his corn model. Stated in modern terms the surplus principle says that, when prices are given, part of the national income accrues to the producers in the form of socially necessary wages. The remainder of the national income represents the social surplus: surplus wages, profits, land rents, and labour rents due to privileges and power positions.

Why are these topics important?

Economic theories aim at the systematic explanation of economic phenomena: value and prices, income distribution, employment levels, growth and business cycles, money and finance, and international trade. These phenomena are interrelated and may be explained in very different ways, according to the theoretical approach one takes, such as classical, neoclassical, Marxian, or Keynesian. For instance, for a neoclassical economist, income distribution is a market problem, whereas it is an issue of power for a Marxian political economist.

The existence of widely differing economic theories provides the basic reason why the study of the history of economic theories is required. John Maynard Keynes (1926) suggested notably that dealing with differing or even contradictory theories of value, distribution, employment and money leads one to independent and open-minded thinking, that is, to the 'emancipation of the mind'. This should enable the student of the history of economic theories to distil the most plausible theoretical principles, on which basis fruitful analyses and sound policy suggestions may then be founded. Hence, a socially useful teaching of economic theory *must* be based on the history of economic theories, as this chapter will show.

Two broad groups of economic theories

To bring fundamental issues in economic theory into the open, two broad groups of theories, economics and political economy, are considered here. David Ricardo's *Principles of Political Economy* and Alfred Marshall's *Principles of Economics* illustrate the relevance of this idea. Throughout this book, other chapters will refer to orthodox or mainstream views in a similar way as this chapter refers to economics, and to heterodox ideas in the way this chapter refers to political economy.

The economics approach

In economics, the great problems – value and prices, distribution and employment – are market issues, meaning that their determination is entirely from within their respective markets. The methodological approach in this regard is basically microeconomic: there are utility-maximizing households and profit-maximizing firms, whose behaviour is deemed 'rational' and is coordinated by markets in a socially meaningful way such that a social optimum prevails, namely, a 'Pareto optimum', defined as a situation where no one can become better off unless someone else is made worse off. In this sense, the macroeconomic general equilibrium is derived from microeconomic rational behaviour through the perfect functioning of markets. Only relative prices (the price of one good relative to another) are determined in neoclassical–Walrasian theory. In this theory, prices are such that the quantities demanded equal the quantities supplied on all markets, which means that an overall market equilibrium is established. Hence, the economy considered here is, essentially, an exchange economy – goods exchange for goods, and money is neutral. This implies that doubling the quantity of money doubles absolute prices (the price level of all goods), leaving relative prices and relative quantities unchanged. Schumpeter called this a 'real economy'. Moreover, money is said to be exogenous, meaning controlled by the central bank (see Chapter 4 for a full discussion). The distribution of income and the determination of the employment level are both market issues. Specifically, the law of supply and demand brings about full employment in competitive conditions. All those willing to work can find a job at the ruling market wage rate.

The neoclassical theory gained prominence and was rendered operable by Keynes's professor, Alfred Marshall, and his supply and demand scheme, which he applied to goods and factor markets.

The political economy approach

The political economy approach stands in sharp contrast to the economics approach. In the political economy approach, the social and circular process of production, which produces a social surplus over socially necessary wages, stands at the centre of things. The fundamental prices of goods are the prices of production based on the cost of producing these goods, not market prices determined by supply and demand. Labour values form the essence of these prices of production and summarize the essential features of the social and circular process of production. As discussed in Chapter 1, social power relations positively govern the distribution of income; in a normative perspective, income distribution becomes an issue of distributive justice, constituting the heart of social ethics. Several problems arise in relation to distributive justice. First, there is the determination of wage structures within enterprises and industries based on the evaluation of work places. Second, trade unions have the task of broadly fixing wage differentials between industries. And, third, socially appropriate profit rates on invested capital entering price calculation have to be fixed within firms and industries. The implementation of these simple principles is, evidently, of immense complexity.

As for the level of employment, it is governed by effective demand. Unemployment is essentially involuntary: workers do not choose not to work, but do not work because no one wants to hire them. Money and finance play an essential role. Money circulating in the real sector enables the production and circulation of goods and services, which are always exchanged against money, not against other goods. Hence, in the real sector, money always has a real-value equivalent, and money is only a representative of value. However, once money leaves the real sector to enter the financial sector, it becomes a store of value in the form of monetary wealth; as such money has *no* real equivalent but, in the course of portfolio diversification, looks for profitable investment in existing real and financial assets. If wealth accumulation is excessive, damaging interactions between the real sector and the financial sector may occur. Given the crucial importance of money, political economy, above all of the classical–Keynesian type, is inherently a monetary theory of production (see Chapter 3 for a full discussion).

Political economy is essentially about the socioeconomic system, made up of a material basis (that is, the economy with the social process of production at the centre), and an institutional superstructure, made up of social, legal, political and cultural institutions, which are given or evolve but slowly (Bortis, 1997, pp. 89–95). The socioeconomic system has laws of its own; most important is the principle of effective demand. Contrary to the economics perspective, there may be strong contradictions between the functioning of the system as a whole and the behaviour of economic agents. Keynes's paradox of thrift is most prominent: if all individuals save more, consumption and the volume of investment both decrease and the economy may precipitate into a slump. This is in stark contrast to the economics approach, where more savings imply more investment and less unemployment.

In the next section, let us turn to the history of economic theories. We start by sketching the historical development of economics. Subsequently we outline the making of political economy. Finally, both strands of thought are assessed to uncover the more plausible approach fit for policy purposes.

The history of economics

Adam Smith is the founder of economics. His theory of value and distribution is dominated by the 'adding-up theorem': all prices of final goods consist of a wage, profit and rent component, meaning that the price of goods is obtained by adding up wages, profits and rents, which are the prices of the factors of production called labour, capital and land.

Adam Smith

Smith's socioeconomic system is grounded on the principle of propriety, a combination of fellow feeling and self-interest (Smith, 1976a). Contrary to modern neoclassical economics, this principle implies that ethics is *on* the marketplace, which means that the fundamental prices are social, and, as such, fair and natural prices (Smith, 1976b). For example, the money wage rate has to be such as to ensure a decent life for workers. And the price of agricultural products would have to be at a sufficiently high level to bring agricultural incomes broadly in line with incomes in industry.

However, in the short run, market prices could fluctuate around their natural level. Hence, there are two prices in Smith: a natural price, determined by the permanently acting socio-ethical principle of propriety, and a market price, which brings about deviations from the natural price, owing, for example, to extraordinary climatic conditions temporarily affecting the output of agricultural goods, to a natural calamity, or to imperfect foresight of producers who have over- or underestimated future demand. However, there is a continuous tendency for market prices to get nearer to their natural level: if the realized profit rate exceeds the natural profit rate, entrepreneurs expand productive capacities, and vice versa, thus narrowing the gap between market and natural prices. Hence, the natural price is a kind of centre of gravitation attracting market prices.

Natural prices also imply natural wages and natural profit rates, as well as natural rents on land. Hence, if all individuals acted according to the principle of propriety, inherent in human nature, a harmonious economy and society would come into being. In such an economy, full employment would naturally prevail, because in Smith's view economic activity is entirely supply determined. Hence, the available quantities of production factors – labour, land and capital – determine the extent of economic activity, not effective demand, that is, the demand for goods and services in terms of money by consumers, producers and the state. This implies that saving is always invested. Given this, Smith explicitly speaks of the virtue of higher saving, which increases investment, hence economic growth, and as the final result enhances the wealth of a nation (Smith, 1976b).

Adam Smith's theory of socio-ethical natural prices did not gain prominence. Instead, the directly visible market prices moved to the fore, giving rise to a vaguely formulated demand and supply theory of price determination. The ethical element was pushed into the background and, as a final result, entirely discarded. This development ended up in the 'Marginalist Revolution' of the 1870s.

Jean-Baptiste Say

In his *Traité d'économie politique* (1803), the French economist Jean-Baptiste Say, an enthusiastic follower of Adam Smith, attempted to rationalize the harmonious and self-regulating property of a market or exchange economy. His famous law, known as Say's Law, explains that 'supply creates its own demand' ($C-M-C'$). It implies that there cannot be an overproduction of *all* goods: any producer sells his or her product (C) against money (M), which in turn is spent on some other product (C') needed by the producer of commodity C. Thus, money is a pure medium of exchange, a veil covering the real transactions ($C-C'$): money is neutral. With the classical economists, David Ricardo in particular, Say's Law was given a macroeconomic interpretation: saving, consisting of profits, is always invested, thus heralding Smith's 'virtue of saving' – higher saving leads to larger investment levels, enhancing economic growth. Hoarding money is irrational, since it does not yield any revenue; given this, saving is always invested, directly or indirectly through banks.

Marginal analysis

As we move into the first half of the nineteenth century, marginal analysis was making its way through underground movements. The notion of marginal utility was developed, giving rise to Gossen's two laws ([1854] 1983), namely the law of diminishing marginal utility and the law of equalization of the marginal utility–price ratios, implying utility maximization. Gossen's first law states that if an additional unit of some good, for example a slice of bread, is consumed, total utility increases, to an ever-smaller extent though; thus, additional (marginal) utility diminishes. According to Gossen's second law, total utility is maximized if, for each dollar spent, the consumer gets the same amount of additional (marginal) utility for the last unit of each good consumed. If for some good the consumer gets a higher amount of additional utility than for other goods, more of the former good will be consumed and, as a consequence, marginal utility provided by additional unity of this good diminishes; in contrast, consumption of other goods is reduced and the marginal utility provided by the last unit consumed increases. This adjustment process goes on until the ratio between marginal utility and price is the same for all goods. At this stage, total utility cannot be increased further, implying that total utility is maximized.

By contrast, the notions of marginal productivity and of marginal costs were still vaguely formulated around 1850. (The marginal productivity of a factor of production is the additional output added by an additional unit of that factor, all other factors being held constant. Marginal costs are the supplementary costs incurred if an additional unit of output is produced.)

These 'marginalist' underground movements finally led to the 'Marginalist Revolution', which occurred broadly between 1870 and 1890 and provided the foundations of the currently still ruling neoclassical mainstream.

The neoclassical school

Among the great founders of the neoclassical school are Stanley Jevons, Carl Menger, Léon Walras and Alfred Marshall. Walras elaborated the general equilibrium model, where all markets are in equilibrium simultaneously, which gradually became the fundamental framework of neoclassical theory. General equilibrium is established by price changes with quantities given, hence already produced. Equilibrium prices have to be such as to equalize the quantities supplied and the quantities demanded for each good. Hence, Walras's basic model is a pure exchange model. Subsequently, production also becomes a matter of exchange. The available quantities of factors of production are combined in each enterprise in proportions such that each dollar spent on labour, land or capital yields the same additional output for a supplementary unit of these factors of production. This implies cost minimization or maximization of profits, which, in turn, goes along with the optimal allocation of resources, that is, the factors of production.

General equilibrium and partial equilibrium approaches

The Walrasian model is of immense complexity, as it describes the demand and supply relationships, based on rational behaviour, and equilibrium conditions across all markets, required to determine simultaneously all prices and quantities. Alfred Marshall then rendered Walras's model operable through the partial equilibrium approach, which deals with supply and demand conditions on specific markets. As a result, each market is considered in isolation in order to be able to set out very simply the way towards equilibrium between supply and demand. This is illustrated by the famous Marshallian 'cross',[1] which is reproduced over and over again in economics textbooks (Figure 2.1).

In Figure 2.1, the demand curve is downward sloping owing to diminishing marginal utility. On the other hand, the supply curve is upward sloping, as marginal costs increase when the quantity produced grows. The equilibrium price (p^*) is determined by the intersection of both curves.

Figure 2.1 The
Marshallian cross

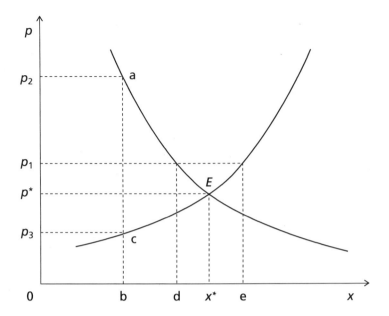

In a Walrasian framework, equilibrium is reached by price adjustments: if the price (such as p_1 in Figure 2.1) is higher than the equilibrium price, the quantity supplied ($0e$) will exceed the quantity demanded ($0d$) and the price will decline until equilibrium (given by price p^* and quantity x^*) is reached. While price adjustments are typical for neoclassical economics, Marshall's route to equilibrium is, however, based on quantity adjustments. For example, to the left of the equilibrium position (E in Figure 2.1), the 'demand price' ($p_2 = ab$ in Figure 2.1), which consumers are willing to pay and producers would get for a certain quantity of goods supplied ($0b$), is above the 'supply price' ($p_3 = bc$) indicating the additional (marginal) costs of production of an extra unit. The difference between the two prices represents an additional profit for firms. Hence, entrepreneurs will produce more until the supply price and the demand price coincide at the point of intersection (E) of the two curves. At this point additional profits are zero and total profits are maximized (if the minimum of the average total costs is below the line p^*E), reflecting rational behaviour of producers.

Since with perfect competition there are a great number of firms in a given market, any firm cannot influence the market price (p^*) and can sell as much as it wants of its goods at this price. Hence, in neoclassical–Marshallian theory output must be determined by supply factors. Indeed, as long as the given market price exceeds the marginal costs incurred in producing an additional unit of the relevant good, the individual firm will expand its production until marginal costs are equal to the (predetermined) market price (p^*). Hence, each firm maximizes the volume of its output, which is determined by scarce resources. This implication of neoclassical–Marshallian partial equilibrium analysis is of paramount importance, because output appears as being determined by supply factors and is, as such, supply-side economics. This is also characteristic of current mainstream economics.

Marshall's *Principles of Economics*, published in 1890, thus became the 'bible' of economic theory. This work represents the basis for the great number of economics' textbooks written after World War II.

Within this Walrasian–Marshallian framework, all the great economic problems are solved on the basis of the principle of supply and demand with all markets being interlinked. As argued by Schumpeter (1954, p. 242, our emphasis):

> the all-pervading interdependence [of markets, hence of prices and quantities] is the fundamental fact, the analysis of which is the chief source of additions that the specifically scientific attitude has to make to the practical man's knowledge of economic phenomena; and that the most fundamental of all specifically scientific questions is the question whether analysis of that interdependence will yield relations sufficient to determine – if possible, uniquely – all the prices and quantities of products and productive services that constitute the economic system. [Walras's] *system of equations*, defining (static) equilibrium in a system of interdependent quantities, *is the Magna Carta of economic theory*.

This statement is of paramount importance and has greatly contributed to establishing the still ongoing supremacy of the neoclassical mainstream. Indeed, most neoclassical economists cannot imagine that one can theorize outside the Walrasian–Marshallian system.

The neoclassical synthesis

Neoclassical economics has dominated the theoretical scene from the 1870s onwards until now. Only in the great cyclical upswing, lasting broadly from 1950 to 1973, the year of the first oil price shock, had neoclassical economics made some concessions to Keynesian economics in the form of Paul Samuelson's neoclassical synthesis, which brings together Keynes's theory of employment determination through effective demand and Marshall's principle of supply and demand applied to the markets of factors of production and of final goods. A kind of mechanical Keynesianism in the shape of fiscal and monetary policies was to bring about full employment; given this, the goods markets would determine the prices of the final products and the associated quantities, and the factor markets regulate distribution, that is, wages, profits and rents at the full employment level.

However, the neoclassical synthesis remained essentially neoclassical economics and, as a consequence, Keynes was to be integrated into neoclassical economics. In fact, in his *General Theory* Keynes claimed that effective demand erected a barrier to the left of the labour market equilibrium. As a result, full employment could not be reached. This becomes understandable if Figure 2.1 is considered to illustrate the labour market, where p represents the average wage rate and x the labour force. The effective demand barrier would be given by the line ab. In a Keynesian perspective, the equilibrium level of employment would be given by 0b and involuntary unemployment would equal bx^*. Entrepreneurs would not hire more than 0b workers, because the additional output produced by these workers, assisted by the existing capital stock or industrial plant, could not be sold, precisely because of limited effective demand.

However, from the 1970s onwards, neoclassical economists began to turn the tables. Positions to the left of the labour market equilibrium were explained by the average wage rate being above the equilibrium wage rate. Unemployment arose because wages (p_2 in Figure 2.1) were too high and had to be lowered in order to bring about a tendency towards full employment at (p^*, x^*). The principle of effective demand was eliminated and the way to fully restoring the reign of supply and demand was open.

Keynesianism indeed collapsed in the 1970s with the advent of inflation, owing to a sharp rise in the price of oil. In the neoclassical view, inflation made some of the basic core assumptions of Keynesianism unsustainable. Increasing the quantity of money, it was argued, did not result in lower interest rates, higher investment volumes and larger output and employment levels, but simply in higher price levels. Given this, from the mid-1970s onwards, monetarism, led by Milton Friedman, triumphed.

Monetarism and new classical economics

Monetarists are a group of economists who believe that competitive markets produce an inherent tendency towards full employment and that the quantity of money decided by the central bank determines only the price level.

Monetarism was developed further in the Walrasian new classical model, where prices are entirely flexible. As a result, there is a continuous market clearing, that is, the quantity supplied always equals the quantity demanded on each market. In regard to Figure 2.1, we are always in a (p^*, x^*) equilibrium situation in *all* markets. However, the behaviour of producers, consumers and states (economic agents) has consequences for the future. Economic agents attempt to come to grips with future developments through taking into account all available information: for example, the best available economic theory (the general equilibrium model), the possible evolution of the oil price, future fiscal policies and the evolution of public debt. However, economic activity is influenced from time to time by unforeseeable external shocks, which may occur either on the demand side (important shifts in demand for some goods) or on the supply side (profound technological changes: the digital revolution, for example). Supply and demand shocks lead to cyclical movements in economic activity, that is, movements in the scale of output and employment. The new classical economists postulate that in the course of business cycles the economy is always in equilibrium too: at market clearing prices, the quantities supplied always match the quantities demanded. Most importantly, there is no involuntary unemployment (which is evident if Figure 2.1 is considered as representing the labour market). All those out of work are voluntarily unemployed, that is, they do not want to accept a job at the prevailing wage rate. Consequently, new classical economics, led by Robert Lucas, is entirely supply oriented. The actually existing quantities of production factors govern economic activity, that is, output and employment. This equilibrium vision of the economy is strictly anti-Keynesian. Indeed, with Keynes, effective demand in money terms by consumers, producers and the state governs economic activity. It increases as the distribution of income becomes more equal, which in turn enhances the spending power of the population. Hence, Keynes and Lucas are, in fact, the great antagonists in modern economic theory.

New Keynesian economics

While new classical economics is equilibrium economics, new Keynesian economics is disequilibrium economics. The new Keynesians assume an equilibrium position does exist (p^*, x^* in Figure 2.1). A disequilibrium (such as p_2 and the quantity 0b in Figure 2.1) may occur and persist, because there is no Walrasian auctioneer to establish the equilibrium price. Indeed, disequilibrium situations may persist for various reasons. For example, the volume of production (0b in Figure 2.1) cannot be increased owing to a persistent shortage of some factors of production or because of a supply cartel, which restricts output. Persistent disequilibria may also exist because some institutions obstruct the functioning of perfect markets as pictured by the demand and supply curves in Figure 2.1. If Figure 2.1 represented the labour market, trade unions would try to shift the labour supply curve upwards and to the left, entrepreneurial associations would attempt to shift the labour demand curve to the left and downwards. A new equilibrium would eventually come into being far to the left of the original equilibrium (E), thereby implying an employment level far below the full employment level $(0x^*)$. All in all, imperfect competition, trade unions, cartels, monopolies and oligopolies may bring about persistent unemployment.

The history of political economy

Considering the history of political economy means leaving the frictionless machine of economics to enter an altogether different theoretical world. What is put to the fore is not the market but the social and circular process of production. The social product – gross domestic product (GDP) – results from a common effort within all industries. Firms can produce only because they receive goods from other firms. For example, the shoe factory receives leather and specific machines; on the other hand, firms producing primary goods (such as iron, steel, electricity and machine tools) deliver their commodities to firms producing intermediate goods and final goods. Hence, the social process of production is a complex system of deliveries and receipts, which is represented by the so-called Leontief quantity system. Given the social nature of production, all the great problems of economic theory – value and price, distribution, employment, money and finance – are social and macroeconomic issues. We will expand on this later.

Political economy also rests on a specific vision of society. The heart of the economy is the social process of production and monetary and financial institutions (the central bank and the banking system). The economy is a monetary production economy that forms the material basis of a society and produces the social surplus, that is, the social product (or GDP) minus the socially necessary consumption by producers – namely, workers.

The social surplus is used up to maintain and to expand the production system through gross investments and, most importantly, to build up political, social, legal and cultural institutions as well as a comprehensive education system. These institutions form the institutional superstructure, and together with economic institutions (enterprises in the social process of production and the banking system) they form a complementary set of institutions. Given the complementarity of institutions, the material basis of a society and its institutional superstructure form a system or a structured entity, which may be called the socioeconomic system or society for short. In political economy, society is primary and the starting point of analysis.

Given this, political economy is essentially about the functioning of the socioeconomic system, not about the rational behaviour of individuals, which is supposed to be coordinated in a socially meaningful sense by competitive markets.

François Quesnay

The political economy strand starts with the French surgeon François Quesnay (1694–1774), whose *tableau économique fundamental* (fundamental economic table) (Meek, 1962, p. 275), first published in 1758, represents for the first time in the history of economic theories the social and circular process of production with flows of goods moving between industry and agriculture, and flows of money moving in the opposite direction to buy the goods. Hence, goods are always exchanged against money, never against other goods. Agriculture delivers necessary consumption goods and raw materials to industry (handicrafts and manufactures), which in turn provides agriculture with industrial consumption goods (cloth and shoes, for example) and various tools (investment goods).

In Quesnay's model, prices are determined within the process of production. These prices of production are known *before* goods arrive on the market, that is, before they enter the process of circulation, as opposed to being determined by supply and demand once they arrive on the markets. All prices are made up of the costs of production and of a profit or rent element.

The expenditures of the state are of the greatest importance for Quesnay. As a physician he considers the state as the heart of the socioeconomic system: through its spending, the state injects money (blood) into the socioeconomic system (body); money is reproduced by the agricultural sector (the stomach) and returned to the heart (the state) in the form of land rent, thereby providing revenues to the state. This emerges from Quesnay's *tableau économique* (Figure 2.2), presented here in an elaborated form. In fact, Quesnay's original figure contains the three central columns (III, IV and V) only (Meek, 1962, p. 275), and, as such, is not easy to understand. To render Quesnay's *tableau* intelligible, columns I, II and VI have been added in Figure 2.2.

Quesnay's *tableau* represents the French economy around 1750 in its sound and natural state. To be able to describe its functioning, a glance at the structure of the French society is required. In pre-revolutionary, eighteenth-century France, the landowners, the nobility, the king and the upper strata of the bourgeoisie also make up the state, which, in addition, comprises the army and the state administration, including the legal

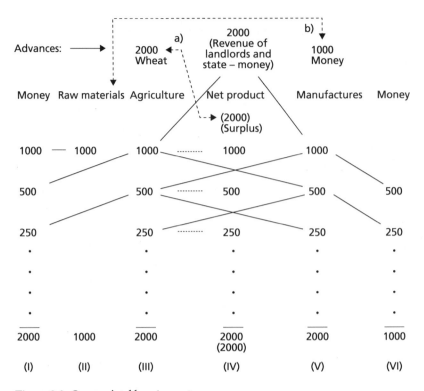

Figure 2.2 Quesnay's *tableau économique*

system. The state revenue (land rents and taxes) amounts to £2000 and appears at the top of column IV. Column III stands for agriculture. Here the tenant farmers dispose of advances in the form of wheat (necessary consumption goods) with a monetary value of £2000. These advances are required to feed the agricultural labour force for the coming production period (a year). The manufacturing sector will use its advances – £1000 in money form (top of column V) – to buy raw materials from the agricultural sector (column II).

The economy, that is, the processes of social production and circulation, is set into motion through the spending of the revenues of the state or the landlords (£2000). Half of the state expenditures (£1000) is spent on agricultural goods (column III), half on manufactured goods (£1000, column V). This demand initiates production with a money value and corresponding income amounting to £1000 in both sectors. Agricultural goods (necessary consumption goods) worth £1000 and manufactured goods worth £1000 now flow to the state to maintain the king and the nobility, government and administration as well as the army. Subsequently, tenant farmers spend half of the newly produced income (£500) on manufactured goods (consumption and (replacement) investment goods, column V); the other half (£500) is put aside in money terms (column I). Similarly, the manufacturing sector buys agricultural goods (necessary consumption goods) from agriculture (£500 in column III), putting aside £500 in view of paying for the raw materials of the next year (column VI). The process goes on as suggested in Figure 2.2.

The surplus column IV remains to be explained. This requires a careful consideration of the figures in column III (£1000, £500, and so on), which have three different meanings. In the first place, these figures stand for the expenditures in money terms of the state (£1000) and of the manufacturing sector (£500) on agricultural (necessary consumption) goods. Second, these amounts represent the money value of inputs in the (productive) agricultural sector. Indeed, the tenant farmers use the sums of money in column III they have received from the landlords (the state) and the manufacturing sector, to pay wages to the agricultural labour force and to buy seeds. The agricultural workers and the tenant farmers spend these amounts of money on the advances of the agricultural sector (wheat worth £2000 at the top of column III). Now, production in the agricultural sector may start. An input of £1000 (labour and seeds) leads to an output of £2000, an input of £500 yields an output of £1000, and so on. Hence, in the third meaning, the figures in column III represent outputs, replacing the inputs incurred. Moreover, owing to the forces of nature, a surplus in terms of wheat amounting to £1000, £500 and so on arises (£2000 in column IV). The surplus in money terms arises in column I (£2000) and consists of half of the sales receipts from the state (£500) and from the sales to the manufacturing sector (£1500): £500 for food sales (columns III and V from the third line onwards) and £1000 for the sale of raw materials. Indeed, the manufacturing sector spends its advances of £1000 in money terms (top of column V) to buy raw materials from the agricultural sector (column II). The surplus in money terms (column I) is used to pay the rents to the landlords (the state); these revenues provide the advances of the state to be spent next year (£2000 at the top of column IV).

Quesnay rightly argues that a surplus can arise in agriculture only, where the goods necessary in the social process of production are produced. In the (sterile) manufacturing sector no surplus can arise. Here output is worth £2000 (column V) and the inputs are delivered by agriculture: raw materials worth £1000 (columns II and V) and food, also worth £1000 (columns III and V). In the manufacturing sector competition is so intense as to reduce profits to zero; given this the value of inputs (£2000) equals the value of output, also £2000 (column V).

Quesnay has been criticized for postulating that land (agriculture) is productive, not labour. This is a misunderstanding. In fact, in the social process of production, land and labour are complementary. Marx said that man (labour) interacts with nature (land) by means of tools and machines. Quesnay looked at production from the land perspective, Ricardo from the labour perspective. The different points of view taken by Quesnay and Ricardo arise from the different problems both were dealing with. Quesnay considered the issues of the scale of economic activity – the level of output (and employment) – and distribution, Ricardo dealt with the issues of value and distribution.

Output and income are thus produced in both the agricultural and manufacturing sectors, enabling both sectors to buy goods from each other. This interaction between both sectors brings the social nature of production, circulation and consumption to the open. This mutual spending of income represents a cumulative process, resulting in the production of agricultural goods worth £5000 in money terms (columns II, III and IV in Figure 2.2) and of manufactures amounting to £2000 (column V). The total output of £7000 is the maximum output, implying full employment. Hence, in a natural and healthy state the appropriate distribution and spending proportions result in the maximum scale of economic activity. Based on the healthy state of the economy, surgeon Quesnay is able to deal with states of economic illness. Most importantly, he worries about landowners not spending the entire amount of their rent (£2000), but engaging in unproductive speculative activities or simply hoarding. Obviously, if the landowners spend less than £2000, economic activity and employment would be reduced, inducing thereby system-caused involuntary unemployment. In 1930, Keynes said that crises arise because money is flowing from the real sector, where production takes place, to the financial sector, in which no income-generating transactions occur. Both Quesnay and Keynes are thereby brothers in spirit.

To be sure, there is no self-regulation of the economic system in Quesnay's *tableau économique*. For Quesnay, the level of economic activity and employment is a political issue, associated with the level of government expenditures and the distribution of national income. Socially appropriate proportions between agricultural rents or the social surplus, the revenues of the farmers, and the wages of the agricultural labour force as well as the industrial wage bill have to be established. For example, the wages in agriculture must be such as to use up the advances in agriculture (£2000). Quesnay explicitly insists on the necessity of paying fair and good wages to agricultural labourers. Not using up the advances would reduce production and bring about a crisis situation.

Classical–Keynesian political economy

The classical–Keynesian supermultiplier to be dealt with at the end of this section, the Leontief quantity system (deliveries and receipts of goods) and Sraffa's prices of production (Sraffa, 1960, p. 11) are straightforward developments of Quesnay's *tableau*. Hence, classical–Keynesian political economy (see Bortis, 1997, 2003, 2013 and 2015) is the elaborated form of Quesnay's *tableau économique* in modern dress. This is perhaps the most important fact in the history of political economy. François Quesnay indeed appears as the founder of political economy.

David Ricardo

Adam Smith, who pushed the social process of production and the state into the background, radically changed the picture and the self-regulating market now eclipses production. With David Ricardo, however, the pendulum of economic theory swung back to political economy: the functioning of the socioeconomic system moves to the fore at the expense of the behaviour of individuals. The social process of production moves to the fore again, with exchange or markets – so important for Adam Smith – being pushed into the background. In contradistinction to Quesnay, however, Ricardo considered the labour aspect of social production. The value of commodities is now governed by direct and indirect labour time – this is what is called the labour theory of value. In other words, what gives value to goods is the amount of labour (or labour time) used in their production. Labour can then be divided into direct and indirect labour. Direct labour is used to produce final products; indirect labour is used for producing the various means of production, namely, used up fixed capital, intermediate and primary goods. Hence, labour values represent the social effort made to produce any commodity.

However, the main problem Ricardo considered is not value but distribution. According to him:

> [t]he produce of the earth – all that is derived from its surface by the united
> application of labour, machinery, and capital, is divided among the three classes
> of the community; namely, the proprietor of the land, the owner of the stock
> or capital necessary for its cultivation, and the labourers by whose industry it
> is cultivated. . . To determine the laws which regulate this distribution, is the
> principal problem in Political Economy. (Ricardo, [1821] 1951, p. 5)

These laws consist of two principles that operate in agriculture, where necessaries, represented by corn, are produced.

First, there is the marginal principle, which determines agricultural rents. The least fertile land just cultivated gets no rent. This is a simplifying assumption required in order to establish the labour value principle. Indeed, with the rent on the least fertile (marginal) land eliminated, the cost of producing corn is determined by direct and indirect labour costs only. This highlights the ingenious method used by Ricardo. He was in fact dealing only with essentials or fundamental causal forces, namely, principles that are absolutely necessary to explain a phenomenon – the value of produced goods in the present instance. Hence, the title of his main work: *On the Principles of Political Economy and Taxation*. In models dealing with fundamentals or principles:

> [only] what is considered to be essential or constitutive to a phenomenon is included in the model, which is a picture, in fact a *reconstruction* or *recreation* of what . . .*constitutes* a phenomenon (for example, prices, quantities and employment levels in political economy). This recreation is performed by reason interacting with intuition and is analogous. . .to the representation of essential information for the user of the underground through a map. (Bortis, 2003, p. 413, original emphasis)

Joan Robinson (1962, p. 33) also compared a theory with a map, adding that a realistic map where the entire reality is represented would be totally useless. Ricardo is very important for political economy, because he was the first to build a logically consistent theoretical model, made up of essentials, in order to be able to explain the immensely complex real world by simple causal models, which, in turn, provide the basis for policy prescriptions.

Hence, Ricardo eliminates rent, crucial for Quesnay, from value formation. This can be generalized: labour values govern prices where the conditions of production are most difficult. This gives rise to various types of rent, occurring when the conditions of production are more favourable.

Now, with rent determined through the marginal principle, another distributional principle, namely the surplus principle, comes in to determine wages and profits in agriculture in real terms, that is, in terms of corn. Ricardo first postulated that the real wage rate is not governed by market forces, that is, by supply and demand, but by social and cultural factors:

> The power of the labourer to support himself, and the family which may be necessary to keep up the number of labourers, does not depend on the quantity of money which he may receive for wages, but on the quantity of food, necessaries, and conveniences become essential to him from habit, which that money will

purchase. The natural price of labour, therefore, depends on the price of the food, necessaries, and conveniences required for the support of the labourer and his family. (Ricardo, [1821] 1951, p. 93)

In this view, profits are merely the surplus over wages of the agricultural output, net of rent. Interestingly, in the view of David Ricardo profits were only justified if they were invested.

In his corn model (Ricardo, 1815) the rate of profits is given by the ratio of corn profits to the agricultural wages sum (circulating capital), also in terms of corn, which stands for necessary consumption goods. This implies two things. First, the agricultural labour force not only produces corn, but also the tools required in production, fixed capital (machinery) being absent. Second, distribution must necessarily be regulated in the sectors producing basic or socially necessary goods, because the natural wage rate, hence the wages sum (circulating capital), are in terms of corn. Given this, the (natural) agricultural profit rate determines the rate of profits in the sectors producing luxuries, silk for example.

Ricardo's corn model was criticized on the grounds that, in an industrial economy, corn was not the only good because there were different consumption and capital goods. Moreover, fixed capital was gaining in importance. A new measure had to be found for the wage goods and for calculating the rate of profits. In his *Principles*, Ricardo proposes measuring the value of all produced goods by direct and indirect labour, which in a way replaces corn. This greatly widens the scope of Ricardo's theory of income distribution, essentially based on the surplus principle. Potentially, distribution becomes positively a matter of social power and normatively an issue of distributive justice.

Reactions against Ricardo and Marx

Given the 'dangerous' and political implications of his theory of value and distribution (recall the discussion in Chapter 1), the reaction against Ricardo set in almost immediately after his death (Dobb, 1973, p. 96) in the form of Smithianism, that is, still vague demand and supply theory. While economics – the precursor of the Marginalist School – grew stronger underground, suddenly in 1867 a powerful piece of political economy was published, that is, the first volume of Karl Marx's *Das Kapital* (Marx, 1973–74), which placed Ricardo's *Principles* in a very wide and profound framework of politics and history. In the mind of many of the time, the two books were considered part of the same theoretical cloth.

This ideological factor was certainly a crucial element in setting off the Marginalist Revolution. In fact, Ricardo and Marx were unable to provide a satisfactory solution to the so-called 'transformation problem', that is, the problem of transforming labour values into prices of production. The difficulty arose first because of the growing importance of fixed capital goods, embodying past labour and having a durability of several years, and second because the rate of profits had in principle to be uniform in all sectors of production to enable the classical mechanism of competition to work properly: capital would always flow to sectors where the realized rate of profits durably exceeded the normal rate of profits, and vice versa. Now, the problem arises if the conditions of production, given by the ratio of the (past) labour embodied in fixed capital to (present) labour embodied in prime costs, is unequal in the various sectors of production (textiles, cars, and so on). Given the uniform rate of profits, the prices of production will exceed the total labour – past and present – embodied in the production of some good if its production is capital intensive, and vice versa. Hence, the prices of production are not proportional to labour values (wage costs) but deviate from them in an unpredictable way. Ricardo and Marx were unable to explain how labour values were transformed into prices of production (this problem was solved by Piero Sraffa in his 1960 book *Production of Commodities by Means of Commodities*). Neoclassical economists considered that classical value theory had moved into a blind alley and as a consequence decided to shift the explanation of value from the social process of production to the market, governed by the marginal principle embodied in the law of supply and demand. This is the essence of the Marginalist Revolution.

and thats all we get

Marshall's *Principles of Economics* (first published in 1890) thus became the 'bible' of economics and the basis of the abundant neoclassical textbooks literature. Subsequently, classical political economy along the lines of François Quesnay and David Ricardo had 'been submerged and forgotten since the advent of the "marginal" method' (Sraffa, 1960, p. v).

A classical–Keynesian counter-revolution

However, in the interwar years 1926–36, Piero Sraffa and John Maynard Keynes produced a theoretical twin revolution, in fact a classical–Keynesian counter-revolution against the utterly dominating neoclassical school. In the mid-1920s Sraffa attacked Marshall's supply curve and argued that marginal costs were not rising, but remained constant when output varied, because capacity utilization increases and money wages are fixed by contracts. Most importantly, however, money wages do not rise when additional workers are hired, because of ever-existing unemployment, which exerts a continuous downward pressure on wages. With marginal or prime costs given, firms may price their goods based on what is called a mark-up approach: prices are determined by imposing a mark-up over costs of production. To have a benchmark price, the mark-up is imposed on prime costs at normal capacity utilization in order to cover fixed costs and to bring about a normal rate of profits. Market prices and realized profits will, as a rule, deviate from these (normal) benchmark prices and actual capacity utilization will differ from normal capacity utilization. If realized profit rates are persistently below the normal profit rate, firms tend to cut back capacities, and vice versa. This is the classical view of competition: the prices of production are determined in the production process and demand determines the quantities produced.

In his 1960 book, Sraffa shows how the prices of production are determined and distribution regulated *in principle* within the social and circular process of production (see particularly p. 11). With the normal prices determined, demand determines the quantities that can be sold. Given this, Sraffa has provided the microeconomic foundations for Keynes's theory of aggregate output and employment as governed by effective demand.

Indeed, in *The General Theory of Employment, Interest and Money* (1936) John Maynard Keynes, the second great protagonist of the twin revolution of the interwar years, for the first time convincingly challenges Say's Law, stating that economic activity is governed by supply factors, that is, scarce resources in the form of labour, land and capital. The Keynesian revolution represents the monetary way to the principle of effective demand (Garegnani, 1983), exhibited by the multiplier relation, explaining how both output and employment are determined in principle:

$$Q = (1/s)\,I = [(1/(1-c)]\,I \qquad (2.1)$$

The economy is set into motion through investment expenditures (I), which subsequently bring about a cumulative process of demand and production of consumption goods. The equilibrium level of output determined by the multiplier $(1/s) = [(1/(1-c)]$ may imply an employment level well below the full employment level ($Q < Q_f$). System-caused involuntary unemployment comes into being. Contrary to Say's Law, general overproduction, that is overproduction of *all* goods, is therefore possible.

The principle of effective demand could be established because saving and consumption mainly depend on current income, and the rate of interest has but a minor and unpredictable effect on them. The rate of interest has the new task of bringing into line the exogenously given amount of money with the demand for money. The supply of money is determined by the central bank. The demand for money is twofold: first for transaction purposes in the real economy where newly produced goods are always exchanged against money, and second for speculative purposes – money is held because of uncertainty about the future course of real and financial assets. For example, when the Dow Jones reaches very high levels, people tend to remain liquid, refraining thus from buying shares, and vice versa.

Outline of the classical–Keynesian system

Above we have suggested that Keynes has been absorbed by neoclassical theory in the form of new Keynesianism. Where, then, do we stand today? Is there an alternative to this neoclassical–Walrasian exchange model? The answer lies precisely in elaborating on and then merging together the insights of Keynes with those of Sraffa as well as Leontief to form a classical–Keynesian monetary production framework (see Chapter 3 for a full discussion).

Such an alternative is captured most appropriately by Marx's scheme of production and circulation of capital (Marx, 1973–74, Vol. II, p. 31):

$$M–C \ldots P \ldots C'–M' \tag{2.2}$$

where M represents money and finance (financial sector), C the means of production, P the social process of production, C' final output (social product), and M' money (effective demand). Keynes, implicitly relying on Marx, explicitly aimed at working out a monetary theory of production to be able to explain the deep crisis of the 1930s. His efforts resulted in *The General Theory*, which is mainly about the sequence $C'–M'$ (effective demand governing output and employment). In earlier works, Keynes dealt with $M–C$ (money and banking); Wassily Leontief was concerned with the quantity flows within the social and circular process of production (P), and finally Piero Sraffa, in close touch with David Ricardo and Karl Marx, considered the principles of price formation and the regulation of distribution within this process. Subsequently, Luigi Pasinetti has decisively contributed to preparing a synthesis of these authors and their followers, clearing thus the way towards a classical–Keynesian system of political economy (Bortis, 2012).

The basic classical–Keynesian model must be made up of the primary principles governing the functioning of modern monetary production economies. Two principles are of classical origin: the labour value principle summarizes the essential features of the immensely complex social process of production to provide the essence of the prices of production, which are the fundamental prices in a monetary production economy (Bortis, 2003, pp. 433–45); the surplus principle of distribution implies that the distribution of income is positively a problem of social power and normatively of distributive justice situated at the heart of social ethics (Bortis, 1997, pp. 158–75). Keynes provided a third principle, namely the principle of effective demand, related to determining the scale of economic activity (Bortis, 2003, pp. 460–67). These three principles imply that money, intimately associated with the financial sector, plays a fundamental role. Indeed, the processes of production and circulation could not go on without money, since production takes time, outlays and receipts are not synchronized, and goods are never exchanged against other goods (as is the case in a neoclassical–Walrasian framework) but always against money, which also acts as a store of value and as such is intimately connected to the financial sector.

It is of the utmost importance to bring together these principles in a coherent theoretical framework that may be set into opposition to the neoclassical–Walrasian framework. Indeed, as emerges from Keynes's economic and philosophical work, to act on the basis of principles is the most appropriate way to act rationally in a complex and rapidly evolving real world of which we have imperfect and probable knowledge only, and where uncertainty about the future always prevails. The great problem is to uncover the most plausible principles on which to base our actions. To make economic analysis fit for purpose requires working out a fundamental classical–Keynesian system of pure theory to bring into the open how monetary production economies essentially function and to compare this theoretical system with the basic neoclassical–Walrasian model.

In fact, it is not sufficient to simply establish the system of classical–Keynesian political economy – the neoclassical theory must still be proven wrong. The neoclassical real theory (that is, the law of supply and demand) has to be attacked at its foundations. This attack was carried out in the course of the Cambridge capital-theoretic debate (Harcourt, 1972). Since this highly important, but immensely complex debate cannot be presented here, only the bare essentials of the argument are set out in what follows.

The capital-theoretic debate

The starting point is the measurement in physical terms of the factors of production (labour, land and capital) as is required by the concept of marginal productivity of a factor of production, essential in neoclassical economics. For example, the marginal product of labour is given by the additional output produced by employing an additional worker for a given unit of time, say a week. Now, the natural factors of production (land and labour) can be measured physically, in acres and labour-hours. However, it is quite evident that it is impossible to measure real capital (machines and factory buildings) physically – in tons of steel, for example. Hence, capital must be measured in money terms. But since capital is a produced factor of production, this requires knowing Sraffa's prices of production. This means, in turn, that the money wage rates and the target profit rate must be known (see also the price equation (2.3) below). Neoclassical economics is now faced with a contradiction: on the one hand, the rate of profit and money wages, hence the normal prices of capital goods, must be known in order to be able to measure the value of capital in money terms; on the other, the rate of profits must be an unknown to be determined on the markets for new capital goods. Here saving, increasing as the rate of interest rises, represents the supply of new capital, and the volume of investment, increasing as the rate of interest decreases, stands for the demand for new capital. This is the well-behaved downward-sloping demand curve for new capital goods: investment increases as the rate of interest decreases.

Now, the basic result of the capital-theoretic debate is that, in principle, *no* well-behaved associations between the volume of investment and the rate of interest need necessarily exist. This implies that the principle of supply and demand is not compatible with the principle of effective demand, since in principle the volume of investment cannot necessarily adjust to full employment saving in the long run, with profit rates being equal in all sectors of production (Garegnani, 1983). However, Keynes's *General Theory* is based on the fact that, in macroeconomic equilibrium, saving always equals investment. This leads to the Keynesian multiplier (equation (2.1) above) and to the classical–Keynesian supermultiplier (equation (2.4) below). The way to effective demand, Garegnani's real way, is thereby definitely cleared and classical–Keynesian political economy may be confidently established.

In the remainder of this chapter we will touch upon two fundamental issues: the formation of prices in relation to income distribution and the determination of the level of output and employment.

The formation of prices

The formation of prices and the regulation of distribution are of immense complexity within the nature aspect of production, considered by Piero Sraffa (Pasinetti, 1977, pp. 71–151). Here the prices of production depend on all the production coefficients making up a technique of production and on income distribution, that is, the money wage rate and the rate of profits. However, moving on to the labour perspective of production leads to a very simple model of value and distribution that can be used for macroeconomic purposes (Bortis, 2003, pp. 436–45). Indeed, each price (p^*) is now given by the product of the money wage rate (w_n), the quantity of direct *and* indirect labour (N) per unit of output $(n = N/Q)$ and the mark-up $(k(r^*))$, which has to ensure a target rate of profits on fixed capital (r^*), which is firmly anchored in the institutional system, a point made by Pierangelo Garegnani time and again. This sectorial price equation leads on to a macroeconomic price equation, based on the labour value principle:

$$p^* = w_n nk = w_n \left(1/A\right) k(r^*) \tag{2.3}$$

Overall labour productivity, A, is the inverse of the macroeconomic labour coefficient, n, with $A = Q/N$ and $n = N/Q$, where N is the (direct and indirect) productive labour force active in the 'profit sector' for specified work hours. The social product, Q, is measured in terms of a bundle of socially necessary consumption goods, of which p^* is the normal price or price of production in terms of money. The coefficient n tells us that in a monetary production economy there are labour costs only, since ultimately labour in the expression $(w_n \, n)$ represents the unit cost in terms of money. As a result, the amount of direct and indirect labour time expended in producing a unit of the social product governs the value of this unit in a Ricardian vein. In a Marxian perspective, the price expresses the value of a product in terms of money. And prices are determined as soon as the money wage rate (w_n) and the mark-up $(k(r^*))$ are fixed. This immediately emerges from equation (2.3).

The money wage rate w_n and the mark-up $k(r^*)$ regulate income distribution, that is, the social surplus (surplus wages, land rents, labour rents owing to social power or to privileges, and, last but not least, profits) over socially necessary wages. Subsequently, the distribution of socially necessary wages and, above all, the distribution of the social surplus among the various social classes becomes a most fascinating problem of political economy, sociology and politics. In general, with given money wages, a larger $k(r^*)$ means that the surplus over socially necessary wages increases, that is, the distribution of income gets more unequal. This has important implications for the classical–Keynesian theory of output and employment to which we now turn.

The determination of long-period or trend output and employment: the supermultiplier

The classical–Keynesian long-period theory of output and employment is given by the supermultiplier relation. The star attached to all independent

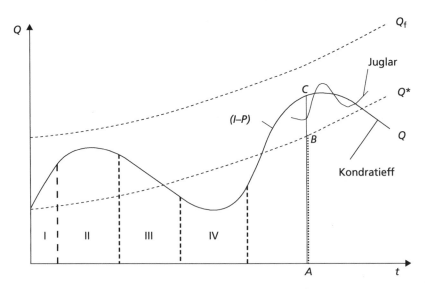

Figure 2.3 The supermultiplier relation

variables and parameters indicates that these are trend values governed by slowly changing factors, that is, technology and institutions:

$$Q^* = \frac{G^* + X^*}{(1 - c^*) + b^* - a^*} \tag{2.4}$$

This relation governs the *position* of the normal, trend or 'equilibrium' output, Q^*, which may be located well below the full employment trend Q_f as Figure 2.3 shows.

The distance between Q_f and Q^* in Figure 2.3 indicates permanent (long-period) involuntary unemployment. The existence of system-governed permanent involuntary unemployment is the most important feature of classical–Keynesian political economy. It is important to note that the super-multiplier determines the level or the volume of employment only. Who is employed or unemployed is more or less uncertain. And who gets jobs, above all the well and very well paid jobs, is a fascinating question of economic sociology.

In the supermultiplier relation (2.4), Q^* is real trend GDP (equal to domestic income) measured in terms of a bundle of necessities having the price p^* (see equation (2.3)). The right-hand side of the supermultiplier equation (2.4) represents effective demand, which governs output and employment. G^* stands for normal government expenditures, resting on parliamentary or government decisions. In highly industrialized countries trend exports X^* are governed, among other factors, by the quality of the education system and by research and development expenditures; c^* represents the trend propensity to consume out of income (C/Q) determined by evolving consumption habits.

Consequently, $(1 - c^*)$ equals the sum of the saving–income ratio $(s = S/Q)$ and the tax rate $(t = T/Q;$ S and T are the amounts saved and paid on taxes respectively. The normal import coefficient (M/Q) is b^* (where M is the volume of imports) and indicates the technological and cultural dependence from the rest of the world. The gross investment–income ratio (I/Q) $= a^*$ is the vehicle through which technical progress is diffused in the form of new and replacement investments (I). The trend rate of growth of effective demand and of GDP (Q^*) is given by the rate of growth of the autonomous variables $(G^* + X^*)$. In light of its definition $(Q = AN)$, potential (full employment) output (Q_f) grows at the natural rate of growth, given by the growth rate of labour productivity (A) – due to technical progress – and the labour force (N). Hence, if the growth rate of effective demand is lower than the natural rate of growth, involuntary unemployment increases. The condition $S = I$ represents the macroeconomic equilibrium condition, which, in a Keynesian vein, must always hold.

The institutionally governed autonomous expenditures – trend government expenditures (G^*) and trend exports (X^*) – set the economy into motion, resulting in a cumulative process of production of both consumption and investment goods, and, simultaneously of income, part of which is spent abroad, giving rise to imports. Hence, the trend volumes of consumption (C^*), of imports (M^*), and, most importantly, of investment (I^*) are all derived magnitudes and determined by long-period effective demand. However, individual investment projects are subject to uncertainty about the future: which investment projects are successful, which ones fail? The fact that long-period (trend) investment $I^* = a^* Q^*$ is determined by trend output, governed, in turn, by long-period effective demand – the right-hand side of equation (2.4) – is highly important: trend investment I^* is stable. Remember that with Keynes, investment is an autonomous variable, governed by long-period expectations, and, as such, psychologically determined and highly volatile (Keynes, 1936, pp. 102–3).

The supermultiplier

The salient features of the supermultiplier relation may now be pictured. Large autonomous variables $(G^* + X^*)$ obviously increase trend output Q^*

as emerges from equation (2.4) and Figure 2.3 (the output and employment trend is shifted upwards). The same is true for a large gross investment–output ratio (a^*): investment volumes are particularly large when great inventions are realized and become innovations.

Government expenditures may increase dramatically in great wars and with armament races. For example, it is well known that it was not President Roosevelt's New Deal that overcame the Great Depression of the 1930s, but World War II. And it is evident that very successful exporters of manufactured products like Germany, Japan and Switzerland, permanently enjoy very high employment levels. On the other hand, trend output Q^* is negatively linked with a strong import dependence, as is reflected in a large import coefficient (b^*). Most importantly, an unequal income distribution is, in principle, associated with a lower level of output and employment: the spending power of the population is reduced and shows up in a low consumption–income ratio (c^*). The inverse long-period link between unequal distribution and output and employment is *the* crucial feature of the supermultiplier relation. This centrally important relationship between unequal distribution and involuntary unemployment represents, according to Schumpeter, the essence of the Keynesian revolution: '[The Keynesian doctrine] can easily be made to say both that "who tries to save destroys real capital" and that, via saving, "the unequal distribution of income is the ultimate cause of unemployment." This is what the Keynesian Revolution amounts to' (Schumpeter, 1946, p. 517).

Given these features of the supermultiplier, classical–Keynesian socioeconomic policies (incomes and employment policies in particular) are fundamentally about social improvement. Hence classical–Keynesian political economy is, in a Keynesian vein, a *moral* science essentially. This stands in sharp contrast to the natural sciences flavour of neoclassical mainstream economics.

Cycles and trend

Business cycles (that is, cyclical movements around the trend as shown in Figure 2.3) represent essentially an interaction between the investment behaviour of entrepreneurs and the socioeconomic system governing the institutional trend (Bortis, 1997, pp. 135–42 and 204–20). Schumpeter (1939, Vol. 1, p. 213) puts the long-period Kondratiev cycles to the fore, around which shorter cycles, for example the Juglar cycles, are situated; the full Kondratiev cycle covers 50–60 years approximately (phases I–IV in Figure 2.3). How the Kondratiev cycle functions in principle can be explained most conveniently with the help of Figure 2.3. Here, trend output

Q^* is governed by trend effective demand, represented by the right-hand side of equation (2.4), whilst realized output Q is determined by actually prevailing effective demand exhibited by the right-hand side of equation (2.5). This equation is a variant of the supermultiplier relation in which both the realized investment–output ratio (a) and the realized consumption–income ratio (c) deviate from their trend values in the course of the cycle for reasons to be explained below:

$$Q = \frac{G^* + X^*}{(1 - c) + b^* - a} \tag{2.5}$$

The mechanism of the cycle is based upon the interaction between the income effect of investment and the capacity effect of investment. The income effect consists in the post-Keynesian interaction between investment and profits, while the capacity effect is grounded upon the relation between productive capacity and the output related to it, and effective demand. The income effect starts from the fact that in the cyclical upswing the realized rate of growth (g) exceeds the trend growth rate (g^*) exhibited in the supermultiplier equation (2.4), implying that realized investment (I) and the realized investment–output ratio (a in equation (2.5)) exceed trend investment (I^*) and the trend investment–output ratio (a^* in equation (2.4)). This implies that in the price equation (2.3) the realized mark-up, associated with the realized rate of profits $(k(r))$ exceed the corresponding normal magnitudes $(k(r^*))$. However, higher realized profit rates (r) will bring about higher realized growth rates and correspondingly larger investment volumes.

A cumulative process based upon the interaction between the investment volume (I) and realized profits (P) is set into motion (I–P in Figure 2.3). Yet, high investment volumes lead on to an expansion of productive capacities. Realized output (Q) gradually rises above the trend output (Q^*) as governed by the institutional-technical system through the supermultiplier equation (2.4). An increasing GDP (Q) exerts a pressure on prices and profits. At $t = A$ in Figure 2.3, the slope of the Q curve equals that of the Q^* curve, implying that a and c in relation (2.5) equal a^* and c^* in relation (2.4). As a result, realized profit equals the target rate $(r = r^*)$. However, realized output Q is AC, exceeding thus effective demand AB. Given this, realized profits in equation (2.5) will now fall short of the normal magnitudes set forth by the supermultiplier equation (2.4). The cyclical movement now changes direction and the downswing is initiated; the interaction between investment and profits $(I$–$P)$ now works in the reverse way in direction of a slump. The economy will pick up again once realized output has declined to a level below the trend output long enough such that the realized profit rate exceeds the normal profit rate implied in the long-term supermultiplier equation. The financial sector may reinforce the cyclical movements. In the upswing new credits grow very rapidly, in the downswing a credit crunch may occur.

The role of the financial sector in a monetary production economy and international trade in a classical–Keynesian perspective would be other important issues to be investigated (on finance see Bortis, 2013, pp. 346–52 and Bortis, 2015; on international trade, see Bortis, 2013, pp. 356–8). In fact, classical–Keynesian political economy enables us to address all-important problems of the modern world in a sensible way.

Neoclassical–Walrasian economics and classical–Keynesian political economy assessed

Which approach, neoclassical–Walrasian economics or classical–Keynesian political economy, is more plausible and hence fit for policy purpose? Theoretical critique and historical-empirical facts strongly speak in favour of Keynesian and classical–Keynesian political economy. On the theoretical side, the above-mentioned capital-theoretic debate (Harcourt, 1972) has shown that there are no well-behaved associations between factor prices and factor quantities in general, and specifically between rates of interest (profits) and quantities of capital. This implies that, in principle, and in the long run, investment *cannot* adjust to full employment saving; hence the market cannot produce any tendency towards full employment at all, even in principle. This is crucial, because principles have to be solid like a rock, otherwise theories are built upon sandy foundations. On the historical-empirical side the great crises of the 1930s and of 2007–08 may be explained convincingly by the classical–Keynesian supermultiplier and the cyclical fluctuations taking place around the long-period trend (Bortis, 1997, pp. 142–220). Given this, Joseph Schumpeter was quite wrong in arguing that Walras's general equilibrium model was the *Magna Carta* of economic theory.

Moreover, devastating internal critique of modern neoclassical economics is being put forward at present. Indeed, the eminent MIT economist Ricardo Caballero writes: 'I am almost certain that if the goal of macroeconomics is to provide formal frameworks to address real economics rather than purely literature-driven ones, *we better start trying something new rather soon*' (Caballero, 2010, p. 87, our emphasis). 'The root cause of the poor state of affairs in the field of macroeconomics lies in a fundamental tension in academic macroeconomics between the enormous complexity of its subject and the micro-theory-like precision to which we aspire' (p. 100). Caballero thus concludes that:

[t]he challenges are big, but macroeconomics can no longer continue playing internal games. The alternative of leaving all the important stuff to the 'policy'-types and informal commentators cannot be the right approach. I do not have the answer. But I suspect that whatever the solution ultimately is, we will accelerate our convergence to it, and reduce the damage we are doing along the transition, if we focus on reducing the extent of our pretense-of-knowledge syndrome. (Caballero, 2010, pp. 100–101)

To this rather pessimistic statement this chapter adds a touch of optimism. Indeed, classical–Keynesian long-period theory, that is, the theory of the long-period output and employment trend, and its implication for the theories of value and distribution as well as the role of the financial sector in a monetary production economy (see Bortis, 1997, 2003, 2013 and 2015) represent the starting point for building up an open-ended classical–Keynesian system of political economy. On the basis of this theoretical system most differing aspects of an evolving real world may be addressed in an altogether different way from the currently dominating mainstream economics.

NOTE

1 Also known as the Marshallian scissors.

 ## REFERENCES

Bortis, H. (1997), *Institutions, Behaviour and Economic Theory – A Contribution to Classical–Keynesian Political Economy*, Cambridge, UK: Cambridge University Press.

Bortis, H. (2003), 'Keynes and the classics: notes on the monetary theory of production', in L.-P. Rochon and S. Rossi (eds), *Modern Theories of Money: The Nature and Role of Money in Capitalist Economies*, Cheltenham, UK and Northampton, MA, USA: Edward Elgar Publishing, pp. 411–75.

Bortis, H. (2012), 'Towards a synthesis in post-Keynesian economics in Luigi Pasinetti's contribution', in R. Arena and P. L. Porta (eds), *Structural Dynamics and Economic Growth*, Cambridge, UK: Cambridge University Press, pp. 145–81.

Bortis, H. (2013), 'Post-Keynesian principles and economic policies', in G.C. Harcourt and P. Kriesler (eds), *The Oxford Handbook of Post-Keynesian Economics, Volume 2: Critiques and Methodology*, Oxford, UK and New York: Oxford University Press, pp. 326–65.

Bortis, H. (2015), 'Capital mobility and natural resources dynamics: a classical-Keynesian perspective', in M. Baranzini, C. Rotondi and R. Scazzieri (eds), *Resources, Production and Structural Dynamics*, Cambridge, UK: Cambridge University Press, pp. 155–73.

Caballero, R. (2010), 'Macroeconomics after the crisis: time to deal with the pretense-of-knowledge syndrome', *Journal of Economic Perspectives*, **24** (4), 85–102.

Dobb, M. (1973), *Theories of Value and Distribution since Adam Smith: Ideology and Economic Theory*, Cambridge, UK: Cambridge University Press.

Garegnani, P.A. (1983), 'Two routes to effective demand', in J.A. Kregel (ed.), *Distribution, Effective Demand and International Economic Relations*, London: Macmillan, pp. 69–80.

Gossen, H.H. ([1854] 1983), *Die Entwicklung der Gesetze des menschlichen Verkehrs und der daraus fließenden Regeln für menschliches Handeln* [The Laws of Human Relations and the Rules of Human Action Derived Therefrom], Boston: The MIT Press.

Harcourt, G.C. (1972), *Some Cambridge Controversies in the Theory of Capital*, Cambridge, UK: Cambridge University Press.

Keynes, J.M. (1926), *The End of Laissez-Faire*, London: Hogarth Press.

Keynes, J.M. (1936), *The General Theory of Employment, Interest and Money*, London: Macmillan.

Marshall, A. ([1890] 1920), *Principles of Economics*, London: Macmillan.

Marx, K. (1973–74), *Das Kapital*, 3 vols, Berlin: Dietz-Verlag; first editions 1867, 1885 and 1894.

Meek, R.L. (1962), *The Economics of Physiocracy*, London: George Allen & Unwin.

Pasinetti, L.L. (1977), *Lectures on the Theory of Production*, London: Macmillan.

Quesnay, F. (1758), *Tableau économique*, Versailles: privately printed.

Ricardo, D. (1810), *The High Price of Bullion, a Proof of the Depreciation of Bank Notes*, London: J. Murray.

Ricardo, D. (1815), *An Essay on the Influence of a Low Price of Corn on the Profits of Stock*, London: J. Murray.

Ricardo, D. ([1821] 1951), *On the Principles of Political Economy and Taxation*, 3rd edition, Cambridge, UK: Cambridge University Press.

Robinson, J. (1962), *Essays in the Theory of Economic Growth*, London: Macmillan.

Say, J.B. (1803), *Traité d'économie politique*, Paris: Déterville.

Schumpeter, J.A. (1939), *Business Cycles – A Theoretical, Historical and Statistical Analysis of the Capitalist Process*, 2 vols, New York and London: McGraw-Hill.

Schumpeter, J.A. (1946), 'John Maynard Keynes, 1883–1946', *American Economic Review*, **36** (4), 495–518.

Schumpeter, J.A. (1954), *History of Economic Analysis*, London: Allen & Unwin.

Smith, A. (1976a), *The Theory of Moral Sentiments*, Oxford: Clarendon Press; originally published 1759.

Smith, A. (1976b), *An Inquiry into the Nature and Causes of the Wealth of Nations*, 2 vols, Glasgow Edition; originally published 1776.

Sraffa, P. (1960), *Production of Commodities by Means of Commodities*, Cambridge, UK: Cambridge University Press.

Walras, L. (1952), *Eléments d'économie politique pure ou théorie de la richesse sociale*, Paris: Librairie Générale de Droit et de Jurisprudence; originally published 1900.

A PORTRAIT OF DAVID RICARDO (1772–1823)

David Ricardo was born into a wealthy Jewish merchant family. He attended elementary school and had some commercial training. At the age of 14 he started to work at the Stock Exchange. In 1792 his conservative father disinherited him because he had married a Christian and converted to Christianity. Being without means, he obtained some loan from friends, which he made skilful use of at the Stock Exchange. At the age of 25 he was said to be richer than his father. Given his comfortable material situation, Ricardo decided to partially retire from business activities to study natural sciences, mainly mathematics, physics and mineralogy.

In 1799 he got to know about Adam Smith's *Wealth of Nations*. Ricardo was deeply impressed and decided to devote his life to the study of political economy. During ten years (1799–1809) he only read and took notes. In 1810 he published his first and much noticed work: *The High Price of Bullion, a Proof of the Depreciation of Bank Notes*. Later (around 1830) his quantity-theoretic views on money and prices were strongly criticized by the Banking School, which advanced a theory of endogenous money creation by banks.

In 1809 Ricardo became a Member of Parliament in the United Kingdom. He was very influential because his clear-cut theoretical vision of the functioning of the economy enabled him to argue simply and convincingly. In 1815 he published *An Essay on the Influence of a Low Price of Corn on the Profits on Stock*, followed in 1817 by the first edition of his fundamental *Principles of Political Economy and Taxation*.

Ricardo died at the age of 51 of an inflammation of the middle ear. His work represents the first logically consistent and complete system of political economy. He may be considered the founder of pure theory, that is, thinking in terms of fundamental principles.

3

Monetary economies of production

Louis-Philippe Rochon

OVERVIEW

In this chapter, we will learn about:

- the neoclassical or mainstream view about the origins of money as linked to barter;

- the heterodox view of the creation and destruction of money through the existence of a monetary circuit of production;

- the theory of the monetary circuit and the role of the banking system.

Readers will thereby understand the differences between a real and a monetary economy, and the relationship between bank credit, debt, money and production.

KEYWORDS

- **Barter theory of money:** According to neoclassical economists, the existence and creation of money are linked to barter and exchange.
- **Bursts of optimism and pessimism:** This expression describes the behaviour of firms or banks with respect to their expectations of aggregate demand in the unknown and unknowable future.
- **Hoarded savings:** The portion of savings that is not channelled through the financial market but represents the final debt of firms toward the banking system.
- **Monetary economy of production:** A money-using economy in which the emphasis in on the production of goods, financed by banks.
- **Reflux:** When money returns to firms through either the consumption of goods by households, or the purchase of private-sector shares on financial markets.

Why are these topics important?

In the opening paragraph of *The General Theory of Employment, Interest and Money,* John Maynard Keynes (1936) warns us that applying policies arising from the teachings of neoclassical theory would be 'disastrous'. We have all seen the consequences of following monetary and fiscal policies derived from such an approach. Indeed, the crisis that erupted in 2007 is the direct result of such policies and, as Keynes warned us, the consequences, which we are still feeling at the time of writing, *have* been 'disastrous'.

Despite this global crisis, many economists still believe that the neoclassical theory is fundamentally sound. Yet, a careful study of this theory reveals that it does not allow for crises to exist. As such, the theory breaks down. While these same economists have claimed that there is no theoretical alternative, the purpose of this chapter is to show that in fact there is a coherent theory capable of explaining precisely how economies break down.

One of the many failures of neoclassical theory is that it is detached from the real world, in particular because it gives no role to money. According to this theory, money is a 'veil' and is not allowed to interfere with the workings of the economy. This approach, however, is clearly wrong – money plays an important role in our economic systems. In this sense, we must study what Keynes has called a 'monetary economy of production'. Money and banks are relevant, and within this 'monetary analysis', we can see the possibilities of crises arising.

The neoclassical/mainstream view

In neoclassical economics, there is no need for money to explain output, employment, consumption, or even prices. You may wonder how one could discuss all these issues without money, yet this is exactly what neoclassical theory does, and when money is added to the story it is as a mere afterthought, a way of making the story seem more realistic. Ultimately, money plays but a minor role in neoclassical thinking.

The origins of money in neoclassical analysis can be found in barter – a situation where two individuals exchange something they each own. There are many stories of barter, even today. For instance, we can imagine a carpenter doing work for a dentist in exchange for a free dental exam. No money exchanges hands, but one commodity or service is traded for the other. How then does money enter into the story?

Neoclassical economists explain the relationship between barter and money in the following way. Imagine a tailor wants a new pair of shoes. He would offer shirts he made to the cordwainer (the person who makes shoes), agree on a price, say three shirts for one pair of shoes, and make the trade. The price of a shirt in terms of shoes is called a relative price. Of course, a shirt would carry many prices, as many in fact as there are goods to trade. For instance, a shirt could be worth two pairs of socks, or one belt. A coat would be more expensive and be worth ten shirts. Relative prices are therefore the price of a good expressed in terms of different goods. This means that a price can be expressed in non-monetary terms: one shirt equals one belt.

If the cordwainer is prepared to accept three shirts, a trade then takes place and both parties obtain what they want. But imagine what happens if the cordwainer is not interested in acquiring shirts; instead, he is looking for a pair of gloves. The tailor must then approach a glover, and propose to trade with him at a price that they agree upon. Once the trade takes place and the tailor has the gloves, he can then go back to the cordwainer and trade the gloves for shoes.

But now imagine the glover is not interested in shirts, but wants a hat. The tailor must now approach the hatmaker to trade shirts for hats at an agreed upon price. Once the tailor has a hat, he can then approach the glover, trade the hat for the gloves, with which the tailor can finally approach the cordwainer and get the pair of shoes, which is all he wanted to begin with.

As one can imagine, this process can be difficult, time consuming, and costly: the tailor would have to invest time in order to go through this long process. If only there was some good that could be acceptable by everyone for trade, then the tailor would avoid all these additional exchanges.

This is where the invention of money enters the neoclassical analysis – to make exchange between individuals easier. There would be no need to exchange several goods to finally end up with the goods you were originally seeking. In this sense, money was invented to make trade easier and to solve what economists call the 'double coincidence of wants'. Stanley Jevons first used this expression in the opening chapter of his book, *Money and the Mechanism of Exchange* (1875, p. 4):

> the first difficulty in barter is to find two persons whose disposable possessions mutually suit each other's wants. There may be many people wanting, and many possessing those things wanted; but to allow of an act of barter there must be a double coincidence, which will rarely happen.

According to this view, money would somehow emerge spontaneously to resolve the problem posed by the double coincidence of wants, and would take the form of a good or commodity that was highly regarded and tradable, such as precious metals – for instance, gold. Money's primary purpose therefore is to serve as a medium of exchange.

There is no doubt barter existed in earlier societies – it is not difficult to imagine a farmer trading chickens for sandals. But the question is whether barter was pervasive and dominated early societies, and then whether money was really invented to make trade easier.

While the economists' story seems plausible, anthropologists and historians, however, are not at all convinced. Instead, they argue that barter, while it did exist among some individuals, was not widespread and certainly did not dominate primitive societies. In fact, it may not even have had an economic purpose.

For instance, anthropologist Caroline Humphrey (1985, p. 49), of the University of Cambridge in the United Kingdom, argues rather convincingly that 'we know from the accumulated evidence of ethnography that barter was indeed very rare as a system dominating primitive economies'. Referring to barter as an 'imagined state', she then adds that '[n]o example of a barter economy, pure and simple, has ever been described, let alone the emergence from it of money; all available ethnography suggests that there never has been such a thing' (Humphrey, 1985, p. 48).

Yet, despite the wealth of historical and anthropological evidence, mainstream economists have steadfastly ignored this evidence, and economics textbooks today still tell students the story of money, trade and the double coincidence of wants.

Heterodox economists, however, have always rejected the story of barter and money. For instance, Dillard (1988, p. 299) argued that:

> [t]he veil of barter must be lifted from general economic theory if we are to have a clear and logical understanding of how our money economy behaves. Economists speak frequently of the 'veil of money' and the 'money illusion' but the more troublesome barter illusion is seldom acknowledged.

But what this mainstream approach shows above all is that the theory of exchange is wholly independent of the theory of money, its creation or existence. Indeed, the cordwainer was able to fabricate shoes, and the tailor was able to produce shirts and then trade them even in the absence of money. They could have even hired some helpers (employment) in their workshops and paid them in shirts and shoes (wages), with which these workers could now go out and barter for goods that they want.

As one can see, in this neoclassical/mainstream view, money is added to the story much later, seemingly like a mere afterthought; money is not allowed to interfere with trade – it simply makes things easier. It is in this sense that neoclassical economists argue that money is neutral: it has no impact on the real economy. This is what Joseph Schumpeter called 'real analysis':

> Real analysis proceeds from the principle that all the essential phenomena of economic life are capable of being described in terms of goods and services, of decisions about them, and of relations between them. Money enters the picture only in the modest role of a technical device that has been adopted in order to facilitate transactions. . . So long as it functions normally, it does not affect the economic process, which behaves in the same way as it would in a barter economy; this is essentially what the concept of neutral money implies. (Schumpeter, 1954, pp. 277–8)

As most undergraduate students learn in studying economics, it is somehow possible to learn about employment, wages, investment, output and economic growth without once referring to the existence of money or the influence of finance. But how can a system where money and finance are so crucial be excluded from the analysis of economics? Is this approach a realistic explanation of the real world we live in?

The heterodox view

The previous section concentrated on the mainstream view of the economic system and showed two important elements: (1) the emphasis was on exchange, not production; and (2) money was invented in order to make barter or trade easier. But a capitalist economy is, by definition, a money-using economy or, more precisely, a monetary economy of production. As such, money must be at the heart of the theory of output and economic growth, otherwise what we are describing is not really a capitalist system.

The heterodox view takes as fundamental the role of money and finance. In fact, in direct contrast to the mainstream view, heterodox economists, and post-Keynesians in particular, consider that it is impossible to explain employment, wages, prices, output, production and economic growth without first and foremost understanding the role money plays in the story. In this sense, the theory of output and economic growth is linked to the theory of money; unlike barter, it is impossible to talk about economics without referring to money. This is one of the most fundamental ideas of the heterodox approach.

While there are various heterodox approaches in economics, this section will concentrate on the contributions of an approach labelled the theory of the monetary circuit, which is a good summary of the heterodox approach in general. It is a 'general theory' of a monetary economy of production that owes much of its central tenets to the views of John Maynard Keynes. Let us expand on this.

The theory of the monetary circuit

The approach known as the theory of the monetary circuit was pioneered by a number of economists, both in France and Italy, in the 1960s. Among the early proponents of this approach, three in particular stand out: Alain Parguez in France, Augusto Graziani in Italy and Bernard Schmitt in both France and Switzerland. All proposed elements of a common idea, and while there exist important differences between their analyses, it is possible to identify a general approach, which has been termed the 'monetary circuit'.

The ideas contained within the monetary circuit approach find their roots mostly in the writings of John Maynard Keynes, notably in some chapters he wrote for his book *The General Theory of Employment, Interest and Money*, which never made it into the final version of this book, as well as some of his other writings both before and after his great masterpiece. Keynes's insights on money and the way money is used within capitalist economies were deep, and recognized even by those who did not always agree with him. For instance, Frank Hahn (1983, p. xi) wrote that 'I nonetheless hold that his insights were several orders more profound and realistic than those of his recent critics'.

This is not to say that the writings of others, such as Knut Wicksell, Karl Marx, Polish economist Michał Kalecki and Cambridge economist Joan Robinson did not influence some of the ideas of the monetary circuit approach, but Keynes certainly remains its main and most important contributor.

The fundamental idea of this approach, as explained below, is that the theory of output and the theory of money are linked. This is the essence of what Joseph Schumpeter called a 'monetary economy', as opposed to a 'real economy' that best describes the exchange economy of neoclassical theory. A monetary economy, according to Schumpeter (1954, p. 278), 'introduces the element of money on the very ground floor of our analytic structure and abandons the idea that all essential features of our economic life can be represented by a barter-economy model'. This is what we stated at the beginning of this section: it is impossible to discuss employment and economic growth without first understanding the role of money.

Keynes, of course, had a similar approach. He wanted to write about the way 'the economy in which we live actually works' (Keynes, 1936, p. 12). In a chapter contained within the first proofs of the *General Theory*, but which did not make it to the final version, Keynes (1979, pp. 67–8) describes his endeavour as follows: 'It is to the theory of a generalised monetary economy. . .that this book will attempt to make a contribution'. Elsewhere, Keynes (1973a, p. 411) makes a similar statement: 'Accordingly I believe that the next task is to work out in some detail a monetary theory of production, to supplement the real-exchange theories which we already possess. At any rate that is the task on which I am not wasting my time'.

For Canadian economist Marc Lavoie (1984, p. 773), a leading heterodox economist, the importance of integrating money from the very beginning of the analysis is paramount: 'The injection of money in the economic system must not be done when output is already specified, as in the exchange economy. . .but rather must be introduced as part of the production process'.

Thus, as the name suggests, the theory of the monetary circuit involves the importance of money and production, within a realist view of our contemporary economies, and, as part of a circuit, it shows how money is first created, then circulated, and then finally destroyed.

Let us begin our analysis of the monetary circuit with a short list of core assumptions. These are as follows:

1. The economy is best described as happening in historical time, meaning that events occur in time and not all at once; events are irreversible. For instance, workers cannot consume before they have found employment that gives them an income from which they can spend and save; corporations cannot hire workers before they have secured the necessary funding to pay for production and wages; once a firm has purchased a capital good (a machine), it cannot reverse its decision.
2. The economy is best described as comprising of various macro-groups (Graziani, 2003). In particular, we can identify four important groups: workers, firms or non-financial corporations, banks, and the govern-

ment. We can add a fifth group to our analysis, that is, the rest of the world. The emphasis therefore is on how these groups interact with one another.

3. Privately-owned firms are also divided into two subsectors, namely, firms that produce consumption goods, and firms that produce investment goods (for instance, machinery).

4. The banking system is at the heart of not only the production process but also of the creation of money through the supply of bank loans; this is the essence of what is called the endogeneity of money – banks make production possible.

5. The analysis is made in terms of a period of production, which is defined as the time between the creation and destruction of money. This is not in calendar years, but rather the logical flow of money.

To further analyse the theory of the monetary circuit, let us consider five specific stages of the circuit (see Rochon, 1999, for further analysis).

Stage one: the planning of production

The circuit begins when non-banking firms plan their production levels, which are based on their expectations of aggregate demand in the near future. In this sense, the supply of goods being produced is dependent on what firms believe the level of demand will be in the not-so-distant future; supply adapts to expected demand. This is the rejection of Say's Law, which states that supply creates its own demand. Obviously, if firms expect demand to increase, they will increase their level of production, or decrease it if they expect demand to weaken.

Once production levels have been determined, firms are in a position to make a number of additional important decisions – for instance, how much of their existing productive capacity will be utilized in the production process, how much labour to hire, and the price of their product.

Firms typically never produce at 100 per cent capacity; the degree of capacity utilization will be less than full. This gives firms the ability to increase production in case demand becomes greater than what the firm anticipated. Imagine, for instance, the production of a new automobile that suddenly becomes very popular. In order to respond to the increased demand, a firm will increase production by increasing its rate of capacity utilization. If demand falls, for instance because of a recession, firms will be able to respond by lowering their degree of capacity utilization.

Firms will then have to decide on how much labour to hire, given their expectations of demand. Given the wage rate, the firm will then know not only the level of labour, but also its wage bill, which is defined as the wage rate times the level of labour.

Finally, firms will be able to set the price of their product or service. This price will be based on the costs of producing the goods, over which they will add some mark-up. For instance, if it costs them US$100 to produce a single unit, they may add a mark-up of, say, 25 per cent, thereby setting the unit price at US$125.

Stage two: bank credit and the creation of money

The next phase of the circuit will move from the planning of production to the actual production of goods. But since firms have not sold anything yet, they typically do not have the necessary funds to start production. In order to do this, they must demand and secure these funds from a bank to cover their costs of production (or some of these costs): production is financed by bank credit. This is what Keynes called the 'finance motive' and what Graziani (2003) called 'initial finance'.

This is an important argument: firms do not have access to prior funds or savings at this early stage. This is why bank credit and the existence of banks is such a crucial component of the monetary circuit: in order to produce, firms must borrow from banks and get into debt. As Seccareccia (1988, p. 51) writes, production is 'a process of debt formation'.

But to secure funds from the bank, the bank must deem the borrower creditworthy; if they are not, the bank will refuse to lend them the funds. Typically, this means that the bank must be satisfied that the borrower, in this case the firm, will be able to reimburse its loan in the future, an argument that we develop in the next section.

Once the bank is satisfied with the creditworthiness of the borrower, it will lend the necessary funds to begin production. This usually takes the form of a line of credit, which the firm draws upon to pay wages and cover other costs related to the production of its goods.

Once wages are paid, money is then deposited into the bank accounts of workers, at which point money is created. Notice how fundamentally linked the theory of money creation is to the theory of output and production, as discussed previously. This is a far cry from the exchange economy of neoclassical economics – in the monetary circuit, money is created when firms agree to get into debt with regard to the banks, and when wages are paid to workers.

Once wages are paid, workers release these funds into active circulation when they consume, a point to which we will return below.

But so far, from the above discussion, two conclusions can be reached. (1) The supply of bank loans is made at the initiation of the borrower. Banks cannot lend if there is no demand for loans. It is in this sense that we say that the supply of loans is demand determined. As Joan Robinson (1952, p. 29) wrote, 'the amount of advances the banks can make is limited by the demand from good borrowers'. (2) Once a loan is made and wages are paid, money is created. The creation of money is not only demand determined and credit led, but it is fundamentally linked to the existence of debt. As Schmitt (1975, p. 160) wrote: money is 'debt which circulates freely'.

Stage three: the bank's decision to lend

Let us revisit in some detail the decision of the bank to grant credit and the criteria it follows to make this decision.

Because we live in an uncertain world, the future is by definition unknown. In deciding to give credit to a firm, a bank faces two sources of uncertainty regarding the firm's ability to reimburse its loan in the future, what I have called elsewhere (see Rochon, 2006) 'micro-uncertainty' and 'macro-uncertainty'.

Micro-uncertainty is the bank's evaluation of the competence of the firm's management. Does it have good leadership, a competent CEO, a good track record, and did it produce a good market study? Banks will typically consider a number of criteria in order to reach a decision, such as past relationship with the firm, the firm's net worth and collateral, debt/equity ratio as well as other financial ratios.

This was well summarized by Barker and Lafleur (1994, p. 83), when they argued that the 'role of banks depends largely on information systems that allow banks to determine the solvency of their customers. Their success will depend heavily on the intuition of their credit officers and their ability to identify the capacity and willingness of borrowers to repay loans'.

But even if the firm is deemed competent at the micro-level, there is another source of uncertainty: the bank's expectations of the macro-environment in the near future. Does the bank forecast a period of strong economic growth or a recession? This is important. If the bank believes a recession is forthcoming, characterized with a decrease in income, then this will make it more difficult for a firm to sell its products and reimburse the bank. The bank will therefore have a very different set of criteria with which to make this other important decision.

So there are two sets of criteria, each aimed at two different objectives: on the one hand to identify the competence of the firm's management, and on the other hand, to identify the competence, so to speak, of the economy as a whole.

What is clear is that banks will lend only to those firms that meet the bank's strict lending criteria. As Keynes ([1930] 1971, p. 327) once said, there will always be a 'fringe of unsatisfied borrowers'.

The two sets of criteria will play a very different role in the bank's decision. Macro-uncertainty will determine the minimum criteria all firms must meet in order to get a loan. Moreover, this bar will move up and down with the bank's expectations of the future levels of aggregate demand. For instance, if the bank becomes more optimistic about the future, it will 'lower the bar', so to speak, making it easier for firms to qualify for a loan. This is because banks are more optimistic, in a growing economy, of a firm's ability to generate income. But if banks become more pessimistic, for instance if a bank expects a recession, then it will raise its criteria, thereby making it more difficult for all firms to qualify for a loan.

But irrespective of where these minimum criteria are set, if a firm meets them, it will be granted a loan (Le Bourva, 1992). The immediate conclusion we reach is that a bank is never constrained in its ability to grant loans. It is only constrained by the number of creditworthy borrowers (see Lavoie, 2014).

Now, what about the criteria used to deal with the micro-uncertainty? These will be used to identify the firm's 'degree of creditworthiness'. If the firm already meets the basic minimum level of creditworthiness, how much more creditworthy is it? This will then be used to determine the rate of interest that will be applied to the firm's borrowing needs. If it meets the minimum level but the bank still sees some uncertainty at the level of the firm, the bank may impose a higher rate of interest than another firm that has a more robust micro-evaluation.

Stage four: the reflux principle and the destruction of money

So far, production has been financed by bank loans, firms have got into debt, and wages have been paid. How will firms be able to recuperate their production costs?

This is done largely during the process of consumption, when households spend their income purchasing produced goods. As they do, money will flow back to the firms. At this point, one can see the circuit forming: money first goes out with the payment of wages, then flows back with the act of consumption, which becomes a source of revenue for firms. As Parguez (1997, p. 5) wrote, '[t]his. . .stage depicts the paramount characteristic of the capitalist economy: firms must be able to recoup money from the sale of their output'. Le Bourva (1992, p. 454) has called this the 'alternating movements of creation and cancellation of money'.

The act of money returning to the firms is known in the monetary circuit approach as the 'reflux phase'. With this revenue, firms are able to pay back at least a part of their loans to banks, at which point, money is destroyed.

Note, however, that firms may not be able to pay back all of their loans. Some firms will amass revenues more than the amount of their wage bill, while others will not. In other words, some firms will make profits while others will make losses, which means that some firms will be in debt toward the banking system at the end of the circuit.

At the macro-level, the overall debt of the system toward the banking system will be equal to the savings of households; collectively, all firms pay out the total amount of their wage bill. The most they can recuperate is the wage bill if households consume all of their income. But if they do not, whatever they save and do not consume will represent the outstanding debt of firms toward the banking system.

A caveat is in order, however, concerning household saving. In fact, only part of the savings will not flow back to firms. Savings can be divided into hoarded savings – that part you keep, say, in your bank accounts – and financial savings – that part of savings used to purchase financial assets on the stock market. These financial savings, when used to buy shares from private sector firms, will also flow back to firms. This is a fundamental conclusion of the monetary circuit, one that did not escape Keynes's attention. For him, 'consumption is just as effective in liquidating the short-term finance as savings is' (Keynes, 1973b, p. 221).

Finally, recall that, earlier on, we argued that money was created along with bank loans. As it is created, money takes the form of a flow – money flows through the economy. At the end of the circuit, however, when firms pay back their loans, some money will stay in bank accounts in the form of hoarded savings. Therefore, there will be an observable stock of money: money now takes the form of a stock. In this sense, money is both a flow and a stock, and this stock corresponds to the portion of their savings households desire to hold as a liquid asset. According to Malcolm Sawyer (1996, p. 51), '[w]hether the money thereby created remains in existence depends on the demand for money as a stock'. Lavoie (1992, p. 156) concurs: 'There is no difference between the outstanding amount of loans and the stock of money'. This is another fundamental conclusion of the theory of the monetary circuit.

Stage five: the planning of investment

So far, we have discussed the importance of bank credit in enabling the production process. There is therefore a natural link between credit, debt, money and production. But we have not yet discussed the role of investment, and how it is financed.

While the issue of how investment is financed is debated among the proponents of the monetary circuit, it is argued here that investment, like production, is financed largely from two sources: the retained earnings of firms as well as bank credit, which is then reimbursed over several periods. But how do firms decide on how much to invest?

If production depends on expectations of sales proceeds in the near future, investment depends on whether firms think these expectations hold into the far future. In other words, if there is an increase in proceeds, firms will typically respond by increasing the degree of capacity utilization of existing capital. But if this increase in demand is deemed permanent, then firms will have to increase their capacity on a permanent basis, which means investing in a new plant or machinery. In this sense, investment decisions are made at the end of the production process in anticipation of the next period of production.

This is why investment is sensitive to changes in demand. This is a very different conclusion from that reached by mainstream economists, who see investment dependent foremost on the rate of interest.

Some implications of the theory of the monetary circuit

The above discussion leads to some interesting conclusions, especially regarding the possibility of an economic crisis.

There are two possible sources of crisis based on the above discussion. First, if banks become very pessimistic, it is clear that they will not be willing to lend. In other words, not many firms will be able to meet the criteria set by the bank. This is problematic. If this occurs, then many production to plans will not be fulfilled, and unemployment will increase.

Take, for instance, the global financial crisis of 2007–08. Irrespective of the precise cause of it, it is clear that once the economy started to deteriorate, banks became increasingly pessimistic, and a sort of self-fulfilling prophecy set in: a collapse of income made banks pessimistic, which led them to cut loans, which depressed the economy even more.

Second, a crisis could occur if the amount of hoarded savings increases. Imagine that households decide to increase the amount of money they hoard. This amount is always a drain on the economy, and if it increases then it will have a greater negative impact on the economic system. Increased hoards could be the result of increased uncertainty about the future. Households may want to save for a rainy day. This translates into a decline in revenue for the firms, as households spend less on consumption goods and also on financial assets. As this occurs, firms will be less able to meet their contractual obligations with the banks. This may translate into an increase of the micro-uncertainty referred to earlier. Seccareccia (1996, p. 16) explained that 'it is only when households choose to withhold their savings from the financial capital markets and seek to hold a significant proportion of their saving in the form of bank deposits that difficulties of reimbursement appear'.

These possible sources of crisis only bring to light the importance of fiscal policy. Indeed, when households or banks are faced with increased uncertainty, they spend less and lend less respectively, thereby depressing the economy. As Keynes tells us, bursts of optimism and pessimism are important in understanding how the business cycle develops.

This then creates the necessity for additional stimulus. If the economy is driven by demand, when demand is weak, we must find a way of increasing it. Now, we cannot force consumers to spend more; we cannot force businesses to invest more; we cannot force foreign countries to buy our goods. All these are sources of demand. So the only remaining thing we have control over is government spending. To increase demand, we can adopt expansionary fiscal policies to stimulate output and economic growth. In other words, fiscal expenditures fill in the aggregate demand void.

The role of the state in the monetary circuit

The above discussion brings us the importance of the state in the monetary circuit.

So far, one issue that stands out is the importance of uncertainty on spending. While the future is always by definition uncertain, the state has a role to play in mitigating its effects. Indeed, fiscal expenditures play on both the micro- and macro-uncertain environments.

In increasing its spending, the government transfers sums of money from its accounts (the public sector) to the accounts of both firms and households (the private sector). In doing so, it makes firms' revenues increase (think of the government hiring a private sector firm to build a new bridge, for instance) and makes the firms more creditworthy at a microeconomic level in the eyes of the banks, by reducing the micro-uncertainty. This will help firms secure funding in the following period.

But by increasing spending, the state also contributes to increasing aggregate demand at the macroeconomic level, thereby reducing macro-uncertainty. This will help banks become more optimistic about the near future and hopefully agree to lend more funds. Also, by reducing macro-uncertainty, firms will also become more optimistic and more willing to borrow.

Conclusion

This chapter presented the theory of the monetary circuit, which describes the natural ebbs and flows of money, between when it is created and ultimately destroyed. This theory places the banking system at the core of its analysis, which finances both production and investment, each depending on expectations of the future. In this framework, uncertainty can play havoc with both activities since expectations can be easily frustrated.

Banks are also subject to this uncertainty and act following bursts of optimism and pessimism. This can be a source of crisis if banks become too pessimistic and refuse to lend, or when borrowers are not willing to borrow. In this sense, the theory of the monetary circuit is not only a theory of credit, money and production, but also a theory of economic crises.

In the end, this theory stands in contrast to mainstream or neoclassical theory, where money is a mere afterthought, added simply to make barter and trade easier. In this sense, money can never be a source of crises. This is why Keynes (1936, p. 3) believed neoclassical economics to be 'disastrous if we attempt to apply it to the facts of experience'.

 REFERENCES

Barker, W. and L.-R. Lafleur (1994), 'Business cycles and the credit-allocation process: an institutional perspective', in *Credit, Interest Rate Spreads and the Monetary Policy Transmissions Mechanism*, proceedings of a conference held at the Bank of Canada, Ottawa, November.

Dillard, D. (1988), 'The barter illusion in classical and neoclassical economics', *Eastern Economic Journal*, **14** (4), 299–318.

Graziani, A. (2003), *The Monetary Theory of Production*, Cambridge, UK: Cambridge University Press.

Hahn, F. (1983), *Money and Inflation*, Cambridge, MA: MIT Press.

Humphrey, C. (1985), 'Barter and economic disintegration', *Man*, **20** (1), 48–72.

Jevons, S. (1875), *Money and the Mechanism of Exchange*, New York: D. Appleton and Co.

Keynes, J.M. (1919), *The Economic Consequences of the Peace*, London: Macmillan.

Keynes, J.M. ([1930] 1971), *The Collected Writings of John Maynard Keynes, Volume VI: A Treatise on Money, Part II: The Applied Theory of Money*, London and Basingstoke, UK: Macmillan.

Keynes, J.M. (1933), *The Means to Prosperity*, London: Macmillan.

Keynes, J.M. (1936), *The General Theory of Employment, Interest and Money*, London: Macmillan.

Keynes, J.M. (1973a), *The Collected Writings of John Maynard Keynes, Volume XIII: The General Theory and After: Part I: Preparation*, London and Basingstoke, UK: Macmillan.

Keynes, J.M. (1973b), *The Collected Writings of John Maynard Keynes, Volume XIV: The General Theory and After: Part II: Defence and Development*, London and Basingstoke, UK: Macmillan.

Keynes, J.M. (1979), *The Collected Writings of John Maynard Keynes, Volume XXIX: The General Theory: A Supplement*, London and Basingstoke, UK: Macmillan.

Lavoie, M. (1984), 'Un modèle post-Keynésien d'économie monétaire fondé sur la théorie du circuit' [A post-Keynesian monetary economics model based on circuit theory], *Economies et Sociétés*, **18** (2), 233–58.

Lavoie, M. (1992), *Foundations of Post-Keynesian Economic Analysis*, Aldershot, UK and Brookfield, VT, USA: Edward Elgar Publishing.

Lavoie, M. (2014), *Post-Keynesian Economics: New Foundations*, Cheltenham, UK and Northampton, MA, USA: Edward Elgar Publishing.

Le Bourva, J. (1992), 'Money creation and credit multipliers', *Review of Political Economy*, **4** (4), 447–66.

Parguez, A. (1997), 'Government deficits within the monetary production economy or the tragedy of the race to balance budgets', University of Ottawa, mimeo.

Robinson, J. (1952), *The Rate of Interest and Other Essays*, London: Macmillan.

Rochon, L.-P. (1999), *Credit, Money and Production: An Alternative Post-Keynesian Approach*, Cheltenham, UK and Northampton, MA, USA: Edward Elgar Publishing.

Rochon, L.-P. (2006), 'Endogenous money, central banks and the banking system: Basil Moore and the supply of money', in M. Setterfield (ed.), *Complexity, Endogenous Money and Macroeconomic Theory: Essays in Honour of Basil J. Moore*, Cheltenham, UK and Northampton, MA, USA: Edward Elgar Publishing, pp. 220–43.

Sawyer, M. (1996), 'Money, finance and interest rates: some post-Keynesian reflections', in P. Arestis (ed.), *Keynes, Money and the Open Economy: Essays in Honour of Paul Davidson, Volume I*, Cheltenham, UK and Northampton, MA, USA: Edward Elgar Publishing, pp. 50–67.

Schmitt, B. (1975), *Monnaie, salaires et profits* [Money, Wages and Profits], Paris: Presses Universitaires de France.

Schumpeter, J.A. (1954), *History of Economic Analysis*, New York: Oxford University Press.

Seccareccia, M. (1988), 'Systemic viability and credit crunches: an examination of recent Canadian cyclical fluctuations', *Journal of Economic Issues*, **22** (1), 49–77.

Seccareccia, M. (1996), 'Post-Keynesian fundism and monetary circulation', in G. Deleplace and E.J. Nell (eds), *Money in Motion: The Post Keynesian and Circulation Approaches*, London and New York: Macmillan and St Martin's Press, pp. 400–416.

A PORTRAIT OF JOHN MAYNARD KEYNES (1883–1946)

Born in Cambridge, England on 5 June 1883, John Maynard Keynes, or simply Maynard to his closest friends, is considered the most influential economist of the twentieth century, and ranks among the greatest economists of all time.

His most important book, *The General Theory of Employment, Interest and Money*, published in 1936, remains one of the most influential books in economics, and is still greatly debated today. The book challenges the core neoclassical belief that markets are self-stabilizing and, if left on their own, would gravitate toward equilibrium, as well as the notion that unemployment was voluntary. Keynes argued that in a money-using world in which uncertainty was a core feature, markets could break down, and could be subject to periods of prolonged recession, during which time unemployment is actually involuntary, that is, independent of the people's willingness to work. Unemployment was not caused by wages being too high, but by the lack of aggregate demand. This view of seeing how markets operate convinced Keynes that governments had an important role to play in promoting economic growth through the use of counter-cyclical fiscal policy.

Keynes started his career as a civil servant in 1906, working in the India Office, but returned to the United Kingdom in 1908, and began lecturing at the University of Cambridge in 1909. From then his reputation grew.

At the beginning of World War I, he began working for the Treasury, and by the end of the war, in 1919, represented the United Kingdom at the Versailles Peace Conference. This is where Keynes's support for the government ended, as he strongly objected to the terms of the Versailles Treaty, arguing that imposing reparations on Germany would be catastrophic. Keynes resigned from the Treasury. He explained his objections to the Versailles Treaty in a famous book, *The Economic Consequences of the Peace* (1919).

With the start of the Great Depression in 1929, Keynes's ideas begin to evolve considerably; in 1933, he published *The Means to Prosperity*, which contained some early ideas that would then reappear in 1936 in his *General Theory*. By now, Keynes's ideas about the use of counter-cyclical fiscal policy would begin to spread. One of Keynes's great accomplishments was to provide a theoretical justification for the use of fiscal policy.

In 1944, Keynes returned to the service of the British government as one of its representative to the Bretton Woods conference, which resulted in the development of what is now known as the Bretton Woods system, and helped create the World Bank and the International Monetary Fund.

In 1942, Keynes became a member of the House of Lords, as Baron Keynes of Tilton, in the County of Sussex. He died on 21 April 1946.

Part II

Money, banks and financial activities

4

Money and banking

Marc Lavoie and Mario Seccareccia

 OVERVIEW

This chapter:

- presents the heterodox approach to money and banking and contrasts it with the mainstream;

- explains why mainstream economists view money as a commodity that takes on the role of medium of exchange, with banks being intermediaries between savers and investors; while heterodox economists view money as a means of payment resulting from a balance-sheet operation within a creditor–debtor relation, with banks being creators of money to finance production;

- focuses on the importance of the creation and destruction of money by the banking system and on the crucial role played by the interbank market for funds and the payment and settlement system;

- points out that credit money creation is demand led and that the mainstream supply-determined perspective on bank lending is erroneous and leads to misguided policies such as the quantitative easing policies implemented in many countries since the global financial crisis erupted in 2007–08.

Readers will thereby understand why money is not a scarce commodity and why the banking sector can create credit money whose only constraint is demand for loans and the creditworthiness of borrowers. Readers will also understand why banks are the source of the finance that initiates the production process, while non-bank financial intermediaries play a role in bringing together savers and business enterprises that have already undertaken investment to address their final financing needs during the reflux phase of the circulatory process.

- **Commercial banking:** Financial institutions engaged in the business of financing, that is, in a process of making out loans, and also accepting deposits whose overall effect is to create or destroy money.
- **Flux/reflux principle:** A basic principle in which bank credit advances constitute the flow while income receipts from these expenditures are the reflux of a corresponding amount that ought to normally permit the removal of the original loans from banks' balance sheets.
- **Means of payment:** In a non-barter system, a payment occurs using a third-party liability, namely that of the central bank or private commercial banks, for final settlement by extinguishing counterparty debt of an equivalent amount.
- **Monetary circuit:** The circular process of advancing credit money and then destroying an equivalent amount once the borrower is able to recapture the principal of a loan for reimbursement, leading to a closure of the circuit.
- **Payment and settlement systems:** National systems for the clearing/settlement of payments within the banking system, in which proper functioning of interbank lending/borrowing increases financial stability through enhanced financial market liquidity, together with a central bank as lender of last resort.

Why are these topics important?

Since money, in its essence, is merely the outcome of a balance-sheet operation, banks play a critical role. Indeed, all aspects of macroeconomic analysis in a modern economy must necessarily involve the monetary system. Monetary relations result from the existence of a group of key institutions in a monetary economy, namely banks, which, together with the central bank, are critical to the modern payment system and are the purveyors of liquidity to the whole economy. It is therefore crucial to understand how banks are the principal creators of money in nearly all modern economies, and why, by their very nature, they are private–public partnerships, especially evident at times of crisis when the public 'trust' that is so critical to their existence is broken, therefore requiring a regulatory framework within which their activity of creators of money is severely circumscribed.

Money, banks, and their origins

The traditional mainstream view

All mainstream economics textbooks introduce money as Adam Smith once described it in his celebrated 1776 opus, *The Wealth of Nations,* as the 'universal instrument of commerce' (Smith, [1776] 1937, p. 28) that was invented in order to facilitate exchange. While someone must have first conceived and designed the wheels of a cart to make it easier to move goods and reduce transport costs as individuals sought to trade more efficiently their commodity surpluses, according to this view so money was invented in order to grease the wheels of commerce so as to engage in commodity exchange with less effort.

Hence, just as individuals at some moment in human history came to recognize the benefits of the division of labour and began to 'truck and barter', so it was, we are told, that they eventually began to use certain commodities, usually precious metals, such as gold and silver, in their new role as money. Money supposedly emerged spontaneously from barter exchange because of these commodities' particular characteristics of divisibility, portability, fungibility, durability and relative scarcity that allowed them to take on the role of medium of exchange, unit of account, and medium of deferment of consumption.

As this tale of money emerging from barter exchange is normally told in mainstream textbooks, money's origin is explained simply as the natural outcome of private cost-minimizing behaviour that had nothing to do with the legal recognition and formal legal actions often taken by the state to ensure money's general acceptability.

money origin

This traditional perspective rests, therefore, on a particularly antiquated vision of money. Money is essentially conceived as a commodity, like grain, cowry shells, or metals, whose metamorphosis into a medium of exchange catapulted this commodity money onto an otherwise pre-existing and privately organized natural barter system. From this, it follows that money's principal purpose was to make this market exchange merely more efficient, thereby surmounting the obstacle of the 'double coincidence of wants' (Jevons, 1875, p. 4) plaguing less efficient barter economies that preceded monetary exchange.

On the basis of this mainstream narrative on the origin of money and monetary exchange that is told repeatedly in economics textbooks, there is often an associated tale of how banks, as particular institutions arising from this profit-seeking behaviour of individual economic agents, first made their appearance and whose history is intertwined with that of money.

Historically, while quasi-banking-related activities of advancing simple credit appeared almost at the same time that humans began record-keeping, one of the tales of modern banking institutions as loan makers/deposit takers and issuers of banknotes goes as follows.

Banks emerged, we are told, very late after the Middle Ages, owing primarily to the conduct of profit-seeking goldsmiths, especially in seventeenth-century England. Banks appear in this traditional story in the following way. As these primitive societies progressed through market exchange, a portion of this overall stock of money in the form of precious metals changed hands at a certain annual turnover rate (or monetary velocity) to acquire and validate monetarily the flow of privately produced commodities. Within these commodity money economies, these transactions generated a flow of money income accruing to the various counterparties in the monetary exchange. Individual economic agents receiving these incomes faced the following options: a portion of this income flow of precious metals could be re-spent, thereby generating a series of consumption flows per period, while another portion could be saved or accumulated as liquid holdings, since other forms of financial assets had not yet appeared.

Banks appear as intermediaries in collecting a community's accumulated liquid savings for safekeeping, for instance, as represented in the textbooks by the stereotypical goldsmith bankers of seventeenth-century England. With time, instead of leaving these stocks of precious metals sitting idle and withholding them from circulation, these profit-seeking goldsmiths began to lend the portion of the community's stock of commodity money stored in their vaults. This saving would then be lent to those more enterprising individuals seeking to borrow money to invest, and charging them interest. Since a portion of the investment expenditures would be returning to the same banks in the form of bank deposits, profit-maximizing banks would then re-lend this money, generating further loans in excess of the initial bank deposits. The effect would be to create bank money, with the latter being the difference between the initial reserves of precious metals (or base money) and the total outstanding deposits, as banks progressively leveraged themselves in relation to their initial gold reserves through a process traditionally referred to as 'fractional reserve banking'.

Ostensibly, the only constraints on this multiple expansion of bank money envisaged within this traditional framework were the desire by profit-seeking banks to hold idle reserves of this commodity money in their vaults exclusively for precautionary purposes and the desire on the part of the public to hold some cash for day-to-day transactions purposes. Moreover, this leveraged banking system could only function as long as only a small portion of depositors withdrew their funds regularly and predictably for transaction needs. Otherwise, if depositors collectively sought to withdraw their gold all at once, as in times of financial panic, this banking 'house of cards' would collapse since there would not be enough 'hard money' in the system owing to the fact that the total money supply (that is, the coins in circulation and bank deposits) would actually be some multiple of the initial commodity money that had originally been deposited for safe-keeping. Moreover, whether individuals hold bank deposits or whether they would hold other forms of bank liabilities, such as privately issued bank notes, the problem would be the same. Whether it is through deposit liabilities or private bank notes, as long as individuals are prepared to hold these two types of bank liabilities (and do not withdraw their precious metal deposits because of lack of confidence), this would allow a bank to issue loans in excess of the original commodity money deposits that initiated the process.

In this traditional story, while banks can create bank money as some multiple of the initial commodity money that was originally deposited in the gold-smiths' vaults and that is re-lent over and over through a circulatory process of deposit/loan expansion, banking institutions are conceived merely as depositories or storehouses of some pre-existing money that was deposited, say, for safe-keeping (Realfonzo, 1998). Regardless of whether this particular tale of banking (resting on either commodity money or surrogates of such commodity money, such as central bank notes) may or may not reflect actual historical reality, this particular perspective on banks as storehouses, whose principal function is that of profit-maximizing intermediation between savers and investors, has changed little in modern times. Instead of resulting from the depositing of precious metals, nowadays we are told that it results from the depositing of exogenous base money initially created and issued by the central bank, which, through bank lending and subsequent deposit creation, leads to a multiple expansion of the money supply – a relation sometimes described as the base money multiplier. Mainstream theorists would argue, therefore, that 'deposits make loans'. Banks are conceived as passive deposit takers that serve the useful function of intermediaries, namely, private institutions whose purpose is to transfer depositors' money (supplied by households that save) to creditworthy borrowers who will use those liquid funds for investment (traditionally business firms seeking credit advances) as is depicted in Figure 4.1, with investment being determined by the rate of interest in the market for loanable funds.

Within this conception of the monetary system, households initiate a process whereby their initial savings are channelled to firms for productive investment through the intermediation role of the banking sector. As described in Figure 4.1, this ensuing business investment generates an income flow, a portion of which is held as savings. These savings then return to the banking sector by starting up a new process as a portion of these savings are accumulated as bank deposits.

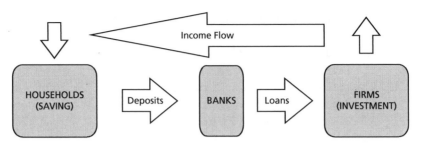

Figure 4.1 The mainstream conception of banks as intermediaries between savers and investors

In their role as intermediaries between savers and investors, banks make out loans to firms to finance their investment, which through the saving process are once again deposited and re-channelled through the banking sector to finance further investment so that the feedback process is propelled forward until the possibility of further loan making from the initial injection of deposits has completely worked itself out. However, the system depicted in Figure 4.1 is, in its essentials, a supply-determined system, whose growth is constrained by the reserves, say, of precious metals, or in modern times by the initial reserves of central bank money that was deposited in the banking system. Hence, for the system to expand, it requires the supply of base money to increase, which then allows the banking sector to serve its crucial allocative role of distributing loanable funds for the purpose of productive investments. Moreover, whether this base money represents the stock of commodity money or of central bank–issued money is of no theoretical significance, since in either case it is the supply of these initial reserves, regardless of their precise forms, that moves the banking system forward in its role as intermediary between savers and investors.

The heterodox perspective

The heterodox theory of money and banking stands this mainstream perspective on the nature and origin on money and the functioning of the banking system somewhat on its head. The notion that money emerged from barter does not find a strong basis in anthropological history. Credit–debit relations stipulated in a particular accounting unit (normally enforced by law or custom) pre-date the appearance of organized market exchange. When money did appear, mostly through the actions of the state, it took on the role of means of payment for the purpose of settling debt obligations, especially tax liabilities (see Peacock, 2013). Within this perspective, and in contrast to the mainstream view, the particular characteristic of the commodity chosen as unit of account was of little significance. What mattered was that money, as an abstract social unit, was sanctioned by the legal apparatus of the state, which would then become the means to discharge liability in a creditor–debtor relation. From this it would ensue that money was not just a particular commodity with some special characteristic feature to facilitate exchange in the context of a previously organized barter exchange system. Instead, the heterodox view suggests that money, as a means of cancelling debt, probably pre-dated organized market exchange itself. Emerging through the expenditures of the state, the legally sanctioned currency entering circulation would eventually not only assume the role as a means of payment in extinguishing debt obligations, but also the role of medium of exchange and a store of liquidity within organized markets, as the latter evolved.

Money, in the sense conceived by heterodox writers, appears in organized markets not as a commodity having some special intrinsic attribute as money, but as a third-party liability having only an extrinsic social value as legal tender, bestowed on it through the legal apparatus of the state either via its monopoly control over the central issuer of the currency (the mint) as during the Middle Ages, or through the state's monetary arm in modern times, namely its central bank (see Parguez and Seccareccia, 2000, p. 101). Banking institutions did not originate primarily from some mistrustful group of profit-seeking goldsmiths who were lending out precious metals while pretending to be holding them in their vaults for safekeeping. Banking institutions existed even before the seventeenth century and these institutions were becoming slowly specialized in the business of finance through double-entry bookkeeping, especially the financing of inventories for long-distance trade, because of the trust they inspired through the public holding of their IOUs, often through the tacit or direct support of the domestic authorities where they were based. In fact, already in twelfth-century Venice and later, such as the Sveriges Riksbank and the Bank of England in the seventeenth century, many early commercial banks actually began as government debt agencies that issued debt certificates, which were then used by merchants and eventually the public as means of payment. However, by the eighteenth and nineteenth centuries, banks typically acquired a charter from the government authorities, which was a certificate or licence authorizing the operation of a bank, whose business involved that of making loans and collecting deposits, but also, during that era, the charter normally gave them the right to circulate their own privately issued bank notes denominated in the currency units established by the state. Because of their convenience, these private bank notes came to compete with the coins produced by the mint, until the mid-nineteenth century, when checking facilities permitted checkable deposits to become more important than private bank notes in circulation. However, because of public distrust in the viability of a payment system that can easily succumb to bank failures, at around the same time during the nineteenth century, governments started to assert monopoly control over the issue of paper currency notes so that by the twentieth century, private bank notes virtually disappeared from circulation in Western countries.

With the decline of primary activities and the rise of modern industrial production, banks extended their activities from the financing of inventories to financing short-term circulating capital requirements to facilitate the process of production. By the nineteenth century, bank credit played a central role in the financing of industrial production. Because of the fears of short-term withdrawals of bank deposits, banks were expected to behave prudently by financing the short-term circulating capital requirements of business enterprises in accordance with the 'real bills' doctrine,[1] but not the long-term funding of fixed capital investment, which instead ought to rely on retained earnings or, through the issuing of securities with the deepening of financial markets, by capturing household saving.

To understand the traditional role of banks within this heterodox approach, let us begin with the fact that much like the state liability issued by central banks, the private banking sector as a whole could create credit money at the stroke of a pen or *ex nihilo* (which is the Latin expression for 'out of nothing'). This is because, contrary to the mainstream tale of goldsmith banking, banks as a whole, and as long as they move closely in tandem in their lending, are not constrained by the amount of reserves arising from their deposit-taking activity. Within this perspective, it is actually loans that make deposits. Indeed, as soon as a bank makes out a loan to a creditworthy borrower, through double-entry bookkeeping a counterparty deposit will appear, initially in the private borrower's account (or in the case of an online credit this would happen instantly), which is then used to meet the borrower's spending need. If the borrower is a business firm, this credit money will go towards the compensation of workers and/or the purchasing of material inputs for the production process. In the archetypal version of bank financing production, this credit gives rise to a circulatory process, as shown in Figure 4.2.

This process of money creation is not driven by some initial deposits entering the banking sector, as with goldsmith banking. If such were the case, then where would the deposit first come from, unless it comes from some outside source, such a government? Within the private banking sector, deposits can only appear when loans are made to either businesses or households. Instead, the initial injection of credit money created *ex nihilo* is sometimes described as the initial finance. These initial credit advances to business enterprises are

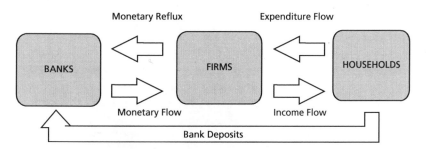

Figure 4.2 The heterodox conception of banks as creators of credit money within the framework of a rudimentary monetary circuit

represented by the 'monetary flow' arrow in Figure 4.2, which generates an 'income flow'. Households, on the receiving end of this income flow, would have a choice to allocate their income towards consumption or saving. In a world with no household saving, all the income is spent, which then allows business firms to capture all of this income generated by the initial bank credit advances (as shown by the 'expenditure flow' arrow), thereby permitting firms to extinguish their debts with regard to the banking sector.

In a world (say, of the nineteenth century) with non-existent (or very shallow) financial markets, the only possible saving is represented in Figure 4.2 in its most unsophisticated form of holdings of bank deposits shown by the return arrow from the household sector to the banks (unless one also considers the option of hoarding bank notes under the mattress or in the cookie jar). As can be seen in Figure 4.2 by the leakage into bank deposits from the household sector, this withholding of consumption spending in liquid form as bank deposits, representing household liquidity preference, can short-circuit the flux/reflux process and prevent the business sector from extinguishing its overall debt to the banks. With a certain portion of the income flow not being spent this would thrust banks into an uncomfortable intermediary role of 'deposits making loans'. Hence, it is only in this crisis situation of incomplete closure of the monetary circuit, with a household saving held in its most liquid form, that the causality between loans and deposits is reversed. However, this is hardly the most realistic scenario, as is shown in Figure 4.3 when organized financial markets exist, reflecting a historically more sophisticated phase of financial deepening.

Indeed, in the heterodox literature, there is an important distinction made between the 'initial' finance of the process of monetary and income expansion and the 'final' finance, which is associated with the reflux phase of this balance-sheet circulatory process (see Graziani, 2003). In Figure 4.2, we have

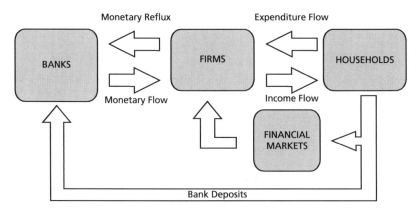

Figure 4.3 The heterodox conception of banks as creators of credit money with organized financial markets

only considered the most elementary case, where the monetary flow from the banking sector gives rise to an equivalent monetary reflux through the consumption expenditures of households, unless households choose to hold savings in the most liquid form of cash or bank deposits, in which case the latter holdings can short-circuit the process.

Let us now consider a world of financial deepening represented in Figure 4.3, where households can choose a whole portfolio of financial assets issued directly by business enterprises, such as corporate stocks or bonds, or other forms of financial instruments offered by investment banks, or even through the intervention of non-bank financial intermediaries, whose liabilities may not be considered good substitutes for commercial bank deposits and thus are not normally acceptable as means of payments. This broad spectrum of institutions constituting the financial markets is depicted in Figure 4.3 as a separate space into which household saving flows out of household income and these institutions do engage in financial interme-diation. However, this intermediation is not between savers and investors, as it is normally described by the mainstream theory of loanable funds, because investment, or the accumulation of capital, has already occurred. After production has taken place, what the financial markets do during the reflux phase is to bring together households who have chosen to save in the form of less liquid assets and firms in search of long-term or 'final' finance in order to allow the latter to extinguish their 'initial' short-term debts with regard to the banking sector. This is described by the arrows going from households choosing to save a portion of their incomes being channelled into the financial markets and firms simultaneously accessing these savings for final finance.

There are numerous complications to this heterodox macroeconomic analysis of banks as creators of credit money that can be added to offer a greater degree of realism, such as when we include in the monetary reflux not only the principal of the loan made out to business enterprises that must be reimbursed but also an analysis of the interest spreads from which banks traditionally make profit. In addition, one can also consider the case where households go into debt with regard to the banking sector to obtain consumer loans or take out mortgages. Also, from the portrait just described of the relation between banks and business firms on the one hand, and businesses and households and the financial markets on the other, we have excluded the role of the government and the central bank. However, these are complications that can and have been analysed by heterodox economists. In order to provide the reader with a more comprehensive understanding of the mechanics of this fundamental relation between banks and the private sector, by considering the case of a consumer loan, but also between commercial banks and the central bank and payment system, let us now describe briefly this process from the standpoint of banks' balance sheets.

Understanding the heterodox approach to banks and the modern payment system from a simple balance-sheet perspective

Most mainstream textbooks treat money just as they would treat commodities: they assume that money should be scarce for it to keep its value, as if money were akin to gold, and they assume that it is the role of the central bank to make sure that this is so. If there is too much money or if the stock of money grows too fast, according to the mainstream story, there will be an increase in the general price level and the value of the domestic currency relative to other currencies will depreciate.

We have seen that mainstream economists assume the existence of a money creation mechanism based on the so-called money multiplier process and fractional-reserve banking system. They assume that in order to be able to create loans and money, commercial banks must first acquire a special kind of money – reserves at the central bank – because financial regulations in a vast number of countries require banks to hold a certain fraction of the money deposits of their customers in the form of a specific kind of assets – reserves at the central bank. According to this story, deposits of agents at banks are thus a multiple of these reserves, roughly speaking the inverse of this required percentage, say, a multiplier of 20, if the required percentage of reserves to bank deposits is 5 per cent. By controlling the amount of reserves that commercial banks have access to, it is said that the central bank has the ability to control the supply of money in the economy.

The causality of this mainstream story is thus the following. Depending on its objectives, mainly concerned with a stable aggregate price level, the central bank creates a certain amount of reserves. This then allows the creation of a multiple amount of loans and deposits, the latter with the addition of banknotes, constituting the supply of money, which hopefully is in line with the needs of the economy.

There are, however, countries where there are no reserve requirements. This obviously makes the mainstream story rather questionable if not meaningless. The creation of money must follow some other mechanism. It is the purpose of the following subsections to examine this more realistic mechanism.

Transactions of the private sector

As we have seen from our analysis of the monetary circuit, the process of money creation is simple yet fascinating. Money creation – the creation of bank deposits – relies on three key elements: the willingness of banks to take risks and grant loans, the creditworthiness of borrowers, and the willingness of borrowers to go into debt and take out a loan. No more is needed. Banks do not need to hold gold and neither do they need to hold reserves at the central bank. Money is created *ex nihilo*.

Suppose that an individual wishes to buy a new car worth 30 000 US dollars and needs to borrow to do so. This person will need to show that she is creditworthy, for instance, by showing that she has a regular income, that this income is likely to be large enough to make the monthly payments, and that interest and principal has been paid on previous loans (that is, the person has a good credit record).

What happens next? As pointed out in our previous discussion, the loan is created at the stroke of a pen, or rather by punching a couple of keys on the banker's computer. As the bank grants the loan, there is a simultaneous creation of a bank deposit: money gets created. This is shown in Table 4.1, which shows the changes in the balance sheet (the T account) of the bank of the borrower: the bank now has US$30 000 more in loans on the assets side of its balance sheet, but simultaneously, on the liabilities side, there is an increase of US$30 000 in bank deposits. The car purchaser now has a bank debt of US$30 000, which from the standpoint of the bank is an asset, but at

Table 4.1 Changes in the balance sheet of a bank that grants a new loan

Bank of the car purchaser

Assets	Liabilities
Loan to car purchaser +US$30 000	Deposit of car purchaser +US$30 000

Table 4.2 Changes in bank balance sheets after the payment is made

Bank of car purchaser		Bank of car dealer	
Assets	Liabilities	Assets	Liabilities
Loan to car purchaser +US$30 000	Debit position at clearinghouse +US$30 000	Credit position at clearinghouse +US$30 000	Deposit of car dealer +US$30 000

the same time the bank now owes a US$30 000 deposit to the car purchaser. This is why it is on the liabilities side of the bank.

What happens next? The individual obtained a car loan because she wanted to buy a car. So the purchaser goes to the car dealer, most likely with a certified cheque, and once all papers are signed, drives off with the car, while the car dealer rushes to deposit the cheque in his bank account. Once this is done and the cheque goes through the payment system, the new balance sheets are as shown in Table 4.2.

All banks are members of a payment and settlement system, either directly or indirectly in the case of small banks that use the account of a larger bank. Indeed, their participation in the payment system is one of the key services rendered by banks. As payments go through banks, bank deposits move from one account to another. These payments are centralized at a clearinghouse, which keeps tabs so to speak. As the cheque (in paper form or electronic form) clears the payment system and goes through the clearinghouse, the US$30 000 are taken away from the car purchaser and end up in the bank account of the car dealer. But now the bank of the car purchaser owes US$30 000 to the clearinghouse, while the clearinghouse owes US$30 000 to the bank of the car dealer, which is what Table 4.2 illustrates.

In all payment systems, amounts due between participating financial institutions must be settled at least by the end of the day. How this will be done

Table 4.3 Changes in bank balance sheets when banks lend to each other

Bank of car purchaser		Bank of car dealer	
Assets	Liabilities	Assets	Liabilities
Loan to car purchaser +US$30000	Loan taken from bank of car dealer +US$30000	Loan to bank of car purchaser +US$30000	Deposit of car dealer +US$30000

depends on the institutional setup, which is specific to each country. In the simplest case, the bank that is in a credit position at the clearinghouse – the bank of the car dealer – will grant what is called an overnight loan (at the overnight rate of interest) to the bank that is in a debit position at the clearinghouse – the bank of the car purchaser. This is the overnight market, also called the interbank market, since it involves banks and a few large financial institutions. Banks will lend to each other as long as participants to the payment system have confidence in each other. Table 4.3 illustrates this situation.

As was the case with the loan to an individual, we see that the banking system relies on trust and creditworthiness. Banks must have sufficient confidence in other banks. When banks start lacking trust, the overnight market so described, where banks in a daily surplus position at the clearinghouse lend funds to banks that are in a negative position, will freeze and banks will decline to lend to each other. This happened in Europe in August 2007, when all financial institutions were afraid to make overnight loans to German banks because of the failure of two German banks. Fears spread to the rest of the world and overnight markets lost their fluidity elsewhere as well, as banks became reluctant to lend large amounts to each other.

What then happens if the overnight market does not function properly or if, for some reason, a bank in a negative position at the clearinghouse cannot get an overnight loan from some other bank? Does the payment made to the car dealer still go through? It will, and this is where the central bank plays its role as a lender of last resort. In this case, using again the two banks described in Tables 4.1 and 4.2, the central bank makes an overnight loan to the bank of the car purchaser, thus allowing it to settle its position at the clearinghouse, as shown in Table 4.4. And what happens to the bank of the car dealer? Well, if it declines to lend its surpluses at the clearinghouse, it has no other choice than to deposit its surpluses in its account at the central bank. The deposits of the bank of the dealer at the central bank are what mainstream authors call reserves; central bankers now refer instead to clearing balances or settlement balances.

Table 4.4 Changes in the balance sheet of banks and the central bank when banks decline to lend to each other

Bank of car purchaser		Bank of car dealer	
Assets	Liabilities	Assets	Liabilities
Loan to car purchaser +US$30 000	Loan taken from the central bank +US$30 000	Deposit at the central bank +US$30 000	Deposit of car dealer +US$30 000

Central bank	
Assets	Liabilities
Advance to the bank of car purchaser +US$30 000	Deposit of the bank of car dealer +US$30 000

Table 4.4 also illustrates the fact that the size of the balance sheet of the central bank will balloon any time overnight markets do not function properly.

As noted previously, there are many possible setups for payment and settlement systems. In the setup assumed so far, unless the overnight market collapses, all the activity occurs in the clearinghouse, which can be run by a private entity, owned by the bankers' association, for instance. Another possible setup, often assumed in textbooks, is that clearing and settlement occurs on the books of the central bank. In that case, payments can only go through, and hence settlement occurs, if the bank making the payment, here the bank of the car purchaser, already has deposits at the central bank (if it has reserves). Table 4.5 illustrates this situation: the bank of the car purchaser sees its reserves at the central bank diminished by US$30 000 while those of the bank of the car dealer get augmented by the same amount.

When an individual bank starts to run out of reserves, it will have to borrow funds on the overnight market, thus borrowing the funds from banks that have a surplus of reserves (this is the federal funds market in the United States); or it might borrow the reserves from the central bank, as illustrated in Table 4.4. Thus the role of the central bank is not to put limits on the creation of reserves; its role is purely defensive – it needs to provide enough reserves to ensure that the payment system runs smoothly. In countries where the clearing occurs essentially through the clearinghouse, and where payments are netted out at the end of the day, there is no need for reserves, and hence, unless some regulation imposes required reserves as a fraction of some measure of assets or

Table 4.5 Changes in balance sheets when the central bank acts as the clearinghouse

Bank of car purchaser		Bank of car dealer	
Assets	Liabilities	Assets	Liabilities
Loan to car purchaser +US$30 000 Reserves at central bank −US$30 000		Reserves at the central bank +US$30 000	Deposit of car dealer +US$30 000

Central bank	
Assets	Liabilities
	Deposit (reserves) of the bank of car dealer +US$30 000 Deposit (reserves) of the bank of car purchaser −US$30 000

liabilities, there will be zero reserves, as is the case with Canada, for instance. By contrast, in countries where the clearing occurs through the central bank and where payments are settled in real time as they go through, banks will have to hold reserves at the central bank, which will then act as the clearinghouse, insuring that there are enough clearing or settlement balances to absorb the fluctuations in incoming and outgoing payments.

Transactions of the public sector

What should be noted is that the total amount of clearing balances (or reserves) in the banking system is a given as long as all transactions occur between private agents. As is obvious from Table 4.5, any increase in the reserves of one bank will be compensated by the decrease in the deposits of another bank. Thus the overall amount of reserves in the banking system can only be changed if a transaction occurs with the public sector, that is, when the central bank is involved in one of the transactions. In fact, such a transaction is already described by Table 4.4. In this case, the central bank provides an advance to the banking sector, thus generating the creation of an equivalent amount of reserves for the banking system. More generally, if the central bank feels that there is a higher demand for reserves by the banking sector, additional reserves can be created by making advances to some banks, for one night, one week, one month, or perhaps even three years as was done by the European Central Bank at the height of the euro-area crisis in 2011.

Table 4.6 An open-market operation when the central bank wishes to increase the amount of reserves or to compensate for a previous fall in reserves

Commercial bank		Central bank	
Assets	Liabilities	Assets	Liabilities
Treasury bills −US$10 000 Reserves at central bank +US$10 000		Treasury bills +US$10 000	Deposit of commercial bank +US$10 000

However, there are other ways in which reserves get created (or destroyed). As reflected in mainstream textbooks, reserves get created whenever the central bank purchases assets from the private sector. Table 4.6 provides such an example. It is assumed that the central bank purchases a government security from the banking sector, for instance a Treasury bill that had been issued earlier by the government and bought by a bank. This transaction, whether it is outright or whether the central bank promises to sell it back within a period of time (in which case it is a repurchase agreement – a repo), leads to the creation of new reserves for the banking sector. This type of transaction is called an open-market operation. Of course, it can go the other way, for instance when the central bank sells the Treasury bills that it holds to the private sector, in which case reserves are destroyed.

The central bank is usually the fiscal agent of the government. This means that the central bank is empowered with the responsibility of selling the securities that the government issues when it borrows funds; it also means that the central bank manages the cash balances of the government, and in particular it implies that the government has an account at the central bank. As a consequence, any time there is an outgoing or incoming payment involving the government deposit account at the central bank, there will be a creation or a destruction of reserves. Central bankers call these the 'autonomous factors' that affect the amount of reserves in the banking system.

Take the example of a civil servant receiving her monthly pay, assuming that it comes from the account of the government at the central bank. Table 4.7 illustrates this case: the bank account of the civil servant will now increase by US$5000. As the payment goes through the clearinghouse and gets settled, the government deposits at the central bank get reduced by US$5000, while the reserves of the bank of the civil servant increase by US$5000. Thus, when the government makes a payment to the private sector, through its account at the central bank, reserves get created. Things go in reverse gear

Table 4.7 Changes in balance sheets induced by government expenditure

Commercial bank		Central bank	
Assets	Liabilities	Assets	Liabilities
Reserves at central bank +US$5000	Deposit of civil servant +US$5000		Deposit of government −US$5000 Deposit of commercial bank +US$5000

if the civil servant has to pay her income taxes, say at the rate of 40 per cent. The deposits of the civil servant will get reduced by US$2000 and, if the proceeds are deposited in the account of the government at the central bank, the reserves of the banking system will be reduced by US$2000 (Wray, 2012, Ch. 3).

The lesson to be drawn here is that commercial banks are the institutions that grant loans and create money *ex nihilo*. There is no constraint on how much can be created, with one exception. A banker must keep the trust and confidence of depositors and of fellow bankers, and so must make sure that the number of 'bad loans' – loans on which borrowers default, thus creating losses for the bank – is minimized, to avoid the arising of suspicion. Commercial banks do not need central bank reserves to grant loans. On the contrary, the role of the central bank is to make sure that there is the right amount of reserves in the banking system, to ensure that the payment system is running smoothly. The central bank will react to changes in the 'autonomous factors' affecting reserves, which we discussed above by either pursuing open-market operations, or by providing advances to the banking sector. To sum up, we may say that the supply of money is endogenous, responding to the demand of the economy, and that the supply of reserves is also endogenous, responding to the needs of the payment system.

Concluding remarks

The heterodox view of money and banking stands on its head much of the mainstream view on the role of money and banks that still reigns supreme in popular textbooks. Money is not a commodity that is dropped exogenously from a helicopter so as to render the exchange of commodities and services more efficient. Money is a means of payment that permeates social relations and allows economic agents in a community to free themselves from the constraints of scarcity that a barter economy imposes. Money is not some predetermined object but, in its essence, is an endogenous creation that is issued by institutions established or licensed by the state. This money emerges through a balance-sheet operation associated with changes in a third-party liability, whether it is the state through its central bank liability, or through the strategic role played by banks via credit money creation reflected in changes in their deposit liabilities. As long as there are creditworthy borrowers, credit money creation is demand driven. It can never be supply constrained as claimed by the mainstream. Moreover, because banks are not reserve constrained as a group and money creation is an outcome of the interaction between an individual borrower and a bank, money cannot be an exogenous variable as normally depicted in the textbooks. Indeed, bank credit follows a circular process of money creation and money destruction and, therefore, in contrast to the mainstream, which emphasizes its role in facilitating exchange, the most crucial social feature of money is associated with its financing of production where commercial banks have played a central role since the nineteenth century.

NOTE

1 The 'real bills' doctrine rested on the belief that prudent banking practices required that commercial banks engage only in short-term lending, in the sense that banks would discount commercial bills or promissory notes on the basis of collateral representing 'real' goods engaged in the production process. This essentially meant that commercial banks should passively accommodate the 'needs of trade' by financing the short-term circulating capital requirement, such as the wage bill, and not to finance the purchases of fixed capital assets. For further discussion see Humphrey (1982).

 REFERENCES

Graziani, A. (2003), *The Monetary Theory of Production*, Cambridge, UK: Cambridge University Press.

Humphrey, T.M. (1982), 'The real bills doctrine', *Federal Reserve Bank of Richmond Economic Review*, **68** (5), 3–13.

Jevons, S. (1875), *Money and the Mechanism of Exchange*, New York: D. Appleton and Co.

Parguez, A. (1975), *Monnaie et macroéconomie: théorie de la monnaie en déséquilibre* [Money and Macroeconomics: Theory of Money in Disequilibrium], Paris: Economica.

Parguez, A. and M. Seccareccia (2000), 'The credit theory of money: the monetary circuit approach', in J. Smithin (ed.), *What is Money?*, London and New York: Routledge, pp. 101–23.

Peacock, M. (2013), *Introducing Money*, London and New York: Routledge.

Realfonzo, R. (1998), *Money and Banking: Theory and Debate (1900–1940)*, Cheltenham, UK and Northampton, MA, USA: Edward Elgar Publishing.

Rochon, L.-P. and M. Seccareccia (eds) (2013), *Monetary Economies of Production: Banking and Financial Circuits and the Role of the State*, Cheltenham, UK, and Northampton, MA, USA: Edward Elgar Publishing.

Smith, A. ([1776] 1937), *An Inquiry into the Nature and Causes of the Wealth of Nations*, New York: The Modern Library.

Wray, L.R. (2012), *Modern Money Theory: A Primer on Macroeconomics for Sovereign Monetary Systems*, Basingstoke, UK and New York: Palgrave Macmillan.

A PORTRAIT OF ALAIN PARGUEZ (1940–)

Alain Parguez is Professor Emeritus at the Université de Franche-Comté, Besançon, France. Together with the late Augusto Graziani, Parguez has been a leading figure of what has been sometimes described historically as the Franco–Italian Circuit School. His ideas are deeply rooted in the works of French Keynesian economists of the post-war period, the most noteworthy being Jean de Largentaye and Alain Barrère. However, his writings find inspiration in the macroeconomic and monetary views of Karl Marx, John Maynard Keynes, Michał Kalecki and Joan Robinson, as well as the monetary ideas of such heterodox writings going back to the Banking School in the nineteenth century.

His ideas on money and the role of banks in the monetary circuit were first espoused in an important book titled *Monnaie et macroéconomie: théorie de la monnaie en déséquilibre* (1975). These ideas on the monetary circuit were further developed in a series of publications that followed his book, particularly in the two French journals *Economie appliquée* and *Economies et sociétés*, where, in the case of the latter, he had edited a special series *Monnaie et Production* that lasted from 1984 to 1996. More recently, a book came out in his honour titled *Monetary Economies of Production: Banking and Financial Circuits and the Role of the State* (Rochon and Seccareccia, 2013), which celebrates his contributions to political economy.

According to Alain Parguez, the mainstream views on money and banking lead to a world of institutionalized scarcity, because they start from the misleading premise that money should be a scarce commodity and that banks are mere intermediaries between savers and investors. In contrast to the mainstream austerity perspective, Parguez starts from the view that there are no supply-side limits to the creation of money, because the latter can be created *ex nihilo*. Therefore, the building of models of modern economies where banks are mere intermediaries whose loan advances depend on the amount of base money created by the central bank, rather than being conceived as creators and destroyers of money, can lead to catastrophic policy consequences. A recent example of this misguided policy based on such erroneous theories of commercial banking is the attempt to kick-start economic growth since the 2007–08 global financial crisis through the policy of quantitative easing, which led to an explosion of reserves in the banking system but without significant effects on economic growth, with the possible exception of sustaining asset prices and, indirectly, perhaps, bank profitability.

In a similar fashion, Parguez has been a staunch critic of the institutional structure of the euro area, because the original architects of the euro tried to create a monetary system not unlike that founded on gold going back to the nineteenth century, with results that have been just as catastrophic. Although Alain Parguez has been an ardent supporter and advocate of the monetary circuit approach, over the years he has done much to promote exchanges with other heterodox theorists of money within the broad post-Keynesian tradition, for instance, with economists such as Paul Davidson and Basil Moore, as well as with neochartalist writers such as Warren Mosler and L. Randall Wray.

5

The financial system

Jan Toporowski

 OVERVIEW

This chapter explains that the financial system:

- is that part of the economy that meets the financing needs of the rest of the economy;

- is very large in key capitalist countries like the United States and United Kingdom;

- is unstable and prone to crisis;

- is not considered in mainstream economics;

- emerges into the modern world with the financing needs of the state, subsequently with the financing needs of infrastructure and industry;

- develops to overcome the financial constraints on modern capitalism, only to impose new debt constraints.

 KEYWORDS

- **Balance sheet:** A financial statement showing the assets (income-generating wealth or claims on other government and other economic units) and liabilities (commitments to pay in the future).
- **Debt:** An obligation to pay money to another person, government, bank, financial institution or firm. Debts are usually eliminated by paying (or settling them) with money, or by cancelling them against other claims, for instance using a bank deposit to pay a debt to the bank, or paying a tax bill with a government bond.
- **Financial wealth:** A claim on another person, government, bank, financial institution or firm, requiring them to pay money. Financial wealth is usually distinguished from other forms of wealth, personal wealth (like jewellery), land or real estate, and productive capital (factories, trucks, and so on) by the fact that financial wealth has no use other than as a claim for a money payment.

- **Interest:** A payment for the use of money during a certain period. Interest is usually calculated over the period of a year. The contract for the use of that money can be a loan, bond or a short-term bill.

Why are these topics important?

Finance is a component of the economy concerned with the financing needs of the whole economy; in other words, it is the set of institutions and practices that contain the financial wealth and obligations of the state, households and firms. This includes banks, investment institutions and the credit operations of capital and banking markets.

In most developed capitalist economies, the financial sector is very large. Indeed, in the case of the United States or the United Kingdom, for instance, its value and turnover are some four or five times the value of national income; in other words, it is four to five times the value of everything that is produced in one year. For many economists, this is excessive, and arises because those who are not bankers and financiers are all becoming 'financialized' and must assume the burden by making payments on this growing debt from national income. So, for example, if total debt is four times the national income, then roughly four times the rate of interest has to be taken out of national income to pay interest on that debt. Yet, this is an incorrect way of viewing this, since most debts are claims on other debts. In other words, the money that a bank pays on its debts comes largely from the money that its customers pay on their debts toward the bank. The net debt (that is, after cancelling out debts backed by other debts) is therefore negligible. So with national income, what is actually taken out of it to service debt is proportionate to net debts rather than the total of all debts.

Most of this size and remarkable activity of the financial system is due to two circumstances. The first is the various processes of 'hedging', which occurs when individuals take financial positions to protect themselves against changes in the value of the assets, or more specifically to offset possible losses or gains, essentially a way in which bankers and financiers make money from each other (see below). The sums involved, at times of economic hardship, expose such individuals to accusations of unfair profiteering from the misery of those affected by that hardship.

The second cause is the growing prominence and international integration of financial markets; capital and banking markets in the United States and the United Kingdom now also serve to transfer capital between other countries of the world – so-called intermediation. Money capital from Russia, for example, appears in New York on its way to Latin America or China. This growing international intermediation makes it appear as if the average Briton or American is supporting a huge amount of debt, when in fact much of it is being serviced by many more people in other countries of the world.

Financial markets have come to the fore in economic discussions since the financial crisis in the United States in 2007–10, and owing to the distinctive role banking and financial markets played in the European economic crisis since 2010. The collapse of Lehman Brothers in September 2008, and the failure of Northern Rock and the Royal Bank of Scotland in Britain, were followed by the deepest economic recession since World War II. The succession of events looked remarkably like the Great Crash of 1929, which was followed by the Great Depression of the 1930s. To be clear, the situation of finance in the twenty-first century's first international economic crisis is complex, with different causal factors at work in different countries. For example, while the US crisis was characterized by a failure of private sector debt, in Europe government debt has been in crisis. This chapter aims to explain some of that complexity.

More generally, a closer examination of economic history over the last 200 years shows us that capitalist economies are unstable and that debt problems and banking crises are common at the very moment economic activity begins to contract, not to mention when a crisis occurs. This makes an understanding of finance crucial for understanding macroeconomics, or the way in which economies as a whole work.

Mainstream economic theory

Mainstream economic theory gives a very poor account of the operations of the financial sector. Several reasons can explain this neglect. Five of them are discussed here.

First, finance appears in textbooks principally as portfolio theory, that is, the theory of 'rational' or 'optimal' portfolio choice, meaning the choice households make about how to allocate their wealth, that is, between, say, bonds or another asset. This choice is supposed to be determined by the 'returns' from holding such an asset. Rational portfolio choice involves getting the highest possible returns from the portfolio, given the possibility of loss that may arise in all uncertain situations (and the future of stock prices is always uncertain).

Portfolio theory is supposed to be a way of calculating how to make the largest possible amount of money out of savings or financial investments. But like any system that promises to make you rich overnight, portfolio theory has all the scientific rigour and insight of seventeenth-century alchemy that promised to turn base metals into gold. The theory has no substantial explanation of how returns are generated in the economy or the relationship of finance and credit to the rest of the economy. Portfolio theory can therefore be safely disregarded. The only reader who may need it is one who will be studying finance for specialist courses. Even then such a reader, who might eventually work in the financial sector, will find portfolio theory virtually useless for guiding actual financial operations. Such operations are determined by the financial strategies of financial institutions, rather than by individual investors' portfolio choices.

Second, the neglect of the importance of finance by mainstream economics is largely due to the success of what is called the Modigliani–Miller theorem in finance and economics, according to which the value of a company is not affected by its financing structure. In other words, the theorem, developed by Modigliani and Miller (1958), claims that the value of a company is independent from the proportion of debt or equity used to finance the company. If this is the case, then there is no need to discuss finance. Yet, this proposition holds true only under very special circumstances or assumptions, such as perfect knowledge of the future, the absence of market 'distortions' such as taxes, and perfect liquidity. But somehow these special circumstances got lost in the process of the acceptance of this theorem into the broader economic curriculum, with the result that the importance of the financing of business was simply forgotten.

Third, another way in which finance appears in mainstream theory is as household savings, resulting from mainstream economists seeking, since the 1970s, to introduce microeconomic foundations (or microfoundations) into the dominant economic theory, an approach that is called 'new classical economics', or the 'new neo-classical synthesis'. But finance is much more complex than simply discussing how households place their savings. A variation of mainstream economics, this new classical doctrine supposes that the economy consists of only households who make calculated decisions about production and exchange, including the sale of their labour, and how much to 'save' for retirement. These savings are then supposed to determine the amount of investment that the economy undertakes, since, according to mainstream theory, savings determine investment. But, since households control all the available resources in the economy, there cannot possibly be any unemployed resources – holding unemployed resources (including labour) would be irrational from the point of view of the household. If there are any unemployed resources, it is merely because households are looking for the next opportunity to trade.

Accordingly, there is no unemployment. And recall that a flexible price system ensures that resources are exchanged to the point where everyone has the goods they prefer. Production is undertaken using only 'real' resources (labour, materials and equipment, but not money), as this is a 'real exchange economy' and not a 'monetary economy of production'. Savings therefore consist of claims on future income from production, that is, entitlements to consumption goods that will be consumed during the saver's retirement.

This new classical theory is only plausible because it plays on the vanity of the university professors who promoted it. After all, this is how rational individuals are supposed to behave in the conditions postulated by the theory. Any other theory must therefore assume that people are irrational, and people, especially university professors, are not irrational!

Unfortunately, this theory became widespread at a time of growing financial and banking instability. The United Kingdom experienced a major stock market crash in 1974, followed by bank failures and then the failure of savings and loan associations in the United States at the end of the 1970s. In 1982, the international banking system nearly collapsed, because many indebted developing country governments, in Mexico, Brazil, Argentina and Poland, could not pay their debts.

How did respectable university professors of economics respond to the financial and banking instability? They did so by arguing that the instability reflected some perceived objective 'risk' of loss that exists in the world. For instance, in a famous model that was supposed to explain how banks work, Douglas Diamond of the University of Chicago and Philip Dybvig of Yale University postulated two types of households (or agents): borrowers and lenders. This model assumed some agents took in the savings of some households (deposits) and then lent them out to other households (loans). A potential problem arises, however, since households are supposed to be able to withdraw their savings at any time. But the savings that were lent to other households (the borrowers) were lent for longer periods of time, and subject to the possibility of loss. So if the deposits were lent out for, say, a period of five years, what happens when the depositor wants to withdraw his or her savings after only one year?

This is supposed to explain bank failures, that is, when banks cannot pay out savings deposited with them (see Diamond and Dybvig, 1983). Bankers, of course, know what makes them fail, so the Diamond and Dybvig model did not offer bankers any new insights. In practice, bankers also have techniques for managing liquidity, giving them the ability to raise cash quickly. But the important thing about the Diamond and Dybvig model was that it showed the conditions under which household banks, run by individuals thinking like university professors of economics possessing rather limited worldly experience, could get into difficulty.

Fourth, at around the same time, Joseph Stiglitz started to publish a series of models arguing that the problems of banks were due to inadequate information on the part of those households/agents on the risk characteristics (ability to repay loans) of their customers. Since the borrowing agents are supposed to know more about their prospects of repaying their debts than the banks, he called this problem one of 'asymmetric information' (see Stiglitz and Weiss, 1981): one party has more information than the other.

This phrase became the call sign of Stiglitz's followers, the so-called 'new Keynesians'. Stiglitz used this information problem of banks to then explain phenomena like unemployment and, later on, the weak development of banking in developing countries. According to Stiglitz, banks based in the United States and the United Kingdom did not know the true economic conditions in the developing countries they had invested in, and those countries did not have financial systems that could cope with these banks' demands to get back their money.

Asymmetric information rose to become a dominant theme of macroeconomics. For instance, by the end of the 1980s, financial and economic instability was sufficiently obvious for (the then) Princeton University Professor Ben Bernanke to get together with Mark Gertler of New York University to attempt to explain this instability. They created a model, relying on asymmetric information, showing how financial markets may affect the economy at large through fluctuations in the 'net worth' of borrowers, that is, the value of their assets, after taking away the value of their liabilities (see Bernanke and Gertler, 1989). Missing from this approach is any attempt to explain the processes by which these changes in 'net worth' arose, other than by reference to the all-pervasive asymmetric information. Net worth decreases when stock and bond prices fall. Not knowing when this will happen is supposed to be due to 'asymmetric information'.

Now, net worth certainly fluctuates with the business cycle, but these processes are of crucial importance for the theory. Only by correctly understanding these processes is it possible to determine whether changes in net worth are symptoms of the business cycle, and determined by them, or, as Bernanke and Gertler (1989) argue, cause business fluctuations. The implications can be very important.

Finally, following the financial crisis that broke out in 2007–08, a certain amount of interest has emerged among economists and bank regulators in what is called 'network theory', according to which the balance sheets of banks and financial institutions, and also those of non-financial businesses, are interconnected; in other words, most of their assets consist of liabilities issued by other financial institutions. If the value of some assets fails, then 'insolvency' arises and spreads through the system (see European Central Bank, 2010). Insolvency occurs therefore when the value of assets in a balance sheet is less than the liabilities. In this situation, a company cannot repay its liabilities from its assets.

The theory arises from the very obvious observation that, when there are interbank markets (in which banks borrow and lend reserves in order to maintain their ability to make payments to their customers), banks end up having a lot of lending to – and borrowing from – other banks on their balance sheets. A bank that is unable to make the payments on its loans from another bank can then easily transmit its difficulties to the other bank. This was certainly a factor in the financial crisis that erupted in 2007–08.

However, precisely because of these interbank markets, bank balance sheets change very quickly from day to day. So network theory may be useful for simulating how a financial crisis arises. But any model built up using real variables very quickly goes out of date, because the balance sheets of inter- mediaries change not only with the business, but also owing to financial and monetary innovation, or the emergence of new kinds of financial intermedi- aries, and 'shadow' banking, which lies beyond the control of regulators and policy-makers.

What is wrong with the textbook approach?

In general, since the financial crisis, there has been a general agreement regarding the importance of finance in explaining the way the economy works, as well as the notion that the views commonly found in economics textbooks give a very poor account of finance in the economy, which are usually founded upon some particular insight that is obvious. For example, wealthy people make portfolio choices; people save for retirement; there is 'uncertainty' about future stock market prices as well as lack of informa- tion about the future of the economy; stock market booms make stockholders wealthier; bank and corporation balance sheets are interconnected. But without an explanation of how the economy as a whole works, these insights remain trivial.

There are at least three reasons why these textbook approaches cannot develop a theory of how the economy as a whole works. First, mainstream approaches reduce all economic activity to the economic choices of individual 'agents', or households that are making production and saving decisions. This, therefore, limits consideration to arguments and decisions that are made only by households; any attempts to deviate from this theory lack 'microfoundations'. To any economist who believes that all private sector economic and financial decisions are made solely by households, this theory would also lack plausibility. Separating their forms of behaviour and roles carries important consequences.

In reality, we cannot conflate all agents together. Households make consumption decisions, with a relatively few wealthy individuals making portfolio investment decisions as well. Firms make production and productive investment decisions that we all depend on, and a third type of 'agents', that is, financial intermediaries, make decisions that affect the structure of the financial system.

Second, textbook approaches confuse saving, or savings, with finance and credit. Saving is simply the *flow* of income that is unspent in a given year or period of time. Savings is the *stock* of financial assets that exists in an economy at any one time. It consists of the *saving* that has been accumulated over a period of time. But it also includes a huge amount of credit that has been advanced on the security of assets (financial and non-financial assets, such as housing, consumer durables, factories, land, and so on). Thus, a bank deposit may be backed in its balance sheet by a loan from the bank to another bank. The second bank's loan (a liability) may be backed by an equivalent asset in the form of a loan to, say, a hedge fund. That hedge fund's liability to its bank may have its asset counterpart in the form of shares of an insurance company. The insurance company may back its shares with assets in the form of shares in an industrial company, or government bonds, and so on.

The financial system, therefore, does not just consist of 'pure' intermediation (transfer of saving) between households with surplus income ('saving') and households with financial deficits (negative 'saving', whose expenditure exceeds their income), except in a very trivial sense. The system consists of a more complex intermediation in the first place between households, but also firms and governments. Adding even further complexity to the system is a more advanced kind of intermediation between financial intermediaries to enable them to match the assets and liabilities in their balance sheets by term (the period of time until a loan or financial contract has to be settled) and by liquidity (the ease with which long-term financial assets, or illiquid assets, like real estate, may be converted into money to make payments on liabilities).

For instance, financial intermediaries, like hedge funds, private equity, or money market brokers, exist to allow wealth holders to have a diversity of assets and liabilities, according to the financing preferences of particular kinds of firms, households and governments.

The most common example of this is a bank that holds short-term deposits, because people prefer to have deposits that can be withdrawn quickly. However, borrowers commonly prefer to borrow for more extended periods of time – years, or even decades. A bank therefore not only collects deposits for lending onto borrowers, but also engages in 'maturity transformation', using short-term deposits to finance long-term loans. Similarly, pension funds and insurance companies hold long-term bonds and shares, which may become illiquid (less easy to sell) and of uncertain value. Private equity funds emerge as an additional kind of financial intermediary that will guarantee the liquidity and profitability of company shares.

This complexity of financial intermediation is almost completely ignored by the textbook approach to financial economics. Yet it has one very important consequence for that key variable in macroeconomics, the rate of interest. Most economists, following Knut Wicksell and John Maynard Keynes, consider the rate of interest as determined in the money market by the demand and supply of money (nowadays in the form of bank reserves). But, in more recent macroeconomics textbooks, the rate of interest is the factor that brings saving (unspent income) equal to investment by the 'laws of supply and demand', with a downward-sloping demand curve for saving to be used for investment purposes, and an upward-sloping supply curve of saving. In other words, most textbooks still adhere to the concept of loanable funds.

In the real world, however, there is a whole constellation of interest rates, or rates of return on financial assets, as stipulated by Joan Robinson (1952). In that world, these rates of interest bring nothing 'into equilibrium'. Rather, imbalances between the preferences of depositors and borrowers are met by another layer of intermediation that will satisfy liquidity and term requirements, rather than by adjustment of these requirements by some rate of interest, in accordance with 'laws of supply and demand'. For instance, there is no rate of interest that will make bank depositors with chequebook accounts prefer to hold long-term deposits that will match the long-term loans that borrowers prefer; or that will make borrowers willing to finance their activities with short-term loans. The margin between short-term and long-term rates of interest is supposed to compensate banks for any difficulties arising from their 'maturity transformation', and banks will borrow and lend among each other to make up any shortfall in money to pay out deposits.

Rates of interest exist to determine the distribution of income or returns around the financial system, or financial surplus among firms, rather than matching needs to provision of finance or money.

In other words, differences in financing requirements and financial investment preferences are accommodated in the financial system not by a rate of interest that brings them into equilibrium but by new forms of expanding financial intermediation. Differences in the various financial market interest rates exist to make such further forms of intermediation worthwhile.

Finally, reality is much more complex than the naive and simplistic narratives put forward in the textbook approaches to finance. Moreover, underlying financial flows are business fluctuations. As a result the financial system is unstable and things are constantly going wrong in terms of unconfirmed predictions and unwanted losses in finance. Financial economics attributes all these untoward events in the system to 'risk', this being the standard cliché with which bankers or financiers, when asked to explain events on which they are supposed to be expert but which they do not understand, claim mystical insight into unexpected events that have befallen the markets. The mathematical approach to financial economics attributes a probability distribution to this 'risk'. This has given rise to a whole cottage industry of mathematical 'modelling' of risk in financial markets. Modelling 'risk' does not make losses any more predictable. But it does help to allay anxieties among financial investors.

The financing needs of modern capitalism

Modern finance emerged out of the financing needs of production and exchange in a capitalist economy. Merchant capitalists in the seventeenth and eighteenth centuries raised 'circulating capital' to finance their cargoes of goods, which they sold around the world. With industrial capitalism, financing needs became massive. In addition to materials and labour, finance was needed to buy or build machines and factories. In the seventeenth and eighteenth centuries, special laws had to be passed to allow canal companies, and later railway companies, to issue shares or bonds to finance the construction of these large undertakings. These were traded on stock exchanges where previously government bonds had been traded. But in manufacturing, for example, the expansion of production and investment was limited by the amount of money that an individual capitalist possessed (his or her own 'capital') and the amount of money that he or she could borrow from banks, usually on a short-term basis, or obtain from partners.

However, things changed when, in the 1860s and 1870s, Britain, followed by most countries in Europe and North America, passed Companies Acts. These revolutionized company finance in two ways. First of all they allowed capitalist businesses to become 'joint stock' companies with limited liability without the trouble and expense of getting the legislature (Parliament or Congress) to pass a special law for each company. All that a business had to do was to have its rules, or 'articles of association', approved by a court of law or company registrar. This allowed companies to obtain long-term finance much more easily. Manufacturing companies went from being financed from personal wealth and short-term borrowing from banks, to being financed with long-term bonds or shares, titles of ownership that gave owners a share of the profits of the company. Of course, financial investors would normally be reluctant to tie up their money for a long time, let alone permanently in the case of shares, with one particular company. A neat arrangement with this new kind of company financing was that any holders of a company bond or share, if they wanted their money back, did not need to demand it back from the company, but could sell their bond or share in the stock exchange. This made it much more attractive to provide long-term finance for companies, because the provider could usually get his or her money back quickly and easily.

The second consequence of this new type of capitalist financing was that it was now possible for companies to match the term of their capital expenditure to their financing. For example, if a company was financing a factory that was expected to generate profits over a 30-year period, the company could finance it with a 30-year bond, a liability whose interest and capital repayments could be paid out of those profits over the lifetime of the capital asset, the factory, that was being financed. This was a huge advantage to capitalists who previously would have had to limit their investments to what they could finance themselves, or to money that they could borrow short term. Such short-term borrowing would have to be 'rolled over' (new borrowing undertaken to repay old borrowing) many times over the course of a capital asset's lifetime. Financing costs, in the form of the interest charged on the borrowing, would be uncertain and, if there was a sudden squeeze on credit and banks became reluctant to lend, capitalists who were unable to repay their debts quickly would be driven out of business. To avoid this kind of crisis, capitalists would have to hold large amounts of money in bank deposits, and this would further restrict investment.

The economic consequences of long-term finance

This easing of financing conditions through 'financial innovation' might have been expected to give rise to a huge investment boom, with rising output and employment. Instead, one by one, capitalist countries, after an initial phase of industrial development, succumbed to economic stagnation and unemployment that, in one way or another, lasted until the middle of the twentieth century.[1] The reason for this was identified initially by the US economist and social critic, Thorstein Veblen (1857–1929), and subsequently by the Austrian Marxist Rudolf Hilferding (1877–1941). The ease of issuing long-term bonds and shares, and trading them in the stock market, also facilitated a rapid concentration of ownership of business. The market for long-term capital also created 'big business' or 'monopoly capital' – firms that were so large that they dominated their markets and suppliers.

So what caused this stagnation? For Veblen, an 'underconsumptionist', economic stagnation arose because, with mass unemployment, wages and employment income were too low to buy all the potential output of the economy. Big business played an important part, because large corporations, with access to the capital market, would stimulate a stock market boom, which in turn would arouse a sense of prosperity, a 'wealth effect' for shareholders who would spend on purchasing luxury goods that would result in a temporary boom. However, in the end, luxury consumption was unable to overcome the gap between employment income and the total value of labour: workers could never be paid the full value of their labour because that would wipe out profits. The deficiency of total demand in the economy would frustrate the realization of expected profits, on which the stock market boom depended. The stock market would crash, and the economy would then revert back to its 'natural' condition of stagnation and mass unemployment (Veblen, 1904).

Rudolf Hilferding had a much clearer idea of how long-term debt markets affected the structure of the capitalist economy. In the first place, monopoly capital was reinforced by coordination with the banking system. He called this alliance between finance and monopoly capital, 'finance capital'. Banks would facilitate the export of capital (foreign loans) to assure demand abroad for the output of the monopolists. By coordinating production and forming cartels, the monopolists would be able to stabilize their markets and production. However, this left another group of capitalists, namely smaller, competitive firms without access to long-term debt markets, whose profits depended on competition with the monopolists. Their precarious position in product markets destabilizes capitalism.

Veblen and Hilferding established the idea that financial operations lie at the heart of the operations of the large business corporations that determine the macroeconomics of modern capitalism. This stands in stark contrast with the fundamental postulate of textbook financial economics and finance theory, which argues that the financial system consists of the saving activity of households engaged in the exchange of 'endowments' or domestic production, where firms do not exist and production using large-scale equipment plays no part.

Veblen and Hilferding were then followed by Michał Kalecki (1899–1970) and Josef Steindl (1912–93). Kalecki, a Polish economist, took up Hilferding's analysis to show that the key factor in determining output and employment in the economy is business investment. Investment also plays a critical role in allowing firms to realize profits.

If what capitalists pay their workers (wage income) comes back to capitalists when workers spend their incomes on consumption, then whose expenditure allows capitalists to realize their profits in money form? Kalecki's (1966) answer was that capitalists do this themselves by their expenditure on their own consumption and on business investment.

The idea originates in the schemes of capitalist reproduction that Marx (1885) put forward in Volume II of *Capital*. It came down to Kalecki through the work of Hilferding and Rosa Luxemburg (1870–1919). Kalecki showed how monopoly capital makes the economy even more unstable. Business cycles become more extreme, because the monopoly profits of big firms allow them to afford to maintain unused capacity in a recession, and the unused capacity discourages the investment that could start off a boom. In a boom, those large firms are likely to overinvest in order to reinforce their dominance in their markets. Small and medium-sized firms, without access to long-term debt markets, have to rely on much more short-term finance, getting themselves into debt in order to invest, and then falling victims to excessive debt in a recession.

In Kalecki's theory, a very particular part is played by the saving of wealthy individuals who do not participate in capitalist production, but live off the income (interest and dividends on shares) that they receive from capitalist enterprise. The income of these 'rentiers' is, of course, paid out of the sales proceeds of capitalist firms. It is a portion of the expenditures of firms that does not come back to capitalist producers if those rentiers save their income, instead of spending it on their own consumption. Kalecki pointed out that this rentier saving serves eventually to depress production and employment, because firms that do not get back in sales revenue all that they spend on costs of production and financing costs (financing costs are the incomes of the rentiers) have to borrow the shortfall from the banks in which the rentiers have deposited their savings. In this way, bank balance sheets (deposits and loans) expand, but productive capitalists get more and more into debt. Eventually this indebtedness makes those capitalists cut back on their investment, and this causes a fall in realized profits, and further reductions in investment, output and employment.

In Kalecki's theory, finance is integrated in the analysis of the firm and the household in the unstable macroeconomics of capitalism.

Josef Steindl developed Kalecki's theory further to show that saving is not just characteristic of highly paid rentier capitalists. Steindl argued that the twentieth-century advanced capitalist economy also contains a large middle class consisting of members of the liberal professions (doctors, lawyers, journalists, and so on), government employees, teachers and public service workers, as well as those employed in financial institutions and the managerial bureaucracies of big business. One way or another, their incomes are derived from income generated in production. If they do not spend overall as much as they receive in income, productive capitalists will be forced into financial deficit, unless capitalists can offset this with their investment. (It is assumed here that capitalists cannot sell abroad, and that the government budget is balanced.) The financial deficit has to be financed by borrowing. So household saving in general must be exceeded by business investment if firms overall are to obtain profits (Steindl, 1989). Like Kalecki, Steindl shows how household saving, far from being automatically matched by investment, as in textbook financial economics, can depress firms' profits and cause recession and unemployment.

Finance in Keynes's analysis

Finally, we get to John Maynard Keynes, another economist who was to incorporate long-term debt markets into the foundations of his macroeconomics.[2]

The key text in which he did this was his most important book, *The General Theory of Employment, Interest and Money*, published in 1936. The long-term debt or capital markets were responsible for setting the long-term rate of interest, that is, the rate of interest on long-term bonds. This is determined by the prices of bonds, which in turn are determined by the supply and demand for bonds. A bond has a rate of interest fixed when it is issued. If the price of the bond goes up, after the bond is issued, then the yield (or the income that may be obtained from a given amount of money invested in the bond) will be reduced. If the price of the bond falls in the market, then the yield, or expected income from the bond, will go up.

The market yield at any one time sets the rate of interest that industrial capitalists must offer if they are to get long-term financing for their investment. According to Keynes, industrial capitalists, or entrepreneurs, calculate the rate of return that they may expect to receive on their investments, and compare this with the long-term rate of interest. If this expected rate of return on business investment is higher than the long-term rate of investment, then it will be worthwhile investing in these projects. Accordingly, this long-term rate of interest and business expectations of profits determine together the amount of investment in any period in the economy (see Keynes, 1936, Ch. 11, and Davidson, 2002, Ch. 7). In turn, as with Kalecki, the amount of investment in a given period determines the amount of output and employment in an economy.

According to Keynes, there are two flaws in the way in which this arrangement works in a capitalist economy. First of all the financiers in the stock market are not truly committed to the enterprises they invest in. They can make more profit from 'speculation', that is, buying bonds or shares in anticipation of an increase in their price, than from the dividends paid on these shares, or interest on the bonds. Such speculation is done by anticipating opinion in the stock market, rather than the profits of companies. This makes the stock market an unreliable source of finance: 'When the capital development of a country becomes a by-product of the activities of a casino, the job is likely to be ill-done' (Keynes, 1936, p. 159). The second flaw is that expectations of future profits, after payment of interest, are based on subjective rather than objective knowledge. Such expectations are therefore volatile, and the resulting shifts in investment are the cause of business cycles (ibid., Ch. 22).

Keynes's solution for this was to use monetary policy to drive down interest rates, including the long-term rate of interest, so that business investment was maintained at a level that would ensure full employment. This policy he called the 'euthanasia of the rentier' (Keynes, 1936, p. 376). Fiscal policy, that is, government expenditure, could also be used to stabilize aggregate demand.

In the end, finance will always escape the simple definition of its relationship with the rest of the capitalist economy. This is because the economy itself is unstable, and finance is merely a part of that instability. Devoted to demonstrating equilibrium, mainstream finance and macroeconomics do not have the necessary concepts or analysis with which to understand – let alone explain – that instability. But the theorists who did were those who thought in terms of business cycles. This is why Keynes, Kalecki, Schumpeter, Hilferding, Steindl and Minsky (an economist who we present at the end of this chapter) are better guides to financial macroeconomics than those who write textbooks in financial macroeconomics.

NOTES

1   This does not mean that there were no new industries, most notably those based on the internal combustion engine (cars, ships, and so on), chemicals and electronics, but these were usually balanced by declining incomes and employment in agriculture and railway construction. See Heilbroner (1961).
2   See also Chapters 3, 4 and 6 in this volume.

REFERENCES

Bernanke, B.S. and M. Gertler (1989), 'Agency costs, net worth, and business fluctuations', *American Economic Review*, **79** (1), 14–31.
Davidson, P. (2002), *Financial Markets, Money and the Real World*, Cheltenham, UK and Northampton, MA, USA: Edward Elgar Publishing.
Diamond, D.W. and P.H. Dybvig (1983), 'Bank runs, deposit insurance and liquidity', *Journal of Political Economy*, **91** (3), 401–19.
European Central Bank (2010), *Recent Advances in Modelling Systemic Risk Using Network Analysis*, Frankfurt am Main: European Central Bank.
Heilbroner, R. (1961), *The Worldly Philosophers: The Lives, Times and Ideas of the Great Economic Thinkers*, New York: Simon and Schuster.
Kalecki, M. (1966), 'Money and real wages', in *Studies in the Theory of Business Cycles 1933–1939*, Oxford, UK: Basil Blackwell, pp. 40–71.
Keynes, J.M. (1936), *The General Theory of Employment, Interest and Money*, London: Macmillan.
Marx, K. (1885), *Das Kapital, Volume II*, Hamburg: O. Meissner.
Modigliani, F. and M. Miller (1958), 'The cost of capital, corporation finance and the theory of investment', *American Economic Review*, **48** (3), 261–97.
Robinson, J. (1952), *The Rate of Interest and Other Essays*, London: Macmillan.
Steindl, J. (1989), 'Saving and debt', in A. Barrère (ed.), *Money, Credit and Prices in Keynesian Perspective*, London: Macmillan, pp. 71–89.
Stiglitz, J.E. and A. Weiss (1981), 'Credit rationing in markets with imperfect information', *American Economic Review*, **71** (3), 393–410.
Veblen, T. (1904), *The Theory of Business Enterprise*, New York: Charles Scribner's Sons.

A PORTRAIT OF HYMAN PHILIP MINSKY (1919–96)

Hyman Philip Minsky came from a poor family in Chicago to study mathematics at the University of Chicago in the years preceding World War II. There, he met Polish Marxist Oskar Lange, who persuaded him that if he wanted an alternative to the Great Depression affecting the United States, he should study economics.

Minsky graduated in economics and, after military service and a short period working on Wall Street in New York, went on to do a PhD under Joseph Schumpeter at Harvard University. After Schumpeter's death in 1950, his supervision was taken over by Wassily Leontief. Minsky's PhD thesis argued that business cycles were also affected by debt in the economy.

Over the following four decades, Minsky developed a theory of financing structures in the economy, where an investment boom would be accompanied by growing indebtedness, which would cause the boom to break down into recession when income was insufficient to service debts. Debt structures would be 'hedged' if payments on them were matched by income flows. However, all business investment went through a period when income fell below debt service payments. He called such financing 'speculative'. Finally, if debt service payments could only be met by additional borrowing, this was 'Ponzi' finance, named after a well-known Boston pyramid-banking operator at the end of World War I. Minsky argued that in any economic boom financing structures would deteriorate, with hedged financing becoming speculative, and speculative financing eventually becoming Ponzi. This would continue until a financial crisis broke out. He called this theory 'the financial instability hypothesis'.

In this way, Minsky solved the problem of where financial 'risk' comes from. At any one time, in an indebted capitalist economy, that economy would require a certain level of investment to generate the income necessary to service these debt structures. The problem was that eventually the build up of debt would induce firms to reduce their investment. This would then cause income, or firms' sales revenues, to fall short of what was necessary to service debts among firms in the economy. Minsky famously suggested that 'stability is destabilizing', because debt commitments increase during periods of economic and financial stability.

6

The central bank and monetary policy

Louis-Philippe Rochon and Sergio Rossi

OVERVIEW

This chapter:

- explains the essential role of a central bank, which is the settlement institution for banks that, together with the central bank, form a banking system, that is, a system characterized by money homogeneity and payment finality for all its members;

- shows that the central bank, like any bank, is both a money and credit provider, as it issues a means of final payment and provides credit to the banking sector, which needs both to avoid financial crises;

- presents monetary policy strategies, instruments and transmission mechanisms in an endogenous money framework, characterized by the fact that money supply is credit driven and demand determined;

- argues that monetary policy goals should go beyond price stability, to also include financial stability and macroeconomic stabilization, with regard to both economic sustainability and employment levels.

These points are relevant to understanding the scope and limits of monetary policy, and to critically discussing both contemporary monetary policies and the regulatory reforms carried out at national and international levels in the aftermath of the global financial crisis that erupted in 2007–08.

KEYWORDS

- **Bubble:** A steadfast increase in asset prices on financial and/or real estate markets that cannot be explained by the economic performance of a country, but results from some forms of speculation induced by banks' behaviour in providing credit.

- **Final payment:** A payment as a result of which the payer settles his or her debt against the payee, who has thereby no further claims on the payer. This provides for monetary order and is a necessary, though not sufficient, condition for financial stability.
- **Monetary targeting:** A monetary policy strategy targeting a publicly announced rate of growth for a given monetary aggregate, in order to make sure that the price level is stable over the long run.
- **Money multiplier:** The ratio between the total money supply and central bank money, which orthodox economists believe exists due to their view of the supposed exogenous supply of the monetary base.
- **Quantitative easing:** A monetary policy intervention whereby the central bank buys a very large volume of financial assets (corporate bonds, government bonds, and so on), in order to lower rates of interest and thereby support economic growth.
- **Taylor rule:** A stylized rule that central banks might use when setting their policy rates of interest, considering inflation and output gaps according to their reaction function against the current or expected macroeconomic situation.

Why are these topics important?

This chapter is important to understanding the role of the central bank in a monetary production economy as well as the scope and limits of monetary policy-making in such a framework. The large majority of the academic literature and of monetary policy interventions fail to consider the particular nature of money and the actual working of a monetary production economy. They are thus unable to deliver the results that are expected.

Further, this chapter provides a systemic view of money and banking, enabling us to understand the monetary–structural origins of the global financial crisis that erupted in 2007–08, particularly after the demise of Lehman Brothers in the United States. It thereby offers an explanation of this crisis based on structural rather than behavioural factors that the regulatory reforms put into practice at national as well as international levels do not and cannot address. This chapter thus highlights the largely ignored fact that a monetary–structural reform of domestic payment systems is required in order to eradicate the factors of systemic crises, which are the hallmark of a monetary disorder affecting the working of our national economies. As a result, the objectives of monetary policy should go much beyond price stability, contributing to re-establishing monetary order and guaranteeing financial stability at systemic level.

The mainstream perspective

The mainstream perspective largely considers the central bank as the originator of the money supply, in the form of 'helicopter money' (Friedman, 1969, pp. 4–5). This means that the central bank is in a position to steer and determine the total amount of money within the economic system, directly (as regards the so-called 'high powered money' [see Friedman, 1969], which is the monetary base issued by the central bank) or indirectly, via the so-called 'money multiplier' (that is, the relationship that orthodox economists believe exists between the monetary base and the total amount of money within the system). This view has given rise to monetary-targeting strategies by a number of central banks once the fixed exchange rate regime decided at Bretton Woods (1944) was abandoned in the early 1970s. Indeed, in the 1980s and 1990s, the majority of central banks implemented their monetary policy with a view to reaching some previously announced target for the rate of growth of a given monetary aggregate (as M0, that is, central bank money, or M3, that is, the total sum of bank deposits across the banking system, including both the central bank and the set of commercial banks).

In this perspective the central bank can increase and reduce the money supply through the 'quantity theory of money' channel, that is, affecting the price level directly via a proportional relationship that this theory establishes between (changes in) the money supply (M) and (changes in) the general price level (P), according to the following so-called 'equation of exchange':

$$MV \equiv PQ \tag{6.1}$$

where V represents the so-called 'velocity of circulation' of money (the number of times that a unit of money is supposed to be used in payments across the economic system during a given period, say a calendar year) and Q is physical output (the bulk of goods and services produced during the same period of time).

Rearranging the terms of equation (6.1) and expressing it in growth rates form, this determines the factors affecting the rate of growth of the money supply, as in equation (6.2):

$$\dot{M} \equiv \pi + g - \dot{V} \tag{6.2}$$

where a dot over a variable indicates its rate of change over time, π is the measured rate of inflation on the goods market, and g represents the growth rate of produced output.

Table 6.1 The monetary-targeting strategy of the German Bundesbank, 1975–98

Year	$\pi^{normative}$ (%)	+$g^{potential}$ (%)	$-\Delta V$	= ΔM^* (%)
1975	5.0–6.0	–	–	8.0
1976	4.0–5.0	2.0	Increasing	8.0
1977	≤ 4.0	3.0	Increasing	8.0
1978	3.0	3.0	–	8.0
1979	Moderate	≈ 1978	Declining	6.0–9.0
1980	3.5–4.0	3.0	Declining	5.0–8.0
1981	3.5	2.5	Increasing	4.0–7.0
1982	3.5	1.5–2.0	–	4.0–7.0
1983	3.0	1.5–2.0	–	4.0–7.0
1984	2.0	2.0	–	4.0–6.0
1985	2.0	2.0	–	3.0–5.0
1986	2.0	2.5	–	3.5–5.5
1987	2.0	2.5	–	3.0–6.0
1988	2.0	2.0	−0.5	3.0–6.0
1989	2.0	2.0–2.5	−0.5	5.0
1990	2.0	2.5	−0.5	4.0–6.0
1991	2.0	2.5	−0.5	3.0–5.0
1992	2.0	2.75	−0.5	3.5–5.5
1993	2.0	3.0	−1.0	4.5–6.5
1994	2.0	2.5	−1.0	4.0–6.0
1995	2.0	2.75	−1.0	4.0–6.0
1996	2.0	2.5	−1.0	4.0–7.0
1997	1.5–2.0	2.25	−1.0	3.5–6.5
1998	1.5–2.0	2.0	−1.0	3.0–6.0

Source: Bofinger (2001, p. 251).

Equation (6.2) has been used to set up monetary-targeting strategies, once the central bank was in a position to determine the three variables on the right-hand side of that equation. The German Bundesbank, for instance, has been implementing this strategy in the 25 years that preceded its adoption of the euro on 1 January 1999 (Table 6.1).

The Bundesbank decided the targeted growth rate of the relevant monetary aggregate (ΔM^*), applying equation (6.3):

$$\Delta M^* \equiv \pi^{normative} + g^{potential} - \Delta V \qquad (6.3)$$

where $\pi^{normative}$ is the desired rate of inflation, $g^{potential}$ is the rate of growth of potential output, and ΔV is the rate of change in money's 'velocity of circulation'.

In fact, monetary-targeting strategies have usually been operationalized via an implicit interest rate rule, which can be written as follows:

$$i_t = i_{t-1} + \alpha \left(\mu_t - \mu^* \right) \tag{6.4}$$

where i represents the policy rate of interest set by the central bank during the relevant period represented by t, α is a positive parameter, μ is the observed growth rate of the targeted monetary aggregate, and μ^* is the targeted rate of growth for that monetary aggregate. This shows that monetary-targeting central banks have been well aware, in general, of the fact that they cannot steer the relevant monetary aggregate through the 'quantity theory of money' channel. In its stead, they operated through interest rate channels, that is, a mechanism centred on the indirect relation between interest rates and demand on the market for produced goods and services, which in the end affects the price level assuming a full employment situation. The causal chain runs like this:

$$\downarrow i \Rightarrow \uparrow C, \uparrow I \Rightarrow \uparrow TD \Rightarrow \uparrow P$$

where C represents consumption, I investment, and TD is total demand on the market for produced goods and services.

If one considers an open economy, that is, an economic system that might import and export a variety of goods and services, one should expand on this interest rate view by including the effects on total demand and the price level that stem from an exchange rate depreciation (appreciation) induced by a reduction (increase) in the policy rates of interest administered by the central bank. This exchange rate pass-through may be particularly important for small open economies whose output is often more focused on a limited variety of products rather than large open economies (whose domestic magnitudes, like the rate of inflation, are less sensitive to the exchange rate channel).

Further, the interest rate channel also affects an economic system's financial stability, as it could inflate an asset bubble on either financial or real estate markets, when the policy rates of interest are kept too low for too long. This induces debtors as well as creditors to increase the volume of credit in order for both to profit, in one way or another, from the inflating credit bubble. In this perspective, the mainstream explanation of the subprime bubble and ensuing crisis observed across the US housing market during the late 1990s and early 2000s is based basically on a too generous monetary policy by the US Federal Reserve in the aftermath of the so-called 'dot.com' bubble.

The explosion of this bubble led the US monetary authority to dramatically reduce policy rates of interest in an attempt to restart the domestic economy, which was also negatively affected by the terrorist attacks of 11 September 2001.

In this light, mainstream economists believe that the policy rates of interest decided by central banks are a powerful instrument with which to affect total demand and, hence, have an impact on the price level in order to guarantee price stability across the economy. The spending behaviour of both consumers and businesses would thus be determined by a variable, the rate of interest, that central banks could influence, if not control, through a reduction or an increase in their own policy rates of interest. This is particularly so with respect to their credit lines: if a central bank (say) reduces its policy rates of interest, banks will reduce (although not one-to-one) their own rates of interest, thereby inducing more consumers and businesses to borrow from the banking sector in order to expand production when the economic system is affected by a recession (such as in the aftermath of a financial crisis).

In fact, as explained by Keynes, reducing (to their zero lower bound) the policy rates of interest may not be enough in order to spur economic growth. As regards firms in particular, their propensity to invest could be impaired by the economic prospects, which, in the case of a deep recession elicited by a global financial crisis, may be so dreadful that firms are unwilling to borrow from banks to finance investment although the borrowing rate of interest is very low. These firms consider that they would not be able to sell the newly produced output because of the bad economic situation as well as its likely evolution over the relevant time horizon.

Nevertheless, the mainstream perspective induced a number of central banks, and in particular the US Federal Reserve System, to try to support economic growth in the aftermath of the global financial crisis that erupted in 2007–08 with so-called 'quantitative easing', that is, an expansionary monetary policy aimed at making sure that banks lend to creditworthy non-financial businesses, in order for the latter to carry out their investment projects and thus expand economic activity, thereby increasing the level of employment. Quantitative easing may take different forms, including the purchase by the central bank of government bonds on the primary market (where these bonds are issued to finance government spending) and the easing of credit standards that banks must fulfil in order to borrow from the central bank (with or without a collateral, that is, a series of eligible assets used as a repayment guarantee for a central bank's loans). Be that as it may, quantitative easing increases the volume of central bank money that banks could spend on the interbank market, but is not enough to induce these banks to provide more credit to non-financial businesses. As a matter of fact, lenders and/or borrowers may have a 'liquidity preference', which means that they decide to abstain from lending or borrowing in light of their own expectations about the future. Indeed, if the economic situation is bad and its expected evolution similar, banks and their potential borrowers are likely to postpone any expansion of credit activities, thus making quantitative easing ineffective in supporting economic growth. Rather than an inflationary pressure, quantitative easing could contribute to deflation, as agents think or observe that such an expansionary monetary policy has no positive effect on prices, which can fall as a result of agents' abstention from both consumption and investment across the economic system.

Further, reducing the policy rates of interest to zero (or even in the negative domain) may not be enough to reduce banks' own rates of interest, particularly on the interbank market. Shortly after the collapse of Lehman Brothers in the United States on 15 September 2008, the US monetary authority reduced the federal funds rate of interest close to zero, but in fact the interbank market rate of interest increased, since banks were reluctant to lend on this market because of their higher uncertainty about the actual financial situation of their counterparts on that market. Indeed, the interest rate channel may not work as monetary authorities expect, although a long period of very low policy rates of interest can have various problematic effects in the financial sector and beyond it. For instance, banks could be induced to borrow from the central bank in order for them to inflate a financial bubble, through a sustained increase in the purchase of financial assets, particularly those assets whose high risks may lead many financial institutions to buy them with the expectation of earning high yields. Also, banks and non-bank financial institutions could inflate a real estate bubble, particularly as a number of middle-class individuals may be attracted by favourable borrowing terms in order to become homeowners. As shown by the subprime bubble that inflated during the 1995–2005 period, which burst in 2006 spurring a series of systemic effects in the United States and beyond it, a number of non-performing loans can increase banks' financial fragility to a point where several financial institutions become bankrupt. In particular, those financial institutions that are 'too big to fail' – individually or as a group – will require an intervention by the public sector, which must bail them out to avoid a systemic financial crisis that will induce a deep recession, if not a depression (like the Great Depression of the 1930s).

This state of affairs has induced many regulatory reforms at national and international levels, such as the so-called 'Basel Accords' signed within the framework of the Basel Committee on Banking Supervision resident at the Bank for International Settlements. The large majority of these reforms aim to affect the banks' behaviour, to limit their risk-taking attitude and provide them with a cushion of safety that should be solid enough to avert a systemic crisis in the case of financial or real estate turmoil.

In fact, however, these regulatory reforms do not and cannot avoid a systemic crisis, as the latter is the result of a structural disorder affecting the payment system, rather than stemming merely from agents' behaviour. The mainstream perspective is not in a position to detect and explain such a systemic crisis, because it considers that any economic system is merely the result of a series of demand and supply forces that the set of economic agents exert on any kinds of market. In this view, therefore, it all boils down to individual behaviour, so that the working of the system as a whole is studied (and can be studied appropriately) with a system of equations that allow to establish the system's 'equilibrium', provided that the public sector does not intervene in the 'market mechanism' – because this intervention would be a matter of hindrance and not a macroeconomic stabilizing factor.

The heterodox perspective

The heterodox perspective on central banking and monetary policy-making is widely different from the mainstream view. The differences stem from a series of different conceptions at both the positive and normative levels. On the one hand, the nature and role of money are essentially different from the mainstream perspective. On the other hand, monetary policy-making has an important influence on both income and wealth distribution according to the heterodox perspective, but its actual impact on the price level should not be overestimated. Hence, interest-rate policies should consider their effects on income and wealth distribution, rather than focusing on the stability of the level of consumer prices, which they cannot influence as claimed by the mainstream.

First, the nature of money, hence also of central bank money, cannot be reduced to a particular commodity or financial asset, whose supply and demand depend on the 'market mechanism' leading to an 'equilibrium' price (or rate of interest, in the case of money). Money is not a commodity or financial asset, but the means of payment in the sense that it allows agents to finally pay their debts on any markets. Each bank in fact issues money in a triangular operation that involves the payer and the payee, as a result of which the latter has no further claim on the former, since he or she obtains the right to dispose of a bank deposit. Contrary to the conventional wisdom, however, the bank deposit does not stem from pre-existing saving whose origin would remain mysterious (as it cannot be explained logically). All bank deposits result, in fact, from a bank loan, and this is why a central bank must exist, to avoid banks moving 'forward in step' (Keynes, [1930] 1971, p. 23) without any endogenous limit to money creation, because this would be a major factor of financial crisis. Indeed, the existence of a central bank closely depends on the book-entry nature of money (see Rochon and Rossi, 2013). Its role is to make sure that all payments on the interbank market are final rather than just promised, as would occur if banks would be allowed to pay simply by issuing their own acknowledgement of debt.

As a result of the book-entry nature of money, the central bank intervenes always and everywhere when there is a payment to be settled between any two particular banks. It is therefore a matter of routine for a central bank to issue its own acknowledgement of debt in order for a payer bank to settle its debt against any other bank on the interbank market. This final payment at the interbank level may also involve the central bank as a financial intermediary, in the sense that the latter provides both money and credit to the paying bank. In particular, the central bank can lend to any bank participating in a domestic payment system the funds that this bank needs in order to settle its debt to a third party. This may occur against collateral (that is, a series of financial assets that the paying bank provides to the central bank as a guarantee of repayment) or it might also occur without collateral (in an emergency situation, particularly when the paying bank is 'too big to fail' without provoking a number of negative outcomes across the domestic or global financial system). When the central bank intervenes in this regard, it plays the role of a lender of last resort, as nobody else is willing to lend to the bank in need of funding its own payments. The central bank may charge a rate of interest to the borrowing bank, which is usually higher than the interbank market rate of interest, as a penalty for the bank not being able to raise funds on that market. This suffices to induce banks to manage their own business in order to limit the number of instances where they need to turn to the central bank as a lender of last resort.

The intervention of the central bank as a lender of last resort confirms that the amount of central bank money is not set by the monetary authority but actually depends on the needs of the set of banks participating in the domestic payment system. The helicopter view of money, hence the money multiplier, cannot account therefore for the working of a monetary economy, thus invalidating the orthodox perspective on factual grounds. The rate of interest set by the central bank is indeed an exogenous magnitude, and does not depend on the market rates of interest; rather, it influences them (although not by a one-to-one relationship and with variable time lags, also depending on the size, type and [private or public] ownership of each bank participating in the domestic payment system).

This empirical evidence against the orthodox perspective is also a critique on the alleged influence that monetary policy can exert on the general price level, hence the doubt about the capacity of a central bank to guarantee price stability through its own rates of interest. The orthodox argument that an interest rate hike reduces demand on the market for produced goods and services, thereby lowering inflationary pressures, can be questioned with regard to the likely impact of monetary policy tightening on banks' own rates of interest. If firms have to pay higher rates of interest because the central bank has raised its own interest rates for banks borrowing from it, then the firms' output will be sold at a higher price (hence an increase in the price level) owing to higher production costs due to bank lending.

Rather than impacting on the price level as claimed by orthodox economists, a central bank's interest rate policy can actually affect income and wealth distribution, making it more concentrated at the top of the relevant pyramid. Consider, for instance, when policy rates of interest diminish, as in the aftermath of the global financial crisis that erupted in 2007–08, with the aim of supporting economic activity and employment levels. In fact, as already pointed out, neither firms nor households will be induced to increase their borrowing from the banking sector if they fear being unable to repay their debt (and the relevant interest) when it matures. Rather, this reduction of interest rates will spur financial transactions, thus inflating an asset price bubble that is further reinforced by the so-called 'wealth effect', which consists in feeling richer when one's assets are priced more on the relevant market. Clearly, wealthy individuals whose assets are priced more as a result of a reduction in policy rates of interest will not increase their spending to buy a series of consumption goods, thereby supporting economic activity, but rather increase their spending on real estate and financial markets, thus increasing the relevant asset prices. Holders of these assets will thereby feel richer, giving rise to an upward spiral that could inflate a bubble, threatening the financial stability of the whole system.

These phenomena are also relevant to criticizing the inflation-targeting strategy that has been in fashion at central bank level and within orthodox circles since the early 1990s, when an increasing number of monetary authorities abandoned monetary targeting for adopting a policy strategy based on an explicit target for the rate of inflation, thereby considered as the principal (if not unique) goal of monetary policy until the financial crisis erupted in

2007–08. Indeed, inflation-targeting strategies and their apparent success in reducing and then keeping inflation rates at a low and stable level across a variety of countries since the early 1990s have not been in a position to avoid a major crisis, in the aftermath of the financial and real estate bubble that burst in the United States in 2006–07. Quite the contrary, these strategies could have been a factor in such a bubble, and the ensuing crisis, as they led a number of central banks, first and foremost the US Federal Reserve, to keep their policy rates of interest too low for too long, thereby inducing several banks as well as non-bank financial institutions to profit from this policy stance in order to increase both their lending volumes and their profits in an unsustainable way for the whole economic system.

The problem in this regard concerns the theoretical framework supporting inflation-targeting strategies. Based on monetarism, this framework considers that a monetary authority should guarantee price stability and nothing else, because this provides the best macroeconomic environment for other categories of agents to contribute to economic growth and maximum employment levels. This explanation argues that rational expectations of agents (firms and households) provide them with the correct model to treat all the newly available information in the right way, independently of the central bank's attempt to surprise these agents with a non-anticipated inflation that should support economic growth via a reduction of real wages and real interest rates (both of which induce firms to increase investment and employment levels, in the view of orthodox economists). These arguments in fact have been instrumental in supporting central bank independence from any government pressures, arguing that these pressures (to 'monetize' public debt when a government's finance minister is unable to balance the public sector's budget through tax receipts or financial markets) eventually lead to overshooting the inflation target – without any positive influence on so-called 'real magnitudes' (like economic growth, labour productivity and employment levels). According to the mainstream view, agents are rational and have rational expectations, so they cannot be led astray by surprise inflation, as in that case they anticipate a rate of inflation higher than the central bank's publicly announced target and thus behave 'as if' the rate of inflation were already higher than the one officially targeted by the central bank (which suffers, therefore, from being dependent on the government, as it does not meet its own objective). This argument has been further reinforced by referring to the so-called 'sacrifice ratio', that is, the ratio measuring output and employment losses as a result of a reduction in the rate of inflation. Mainstream literature points out that these losses are lower when the central bank is independent of the government, arguing that a central bank's independence enhances monetary policy credibility, which is instrumental in making sure that an inflation-targeting strategy elicits no output and employment losses, as shown by expression (6.5):

$$Y_t = Y^* + \beta \left(\pi_t - \pi^e \right) \tag{6.5}$$

where Y_t is current output, Y^* is full employment (or potential) output, β is a positive parameter, π_t is the current rate of inflation, and π^e is the rate of inflation expected by economic agents. A central bank's credibility would be instrumental in order to make sure that inflation is on target without generating output and employment losses (in that case $Y_t = Y^*$). As a result, a restrictive monetary policy stance aimed at reducing the measured rate of inflation would give rise to no output and employment losses, if the central bank is independent of the government, as this is enough to make sure that both the central bank and its policy stance are credible.

Now, the problem is that agents are not 'always and everywhere' rational, as they do not have all the information and the knowledge required to be rational. Rather, as Keynes pointed out, the future is unknown and unknowable. Further, there are too many variables and reciprocal influences among their set to be able to appraise the actual working of the whole economic system with a particular model or series of models. Hence, the 'pretense-of-knowledge syndrome' (Caballero, 2010) that affects mainstream economics and the ensuing monetary policy-making is a dangerous factor of financial instability and economic crisis, as it gives a false perception of security in simply targeting price stability on the goods market by contemporary central banks. In fact, as heterodox economists have pointed out, inflation-targeting central banks have been inflicting an anti-growth bias to their economic systems, without preserving the latter from financial bubbles that gave rise to system-wide crises once they burst. A clear example is the monetary policy stance of the European Central Bank. Before the euro-area crisis erupted towards the end of 2009, its inflation-targeting strategy inflated a credit bubble in a variety of so-called 'peripheral' countries across the euro area, while it hindered economic activities as the monetary policy rates of interest were not reduced until measured inflation had fallen below 1 per cent, but increased as soon as expected inflation (a virtual magnitude) was close to 2 per cent, even though measured inflation was much lower than that (see Chapter 14 for analytical elaboration on this).

Heterodox economists argue in favour of a very different monetary policy stance. In their view, any central bank should contribute to achieving the various goals of general economic policies, including output stabilization, employment maximization, as well as sustainable economic growth, also considering the impact of interest rate policy on income and wealth distribution across the economic system, without neglecting the fact that it should contribute to financial stability for the system as a whole. This puts the conventional policy tools used by central banks (namely, interest rates, open-market operations, repurchase agreements, and reserve requirements) under stress, as they are not appropriate, individually and as a whole, to ensure that the above set of policy goals are fulfilled adequately.

In this regard, heterodox economists criticize the so-called 'Taylor rule' (Taylor, 1999), which aims at setting policy rates of interest according to equation (6.6):

$$i_t = r + \pi_t + \alpha(\pi_t - \pi^*) + \beta[(Yt - Y^*)/Y^*] \qquad (6.6)$$

where r is the so-called 'natural' (or equilibrium) rate of interest, π^* is the target rate of inflation, and α and β are positive parameters reflecting the importance of inflation and output gaps respectively in the central bank policy reaction function.

This rule has been criticized on several grounds. First, it integrates neither exchange rate issues nor the problems stemming from financial instability, perhaps because it is difficult to determine exchange rate misalignments and to define financial instability. Second, the notion of a 'natural' rate of interest is a figment of the imagination, as it stems from a dichotomous view of the working of an economic system that is conceived as made up of a 'real' sector and a 'monetary' sector that would be separated from each other. In the first sector, equilibrium would be attained when savings are equal to the amount of firms' desired investment, thereby determining the 'natural' interest rate. In the second sector, by contrast, money supply and money demand (two separate and independent forces in the orthodox view) would determine, at equilibrium, the market rate of interest – which may thus differ from the 'natural' rate, thereby generating an inflationary or deflationary pressure across the whole economic system. Third, the 'Taylor rule' ignores the fact that interest rate policies affect both income and wealth distribution across this system, which is a major issue for financial stability as well as for macroeconomic stabilization as explained above. In light of all these critiques, the heterodox approach to interest rate policy offers two alternative views: one that has the merit of including macroeconomic stabilization in a central bank's objectives, and another that focuses on the distributional impact of changing the rates of interest set by the monetary authority. In the former view, central banks are important actors in influencing the economic performance of the relevant countries, as monetary policy is in a position to support or hinder economic growth not just through its impact on price stability, but also via output and employment stabilization. In the latter view, by way of contrast, monetary policy impacts income and wealth distribution via the setting of interest rates, which tends to favour the owners of financial capital (the rentiers) in that the targeted rate of inflation is lower (and the policy rates of interest are higher) than what is needed in order to reduce the income share of rentiers and to increase the income share of wage earners with a view to induce economic growth in a sustainable way for the whole system.

All these issues show that monetary policy cannot be considered merely a technical matter that should be left to 'technicians' or perhaps to an automatic pilot, without any political economy consideration. This echoes the famous argument already raised in the 1930s by Ralph George Hawtrey, who wrote that monetary policy is an art rather than a science (Hawtrey, 1932, p. vi). As such, and in light of their socioeconomic consequences, monetary policy decisions should be taken as a result of a systemic appraisal of their effects and considering the common good, that is, the well-being of the whole population affected by them.

 REFERENCES

Bofinger, P. (2001), *Monetary Policy: Goals, Institutions, Strategies, and Instruments*, Oxford, UK: Oxford University Press.

Caballero, R.J. (2010), 'Macroeconomics after the crisis: time to deal with the pretense-of-knowledge syndrome', *Journal of Economic Perspectives*, **24** (4), 85–102.

Eichner, A. (ed.) (1979), *A Guide to Post-Keynesian Economics*, Armonk, NY: M.E. Sharpe.

Eichner, A. (1987), *The Macrodynamics of Advanced Markets Economies*, Armonk, NY: M.E. Sharpe.

Friedman, M. (1969), *The Optimum Quantity of Money and Other Essays*, Chicago, IL: Aldine Publishing.

Hawtrey, R.G. (1932), *The Art of Central Banking*, London: Longmans, Green and Company.

Keynes, J.M. ([1930] 1971), *A Treatise on Money, Volume 1: The Pure Theory of Money*, reprinted in *The Collected Writings of John Maynard Keynes, Volume V*, London and Basingstoke, UK: Macmillan.

Lavoie, M., L.-P. Rochon and M. Seccareccia (eds) (2010), *Money and Macrodynamics: Alfred Eichner and Post-Keynesian Economics*, Armonk, NY: M.E. Sharpe.

Rochon, L.-P. and S. Rossi (2013), 'Endogenous money: the evolutionary versus revolutionary views', *Review of Keynesian Economics*, **1** (2), 210–29.

Taylor, J.B. (1999), 'Monetary policy guidelines for employment and inflation stability', in R.M. Solow and J.B. Taylor (eds), *Inflation, Unemployment, and Monetary Policy*, Cambridge, MA: MIT Press, pp. 29–54.

A PORTRAIT OF ALFRED S. EICHNER (1937–88)

Born in the United States on 23 March 1937, Alfred Eichner was a leading post-Keynesian economist who contributed to the advancement of pricing theory, the theory of economic growth and income distribution, and monetary theory and policy. He is considered by many as one of the founders of the US post-Keynesian school.

Eichner received his doctorate from Columbia University in New York, and taught at Columbia University, State University of New York in Purchase (SUNY), and at Rutgers University. He died on 10 February 1988.

Eichner has written numerous articles and books, but is perhaps best remembered for two books in particular: his *Guide to Post-Keynesian Economics*, published in 1979, which offered for the first time a complete and concise introduction to various themes within post-Keynesian economics, as well as *The Macrodynamics of*

Advanced Market Economies, published in 1987, which contains certainly his most important insights into the workings of an advanced market economy.

Eichner was not only an avid author and professor, but also somewhat of an activist, having testified numerous times on Capitol Hill before several Congressional and other legislative committees.

With respect to pricing theory, Eichner rejected the neoclassical theory of supply and demand, and argued instead that prices were determined by a mark-up over the costs of production.

Eichner's most important book, *The Macrodynamics of Advanced Market Economies* (1987), contains chapters on monetary theory and an interesting account of central banking practices, which in many ways foreshadowed several discussions held some two decades later (see Lavoie et al., 2010).

Part III

The macroeconomics of the short and long run

7

Aggregate demand

Jesper Jespersen

OVERVIEW

This chapter explores the following:

- That aggregate demand comprises private consumption, private investment, government expenditure, and net exports.

- That neoclassical economists consider aggregate demand rather unimportant. They argue that output (GDP) is determined mainly by the supply of labour and capital. The market system is considered self-adjusting, which makes them conclude that in the long run 'the supply of goods creates their demand'.

- That, according to heterodox economists and Keynesian macroeconomic theory, aggregate demand is an important analytical concept. It is the major driving force behind the development in output and employment in the short and longer run. This consideration makes demand management policies instrumental for creating macroeconomic stability and economic growth.

- That Richard Kahn was one of the first Keynesian economists who contributed to the theory of aggregate demand. He invented the analytical concept of the 'multiplier' as a short-run dynamic phenomenon.

KEYWORDS

- **Aggregate demand:** It is an important theoretical concept used intensively by Keynesian macroeconomists in opposition to the neoclassical proposition that 'supply creates it own demand'.
- **Demand management policies:** They are undertaken by governments (fiscal policy) and central banks (monetary policy) with the aim of making the macroeconomic development more stable and to reduce unemployment rates.
- **Income multiplier:** It is the relation between a change in an exogenous part of aggregate demand and the resulting change in output. The size

of the income multiplier is determined by the marginal propensity to consume, the marginal tax rate, social benefits, and marginal propensity to import. The magnitude varies between countries and during the business cycle and lies usually between 1.5 and 0.7 on a yearly basis.

• **Private consumption and investment:** These are the dominant demand components and the main drivers of macroeconomic dynamics making the causality run from decisions on production to employment in the short run (business cycles) and the longer run (growth).

Why are these topics important?

Aggregate demand is key for Keynesian economists, but essentially unimportant for the mainstream view. When aggregate demand is lower than potential GDP, there is a room for demand management policies, particularly fiscal and monetary policies. According to Keynesian economists, demand management policies can close output gaps and make the whole economic system more stable. By contrast, the mainstream of the economics profession considers demand management policies as superfluous or counterproductive. This scepticism builds on the assumption that the market-based economic system is self-adjusting. If wages are fully flexible, then the labour market will adjust by itself to full employment. In such cases aggregate demand also by itself adjusts to potential output via changes in real wealth and/or changes in net foreign trade. The reason for these different analytical outcomes is to be found in the choice of the theoretical macroeconomic framework. Keynesian aggregate demand analysis considers that the future is radically uncertain, which creates room for demand management policies. By contrast, the neoclassical assumption of automatic market adjustment makes aggregate demand equal to potential output over the long run, provided that the public sector does not intervene to affect the free-market equilibrium.

The National Accounting System: some principles and definitions

Macroeconomic analysis is statistically based on the National Accounting System (NAS). The general principles behind the NAS were established in the 1930s as a result of the Great Depression, which caused a steep fall in production and a rise in unemployment. At the time, governments felt an urgent need for more precise information about the overall status of the general economic situation. As a result, they established a standard for the statistical principles of the NAS, since the latter were accepted internationally, overlooked by the United Nations' organization and agreed to be followed by its member states.

The basic principles of the NAS are quite simple and aim to give an objective picture of economic activity in a country. Registrations are based on statistics covering economic transactions, which have a market price and/or create money income (so-called factor income).

Aggregate demand is defined by the NAS as the sum of several specific economic transactions, which adds up to final demand. The NAS is organized in such a way that factor income (wages and profits), gross domestic product (GDP), and final demand by definition are made similar.

The focus point in macroeconomic[1] analysis is usually aggregate demand and production, which are important factors determining employment as well as unemployment.

Aggregate demand consists of a number of subcomponents. They are usually defined and categorized within the NAS by, on the one hand, the characteristics of the produced goods and services and, on the other, by the actors (households, firms, government sector, or those living abroad), who have undertaken the demand (by ordering and purchasing the produced goods and services) registered within the statistics. Aggregate demand refers to items and activities that cause physical production (real economic activities), which employ labour and involve the use of physical capital. As a consequence of this production, these factors receive (factor) income usually in the form of money wages and profits, which are eventually spent in purchasing goods and services.

Aggregate demand (consisting of newly produced goods and services) is divided within the NAS into a number of analytically relevant demand components: private consumption, private investment, government consumption and investment, and net exports.

Within the private sector, it is assumed that households, mainly wage earners, decide on consumption, which (statistically) consists of items such as food, clothes, entertainment, travel, cars, and house rent. Private houses, although usually bought by households, are considered as an investment, because newly produced houses are (like firms' investment) long-lasting.

Private firms decide on investment, which, as a part of aggregate demand, is defined as only *newly* produced buildings, infrastructure, vehicles and machinery. Likewise, the government contributes to aggregate demand by public consumption and investment in the form of employing people in the public sector and/or demanding goods and services produced in the private sector. Finally, exports of goods and services are the part of aggregate demand that is sold abroad.

It has become standard to present aggregate demand (AD) in analytical models as follows:

$$AD \equiv C + I + G + E \tag{7.1}$$

where C represents private consumption, I private investment, G government consumption and investment, and E exports of goods and services.

Further, it is a statistical convention that aggregate demand is made equal to the supply of goods and services, which are either domestically produced (that is, the Gross Domestic Product, GDP) or produced abroad by foreign firms and called import (M). The national accounting identity is as follows:

$$AD \equiv GDP + M \tag{7.2}$$

Domestic production is assumed to be carried out by private and public firms or public institutions. GDP is physically produced by employing labour and physical capital (land, buildings and machinery) in the economic system. The value of production, GDP, measured at market prices, is the remuneration that the factors of production obtain in the form of wages (labour) and profits (physical capital). The sum of wages (W) and profits (P) is called gross factor income (Y).

These statistical conventions bring us to another important National Accounting identity, as follows:

$$W + P \equiv Y \equiv GDP \equiv C + I + G + E - M \tag{7.3}$$

Identity (7.3) shows that factor income and output are by definition identical and add up to aggregate demand minus imported goods and services at the macroeconomic level.

From statistical concepts to macroeconomic theory

Macroeconomic figures are important. They allow us to understand the overall economic development during a given period of time. Although the main concern usually is directed towards GDP, the statistical records of the NSA contain very detailed information about many other important macroeconomic variables, like employment, balance of payments, inflation, and public sector budgets, just to mention those variables that usually cause political concern.

The overlying task for macroeconomists is to establish plausible explanations of the statistical development of the major macroeconomic variables through time. For that purpose macroeconomists set up hypotheses about the causalities and dynamic structures within the economic system.

As regards macroeconomic theory, there are two dominant and competing hypotheses of how to explain the evolution of GDP, employment, inflation, and so on. Both theoretical explanations take their departure from equation (7.3). In the previous section, this equation was presented as an identity, which is useful in securing consistency within the NAS, but it does not give any information about causality. This is where Keynesian macroeconomists deviate from the conventional neoclassical explanation of how GDP is determined.

To put it briefly, as explained in Chapter 2, neoclassical economists argue that the supply of production factors (labour and real capital) together with technological capability (productivity) determine (mainly) the potential level of output and, under ideal market conditions, the actual level of production. This amounts to saying that neoclassical economists assume that 'the supply of goods creates their own demand' (Say's Law).

By contrast, Keynesian economists argue that it is the aggregate demand for goods and services that makes firms undertake production and employ labour (and capital). In other words, Keynesian economists argue that aggregate demand is a necessary (but not always sufficient) condition to make firms produce (Box 7.1).

BOX 7.1

TWO ALTERNATIVE MACROECONOMIC THEORIES (CAUSAL RELATIONS) OF PRODUCTION, EMPLOYMENT AND AGGREGATE DEMAND

Neoclassical theory: supply of labour ➜ (full) employment ➜ GDP ➜ aggregate demand

Keynesian theory: aggregate demand ➜ GDP ➜ employment (unemployment)

Hence, aggregate demand plays a much more prominent role in Keynesian macroeconomic theory than in neoclassical economics. Therefore, the next section on the role of aggregate demand in neoclassical theory will be rather brief compared to the discussion of the determinants of aggregate demand in Keynesian macroeconomics, which takes a lot of inspiration from John Maynard Keynes's original contribution in *The General Theory of Employment, Interest and Money* (1936).

The neoclassical theory of aggregate demand

Aggregate demand plays an unobtrusive role in neoclassical macroeconomics. As shown in Box 7.1, the assumed causality within the economic system runs from the supply of factors of production via a well-functioning labour market with flexible money wages to the size of GDP. Further, it is assumed within this macroeconomic framework that 'the supply of goods creates their own demand', which means that aggregate demand for goods and services always adjusts to potential output. Hence, it is not total output but only the division of output between consumption and investment goods that is determined by the subdivision of aggregate demand undertaken by consumers (households), investors (firms), and the general government sector.

The theoretical arguments build on microeconomic principles of individual optimization (utility and profit-maximizing behaviour) and single market adjustment (usually under the condition of perfect competition) put into a macroeconomic framework of general (that is, total) market clearing.

The causal starting point of the theory of aggregate demand in neoclassical economics is the neoclassical labour market, where the demand and supply of labour are derived from aggregated individual optimization behaviour (Figure 7.1). Employment is determined by the intersection point of L_d and L_s functions, which stand for the demand and supply of labour respectively. Their intersection marks the equilibrium within the labour market.

Yet, the occurrence of this equilibrium can be impeded by rigidities of real-wage adjustment, caused by external market forces such as a minimum wage set by the government or market power exercised by trade unions. If the real wage is too high, that is, above the equilibrium real wage, there will be a discrepancy between labour demand and labour supply: workers will offer more labour than what firms are ready to demand at that real wage, resulting in so-called involuntary unemployment – involuntary because individuals do not have the power of reducing the real-wage level (set by external forces) or the possibility to improve their employment situation in another way.

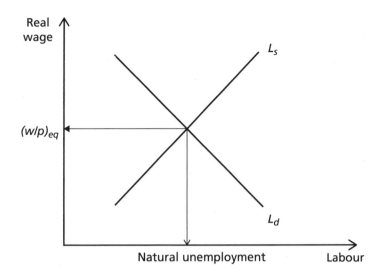

Figure 7.1 The neoclassical labour market

In some versions of neoclassical theory, temporary unemployment is also explained by a sluggish adjustment of the real wage owing to a lack of information, employment contracts and social security systems. In other words, the real wage will move toward the equilibrium only slowly, because of frictions or imperfections. This adjustment process might even take several years to complete. But the labour market is assumed to eventually reach the market clearing equilibrium, with a *natural rate of unemployment*, in the longer run. Output will grow as a consequence of the expansion of employment, because it is assumed that supply creates its own demand.

When the labour market has adjusted to its equilibrium, any further expansion in output is explained within the neoclassical growth model (see Chapter 10). In that model, it is the development in productivity and labour supply that determine the long-run growth rate of output. Households decide on how to divide factor income between current consumption and savings (deferred consumption). It is assumed that financial savings are transformed automatically into productive real investment via a perfectly functioning credit market. In this model, savings are always identical to investment and, therefore, do not cause any drain on aggregate demand. Further, it is assumed that savings determine investment.

Neoclassical aggregate supply: the AS model

Neoclassical models of output determination have their causal starting point on the labour market. As discussed above, the crucial assumption is

Figure 7.2 The neoclassical output model

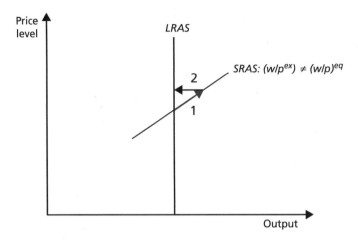

that, owing to market forces, the labour market will adjust by itself to an equilibrium, that is, the intersection point of L_d and L_s curves in Figure 7.1, the point that Milton Friedman dubbed the 'natural rate of unemployment' (that is, no involuntary unemployment). Given the labour market structural conditions and the social security system, unemployment cannot be reduced further without causing wage (w) and price (p) inflation. Hence, the longer-run output level (the *LRAS* curve in Figure 7.2) is determined by labour market equilibrium and is assumed to be constant (while disregarding changes in capital stock and productivity).

If firms erroneously expect the price level of output in the next period to increase, they will react as if the real-wage level (w/p) has fallen, since an increase in the price level decreases the real wage. As a result, they will employ more people and expand output according to their short-run aggregate supply curve (*SRAS* in Figure 7.2). Employment is, in this case, increased temporarily and unemployment reduced below its natural level, which will shortly make money wage begin to rise, thereby increasing the real wage. Firms will realize at the end of the period that their expectations had been wrong, since the real wage has not fallen as much as they expected. They will therefore start to reduce output and employment in the following period(s) in accordance with the new information on prices and wages. At the end of the adjustment process, output and employment will be unchanged (predetermined by the long-run aggregate supply, *LRAS* curve); but the price level might have increased permanently.

Something similar is assumed to happen if governments try to increase the level of employment by expansionary monetary or fiscal policies (see Chapter 9). Increased public sector employment might temporary increase total output, but money wages go up and squeeze private sector production, leaving the overall GDP (output) unchanged at the end of the adjustment period. The same labour market development occurs when increased public investment is undertaken. Public investment drains private savings and raises the rate of interest (see Chapter 6). Hence, private investment will fall *pari passu*. In neoclassical economics this mechanism of public expenditures substituting private consumption or investment is called the 'crowding out effect'. It changes the composition of aggregate demand, but leaves total GDP (output) unchanged.

In general, neoclassical economists dispute the beneficial effects of expansionary demand management policies. They claim that the market system in principle is self-adjusting. Hence, in the case of unemployment there is no need to undertake an expansionary demand policy. Rather, the economic system and especially the labour market should be made more flexible, and the wage level more responsive to unemployment. Neoclassical economists claim that an output gap is not caused by a lack of effective demand but is more often caused by rigidities in the labour market, which therefore should be reformed.

The Keynesian theory of aggregate demand and output

Changes in output are decided by firms (and governments) in light of effective demand, which means the expected sales of goods and services by private firms produced at a positive profit margin. Expectations concerning the future are always based on *uncertain* information. Proceeds from future sales cannot be calculated with certainty. In practice, these expectations are subjectively formed partly on historical data and partly on vague information on what might happen in the future, often influenced by waves of optimism and pessimism.[2] On the other hand, a number of firms produce only in response to specific orders from other firms or from the public. In these cases it is the actual demand that gives rise directly to production and employment (Jespersen, 2009).

The statistical aggregation of these millions and millions of daily/monthly transactions caused by consumption and investment (domestically and internationally) will, together with information about likely future events, comprise the backbone of expected aggregate demand and will, therefore, dominate the firms' production decisions. History and qualified information are essential for the formulation of the aggregate demand function in a Keynesian macroeconomic model.

Private consumption

Private consumption is the largest of the subcomponents of aggregate demand accounting for more than half of GDP. Disposable current household income (factor income plus social benefits minus taxes) is assumed to be the major determinant of private consumption. The population, on average, is assumed to spend a certain and relatively stable proportion of changes in its current disposable income on consumption. This marginal propensity to consume determines the division of changes in household income into consumption and savings in the aggregate consumption function:

$$C = C_0 + c_1 Y_d \qquad (7.4)$$

where c_1 represents the marginal propensity to consume,[3] Y_d is disposable income (factor income (Y) + social benefits – taxes), and C_0 is that part of consumption that does not depend on income. The latter is referred in most textbooks as autonomous consumption.

Of course, private consumption is influenced by many factors other than just disposable income. It has become common practice in recent years also to add a wealth variable, WE. In other words, consumption today is assumed to depend on current disposable income and wealth. The wealthier society becomes, the larger a share of current income it can afford to spend:

$$C = C_0 + c_1 Y_d + c_2 WE \qquad (7.5)$$

Further, distribution of income and credit facilities also matter with regard to private consumption. The variable C_0 in equation (7.5) represents all these factors besides disposable income and wealth, which make the consumption function shift from time to time. These factors are many and partly unknown, partly unstable, and partly of minor importance.

The part of private disposable income that is not used for consumption is saved. Hence, savings is income not spent on consumption and instead put into banks as deposits or into pensions schemes for consumption in old age. The point here is that savings do not form a part of aggregate demand. In fact, the immediate effect of increased financial savings is a reduction of private consumption, which has a negative impact on output. Hence, the larger the propensity to save, the smaller the propensity to consume, because private consumption (C) and private savings (S) add by definition to disposable income. In other words, the marginal propensity to consume and the marginal propensity to save must add to 1. Hence, we have:

$$C + S \equiv Y_d \qquad\qquad (7.6)$$

Private investment

Private firms undertake investment when they buy new machinery or vehicles, construct new buildings for factories or offices, or create infrastructure. In macroeconomics, the word 'investment' is reserved for economic activities that increase the stock of physical capital. This is so for three analytical reasons:

- Investment gives rise to output and is part of aggregate demand. Hence, investments are recorded within the NAS as newly physically produced goods. In this respect, investments in the NAS are very different from financial investments (for instance, when one buys stocks on the stock exchange market) or the purchase of already produced physical capital, not to mention land (and other non-producible assets).
- Private investments and private savings are two absolutely distinct economic activities, undertaken by two different groups in society. Firms undertake investment, and do so to be more productive, whereas households save for old age or for the uncertain future. Investment is part of aggregate demand; savings is non-consumption and therefore not part of aggregate demand. This leads to what is called the paradox of thrift: increases in the propensity to save out of disposable income by private households (and firms) lead to a decrease in aggregate demand and output.
- Since investment gives rise to newly produced assets, once it has been undertaken the size of physical capital will increase. As such, the productive capacity of the economic system increases, which in turn increases the growth potential of GDP (see Chapter 10).

As stated above, private firms undertake investment, and do so with the purpose of making a profit in the future. Hence, they calculate what they can expect to add to their profits in the future by undertaking investments in physical capital today. These calculations, however, are very uncertain. Over and over again in *The General Theory* Keynes emphasized that such calculations are by nature uncertain and will at the end depend considerably on the psychology of the manager and of the business mood in general. Bursts of optimism and pessimism spread in society with a self-reinforcing effect owing to, among other things, what Keynes called 'animal spirits'.

So why would a firm undertake investment? New capital is needed to substitute used and worn-out capital. Real assets do not last forever and new technology requires that the existing capital equipment is renewed and updated. These investments replace old capital and are called amortization;

they represent the largest share of private investment in the NAS. Yet, this has no impact on the size of the physical capital stock: amortization simply replaces old machines and equipment.

Although amortization goods (re-investment) are produced and make up a part of GDP, they are, as mentioned, only replacements for worn-out capital. If amortization investment did not take place, the capital stock would shrink and society would eat up its physical wealth. A number of amortization decisions are made rather mechanically, because a broken machine, an outdated vehicle or an old-fashioned technology has to be replaced to make the economic system productive and competitive. Therefore, amortization is a part of the costs of production during the period under consideration that firms have to pay. For that reason, it has become practice to separate between gross profit and net profit in the NAS.

By contrast, decisions on investments that enlarge the size of the real capital stock are much more dependent on future production. As explained above, they rely heavily on uncertain expectations of future proceeds from an expanding aggregate demand. The foundation of this calculation regarding the future is by nature quite uncertain and depends on the state of confidence: 'There is, however, not much to be said about the state of confidence *a priori*. Our conclusions must mainly depend upon the actual observation of markets and business psychology' (Keynes, 1936, p. 149).

Real investments are long-lasting and can usually not be financed by current profits only. Therefore, when firms have made up their mind with regard to the expected return on new investments, they have to confront the expected return with the rate of interest that they have to pay to obtain the necessary finance. This suggests two things: investment depends on the difference between the expected rate of return and the banks' rate of interest; second, monetary policy as practised by central banks could have an influence over investments by making credit facilities more easily available and by reducing the rate of interest (see below and Chapter 6).

Government expenditures on goods and services

As we can see from equation (7.3), government expenditures, G, that is, when governments consume and invest, are part of aggregate demand. In the 1930s their share was less than 10 per cent of total aggregate demand. Today, depending on the country, this share has risen to 20–30 per cent. Unfortunately, macroeconomic theory has not that much to say about this expansion of the public sector, because it was mainly initiated by political considerations, especially when building up the welfare state. We will consider the government demand for goods and services when demand management policies are analysed (see below and Chapter 9).

Another important part of public expenditures is social income transfers (benefits and subsidies), which do not appear in the definition of aggregate demand. This is so because these expenditures are not paid to households in exchange for real goods and services. They are instead paid according to specific social criteria, usually with the aim of protecting people against material starvation. In macroeconomic analysis social benefit is considered a part of disposable income, Y_d, in equations (7.4) and (7.5), and will therefore only have an impact on aggregate demand when they are spent on private consumption.

Public expenditures are mainly financed by taxes (income, consumer and real estate taxes), which, similarly to social income transfers, do not appear in the definition of aggregate demand, because a tax is by definition not a payment for a specific good or service. On the other hand, taxes reduce disposable household income and thereby reduce private consumption. Although the impact on aggregate demand and output is indirect, a change in the tax rate is considered as one of the major instruments of demand management policies, as explained below.

International trade

Looking at equation (7.3) two items related to trade appear: exports and imports of goods and services. They have both a direct impact on GDP. In larger countries like the United States, exports amount to approximately 20 per cent of GDP, whereas in small open economies like the Netherlands exports come close to 80 per cent of GDP.

Exports are determined by the demand by households and firms in other countries. For instance, when Chinese importers purchase goods produced in the United States, these are considered exported goods in an equation determining US aggregate demand. Increased purchasing power abroad, especially in neighbouring countries, has a positive impact on exports: when households in these countries consume more, they also import more foreign goods and services. Similarly, domestic aggregate demand is not only directed towards domestically produced goods and services, since we also consume goods and services produced abroad and recorded as imports in the national accounting system (see equation 7.3). Imports therefore play a significant role when aggregate demand is divided between domestic and foreign output.

Some goods (like coffee and bananas) cannot be produced in all countries owing to climatic conditions. Some countries are too small to have an efficient production in all industries (cars, airplanes, advanced electronics, and so on). But even in countries that have their own production of nearly all goods, one may see apparently similar goods being imported. Wine from all over the world can also be bought in wine-producing countries. Cars are imported and exported in and out of all major industrial countries. The reason for this is partly specific preferences, partly different costs of production and of delivering. Depending on the type of product (or service) under consideration, its costs of production have a rather important impact on firms' international competiveness, which will make especially in the longer run an impact on trade flows in and out of the country and therefore on its output.

Imbalances between exports and imports show up in the current account of the balance of payments. A surplus has a positive impact on GDP (and employment), because exports exceed imports in that case.

The income multiplier

The original simple multiplier

The marginal propensity to consume (see equations (7.4) and (7.5)) plays a major role in all macroeconomic models. It determines the expansionary effect of an increased income inside the system. When an extra unit of income is earned, the propensity to consume tells us the share of this extra income that is spent on consumption. The extra consumption has to be produced, which we know from equation (7.3) creates an equivalent amount of factor income. A part of this extra income is spent on consumption creating more factor income, which is partly spent and so on. This expansionary effect, however, will not go on forever. Each time extra income is created, a part of it is saved and therefore withdrawn from aggregate demand. This dynamic development is called the 'income multiplier'. It was first introduced into macroeconomic theory by Richard Kahn and is illustrated in Box 7.2.

BOX 7.2

THE SIMPLE INCOME MULTIPLIER

$\text{MULT} = 1/(1 - c)$ or $\text{MULT} = 1/s$ (7.7)

where c is the marginal propensity to consume out of disposable income and

s the marginal propensity to save out of disposable income, because $c + s \equiv 1$.

The calculation of the income multiplier within a simple macroeconomic model, where only private consumption is considered, is quite simple. The multiplier effect depends only on the propensity to consume. The larger the propensity to consume, the more income is spent on consumption (and output) each time an extra unit of income is earned.

For instance, if the marginal propensity to consume is estimated to 0.9, then the income multiplier will be equal to 10. This means that each time a household receives $100 extra, it will consume $90 worth of goods and services. This $90 is then spent and thereby becomes someone else's income, who will then spend $81 worth of goods (90 per cent of $90). This $81 is also someone else's income, who will spend 90 per cent of that, hence $72.90, and so on. As one can see, an initial increase in consumption, which increases output, has a 'multiplying' effect on output.

The theoretical explanation of the multiplier principle is one of Keynes's most fundamental contributions to macroeconomic analysis.

The elaborated multiplier

Modern welfare states are primarily financed by income and consumption taxes. Since taxes are paid out of current income, tax revenues (net of social benefits) reduce disposable income and thereby private households' consumption, which is thus a drain on aggregate demand. The higher the income (and consumption) tax rate, the larger the drain. In this respect taxes will, like private savings, reduce the size of the multiplier, because an extra unit of factor income is taxed quite highly, in some countries by 40 or 50 per cent. This tendency of a diminished income multiplier is reinforced further by social benefits being dependent on changes in unemployment, which increases the marginal net tax rate (the tax rate plus the unemployment benefit rate). Hence, within the modern welfare state the size of the income multiplier is reduced substantially compared to the 1930s, and much more in the Scandinavian countries than in the United States.

Further, the income multiplier is reduced by imports of goods and services. When domestic aggregate demand is increased, especially private consumption and firms' investment, imports will go up and some income will thus leak abroad and cause no further domestic multiplier effect. Hence, the higher the marginal propensity to import, the smaller the income multiplier becomes.

In general, small(er) countries are more dependent than big countries on imports owing to both international specialization and economies of scale. This means that the marginal propensity to import usually is larger in small(er) countries than in larger and more self-sufficient countries. The higher the marginal propensity to import is, the smaller the income multiplier becomes. In a number of the smaller countries with rather extended welfare states the income multiplier has become smaller than one owing to high taxes, social benefits and imports.

Expected aggregate demand and supply: effective demand

Aggregate demand (AD) represents the proceeds producers as a whole expect from future sales. The slope of the AD curve in Figure 7.3 is determined by the marginal propensity to consume out of disposable income (see equations (7.4) and (7.5)), where disposable income is defined as factor income (Y) plus social benefits minus taxes, as explained above.

The aggregate supply (AS) curve represents the variable costs of production (wages and raw materials) plus a normal business profit.[4] The cost-determined AS curve bends upwards following the convention that in the short run it becomes more expensive to increase output, because firms have to pay extra wages when labourers work more than normal hours,[5] and sometimes less efficient machines are used for a (quickly) increased production. In the long run the shape of the cost curve might be quite different depending on new technology and increased productivity (see Chapter 10).

The intersection point between the AD curve and the AS curve represents the short-run equilibrium level of output, which fulfils the producers' expected proceeds and gives a normal rate of profit. Keynes called this intersection point 'effective demand'. When producers have decided on output for the coming period, they also know how many people to employ. Hence, employment is determined by effective demand, which is represented in Figure 7.3 by the vertical line connecting output of goods and services (upper part of the figure) with the labour market (lower part).

In the lower part of Figure 7.3, illustrating the labour market, we have also drawn the conventional short-run demand (L_D) function for labour. Keynes accepted in many ways the relevance of this very conventional labour demand curve, assuming individually profit-maximizing firms, decreasing productivity of labour, and perfect competition among producers in the labour market. Under these admittedly very unrealistic assumptions the real wage would be determined by effective demand for output following the arrows marked A.

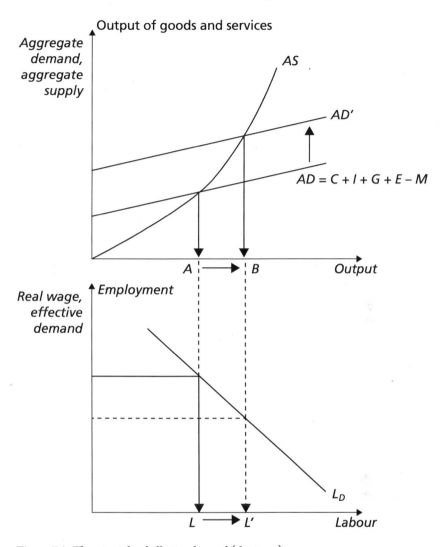

Figure 7.3 The principle of effective demand (short run)

When producers and/or trade unions execute market power in the wage-setting process, which they often do, the real wage is not only determined by market forces but also dependent on the relative strength of labour market organizations and of the size of unemployment (see Chapter 8).

An expansionary demand management policy causes an upward shift in the *AD* curve in Figure 7.3. The new intersection point between aggregate demand and aggregate supply determines how much output and employment will increase according to the model. It is the slope of the *AD* curve that determines the dynamics of the adjustment process, that is, the size of the income multiplier. The steeper the *AD* curve is, the larger is the multiplier.

Demand management policies

As discussed earlier, post-Keynesian economists do not share the neoclassical precondition of a self-adjusting market mechanism that moves the economic system toward full employment. Without this mechanism, the economy can easily get stuck at a high level of unemployment. This was precisely the case in the interwar period, when unemployment remained high for long periods of time. This cannot be justified using neoclassical economics, which only sees unemployment as transitory.

Keynes, however, saw neoclassical theory as a special and usually irrelevant case, because the general case was persistently high unemployment. This explains the historical context in which Keynes wrote his *General Theory*.

Yet, empirical evidence shows that periods of persistent unemployment are not limited to the interwar period. In fact, a high rate of unemployment has been the case since the early 1990s both in Europe and in the United States although somewhat more fluctuating in the latter country. Hence, economic systems do not converge to a low rate of unemployment by themselves.

In these long periods when the rate of unemployment is above any reasonably defined level of full employment, there is a gap between actual and potential output. Private effective demand is not enough to fill that gap. In these long-lasting periods, demand management policies can be useful to expand aggregate demand by monetary and/or fiscal policies.

Monetary policy is conducted by the central bank. The main monetary policy instruments are the short-term rate of interest, extended credit facilities, and open-market operations (buying long-term bonds from banks) with the aim of reducing the long-term rate of interest (see Chapter 6). Lower rates of interest and easier access to credit are expected to have a stimulating effect on private investment and to some, but lesser, extent on private consumption. Further, countries with a flexible exchange rate regime may experience a currency depreciation as a consequence of lower rates of interest and 'quantitative easing'. In this case, exports go up and imports down, which will increase aggregate demand and domestic output. A lower rate of interest will also reduce public sector interest payment, which will relieve liquidity constrained public sector budgets.

Fiscal policy is undertaken by governments to correct macroeconomic imbalances in the private sector, especially when unemployment is high. In such cases the government can increase public expenditures (G in equation (7.3)) and/or lower taxes and/or increase social spending. These kinds of expansionary fiscal policy will have a positive, but quite different impact on aggregate demand, depending on what instruments are used. There is a vast difference in the size of the income multiplier related to change in specific policy instruments. Usually, public consumption is considered as the instrument with the largest multiplier effect, because the first-round income effect is mainly domestic with very little content of imports. Similarly, social benefits have a rather high multiplier, because very little, if anything at all, is saved in the first round. People with low income spend what they earn, whereas tax reliefs to people with high income have little impact on consumption, output and employment.

Unfortunately, demand management policies are not always simple to undertake. There is a time lag from the adoption of the relevant policy instrument until private firms revise their production plans. In general, monetary policy can be decided relatively quickly, contrary to discretionary fiscal policy, which has to be approved by Parliament. Further, expansionary fiscal policy will often leave the public budget with a deficit, which has to be financed by increasing the money supply and/or selling bonds to the private sector (or abroad) (see Chapter 9).

The importance of aggregate demand in macroeconomic analysis was one of the theoretical novelties exposed by Keynes's *General Theory*. It has been a long-lasting process, because already in the early 1930s Richard Kahn had demonstrated, using public investments (in housing) as an example of active demand management policies, how the government could counterbalance and correct an imbalance in the private sector between savings and private investments, if the rate of unemployment was unacceptably high (see Kahn, 1984).

NOTES

1 In fact, the expression 'macroeconomics' related to the aggregated National Accounting items was not established until the second half of the 1930s.

2 'State of confidence' is an expression often used by Keynes in this regard.

3 It is called 'marginal' because it settles how much consumption will increase, if disposable income goes up by one extra (so-called 'marginal') unit of income.

4 'Normal business profit' is not a well-defined concept, but is related to the ruling rate of interest plus a risk premium, which might vary from industry to industry.

5 A more thorough argument at the macroeconomic level would refer to the Phillips curve. Here it is assumed that the lower the rate of unemployment, the higher the rate of wage inflation causing the cost level to rise (see Chapter 8).

REFERENCES

Jespersen, J. (2009), *Macroeconomic Methodology: A Post-Keynesian Perspective*, Cheltenham, UK and Northampton, MA, USA: Edward Elgar Publishing.

Kahn, R. (1929), *The Economics of the Short Period*, Cambridge, UK: King's College.

Kahn, R.F. (1931), 'The relation of home investment to unemployment', *Economic Journal*, **41** (162), 173–98.

Kahn, R.F. (1984), *The Making of Keynes's General Theory*, Cambridge, UK: Cambridge University Press.

Keynes, J.M. (1930a), *A Treatise on Money, Volume I: The Pure Theory of Money*, London: Macmillan.

Keynes, J.M. (1930b), *A Treatise on Money, Volume II: The Applied Theory of Money*, London: Macmillan.

Keynes, J.M. (1936), *The General Theory of Employment, Interest and Money*, London: Macmillan.

A PORTRAIT OF RICHARD KAHN (1905–89)

Richard Kahn was educated in mathematics, physics and economics at the University of Cambridge, United Kingdom. He was associated with King's College from the very beginning. He was elected fellow in 1930 and succeeded Keynes as bursar in 1946. He had appointments in the Faculty of Economics and Politics from 1933, and became a full professor in 1951, at which point he succeeded Dennis Holmes Robertson.

Kahn was Keynes's closest collaborator while Keynes wrote *The General Theory of Employment, Interest and Money*. Kahn was one of the five members of the so-called Cambridge Circus, together with Joan Robinson, Austin Robinson, Piero Sraffa and James Meade, whose principle mission, starting in autumn 1930, was to discuss Keynes's newly published *A Treatise on Money*, a two-volume book (Keynes, 1930a, 1930b). Kahn reported once a week to Keynes on the findings of the 'Circus'.

Kahn's most notable contribution to economic analysis was his principle of the income multiplier. This multiplier is the relation between an increase in aggregate demand and the related increase in output. His findings on the multiplier were first published in his seminal 1931 article, 'The relation of home investment to unemployment' in the *Economic Journal*. This paper was developed from his fellow dissertation *The Economics of the Short Period*, submitted to King's College in 1929. Keynes quickly picked up the idea of the multiplier and elaborated on it in several cases before he made it an integrated element of his *General Theory*.

During World War II, Kahn worked as a civil servant in a number of different ministries, which gave him a lot of practical experience concerning real-world economics, planning and the role of economic policies. In 1946 he returned to Cambridge. Although he was appointed full professor in 1951, he did not really make a lasting impact on the Department of Economics and Politics. When he retired in 1972 his chair in economics was taken over by the neoclassical economist Frank Hahn.

8

Inflation and unemployment

Alvaro Cencini and Sergio Rossi

 OVERVIEW

This chapter:

- provides a correct definition of inflation;

- shows that a distinction must be made between inflation and the cost of living;

- shows that the consumer price index is a poor indicator of the rate of inflation and that inflation cannot be identified with a persistent rise of the general price level;

- explains the monetary–structural origin of inflation;

- introduces Keynes's distinction between voluntary and involuntary unemployment;

- shows that involuntary unemployment is pathological and cannot be imputed to economic agents' behaviour;

- proves the existence of a close relationship between involuntary unemployment and deflation, and points to the role played by both the rate of interest and the process of capital accumulation in the rise of unemployment;

- shows that inflation and unemployment are twin effects of the same cause;

- outlines a reform that can solve both pathologies and enable a transition from a disorderly to an orderly system of payments.

KEYWORDS

- **Frictional unemployment:** The unemployment that occurs owing to the normal working of an economic system, where some people are temporarily unemployed until they are able to find another job.
- **Inflation:** Caused by a pathological change altering the relationship between national money and national output, inflation is a disorder causing the loss in the purchasing power of each money unit.
- **Involuntary unemployment:** The pathological unemployment caused by a monetary disorder arising from the actual process of fixed capital formation and the ensuing deflation.
- **Standard of living:** Measures the purchasing power of households over a basket of domestic and foreign commodities. It must be clearly distinguished from inflation.
- **Voluntary unemployment:** The frictional unemployment accompanying the normal working of our monetary economies of production.

Why are these topics important?

The negative consequences of inflation and unemployment should be self-evident. The economic and social problems induced by unemployment affect an increasing number of industrialized countries. The consequences of this disorder are well known: increase in poverty, spending cuts in public services, increased indebtedness (public and private), and social unrest are only some of the negative consequences endured by populations all over the world.

Inflation is only superficially a less disruptive disorder. If we bear in mind that inflation brings about a decrease in the purchasing power of money, we can easily realize that it affects the standard of living of all those people whose income is fixed over time (such as pensioners, beneficiaries of public assistance, owners of non-indexed bonds, and so on).

The failure to address these pathologies correctly has led to a worsening of the disorder, of which the economic and financial crisis that erupted in 2007–08 is a dramatic manifestation at the global level. Inflation and involuntary unemployment are in fact at the core of this macroeconomic disorder, and a correct understanding of their cause is an essential step towards a new, orderly system.

Inflation

The traditional analysis of inflation

Definition

Conventionally, economists define inflation as a persistent increase in the general price level. This means that whenever the price level increases over time, it signals that some inflationary pressures have been pushing a variety of prices upwards. Defining inflation by simply referring to changes in price levels implies that inflation is a result of supply and demand forces: if, on any given market for produced goods or services, there is an increase in demand and/or a reduction in supply, and if the elasticity of supply is low (that is to say, supply does not easily adjust to increases in demand), the prices of the relevant items will be higher as a result of the price determination process. Now, since there are thousands of goods and services, whose prices may move up and down at different rates of change in any given period, inflation is usually measured by referring to an index number, that is, a numerical index that is meant to subsume a great number of items whose prices may change differently during a given period of time (say, between last year and this year).

Measurement

Generally speaking, national statistical offices measure inflation through the Laspeyres price index. The relevant formula is as follows:

$$P_L \equiv \frac{\sum_{i=1}^{n} p_i^1 q_i^0}{\sum_{i=1}^{n} p_i^0 q_i^0} \times 100 \tag{8.1}$$

where P_L is the Laspeyres price index, i represents a good or service (for $i = 1, \ldots, n$), pi_1 is the price of item i in the current period (1), pi_0 is the price of the same item in the reference period (0), and qi_0 is the quantity of item i purchased in the reference period.

Now, '[the Laspeyres index] assumes no consumer substitution occurs in response to changes in relative prices, an assumption that is extreme, unrealistic and unnecessary' (Boskin et al., 1998, p. 7). In fact, when the prices of substitutable goods change over time, consumers tend to substitute the good whose price has increased more with the good whose price has increased less. Suppose, for instance, that the price of beer X is increasing more than the price of beer Y: assuming that these beers are similar, one is led to reduce or stop purchasing beer X and to increase consumption of beer Y. If so, then the Laspeyres index does not capture this shift in consumers' behaviour, because it considers the quantities of beers X and Y bought in the reference period (0) rather than those purchased in the current period (1). Generalizing this stylized example allows one to understand that the Laspeyres index leads us to overstate the upward movement of prices (see Rossi, 2001, Ch. 1 for analytical elaboration on this).

Causes

There are several causes for an increase in price levels. Neoclassical economists focus largely on the demand side of the economic system, and point out the following:

- Inflation is said to occur whenever the public sector increases government expenditure, as it exerts an upward pressure on the price level by increasing demand on the market for produced goods and services. This implies that, prior to government spending, there was a full employment equilibrium on the goods market: if the public sector is now demanding more goods or services, their market prices will increase, since there can be no general increase in output once all production factors are fully employed.
- Inflation would occur whenever consumers change their forms of behaviour abruptly, and decide to save less in order to consume more goods or services. This may occur, for instance, after a war, when people are relieved to see that the situation has improved and are therefore keener on spending rather than saving. On the assumption that full employment prevails, such an increase in consumption brings about an increase in a number of market prices, hence also an increase in the relevant price level.
- Inflation, it is also claimed, may occur when either the public sector or the private sector obtains more credit from the banking system. In both cases, demand on the goods market increases, leading to an increase in the general price level or, at least, in expected inflation. For instance, the dramatic increase in the money supply as a result of the unprecedented intervention by several central banks in the aftermath of the global financial crisis that erupted in 2007–08 has led many to fear a resurgence of inflation in those countries where monetary authorities have carried out either credit easing or quantitative easing programmes – most notably across the euro area and the United States (see MacLean, 2015 and Werner, 2015).

These causes of inflation, in neoclassical economics, are closely linked to the quantity theory of money, which considers that any increase in the money supply leads to some increase in the relevant price level over time (see Mastromatteo and Tedeschi, 2015). In short, orthodox economists believe that the quantity of money and the amount of credit are supply driven and determined by the central bank. Monetary policy should therefore aim at price stability on the market for produced goods and services, and nothing else.

Now, heterodox economists take a different position. Although many of them adhere to the definition of inflation by its effect on the price level, these economists argue that the causes of inflation are to be found in the never-ending struggle over income distribution between firms (profits) and workers (wages). This is the conflict theory of inflation (see Rowthorn, 1977). As Palley (1996, p. 182) observes, this approach stems from the cost-push theory of inflation developed in the 1950s. In fact, the most widely mentioned source of 'cost-push inflation' arises from 'inconsistent claims on income that emerge from the income distribution struggle between workers and firms' (ibid., p. 182). In this view, the two parties' claims on income may exceed available output in the economy as a whole. So, the excess of income claims over national output originates an increase in prices on the market for produced goods and services. Wage earners try to counteract this upward pressure by bidding for higher wages, thereby setting forth a price–wage or wage–price spiral in which each party seeks to obtain, or to maintain, its targeted income share (see Rossi, 2001, Ch. 5 for analytical elaboration on this).

Some criticisms

Even though the conventional definition of inflation seems uncontroversial, it remains superficial, as it focuses on a surface phenomenon, that is, an increase in some relevant price level. In fact, essentially, inflation is a decrease in the purchasing power of money, as a result of which the general price level increases.

This essential definition needs to be clarified. In particular one has to make clear where the purchasing power of money comes from, and what are those goods and services that determine the purchasing power of any given national currency.

How is it that a national currency can be endowed with a positive purchasing power? The answer is straightforward: it is production that gives a purchasing power to money. One may indeed have a lot of money, but if there is nothing to purchase (as a result of production), one has in fact no purchasing power at all. This simple thought experiment is enough to establish that the purchasing power of any national currency is determined with regard to the goods and services produced by the corresponding national economy. Hence, the US dollar's purchasing power is defined with respect to US national output, the British pound's purchasing power defines those UK goods and services that can be purchased by the British currency, and so on. In other words, through production each national economy gives its national money a physical content, represented by currently produced goods and services, which are the real object of its purchasing power.

Inflation is therefore the result of an anomaly that affects the initial relationship between money and output established by production. In this sense, inflation is the manifestation of a pathology that increases the number of money units without increasing production.

Let us expand on this by critiquing the traditional explanations of inflation as presented above. Having defined inflation as a persistent rise in the price level, orthodox economists explain it by referring to the general price level. According to general equilibrium analysis, prices are relative. Goods are exchanged against goods on the commodity market, and it is through their exchange, so the orthodox story goes, that their relative prices are determined. Hence, orthodox economists claim that the price of any given commodity can only be expressed in terms of another commodity against which the former is exchanged. But how can this conception of prices be reconciled with the undisputable fact that the general price level is expressed in terms of money? Their answer is simply that money itself is essentially a commodity, that is to say, an asset that is exchanged against the goods and services offered in the market. The general price level would then be nothing but the relative price of money in terms of a representative bundle of goods and services defined as a composite commodity. In fact, in the quantity theory of money, the price level is determined by relating the quantity of money to the available quantity of produced goods and services.

Hence, advocates of the quantity theory of money, also known as 'monetarists', argue that variations in the price level are due to adjustments between two distinct stocks: the quantity of money as determined by monetary authorities (essentially central banks) and the quantity of available output as determined by current production. Inflation would therefore result from an excessive growth of the money supply, which increases the quantity of money without being offset by a corresponding rise of the composite commodity. To avoid an inflationary increase in the general price level, monetary authorities would have to control the growth of the money supply, keeping it in line with variations in the quantity of produced goods and services.

Modern monetary analysis, which proves the inadequacy of the quantity theory of money and its failure to explain inflation, has shown that this old-fashioned way of looking at money as a stock is wrong. The idea that money can be created as a net asset by central banks is far-fetched to say the least. Neither human beings nor any of their institutions can create a positive asset out of nothing. Bank money is issued by means of double-entry bookkeeping and can thus only be defined as an asset–liability in accordance with the principle of the necessary balancing of assets and liabilities. If money can nevertheless be endowed with a positive value, its purchasing power, it is because it is associated with production. It is because of its 'integration' with output that money acquires a positive purchasing power. A correct explanation of inflation has to be consistent with the bookkeeping nature of bank money. What has to be investigated is how the strict relationship established by production between money and output can be altered.

Inflation and the price level

A first point that has to be clarified concerns the conventional definition of inflation as a persistent increase in the general price level and its measurement through the Laspeyres formula (see above). In fact, any increase in the price level does not necessarily imply a variation in the relationship between money and output. Indeed, it can easily be shown that: (1) there are persistent increases in prices that do not reduce the purchasing power of money in the least; (2) stability of the general price level can mask the existence of inflation.

The first example is provided by the state's decision to substantially increase indirect taxation, say through an increase in taxes on fuel. The ensuing sharp rise in the price of fuel would certainly have an impact on the purchasing power of many households, yet would it also reduce the purchasing power of money? The answer is no, because what would be lost by these households would be earned by the state, so that the totality of economic agents (state included) would still enjoy the same purchasing power. The result of the increase in indirect taxation is thus an increase in prices that is not of an inflationary nature. Money would be redistributed among the different categories of economic agents, but its purchasing power would not be reduced.

Our second example concerns the impact of technological progress on costs and prices. It is a fact that technological improvements generally reduce production costs so that, in the absence of inflation, prices should decrease over time. Let us suppose that, despite the generalized presence of technological or structural improvements, the level of prices remains constant. By identifying inflation with a rise in the general price level, orthodox economists are bound to conclude that there is no inflation, as the price level is the same across the relevant periods. In reality, the correct conclusion would be that it is due to inflation that the price level, which should have decreased because of the consequences of structural change, has remained constant.

Inflation and the cost of living

Orthodox economists use the consumer price index (CPI) to measure inflation. The CPI is a numerical index (calculated with the Laspeyres formula) attributed to a standardized basket of goods and services that is supposed to include the commodities purchased by a representative household during a given period of time. The use of the CPI has often been criticized by stressing the fact that a comparison between consumer price indexes calculated at different points in time requires the basket to be made up of the same goods in the same proportion. This is obviously not the case, which makes it difficult if not altogether impossible to compare heterogeneous baskets.

But this is not the only criticism that can be levelled against the use of the CPI. The fact that among the goods and services introduced in the representative basket are goods and services produced abroad is another critical element, which shows that the CPI cannot be considered an appropriate measure of the rate of inflation. In fact, foreign goods and services have nothing to do with the definition and determination of the purchasing power of a national currency. Only domestically produced goods and services enter the definition of the output whose production attributes a purchasing power to a country's national currency. It therefore follows that, since variations in the prices of imported goods and services do not bring about any change in the relationship between domestic currency and domestic output, they cannot cause inflation.

While it is true that a significant increase in the prices of imported goods and services may lead to a persistent rise in the CPI, it is also certain that this has nothing to do with inflation. It is therefore clear that the CPI must be considered in fact as a measure of the variation in the cost of living rather than a measure of inflation. A rise in the CPI indeed entails a fall in the standard of living of all those people who cannot easily modify their consumption habits. It could even entail a generalized reduction in the standard of living of every resident. Yet it would be wrong to conclude that it also reduces the purchasing power of the domestic currency as defined by its relationship to domestic output. If the rise in the CPI were caused by a rise in the prices of imported goods and services, this would mean that imports would cost more in terms of exports. Such a change in the terms of trade could be a problem, but it cannot modify the relationship, established by domestic production, between national money and domestic output.

Before investigating how the relationship between money and output can be altered, let us consider the second anomaly examined in this chapter.

Unemployment

Definition

A first, broad and rather obvious definition of unemployment is that of a state of the economy where part of the working population can no longer be employed and has to be laid off.

What immediately appears to be a central element in the analysis of unemployment is the determination of its causes. Indeed, it was by distinguishing between its possible causes that Keynes introduced two categories of unemployment – voluntary and involuntary – whose conceptual distinction is of the foremost importance for understanding this major economic disorder.

Voluntary unemployment

Let us immediately clarify that the adjective 'voluntary' shall not be taken in its literal sense. Voluntary unemployment is not that brought about by free choice; it is not merely due to the decision of people not to work. Keynes provides a series of examples that help us to understand that by voluntary unemployment he identifies a side-effect created by the 'normal' working of a capitalist economy.

Frictional unemployment is one of these examples. People who decide to change their working place (either continuing in a given activity or switching from one to another) or who have to leave it may not immediately find another working place or another job because of imperfect information or other distortions in the labour market. Unemployment due to industrial structural changes is another example. Because of technological changes, firms are often led to lay off part of their work force and only very rarely can the latter immediately find another job.

In what sense is it appropriate to qualify these examples as cases of voluntary unemployment? The choice of the word 'voluntary' is meaningful only if it is taken to define the free choice of an economic system, whose normal workings entail temporary, sectorial adjustments that affect employment. A monetary economy of production based on capital accumulation is a dynamic system, whose changes may have negative, albeit temporary, effects on employment. By choosing such an economic system, in a certain sense we have also chosen to embrace its unintended consequences, and this is why we define the situation in which people are 'frictionally' or 'technologically' out of work as 'voluntary' unemployment.

Now, contrary to what might be thought in the first place, voluntary unemployment is not a serious disorder and explains only an extremely small fraction of the overall level of unemployment. Indeed, if voluntary unemployment were the only disorder our economic system suffered from, we would have nothing to worry about. This can be better understood by observing that technological evolution often brings with it a possible solution to the unemployment it creates. This is so because technological improvement increases physical productivity, reduces costs, and creates the conditions necessary to reduce the number of working hours per worker without reducing the number of employees. It is true that today this solution is not feasible, but this is because our economic systems remain infected by the two serious pathologies of inflation and involuntary unemployment. Let us turn our attention to this latter form of unemployment.

Involuntary unemployment

Unfortunately, no definition of involuntary unemployment is given in Keynes's work, yet it can be derived from his definition of voluntary unemployment. Since voluntary unemployment is a temporary form of unemployment resulting from the normal imperfections of our economies, involuntary unemployment can only be the persistent form of unemployment caused by the pathological working of our economic systems. The crucial demarcation is that between order and disorder. Any kind of frictional unemployment consistent with an orderly economic system is but an instance of voluntary unemployment. On the other hand, any form of persistent unemployment due to a structural disorder of the system is a pathology pertaining to involuntary unemployment.

The question that has to be asked now is: what are the criteria by which we can distinguish an orderly from a disorderly economic system? The answer to this question as given by orthodox economics differs substantially from that advocated by modern monetary macroeconomics. Let us first introduce, critically, the orthodox point of view.

Unemployment as the consequence of labour markets' rigidities and changes in consumers' demand

Economists of all schools are unanimous in considering deflation as one of the main causes of unemployment, where deflation is a situation in which demand falls short of supply on the market for produced goods and services, so that part of current output cannot be sold at current prices. Orthodox economists maintain that this situation can be brought about by variations in economic agents' behaviour, for example a reduction in consumption. If, for whatever reason, income holders were to persistently reduce their propensity to consume, the reduction in demand would force firms to produce less, and the ensuing tendency to lay off workers would be offset only if money wages were perfectly elastic downwards. If not, unemployment would set in and the economy could enter a phase of recession.

This traditional, neoclassical analysis of unemployment also emphasizes the role played by workers and their associations. In the presence of deflation or of any other obstacle impeding firms to 'clear the market' (that is, to sell all their output), equilibrium could be preserved, neoclassical economists maintain, if money wages were free to fluctuate. According to their analysis, unemployment is the consequence of workers', trade unions' and states' unwillingness to let nominal wages fall to the level that would preserve full employment.

Besides ethical and socio-political considerations, this analysis has to be rejected on conceptual and analytical grounds. Its main shortcoming is to consider labour as a commodity and to assume that wages are its price, determined on the labour market by the traditional forces of supply and demand. Orthodox economists seem unaware of the fact stated by Smith, Ricardo, Marx and Keynes, among others, that labour is the source of value and that, as such, it cannot itself have a value. Analogously, being at the origin of commodities, it cannot itself be identified as a commodity. Moreover, since money is given a positive value or purchasing power by production, wages provide the original income in an economic system. A reduction in nominal wages advocated by orthodox economists would only modify the numerical expression of production without touching on the pathology at the origin of involuntary unemployment. Income would be reduced to the same extent as wages, and deflation would essentially remain unchanged.

Orthodox analysis is indeed wrong, since it rests on a wrong conception of bank money, considered as an asset, and on the belief that savings can be hoarded as if money income were a physical quantity that can be taken out of circulation. In reality, the nature of bank money and the principle of double-entry bookkeeping are such that the totality of income necessarily takes the form of bank deposits. Since bank deposits cannot be hoarded, it immediately appears that saving does not reduce the amount of income available in a given banking system. It thus follows that neither labour markets' rigidities nor saving can be the causes of involuntary unemployment.

Towards a monetary macroeconomic analysis of inflation and unemployment

In this section we introduce the elements for a new analysis, emphasizing the existence of a disruptive inconsistency between the nature of money, income and capital on one side, and the way transactions leading to the formation of money, income and capital are entered in banks' ledgers on the other. We will show that, because the present accounting system of national payments cannot consistently distinguish between these three fundamental conceptual entities, a pathology arises that engenders both inflation and deflation.

On money and income

Money is a spontaneous acknowledgement of debt issued by banks. It is because banks issue it by using double-entry bookkeeping that money is an acknowledgement of debt. Yet, its emission would be meaningless if the object of this debt was bound to remain money. In other words, the emission of money acquires all its significance only if it is associated with an economic transaction endowing it with a positive value. The idea that money can be issued as a positive amount of income irrespective of production is thus wrong. It would amount to claiming that banks can create a positive value out of thin air. In reality, money is transformed into income only if it is associated with production, that is, once goods and services are given a monetary form and are thus transformed from physical objects into economic products (see Schmitt, 1960 and 1972; Cencini, 2001 and 2005).

Figure 8.1 represents the result of production.

As shown in Figure 8.1, income is the result of a transaction whereby output becomes the real 'content' or 'object' of money. A positive income is the result of production and constitutes the strictest possible relationship

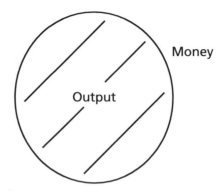

Figure 8.1 Production as the association between money and output

between money and physical output. This means that production generates the income that defines economic output, which is to say that it is through production that money obtains its purchasing power.

From the distinction between money and income we can derive as a first conclusion that economic purchases can be financed only out of positive incomes. Being deprived of any value whatsoever, money as such should never be used to 'finance' a purchase or to cover a financial deficit. The logical distinction between money proper and income should materialize in a distinction between a monetary and a financial department at the banking level, which would guarantee the practical impossibility for money to substitute for income.

Two simple examples show how inflation would arise each time money is issued to 'finance' a purchase or cover a deficit. The first example refers to what would happen if a central bank were to issue money in order to reduce a country's public deficit. The creation of what we could call 'empty' money (that is, a money with no real content derived from production) increases the number of money units available in the country, but leaves the amount of physical output unaltered. As a result, the same output would be distributed over an increased number of money units, leading to the decrease in each money unit's purchasing power (that is, of its real content) (Figure 8.2).

The second example is slightly more complex and refers to the role played by banks as financial intermediaries. The golden rule banks have to follow when lending the income deposited by their customers is that the sum of loans must equal the sum of deposits. Unfortunately, this rule is not enough to avoid the conflation of a monetary emission with banks' financial intermediation.

Let us imagine a commercial bank, B, with a deposit of 100 units of money income, whose object are the goods and services produced by firm F and

Figure 8.2 Inflation as the addition of 'empty money' to income generated by production

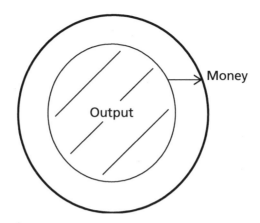

financially deposited on the assets side of the bank's balance sheet. Let us consider a given period of time and suppose that a client of B asks for a loan of 110 money units in order to purchase, at a price of 110, the goods and services produced by F. Would bank B, consistent with the 'golden rule', be allowed to lend 110 money units to its client C? Apparently no, yet it is enough to write down the bookkeeping entries corresponding first to production and then to the payment that B would carry out on behalf of C and to the benefit of F to realize that the loan of 110 money units would not be in contrast with the 'golden rule' (Table 8.1).

The first entry represents the payment of F's costs of production by the bank and the corresponding formation of 100 units of money income. F is entered on the assets side of B's balance sheet, because it is indebted to the bank following the payment made by B on its behalf. Since F's output is the object of F's debt to B, goods and services are financially owned by the bank. On the liabilities side of B's balance sheet we find the income generated by the payment of F's costs of production and owned by income earners, IE. This means that bank B is indebted to IE and this is so because IE are the owners of 100 units of money income deposited with B. The deposit is a loan granted

Table 8.1 Inflation as caused by banks' excessive lending

Bank B

Assets		Liabilities	
(1) Firm F	100	Income earners (IE)	100
(2) Client C	110	Firm F	110

by IE to B, whose object is the product that F owes B, so that income earners are the true initial owners of F's output. This cannot come as a surprise, because the value of money income is precisely given by its purchasing power over current output.

The second entry corresponds to the payment of 110 money units carried out by B to the benefit of F on behalf of C. B's client obtains a loan and spends it in order to purchase F's output; this is why the bank's client is entered on the bank ledger's assets side, while F is entered on its liabilities side. Now, it is the entry of 110 money units on the liabilities side of B's balance sheet that justifies the loan of 110 money units granted by B to its client. The 110 money units earned by F define a deposit formed with B, and it is this deposit that covers the loan of 110 money units.

The 'golden rule' is undoubtedly complied with, yet an inflationary gap of 10 money units is formed that brings about a decrease in each money unit's purchasing power. Indeed, the income created by production has remained equal to 100 money units, and this is what the bank should have lent. The 10 money units lent by B on top of the 100 units of money-income deposited by income earners have no real 'content' at all: it is 'empty' money that derives its purchasing power from that of the 100 money units associated with production.

The distribution of 100 units of income over 110 money units implies a loss of purchasing power for each unit of money, and the cause of this inflationary decrease is the superposition of a monetary emission on a financial intermediation. Indeed, bank B feeds part of its loan through money creation. Up to 100 money units, its loan is a transfer of income, namely a financial intermediation, while the remaining 10 units result from a creation of money.

This example is far from providing an all-encompassing explanation of inflation. The inflationary gap formed because of B's excess lending is indeed bound to be neutralized when C reimburses its debt (technically, the inflationary gap is not cumulative in time) and banks tend to control their lending activity very strictly in order to avoid interbank indebtedness. Yet, this example shows how a monetary disorder may arise out of a structural lack of respect for the logical and factual distinction between money and income. The next fundamental step is to show that inflation and deflation are the twin effects of a process of capital formation in which the essential distinction between money, income and fixed capital goes unrecognized.

The logic of fixed capital formation

As acknowledged by the greatest economists of the past, the first necessary step leading to fixed capital formation is saving. This simply means that in order to have fixed capital goods, part of current income has to be saved and invested in a new production of instrumental goods. If the totality of currently produced income were spent for the final purchase of current output, no fixed capital could be formed and the entire production would consist of consumption goods only. Hence, by subtracting part of current income from consumption, saving creates both a monetary fund that can be invested in the production of instrumental goods and a stock of consumption goods that will be sold in a later period to income earners.

In any monetary economy of production saving required for the formation of fixed capital takes the form of invested profit. Instead of being spent for the final purchase of current consumption goods, part of current income is transferred to firms and used by them to finance a new production. Now, like any other production, that of instrumental goods leads to the formation of a new income. What happens then to the income transferred as profit to firms and invested by them? The only logical answer coherent with the fact that production is at the origin of income is that it is transformed into fixed capital. The production of consumption goods creates the income required for their final purchase, whereas the production of instrumental goods transforms saved up income into fixed capital. At the same time, the new income formed by the production of instrumental goods gives income earners the power to purchase the consumption goods previously stocked by firms.

Let us illustrate this process by a numerical example. Suppose the initial production of consumption goods to be equal to 100 money units. If firms were to sell these goods at the market price of 125 and if income earners were to spend all their income to this effect, firms would obtain 100 money units and give up consumption goods worth 80 money units. The difference between firms' inflows (100 money units) and outflows (goods worth 80 money units), equal to 20 money units, would define their profit. The investment of this profit would have a double effect: it would transform it into a fixed capital equal to 20 money units, and give rise to a new income of 20 money units. Fixed capital would define the monetary face of the newly produced capital goods, while the new income would give IE the right to purchase the 20 money units of consumption goods still unsold by firms.

Table 8.2 The bookkeeping distinction between income and fixed capital and the investment of profit

Bank's financial department (II)

Assets		Liabilities	
(1) Stock of consumption goods	20	Firms	20
(2) Firms	20	Department III	20
(3) Firms (instrumental goods)	20	Income earners	20
Firms (instrumental goods)	20	Department III	20
Stock of consumption goods	20	Income earners	20

Bank's fixed capital department (III)

Assets		Liabilities	
(2) Department II	20	Firms	20

If banks practised double-entry bookkeeping consistently with this logical process of fixed capital formation, the investment of profit would be entered as shown by Table 8.2.

The first thing to observe is the distinction – introduced by Schmitt (1984) – between a financial department (department II) and a department of fixed capital (department III), the first department, which we do not explicitly introduce here, being the money department. Book-entry (1) results from the formation of a profit, owned by firms, whose real object is the product formed as a stock of still unsold consumption goods. The investment by firms of all their profit, equal to 20 money units, gives rise to book-entries (2) and (3), where entry (2) represents the transformation of profit into fixed capital through its transfer from department II to department III, whereas entry (3) shows the formation of a new income generated by the new production of instrumental goods. As a result of the whole process, income earners own the income necessary to purchase the stock of consumption goods and firms own the fixed capital deposited in the third department, whose real object is a set of instrumental goods that will be used to increase physical productivity.

The actual process of capital formation

The substantial gap between the logical and the actual process of capital formation lies in the present lack of a distinction between financial and fixed capital departments. Having failed so far to understand the need for a

Table 8.3 The actual bookkeeping entry relative to fixed capital formation

Bank

Assets		Liabilities	
(1) Stock of consumption goods	20	Firms	20
(2) Firms (instrumental goods)	20	Income earners	20

clear and rigorous conceptual and practical distinction between income and capital, economists and bankers keep entering the transactions that we have described in the previous subsection in one and the same banking department. The bookkeeping entries defining the formation of fixed capital that we can find today in the stylized banks' balance sheet are shown in Table 8.3.

As entry (2) shows, the investment of profit corresponds to its expenditure on the factor market. Profit feeds the payment of the costs incurred by firms for the production of instrumental goods. Instead of being transformed into fixed capital and preserved as such in department III, profit is spent on the factor market. The consequences of this expenditure are the following: (1) instrumental goods are lost to income holders and appropriated by what Schmitt (1984) calls 'disembodied firms'; (2) money units obtained by wage earners are deprived of their physical content.

The presence of disembodied firms characterizes the pathological state of our economic system, where the existence of fixed capital denotes a process of alienation whereby the production of instrumental goods leaves income earners empty handed.

A simple and straightforward question may help to clarify the matter: is it logical for an income transformed into fixed capital to remain available on the financial market? The answer is clearly no. However, this is precisely what happens in the actual system of national payments: the profit invested in the production of instrumental goods reappears as a bank deposit owned by income earners and lent by banks. The result is that fixed capital is spent while it should be saved up in the banks' third department, and a money deprived of its 'real' content is lent on the financial market.

In a textbook for undergraduates the analysis can only aim at clarifying the terms of the problem and provide the conceptual elements required for its further development. We will therefore conclude this chapter by summarizing the remaining steps leading to a full explanation of inflation and unemployment:

1. The empty money formed as a result of the investment of profit is clear evidence of the inflationary character of the actual process of fixed capital formation. Yet inflation settles in when instrumental goods are used in the production of new goods and services and have therefore to be amortized.

2. Amortization, in its strict macroeconomic sense, implies the production of amortization goods and modern monetary macroeconomics shows that, when fixed capital is formed pathologically, amortization has two consequences, namely inflation and overaccumulation of instrumental goods. If fixed capital could accumulate boundlessly, inflation would be a minor disorder, because the loss of money's purchasing power would not impede the substantial rise of our standard of living owing to capital overaccumulation.

3. The problem is that capital has to be remunerated and that this is done out of profits. A constant increase in capital requires a corresponding rise in profits. Now, albeit rising in absolute terms, profits grow at a lower rate than capital, which is why the rate of profit (the ratio between total profit and total capital) has been steadily declining in recent years.

4. The fall in the rate of profit becomes worrisome when it comes to a level close to that of the market rate of interest. From that moment on, national economies have to slow down their capital accumulation, otherwise they would no longer be able to remunerate their capital. The reduction in fixed capital accumulation means that firms must reduce their investment in the production of new instrumental goods. This can be done by investing part of their profit either on the financial market or on the production of new consumption goods. In the first case a rise in unemployment would be the immediate result.

5. If firms were to invest part of their profit in the production of consumption goods, deflation would settle in. Indeed, the supply of consumption goods on the commodity market would increase without being matched by a rise in the income available to finance their purchase. The production of new consumption goods, in this case being financed by the investment of profit, would give rise to empty money, that is, money with zero purchasing power. The difference between total supply (increased by newly produced consumption goods) and total demand (which remains unaltered) defines a deflationary disorder that will inevitably lead to a further increase in unemployment.

6. The solution consists in a reform of the system of national payments and implies the implementation of a bookkeeping distinction between the departments of money, income, and fixed capital.

REFERENCES

Boskin, M.J., E.R. Dulberger and R.J. Gordon et al. (1998), 'Consumer prices, the consumer price index, and the cost of living', *Journal of Economic Perspectives*, **12** (1), 3–26.

Cencini, A. (2001), *Monetary Macroeconomics: A New Approach*, London and New York: Routledge.

Cencini, A. (2005), *Macroeconomic Foundations of Macroeconomics*, London and New York: Routledge.

MacLean, B.K. (2015), 'Quantitative easing', in L.-P. Rochon and S. Rossi (eds), *The Encyclopedia of Central Banking*, Cheltenham, UK and Northampton, MA, USA: Edward Elgar Publishing, pp. 414–16.

Mastromatteo, G. and A. Tedeschi (2015), 'Quantity theory of money', in L.-P. Rochon and S. Rossi (eds), *The Encyclopedia of Central Banking*, Cheltenham, UK and Northampton, MA, USA: Edward Elgar Publishing, pp. 419–22.

Palley, T.I. (1996), *Post Keynesian Economics: Debt, Distribution and the Macro Economy*, London and New York: Macmillan and St. Martin's Press.

Rossi, S. (2001), *Money and Inflation: A New Macroeconomic Analysis*, Cheltenham, UK and Northampton, MA, USA: Edward Elgar Publishing (reprinted 2003).

Rowthorn, R.E. (1977), 'Conflict, inflation and money', *Cambridge Journal of Economics*, **1** (3), 215–39.

Schmitt, B. (1960), *La formation du pouvoir d'achat* [The Formation of Purchasing Power], Paris: Sirey.

Schmitt, B. (1972), *Macroeconomic Theory: A Fundamental Revision*, Albeuve, Switzerland: Castella.

Schmitt, B. (1975), *Théorie unitaire de la monnaie, nationale et international* [Unitary Theory of Money, National and International], Albeuve, Switzerland: Castella.

Schmitt, B. (1984), *Inflation, chômage et malformations du capital* [Inflation, Unemployment and Capital Malformations], Albeuve, Switzerland and Paris: Castella and Economica.

Werner, R.A. (2015), 'Credit easing', in L.-P. Rochon and S. Rossi (eds), *The Encyclopedia of Central Banking*, Cheltenham, UK and Northampton, MA, USA: Edward Elgar Publishing, pp. 121–3.

A PORTRAIT OF BERNARD SCHMITT (1929–2014)

Bernard Schmitt was born in Colmar (France) on 6 November 1929, and died in Beaune (France) on 26 March 2014. After his graduate studies he obtained his PhD in Paris and spent a year in Cambridge, United Kingdom, where he worked with Dennis Robertson, Piero Sraffa and Joan Robinson. He was a Professor of Macroeconomics and Monetary Economics at the Universities of Burgundy (France) and Fribourg (Switzerland) for several decades. His research work has been awarded a silver and a bronze medal by the *Centre National de la Recherche Scientifique* in France.

It was while writing his doctoral dissertation (Schmitt, 1960) that he had his first intuition about the double-entry nature of bank money and the logical distinction between money and income. Through rigorous analysis he was able to show that, since money's purchasing power is generated by production, the identity between output (macroeconomic supply) and income (macroeconomic demand) is the fundamental law on which macroeconomics has to be founded. Income and output are the twin results of production, which means that if a difference appears between macroeconomic demand and supply, it can only be of a pathological nature. It is in his 1984 book, *Inflation, chômage et malformations du capital* (Inflation, Unemployment and Capital Malformations), that Schmitt provides a full analysis of these two pathologies. In what is one of his masterpieces, he shows that today the investment of profit leads to the formation of a fixed capital that is not owned by income holders. This 'expropriation' is caused by a lack of consistency between the actual system of national payments and the logical distinction between money, income and fixed capital. This analysis allowed Schmitt to explain inflation and unemployment as the consequences of fixed capital amortization and to propose a reform to resolve the inconsistency.

The originality and relevance of Schmitt's analysis lies in a truly macroeconomic conception of macroeconomics and in the development of a quantum monetary theory of production and exchange. The concept of quantum time introduced by Schmitt has no parallel in economics. It establishes macroeconomics as a science and provides the foundation for a new approach based on absolute instead of relative exchange.

The other field covered by Schmitt's analysis is that of international payments. Since the 1970s he provided a series of writings on the logical shortcomings of the actual (non-)system of international payments and on a critical assessment of European monetary union. Of a particular interest is his 1975 book on the circuits of national and international money, which was followed by numerous post-Keynesian contributions to the so-called theory of the monetary circuit.

Schmitt's long-lasting research on countries' external debts deserves a central place in his most important contributions. Thanks to an in-depth analysis of the role of money in the payment of a country's deficit, he shows that the sovereign debt crisis that so deeply affects our economies at the time of writing is of an entirely pathological origin due to the imperfect understanding of the principles of international transactions. Developed since the 1970s, this analysis is Schmitt's latest legacy and provides both an explanation of and a remedy for the very formation of countries' sovereign debts.

9

The role of fiscal policy

Malcolm Sawyer

 OVERVIEW

This chapter:

- explains that fiscal policy relates to the balance between government expenditures and tax revenues;

- argues that fiscal policy seeks to set that balance to influence the overall economy – more specifically, but not exclusively, output and employment;

- points out that the need for fiscal policy arises from the perspective, denied by mainstream economists, that the capitalist economy is subject to cyclical fluctuations and unemployment arising from inadequacy of aggregate demand, as discussed in Chapter 7.

 KEYWORDS

- **Automatic stabilizers:** These concern the effects of falling (rising) tax revenues and rising (falling) transfer payments (notably unemployment benefits) on damping down the effects of a fall (rise) in demand on the level of economic activity.
- **Budget deficit:** The difference between government expenditure and tax revenues.
- **Crowding in:** This reflects the post-Keynesian view that an increase in government expenditure leads to a higher level of private demand, stimulating economic activity.
- **Crowding out:** This reflects the mainstream view that an increase in government expenditure, increasing the budget deficit, would reduce investment expenditure (through, for example, upward pressure on interest rates) and other forms of private expenditure.
- **Fiscal policy:** The economic policy with regard to the size of the budget deficit and its impact on the level of economic activity.

Why are these topics important?

Fiscal policy is concerned with public expenditures on the one side, and tax revenues on the other, and more specifically about the balance between them, that is, the overall position of the government budget whether in deficit or surplus.

The government budget position is the difference between government expenditures and tax revenues. When expenditures are greater than tax revenues, governments have a deficit, whereas a surplus occurs when governments raise more tax revenues than they spend.

Government expenditures can be divided into four different categories: (1) current expenditures on goods, services and employment; (2) capital expenditures (often referred to as public investment); (3) transfer payments (social security and welfare payments); and (4) interest on debt. Dividing fiscal expenditures into these four categories is relevant to fiscal policy for the following three reasons. First, both current and capital expenditures are of particular importance, as each of these expenditures leads directly to the use of resources including labour. Second, these distinctions enable us to set up the primary budget position, which is defined as the difference between government expenditures and tax revenues, but excluding interest payments. Third, the argument is often made that governments can borrow for investment purposes but not to cover current expenditures. In doing so, critics try to apply the same analysis to public finances that is discussed with respect to private finances. In other words, they attempt to compare the government to a firm (or a household) that borrows for investment in the hope that the investment will yield future profits. Current expenditures plus transfers and interest payments, minus tax revenues, then give the current budget position. For the purposes of fiscal policy it is the overall deficit that is relevant.

Is there a need for fiscal policy?

Fiscal policy affects the level of aggregate demand in the economy, and thereby the level of economic activity. In turn there can be a range of reasons (stated or unstated) for concern over the level of aggregate demand – for its impacts on the levels of unemployment and employment, the current account position, and so on. Discussion of fiscal policy has to involve (often implicitly) a theoretical framework of how a capitalist economy operates. A simple illustration of this relates to the question of whether a market economy is stable or is subject to major fluctuations and whether there are strong forces within such an economy that quickly move the economy to full employment. If the answer to these questions is stable and yes, then there is little need for fiscal policy. If the answer is lacking stability and no, then there is considerable need for fiscal policy.

We focus here on a closed economy, that is, one that does not engage in international trade, to highlight the key issues. There is a basic relationship between the private sector and the public sector, which states:

$$S^a - I^a = G^a - T^a \tag{9.1}$$

where S is private saving, I private investment (the left-hand side of the equation can thus be referred to as net private saving), G is government expenditures and T tax revenues. Government expenditures here include current expenditures, public investment, social transfers and interest payments on public debt. The equation can be viewed as a national income accounts identity when it refers to outcomes. This is done by adding the superscript a after each variable, signifying outcome (often referred to as an ex post relationship).

The relationship between the public sector (the government) and the private sector (firms and households) can also be considered as an equilibrium relationship when, for example, savings behaviour is the desired behaviour, given other conditions such as the level of income and interest rate. This is written as:

$$S(r,Y) - I(r,Y) = G - t(Y) \tag{9.2}$$

where r is a representative interest rate, Y is income, tax revenues, represented by the tax function $t(Y)$, are related to the level of income (for given tax rates, t), and G is government planned expenditures. Hence, in this equation, both savings and investment are made to depend on the rate of interest and on income, and $G - t(Y)$ is the government budget.

It can easily be seen that if the left-hand side of the equation is zero, then the right-hand side will be zero. Hence, if intended saving and investment are in balance, then the public deficit would be zero.

The neoclassical model

In Figures 9.1a and 9.1b, two representations of equation (9.2) are provided. In the first representation (Figure 9.1a), desired savings and desired investment are each drawn as a function of the rate of interest, with the level of

Figure 9.1a Portrayal of the 'loanable funds' approach

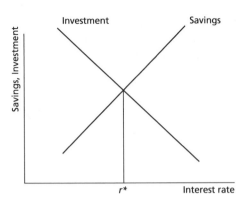

Figure 9.1b Investment and savings linked with income

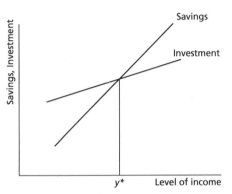

income held constant at the full employment level, with the savings function shown as a positive relationship to the rate of interest, and the investment function as a negative relationship. In other words, as the rate of interest rises, the desire to save increases but the desire to invest decreases. There is then seen to be an equilibrium interest rate r^* (sometimes referred to as the 'natural rate of interest'), which would ensure the equality between savings and investment at full employment, Y^*.

In the second representation (Figure 9.1b), savings and investment are now drawn as a function of income. Now, both functions are positively sloped, which means that as income increases, both savings and investment would increase, although at different rates. Given the slopes, it is clear that as income increases, savings would increase faster. Nevertheless, a given r^* would ensure an equilibrium level of income, Y^* as indicated.

The key proposition from the mainstream is that full employment income can be obtained through a suitable choice of the interest rate. In other words, there is only one level of interest rate, that is, the 'natural' level r^*, which guarantees full employment income, Y^*. The general level of interest rates is guided by the policy rate of interest set by the central bank, and the achievement of an interest rate corresponding to r^* would depend on central bank decisions. It requires that r^* is indeed positive, as it is generally difficult to generate negative interest rates (the nominal interest rate is generally regarded as subject to a lower bound of zero, and negative real interest rates then require significant inflation). But there is another strong assumption built into this analysis, namely, that the tendencies to save and to invest are broadly similar.

The post-Keynesian critique

In the post-Keynesian view, three points stand out. The first is that savings and investment are determined by many factors, of which the rate of interest is only a minor player. Insofar as figures such as Figures 9.1a and 9.1b have any validity, the intersection of S and I may often take place at a negative (hence unobtainable) rate of interest. The situation over the past few years in many industrialized countries (which continues at the time of writing in late 2014) shows this: interest rates have been close to zero, yet there are high levels of unemployment. The second point is that interest rates are not set by what is termed the 'loanable funds' approach (in effect represented in Figures 9.1a and 9.1b), but by the actions of the central bank and by 'liquidity preference' (that is, the relative preference for more liquid assets such as money compared to less liquid ones), as discussed in Chapters 4 and 6.

The third point is that different people undertake different saving and investment decisions (households and firms in the case of savings, firms in the case of investment) and that the forces influencing these decisions are quite different. There is little reason to think that the general tendencies to save and to invest will be in alignment. Let us illustrate this as follows. The purpose of investment is to make additions to the capital stock in order to produce and sell a higher output (and making higher profits in the process). Investment enables the capital stock to grow broadly in line with the growth of expected demand, and the underlying growth rate of the economy. If the trend growth of expected demand is g, and the capital–output ratio is v, then the growth of the capital stock required would be gv (see Appendix A for details). For instance, if the expected rate of growth of the economy is 2.5 per cent, and the capital–output ratio is 4, then we expect a net-investment-to-GDP ratio of 10 per cent. Gross investment, however, would be larger, as it covers the depreciation of existing capital assets.

Now, consider savings. First, let us write the savings function of the economy as a whole – that is, the savings of both households and firms (households save out of their disposable income, and firms save through retaining a part of their profits).

The saving function can be written as:

$$S = s_w W + s_p P \qquad (9.3)$$

where W is wages and P profits, with s_w and s_p the propensities to save out of wages and profits respectively. It may be expected that the saving propensity of households out of wages would be rather lower than the saving propensity of firms out of profits.

Dividing this equation through by Y, we get the average propensity to save, which is:

$$S/Y = s_w(W/Y) + s_p(P/Y) \qquad (9.4)$$

One feature of particular interest is that the average propensity to save depends on the distribution of income between wages and profits. Since $s_p > s_w$, the average propensity to save is expected to be higher with a larger share of profits in national income. But the major argument to understand is the lack of reasons to believe that the propensity to save and the propensity to invest are aligned. What would then be the result of a lack of alignment? In this case, the excess of savings over investment would create a downward deflationary spiral: in the circular flow of income, leakages would exceed injections, and income would fall. When the share of profits increases (at the expense of the share of wages), as happened in many countries in the past decade or so, this can give rise to a shortfall of demand as the average propensity to save rises.

A crucial question regarding budget deficits and their impact on economic activity is how would savings and investment intentions respond to government expenditures, tax rates and the size of the budget deficit? In fact, many of the differences between mainstream and post-Keynesian views come precisely from the answers given to this question. According to the mainstream, increased budget deficits would lead to 'crowding out': increased public expenditures would lead to a direct decrease in private expenditures; households would save more (consume less) and firms would invest less in response to an announced intention to increase the budget deficit, then there would be little if any stimulus to economic activity.

The post-Keynesian perspective, however, is quite different: an increase in government expenditures can have 'crowding in' effects. It works like this:

increases in public expenditures stimulate investment through its direct effects on the level of demand, and its indirect effects on opportunities for investment. It also stimulates consumer expenditures; as a result, economic activity would increase.

How can we explain this stark difference between the two approaches? An important part of the mainstream view comes from the idea of what is called the 'Ricardian equivalence', which can be expressed as follows. A budget deficit involves borrowing and the accumulation of public debt, which in turn has implications for future interest payments on the public debt and the repayment of the principal. In other words, any deficits incurred today must be reimbursed at some point in the future. To pay the deficit, the government may sell bonds, and those who have lent to the government will have acquired assets (bonds) and will benefit from the interest payments on these bonds in the future. But on the other side, the government now has a liability (bonds) and obligations to pay interest on these bonds for many years. Taxpayers anticipate that there will be future tax obligations to meet these interest payments, and as a result taxpayers will be worse off. They will respond to that by reducing their expenditures today. The full Ricardian equivalence occurs when the taxpayers' response is so strong that they cut back on their consumer expenditure to the extent that it matches the stimulating effect of the increase in public expenditure that had given rise to the higher budget deficit. In the end, the net effect on the economy is nil: there is no multiplier effect.

The mainstream view had been extended even beyond Ricardian equivalence to argue for 'expansionary fiscal consolidation'. This was the idea that a planned reduction in the budget deficit would have such an impact on confidence and interest rates that private expenditure would increase and do so more than the reduction in public expenditure. Overall expenditures and hence economic activity would expand.

It cannot be denied that a rise in investment expenditures, for example, will lead to a decline in the budget deficit – consider equation (9.1). But the 'expansionary fiscal consolidation' proposition reverses the causality and argues that it is a decline in budget deficits that leads to a rise in investment expenditure, which more than compensates for the decline in public expenditure or increase in tax rates.

The post-Keynesian proposition, however, would be that when there is a revival in investment activity then the budget deficit declines. The revival in investment activity can come from a variety of sources including a rise in confidence and 'animal spirits', opening up of new technological opportunities, or the recognition that investment is inherently cyclical. Further, attempts to reduce a budget deficit through austerity programmes may well be counterproductive: declines in public investment on infrastructure and declines in employment levels are not conducive to higher investment.

The role of automatic stabilizers

Fiscal policy operates as an automatic stabilizer in that it helps to mitigate the effects of fluctuations in economic activity. When economic activity falls and unemployment rises, then tax revenues (being based on income and sales) decline, and some social transfers such as unemployment insurance benefits rise. The decline in tax revenues and the rise in social transfers help to limit the fall in economic activity.

The scale of budget deficits will move with fluctuations in economic activity. Lower economic activity will widen the budget deficit as tax revenues fall and social transfers rise; higher economic activity will narrow the budget deficit (or increase budget surplus).

Estimates suggest that a 1 per cent lower output is associated with a rise in budget deficit of the order of 0.5 per cent of GDP. The fall in tax revenues cushions the fall in economic activity (as compared with what would happen without taxation). The degree of cushioning would depend on how tax revenues responded to changes in economic activity – this depends on the progressivity of the tax system. A progressive tax system is one in which, taking the full range of taxes into account, higher-income individuals pay more tax relative to their income compared with lower-income individuals. In a progressive tax system, tax revenues would rise faster than income.

While automatic stabilizers can damp down the fluctuations in economic activity, they do not eliminate them. Automatic stabilizers can be augmented by discretionary changes: for example, when there is the prospect of a downturn, government expenditures are increased and tax rates decreased, and the downturn contained or eliminated. The idea that fiscal policy should operate in this way became seen as 'fine-tuning'. As such, it ran into a range of criticisms from mainstream economists.

First, it relies on accurate forecasting of future fluctuations in economic activity, so that changes in fiscal policy can be implemented in response. Second, if fine-tuning was used, it would impact economic activity in such a way that the outcome would differ from that forecast, and thereby it becomes impossible to validate the forecasts. Third, there would be also a number of lags: lags in recognizing what is happening to economic activity, lags in decision-making, lags in the implementation of the decision, and lags in the impact of the decisions on economic activity. These lags can mean that the impact of the policy arrives too late. There is though some inevitable degree of fine-tuning involved with fiscal policy in the sense that budget decisions are made on an annual basis (and sometimes more frequently).

Given the criticism above, two questions arise here. The first is whether it is worthwhile seeking to reduce the degree of economic fluctuations. After all, it has been argued that the social welfare gains from reducing (eliminating) fluctuations are rather small. The simple reason for this thinking is that with fluctuations, sometimes output is 'too high' and sometimes 'too low', but they broadly cancel out over the cycle.

In contrast, post-Keynesians argue that not only can fluctuations be substantial (witness the 'Great Recession' starting in 2007–08) but also that full employment is at best reached at the top of the economic cycle, and attempts at limiting the scale of fluctuations would only result in lifting the average levels of output and employment.

The second question asks whether the automatic stabilizers can be enhanced. As hinted above, a more progressive tax regime would raise the power of the automatic stabilizers: a rise in economic activity would increase tax revenues more substantially, and in the other direction a fall in economic activity would reduce tax revenues substantially and cushion the effects of the fall in demand. A further step could be building in some automatic variations in the tax rates: for instance, social security rates could be linked with the level of economic activity. For example, when the unemployment rate rises by more than a prespecified amount in a quarter, the social security contribution rates would be reduced in the following quarter in order to provide a boost to demand and lower the cost of employing labour.

Functional finance and the post-Keynesian approach to fiscal policy

The post-Keynesian approach to fiscal policy is particularly based on the ideas of Abba Lerner and Michał Kalecki (see a profile of Kalecki at the end of this chapter). It is based on two pillars. The first concerns what should be the purposes of fiscal policy and budget positions. In Lerner's words (1943, p. 355), we should reject 'the principle of trying to balance the budget over a solar year or any other arbitrary period'. From this point of view, the purpose of fiscal policy is first and foremost to pursue a sustained and high level of economic activity and to move the economy as close as possible to full employment. Budgets should not be balanced for the sake of balancing them. Of particular importance, therefore, is the objective we set for fiscal policy.

Lerner's reference to the time period ('a solar year or any other arbitrary period') is also relevant, because while most economists would accept that in the face of an economic downturn governments should not seek to balance the budget in the year concerned, mainstream economists would generally argue that over the business cycle the budget should be balanced. This can be alternatively expressed, and a common idea now is that the cyclically adjusted budget (often referred to as the 'structural budget') should be balanced. Irrespective of whether we balance over a year or a business cycle, such policies are harmful to economic activity and employment.

An example of the view of balancing a budget over a business cycle is the Stability and Growth Pact of the European Monetary Union, which states that the public budget should be balanced over the business cycle with an upper limit of 3 per cent of GDP for the fiscal deficit in any year. In the so-called 'Fiscal Compact' (formally the Treaty on Stability, Coordination and Governance) agreed to by most member countries of the European Union, this has been amended to read a balanced 'structural budget'.

The second pillar is that an unbalanced budget will generally be required to correspond to full employment. The more usual case would be that a budget deficit will be required in this regard, which from equations (9.1) and (9.2) would correspond to a situation where saving intentions tend to exceed investment. The case where a budget surplus would be required is not ruled out, and of course would correspond to investment intentions exceeding savings.

Figure 9.2 shows the budget positions for some major countries (and for the countries of the European Union as a whole) since 1998.

Two clear pictures arise from Figure 9.2. First, what is apparent is that the budget position varies considerably over time; many of these variations are related to the business cycle – notice particularly the sharp rise in public deficits around 2008 and 2009 as the 'Great Recession' struck. Second, the budget position is more often in deficit than it is in surplus: budget deficits are the norm. Indeed, if they were not the norm, then the scale of public debt would tend to zero. The persistence of budget deficits could be interpreted, as done by the mainstream, as the profligate nature of governments,

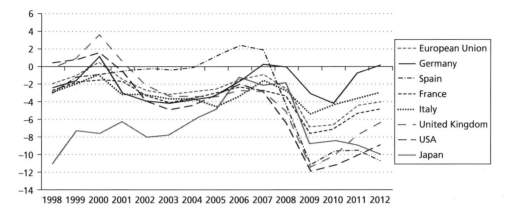

Source: Calculated from Eurostat data.

Figure 9.2 Budget deficits as a percentage of GDP in selected countries, 1998–2012

since a budget deficit means that more public services are being provided than is paid for by tax revenues. The alternative interpretation, however, is that budget deficits are generally required to sustain reasonable levels of economic activity, even though full employment itself was not achieved in general. In the countries in Figure 9.2 there is little (or no) evidence that there was overheating of their economies during the years of public deficits. Indeed, to the contrary, public deficits are larger in years of 'underheating', and fall or become surpluses when the economy booms.

In terms of Figure 9.3 (the foreign sector is omitted for convenience), equilibrium between savings and investment would lead to a level of income $Y^\wedge$.

With saving intentions exceeding investment intentions, a budget deficit would be required to reach full employment income Y^*. The 'functional finance' approach would advocate seeking to set the fiscal policy and budget position of the government such that full employment income is attained. The budget deficit would be the dotted line from A to B. It can be noted that savings and investment would be higher with a budget deficit than without it. When, say, the desires to investment change, represented by a shift in the investment schedule in Figure 9.3, then the required budget deficit would also change.

Answering the critics

When fiscal policy is operated from a 'functional finance' perspective, then many of the objections raised against the use of budget deficits fall. The first is the 'crowding out' argument – that budget deficit and government

Figure 9.3 Illustrating the power of fiscal policy

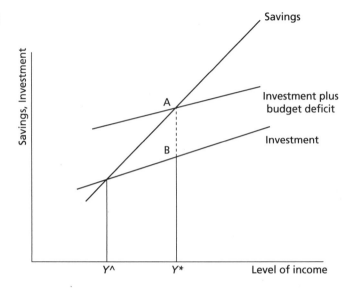

expenditure 'crowd out' private sector economic activity. But crowding out can only occur in situations of full employment: if the economy is operating at full employment, then more employed people in the public sector must necessarily come from the private sector. Society would then have to judge and argue over whether public sector activity is more or less beneficial than private sector activity. But full employment remains at best an illusive dream, and unemployment is the usual economic condition. In these circumstances, there is no crowding out: public sector activity in fact 'crowds in' private sector activity. Public sector employment is thus higher; the wages of the public sector employees are spent and that creates further employment in the private sector.

Another frequently heard argument against a budget deficit is that debt is being accumulated that will be a burden to our children and grandchildren. The government debt takes the form of bonds paying interest, and these bonds are assets for the members of the public who own them. The interest payments on government debt are a transfer from taxpayers to bond-holders.

A frequently asked question in connection with a budget deficit is: 'Where is the money coming from?' There are two aspects to this question. First, any expenditure, whether by individuals, firms or government, can only take place if there is prior possession of spending power – that is, money. But since the government holds an account with the central bank, it can spend from that account through the issuance of central bank money, which is then spent by the government.

The second part can be termed the 'funding of the deficit'. At the end of an accounting period, the government's accounts (in this regard similar to any individual's) obey the requirements, namely that expenditures equal receipts plus borrowing. The government borrows in the form of issue and sale of bonds, and this may change the monetary base (that is, money issued by the central bank, which is the sum of cash and notes held by the public and reserves held by banks with the central bank; see Chapter 4). The consolidated balance sheet of government including the central bank would read as follows:

$$G - T = \Delta B + \Delta M \qquad (9.5)$$

where Δ signifies a change in the relevant variable, G is government expenditures, T is total tax receipts, so $G - T$ is the public sector deficit; B is the supply of bonds, and M is the monetary base. Note that the government sells bonds but some of these bonds will be bought by the central bank through open-market operations.

Now, can we explain how the public deficit is funded? To answer this question, we must understand what individuals do with their savings. On the private sector side (firms and households), savings are necessarily held in a variety of assets: financial assets, which include deposits with banks and other financial institutions, bonds, or shares in corporations. Much of the savings will be lent to other parts of the private sector, for instance households are lending to firms, sometimes directly and more often indirectly. But what happens when saving intentions exceed investment intentions? At that point, the saving intentions can only be realized if the government runs a budget deficit, which will generate bonds that households can then purchase. Indeed, in the absence of a budget deficit there would not be an outlet for the excess savings.

Thus, when a budget deficit is operated along functional finance lines, the conditions in which a budget deficit would be required are precisely the conditions in which there is the potential availability of funds. But these funds can only be realized if there is a budget deficit. This point was well made by Kalecki (1990, p. 360): 'Thus the question of how it is possible to increase government expenditure if expenditure on private investment and personal consumption is cut is answered by the fact that there will always be such an increase in incomes as to create an increase in savings equal to the increase in the budget deficit'. In other words, the public deficit generates the necessary savings to fund it. Thus it cannot be argued that public borrowing will place upward pressure on interest rates.

Of course, a budget deficit leads to borrowing and hence to a rise in the outstanding debt of government. This raises two issues: first, there is the possibility of escalating debt; second, the budget deficit could become unsustainable. But there is no reason to believe that either statement is true, and here is why (see Appendix B for the algebra to support this analysis). First, consider a deficit relative to GDP of d, which we can write as a debt ratio (to GDP) of $b = d/g$, where g is the nominal rate of economic growth. In other words, if there is a budget deficit of 3 per cent of GDP, this leads to a debt ratio of 60 per cent if the nominal GDP growth rate is 5 per cent; that is, $0.03/0.6 = 0.5$. If $b = d/g$, we can rewrite this as $d = bg$, which will be useful below.

However, what is relevant for the level of demand and the one that appears in the equations above is the overall budget, which can be written as $d = pd + ib$, where pd is primary deficit (negative if it is a surplus) and i is the interest rate, so ib is the interest payment the government must pay on its level of debt. Recall that the primary deficit is government expenditures minus tax revenues. So when government expenditures are greater than tax revenues, pd is positive, which means a deficit.

Rearranging, we can write that $pd = d - ib$. Recall from above that $d = bg$, so we can write $pd = gb - ib$. This leads us to write $pd = (g - i)b$: there would be a primary deficit only when the growth rate of nominal GDP is greater than the interest rate, and a primary surplus when the rate of interest exceeds the nominal GDP growth rate. When the growth rate and the interest rate are equal then the primary budget would be balanced, and in effect the government would be borrowing to cover interest payments.

Second, a sustainable public deficit as just indicated may involve a primary surplus, deficit or balance. The primary budget is the budget excluding interest payments. This could be regarded as a summary statement of what the government spends on goods and services and transfer payments relative to the tax revenues raised: the former represents the benefits provided to citizens and the latter the costs involved. This view clearly places no value on the interest payments received but which form an income so far as the bondholders are concerned.

The key point here is that fiscal policy should be set to achieve a high and sustainable level of demand in the economy rather than seeking to achieve a balanced budget. As shown here when fiscal policy is used in that manner, the arguments deployed against fiscal policy and budget deficits are invalid.

Conclusion

The essential argument here is that in an economy in which private demand fluctuates and is insufficient to provide full employment, fiscal policy has a crucial role in dampening the fluctuations and in providing sufficient demand to achieve high levels of employment. But while the use of fiscal policy is a necessary condition for high levels of employment, it is not a sufficient condition.

 REFERENCES

Kalecki, M. (1944), 'Three ways to full employment', in *The Economics of Full Employment*, Oxford, UK: Blackwell, pp. 39–58.

Kalecki, M. (1990), *Collected Works of Michał Kalecki, Volume 1*, Oxford, UK: Clarendon Press.

Lerner, A. (1943), 'Functional finance and the federal debt', *Social Research*, **10** (1), 38–51.

Appendix A

The relationship between (capacity) output and capital stock is given by $K = vY$; hence $\Delta K = v\Delta Y$, where Δ is the change in the corresponding variable. Then $\Delta K/Y = v\Delta Y/Y$, and since (net) investment (I) is the change in the capital stock, this gives the share of (net) investment in output $I/Y = gv$.

Appendix B

The budget deficit can be written as $D = PD + iB$, where D is the overall deficit, PD is the primary deficit (negative if there is a surplus), i is the interest rate on public debt.

The change in the debt ratio is given by $\frac{d}{dt}\left(\frac{B}{Y}\right) = \frac{1}{Y}\frac{dB}{dt} - \frac{B}{Y^2}\frac{dY}{dt} = \frac{1}{Y}D - \frac{B}{Y}\frac{1}{Y}\frac{dY}{dt}$ where Y is the level of income since the change in debt is equal to the public deficit (including interest payments) and the debt ratio is stable when the change in the ratio is zero, which would imply $d - bg = 0$ and hence $b = d/g$. The overall budget deficit can be written $d = pd + ib$, where pd is the primary deficit (negative if a surplus) and i is interest payment on debt. Then $d = pd + ib$, hence $pd = (g - i)b$: there would be a primary deficit when the nominal GDP growth rate is greater than the interest rate, and a primary surplus when the rate of interest exceeds the nominal GDP growth rate. When the latter rate and the interest rate are equal then the primary budget would be in balance, and in effect the government would be borrowing to cover interest payments.

A PORTRAIT OF MICHAŁ KALECKI (1899–1970)

Michał Kalecki was born in Lodz, in the Russian-occupied Kingdom of Poland in 1899, and died in Poland in 1970. He was self-taught in economics after training in engineering and mathematics. He obtained his first quasi-academic employment in 1929 at the Research Institute of Business Cycles and Prices in Warsaw. Following the award of a Rockefeller Foundation Fellowship, he travelled to Sweden and England, where he remained for the next ten years, including employment during World War II at the Oxford University Institute of Statistics. After working for the International Labour Office in Montreal, Canada, Kalecki was appointed Deputy Director of a section of the economics department of the United Nations Secretariat in New York at the end of 1946, where he stayed until 1954. He returned to Poland in 1955, where he was heavily involved in the debates over the role of decentralization and of workers' councils, the speed of industrialization and the relative size of consumption and investment, and problems of economic development.

Kalecki discovered many of the key ideas of post-Keynesian economics, along with Keynes, both of whom were writing during the 1930s. He developed the ideas that the level of demand was crucial for the level of economic activity, and that fluctuations in investment were a key ingredient in the generation of cycles in economic activity. He also saw that the market power of firms allowed them to charge prices higher than wages (and hence depress real wages, which are the ratio of wages to prices), and thereby influenced the share of profits, since profits depend on the difference between revenue (price times quantity) and wages. He introduced the 'principle of increasing risk', whereby the risk of default on a loan rises with the size of the loan (relative to the own capital of the firm), which helps explain why loans are rationed by banks. His portrayal of a capitalist economy was one in which unemployment and spare capacity were endemic. In light of the 'principle of effective demand', he argued that the economic tools to overcome unemployment were available, but the achievement of sustained full employment would encounter major political and social constraints (Kalecki, 1944).

10

Economic growth and development*

Mark Setterfield

 OVERVIEW

This chapter reviews the historical record of economic growth and Keynesian growth theory.

- It shows that economic growth is a relatively recent phenomenon that has resulted in divergence between the incomes of fast-growing rich economies and slower-growing poorer economies.

- It contrasts supply-led, neoclassical growth with demand-led, Keynesian growth.

- It outlines three Keynesian economic growth theories (Harrodian, Kaleckian and Kaldorian). They are shown to differ according to whether investment spending or export demand is the key 'driver' of demand formation and growth.

- It identifies the properties of Keynesian growth, including the relationship between saving behaviour and economic growth, the effects of income redistribution on GDP growth, the relationship between technical progress and economic growth, and the interaction of supply and demand in the economic growth process.

 KEYWORDS

- **Demand-led growth:** Keynesian macroeconomics suggests that the enlargement of aggregate demand – owing to investment spending or export demand – is a critical determinant of economic growth.
- **Divergence:** The economic growth record shows that rich countries have 'forged ahead' while poor countries have 'fallen behind', increasing global income inequality in the course of growth.
- **Economic growth:** The process by which real income per capita rises over a protracted interval of time.

Why are these topics important?

Economic growth is defined as an increase in real income over a protracted interval of time, say one year. Growth is usually measured as a percentage rate of change of income within a given period of time. For instance, we might say that the economy grew at 3 per cent in one year, meaning that GDP is 3 per cent higher this year than it was at the same time last year.

Of particular interest to economists is the expansion of real per capita income – that is, the growth in income per person. When per capita income expands, everyone becomes better off on average, at least in terms of their ability to consume material goods and services.[1] It is important to note the reference in the previous sentence to individuals being better off *on average*: it need not be the case that *every* individual is better off (or even no worse off) when per capita income rises. This immediately draws attention to the important connection between the growth of income and its *distribution* (between individuals, families and social classes) – a topic we will return to later in this chapter.

Economic development is a broader term that is commonly used to refer to the processes of economic growth and structural change in lower-income or less-developed countries, such as Brazil, Mexico or China. Development economists often look at the broader impacts of economic growth on factors such as health outcomes, demographics and political institutions. The idea that economic growth is also accompanied by wholesale social transformation – including not only the sectoral composition, technology and institutions of the economy itself, but also aspects of civic life such as the division of time between work and home, or the physical location of a country's population – has a longstanding pedigree in economics, which can be traced back to the classical economics of Smith, Malthus, Ricardo and Marx. Since the early twentieth century, however, the study of economic growth has focused more exclusively on the causes of growth narrowly defined, as sustained increases in the level of real per capita income.

The remainder of this chapter is organized as follows. We begin with an overview of the historical growth record. Three salient features of the historical record are emphasized: (1) the extent and unevenness of growth; (2) the unbalanced nature of growth (resulting in structural change, as exemplified by deindustrialization); and (3) fluctuations in the pace of growth over time. The chapter then considers whether growth is a supply-led or demand-led process, contrasting mainstream neoclassical (supply-led) and alternative Keynesian (demand-led) views.

Next, the chapter explores in greater detail the Keynesian (demand-led) view of growth. Harrodian, Kaleckian and Kaldorian growth theories are outlined (named after Roy Harrod, Michał Kalecki, and Nicolas Kaldor), using simple analytics that draw on expenditure multiplier analysis of the sort commonly used in short-run macroeconomics (see Chapter 7). The discussion draws attention to the different sources of autonomous demand that each theory considers to be the key determinant or 'driver' of long-term growth. Various properties of economic growth associated with the Keynesian view of the growth process are then considered. These include the paradox of thrift (an increase in the saving rate is harmful to economic growth), the influence of changes in the distribution of income on growth (including discussion of the possibility that raising the share of profits in total income may be harmful to growth), the relationship between technical progress and growth, and the interaction of supply and demand in long-term growth. Finally, the chapter ends with a portrait of Nicholas Kaldor, one of the progenitors of Keynesian growth theory.

Economic growth: the statistical record

Economic growth is a relatively recent phenomenon, confined to the last few hundred years of human experience. This is clearly illustrated in Figure 10.1, which shows economic growth over the last two millennia in selected countries from five different continents.

It is evident from Figure 10.1 that prior to the eighteenth century there was little evidence of economic growth anywhere. Since then, however, economic growth has taken off around the globe – although exactly *when* and to *what extent* differs markedly between different countries. For instance, the United Kingdom experienced the first Industrial Revolution and exhibited significant signs of growth even before 1800. In countries such as Japan and Brazil, however, economic growth is only really evident during the twentieth century – and whereas Japan has already made up ground on earlier industrializers such as the United Kingdom and the United States, Brazil has not.

These observations draw attention to several properties of the historical growth record associated with the extent and unevenness of growth during the post-seventeenth-century 'growth era'. They suggest that processes of 'forging ahead', 'catching up', and 'falling behind' have marked the growth experience of different economies. Table 10.1 shows the extent of growth over the past two centuries in representative advanced, middle-income, Latin American and Asian economies.

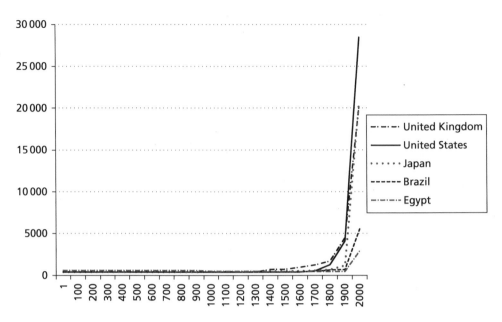

Note: The vertical scale measures per capita GDP in 1990 Geary-Khamis dollars.

Source: Maddison (2008).

Figure 10.1 Economic growth in the very long run

To give some idea of the significance of the growth rates reported in the last two columns of Table 10.1, consider the average annual rate of growth since 1820 in the advanced economies (those that currently have the highest per capita incomes and that, in general, also have the longest histories of economic growth). This growth rate is sufficient to ensure the doubling of real per capita income roughly every 40 years – that is, within the working lifetime of each generation. Table 10.1 also shows the unevenness of the growth experience. Note, for example, that the advanced economies were already the richest economies in 1820, and grew faster than any other group of economies over the ensuing period of almost two centuries. As a result, they were even richer (in both absolute and relative terms) by comparison with the rest of the world by 2007. This is reflected in the figures in Table 10.1, which report the real per capita income of middle-income economies, of Latin American economies, and of Asian economies as a percentage of advanced economy real per capita income. Without exception these figures fall over the period 1820–2007 as a whole. The unevenness of growth is also illustrated in Figure 10.2, which shows the widening gap between the advanced economies and the rest of the world from 1820 to 2007.[2]

Over the past two centuries then, the general growth experience has been one of divergence: the early start and relatively rapid growth of the advanced

Table 10.1 Real per capita income (1990 Geary-Khamis dollars), 1820–2007[a]

	1820	1870	1913	1950	1973	1989	2007	Average annual growth rate 1820–2007 (%)	Average annual growth rate 1950–2007 (%)
Advanced economies[b]	1095	1989	3653	5832	12959	17835	24346	1.65	2.10
Middle-income economies[c]	774 (70.63)	1413 (71.05)	2357 (64.51)	3592 (61.59)	7641 (58.96)	9768 (54.77)	13696 (56.25)	1.53	1.97
Latin American economies[d]	700 (63.88)	997 (50.12)	2332 (63.84)	3173 (54.41)	5432 (41.92)	5981 (33.54)	9367 (38.47)	1.38	1.59
Asian economies[e]	579 (52.87)	559 (28.10)	740 (20.26)	697 (11.94)	1659 (12.80)	3938 (22.08)	9108 (37.41)	1.47	3.78

Notes:

a. Percentages of advanced economies' real per capita GDP are shown in parentheses.
b. Australia, Austria, Belgium, Canada, Denmark, Finland, France, Germany, Italy, Japan, Netherlands, Norway, Sweden, Switzerland, UK, USA.
c. Former Czechoslovakia, Hungary, New Zealand, Portugal, Spain, Former USSR.
d. Argentina, Brazil, Chile, Mexico.
e. Bangladesh, China, India, Indonesia, South Korea, Taiwan.

Sources: Author's calculations based on Maddison (2008), and also Maddison (1991, Table 1.1, pp. 6–7); Maddison (1991, Table 1.5, pp. 24–5).

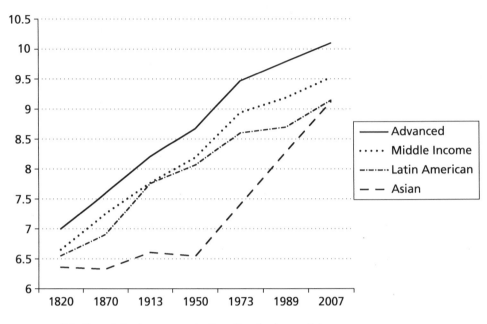

Note: The vertical scale measures natural logarithm of real per capita income.

Source: Author's calculations based on Maddison (2008).

Figure 10.2 Forging ahead, catching up, and falling behind: the general experience

economies has seen them 'forge ahead', while the experience of the rest of the world has involved a process of 'falling behind'.

Table 10.1 and Figure 10.2, however, also show some evidence of 'catching up'. The final column of Table 10.1 shows that since 1950 the Asian economies have grown almost twice as quickly as the advanced economies. As reflected in Figure 10.2, this has closed the relative per capita income gap between these economies since the middle of the twentieth century. As illustrated in Figure 10.3, this catching up process is particularly evident in a small number of very successful economies. A good example is South Korea, which according to Figure 10.3 has grown so rapidly since the 1950s that it has now essentially joined the 'club' of advanced economies that enjoy the highest per capita incomes.

Two other features of the historical growth record that are not evident from Table 10.1 but that are nevertheless worth emphasizing are the tendency of growth to be 'unbalanced' and 'unsteady'. Growth is unbalanced in the sense that different sectors of the economy grow at different rates, with the result that economies experience what is called 'structural change', meaning the composi-

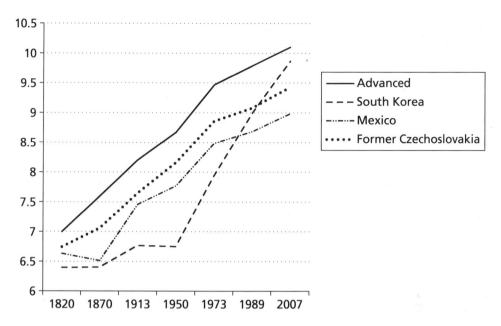

Note: The vertical scale measures natural logarithm of real per capita income.

Source: Author's calculations based on Maddison (2008).

Figure 10.3 Forging ahead, catching up, and falling behind: country-specific experiences

tion of economic activity changes over time. The most obvious symptom of this process is the changing composition of employment. Over the last two centuries, all of the advanced economies in Table 10.1 have experienced a continuous decline in the share of the workforce employed in agriculture and a continuous increase in the employment share of the service sector. These trends have been accompanied by a rise and then – since the middle of the twentieth century – decline of the employment share in the manufacturing sector – a phenomenon referred to as 'deindustrialization'. There is considerable debate as to whether deindustrialization is due to a 'normal' transformation that accompanies growth beyond a certain level of real per capita income (the maturity hypothesis) or, at least in some instances, the result of competitive and/or policy deficiencies, such as persistently overvalued exchange rates (the failure hypothesis).

Growth is said to be unsteady because, rather than being constant, GDP growth rates fluctuate over time. Some economists argue that these fluctuations are sufficiently regular as to constitute cycles. The existence of a Juglar or business cycle is widely accepted, but cycles of longer duration such as Kuznets swings (over periods of 25–30 years) or Kondratieff waves (over periods of 40–50 years) have also been proposed. This means that over, say, 50 years, the economy will experience a long (20–25-year) boom period of fast growth, followed by a similarly long slump period marked by slower growth, before again experiencing a long boom of faster growth, and so on. Other economists argue that fluctuations of longer duration exist, but that these represent irregular and historically specific episodes or phases of growth rather than a well-defined cycle.[3]

Having considered the historical record of growth, let us now turn our attention, in the following section, to the specific factors determining economic growth. We first explore growth from a neoclassical perspective, and then outline the Keynesian view of the growth process.

Supply versus demand in the determination of long-run growth

According to mainstream neoclassical analysis, economic growth is a supply-side process. In other words, it results from the increased availability and/or productivity of the factors of production (such as labour or capital goods), which determine expansion of the economy's potential output.[4] In this view, there is no room for the demand side to play a significant role. Say's Law is supreme: demand will simply adjust to the needs of supply.

Keynesian economists, however, reject Say's Law, arguing that there is no mechanism in the economy that causes aggregate demand to automatically adjust to the level required by potential output. The substance of this proposition in the short run has been discussed earlier in this book (see Chapter 7). For Keynesians, the same issues and concerns carry over to the longer term, with the result that economic growth is understood to result from the growth and development of aggregate demand over time. In other words, changes in aggregate demand drive economic growth.

Figure 10.4 illustrates these opposing views using the concept of a production possibility frontier (PPF). The PPF shows what combination of any two goods the economy can produce when it fully utilizes all of its available resources.

In the neoclassical growth process, increases in the quantity and/or productivity of factors of production (labour or capital goods) push the PPF out, from PPF_1 to PPF_2 and PPF_3. Actual output expands in tandem with these developments (from A to B to C) in accordance with Say's Law ('supply creates its own demand'). In other words, increases in the availability and/or productivity of labour or capital goods means that we both *can* and *do* produce more goods of all kinds.

Figure 10.4
Neoclassical and
Keynesian growth
processes

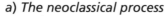

a) The neoclassical process

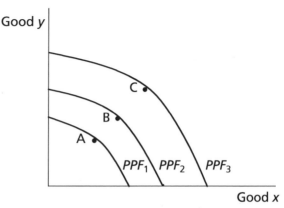

b) The Keynesian process

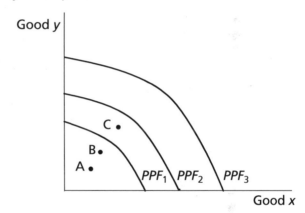

In the Keynesian growth process, increases in the quantity and/or productivity of factors of production again push the PPF out from PPF_1 to PPF_2 and PPF_3. This time, however, *actual* (as opposed to potential) output expands independently of these developments, from A to B to C. This is because aggregate demand – not the availability of capital and labour – explains the level of output at any point in time, and hence the expansion of output (economic growth) over time. In the real world, productive resources will be chronically underutilized as a result of the Keynesian growth process: the economy will almost always operate in the interior of its PPF (that is, at an actual level of output below potential output). In other words, there will usually be unemployed labour and idle capital.

Figure 10.5
Neoclassical and
Keynesian growth
trajectories

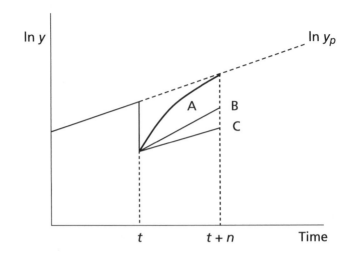

Figure 10.5 illustrates typical growth trajectories produced by the neoclassical and Keynesian growth processes outlined above.

Let us assume that the economy progresses along its potential output path (denoted as $\ln y_p$) until time period t, at which point output is reduced by a recession. In the neoclassical case, output recovers quickly and automatically to its potential level (path A), so that by period $t + n$ the economy is once again on its potential output path. But in the Keynesian case, many possible trend expansion paths are possible after period t. For example, the economy may begin a slow adjustment back towards potential output (path B). Other things being equal, this would mean that the potential output path is eventually regained. However, the economy may expand at or even below potential (along path C, for example). In this case it will experience what is known as 'secular stagnation' – a prolonged period of slow growth coupled with high or even rising unemployment. Given these two possibilities, one important conclusion is that, in the Keynesian case, the growth trajectory subsequent to period t in Figure 10.4 is not predetermined by the economy's potential output, so that there is no guaranteed return to the potential output path by $t + n$ (or any other point in time thereafter).[5]

What forces shape demand formation and growth in the long run?

If the Keynesian growth process is demand driven, the question arises as to what forces shape aggregate demand formation and hence the pace of economic growth in the longer term. Historically, these forces have been idiosyncratic. The US economy provides a good example of this.[6] Following the

Great Depression, almost a decade of weak economic growth ensued during the 1930s, before massive rearmament in response to the advent of World War II eventually boosted demand to the point of fully employing all available resources by the early 1940s. Immediately after the war, the United States experienced a long economic expansion that was propelled and sustained by large-scale infrastructure projects (in particular, the construction of the interstate highways), military spending as a result of the Cold War, and the expansion of international trade. Demand growth faltered during the 1970s and 1980s, but recovered strongly in the mid-1990s, based first on a new wave of investment spending on information and communication technologies following the commercialization of the Internet, and subsequently by residential construction and an associated debt-financed consumer spending boom. Since 2007–08, of course, the dynamics of this demand-generating process have unravelled in the wake of the financial crisis and Great Recession, from which neither demand formation nor (as a result) the US economy have yet recovered.

Demand formation in Europe has followed similar patterns to those observed in the United States since the early twentieth century, although once again the precise forces responsible for the expansion of demand have been idiosyncratic. Demand growth after 1945, for example, was propelled in large measure by reconstruction following World War II, with an important supporting role played by the large-scale expansion of the welfare state. More recently, meanwhile, austerity policies throughout Europe that have focused on cutting public expenditures in response to rising public sector deficits and debt have impeded demand formation in the aftermath of the Great Recession.

Beyond these historical generalities, Keynesian macroeconomic theory suggests that the answer to the question posed at the start of this section ('What shapes demand formation?') boils down to a distinction between internal and external sources of autonomous demand, or, in other words, whether investment or exports can be seen as the main 'driver' of aggregate demand formation and hence economic growth. Hereafter we will refer to these as the 'Harrodian/Kaleckian' and 'Kaldorian' views, respectively, named after the three famous Keynesian economists they are associated with: Roy Harrod, Michał Kalecki and Nicholas Kaldor. These views, and their implications for economic growth, can be developed by building on the simple income determination analysis used to describe the short run (see Chapter 7).

Before we go on, it is important to note that, in what follows, the emphasis is on *aggregate* demand formation and the key sources of autonomous demand responsible for this. But sustainable growth and development may also require a certain *composition* of demand. For example, sufficient investment in specific types of capital (private, public, environmental and social), rather than just sufficient investment in total, may be required. These and other themes related to sustainable growth and development are pursued in detail in Chapter 17.

Keynesian growth theory

Harrodian growth theory

As mentioned in the previous section, Harrodian growth theory is associated with the idea that investment by firms is the key source of autonomous demand responsible for the formation of aggregate demand. The Harrodian view can be developed as follows. We begin with three equations describing investment by firms, saving by households, and the relationship between saving and investment necessary for macroeconomic equilibrium (equality of aggregate supply and demand) in a closed economy with no fiscally active government sector:

$$I = \beta Y_{-1} \tag{10.1}$$

$$S = s_\pi \pi Y \tag{10.2}$$

$$S = I \tag{10.3}$$

In equations (10.1), (10.2) and (10.3), I denotes investment, Y is total output, S is total saving by households, and π is the profit share of income. Equation (10.1) is an investment function in which investment increases (with a lag) in response to rising output. This is known as the 'accelerator effect'. It suggests that firms invest in order to ensure that their productive capacity keeps pace with economic expansion. Equation (10.2) describes household saving behaviour. Note that saving takes place out of profit income only (at a rate determined by the propensity to save out of profits, s_π): workers are assumed to spend all of their (wage) income, so they do not save. This simplifying assumption captures the idea that wage earners are generally among the less affluent households in the economy (associated with the bottom 80 per cent of the size distribution of income), and therefore have the highest marginal propensities to spend. Equation (10.3) states the condition necessary for macroeconomic equilibrium.

Combining equations (10.1), (10.2) and (10.3), we arrive at:

$$s_\pi \pi Y = \beta Y_{-1}$$

and solving this expression for Y gives us:

$$Y = \frac{\beta}{s_\pi \pi} Y_{-1} \qquad (10.4)$$

By subtracting Y_{-1} from both sides of equation (10.4), we arrive at the following expression for the *change* in output over time – which, in this simple framework, we can associate with economic growth:

$$\Delta Y = \left(\frac{\beta}{s_\pi \pi} - 1 \right) Y_{-1} \qquad (10.5)$$

Now suppose that $Y_{-1} = Y_0$ and that $\Delta Y > 0$. It follows that we will observe $Y_1 > Y_0$, which, according to equation (10.5), will cause ΔY to increase subsequently. Alternatively, if $Y_{-1} = Y_0$ and $\Delta Y < 0$, then we will find that $Y_1 < Y_0$ and, in equation (10.5), ΔY will decrease from one period to the next. This suggests that investment-driven growth is 'unsteady'. As noted earlier in this chapter, the growth rate is unsteady if it varies over time, increasing or decreasing from period to period rather than remaining constant. Note that if the economy *alternates* between increasing and decreasing growth, then economic growth will fluctuate in a cyclical fashion. The economy will then experience booms and slumps marked by faster and slower growth (respectively) over protracted intervals, giving rise to the business cycles, Kuznets swings, and/or Kondratieff waves described earlier.

Kaleckian growth theory

Kaleckian growth theory is also associated with the idea that investment by firms is the main 'driver' of aggregate demand formation. The Kaleckian view can be developed by once again beginning with three equations that describe investment by firms, saving by households, and the relationship between saving and investment necessary in equilibrium:

$$I = \alpha + \beta Y + \gamma \pi Y \qquad (10.6)$$

The difference between the Harrodian and Kaleckian models boils down to the investment equation (10.6), which now suggests that investment increases in response to rising output, Y, and rising profits, πY. Note that in equation (10.6) investment can also vary independently of either output or profits owing to variations in α. This captures the influence on investment spending of 'animal spirits', that is, the willingness of firms to act spontaneously in the face of fundamental uncertainty regarding the future.[7] Equations

(10.2) and (10.3) again describe household saving behaviour and the conditions necessary for macroeconomic equilibrium, respectively.

Combining equations (10.2), (10.3) and (10.6), we arrive at:

$$s_\pi \pi Y = \alpha + \beta Y + \gamma \pi Y$$

and solving this expression for Y results in the following expression:

$$Y = \frac{\alpha}{(s_\pi - \gamma)\pi - \beta} \tag{10.7}$$

It follows from equation (10.7) that the *change* in output over time – and hence economic growth – can be described as follows:

$$\Delta Y = \frac{\Delta \alpha}{(s_\pi - \gamma)\pi - \beta} \tag{10.8}$$

Equation (10.8) tells us that changes in 'animal spirits' – the exogenous determinant of investment spending in equation (10.6) – drive the expansion of aggregate demand and hence output.

Kaldorian growth theory

One of the hallmarks of Kaldorian growth theory is its insistence on open-economy analysis – an approach that ultimately identifies export demand as the critical source of autonomous demand guiding aggregate demand formation and growth. The Kaldorian view can be developed by first extending equation (10.3) to allow for international trade. In this case, the macroeconomic equilibrium condition can be stated as follows:

$$S + M = I + X \tag{10.9}$$

where M and X denote imports and exports, respectively. Imports are added to savings because they represent an additional 'leakage' from the circular flow of income (that is, a reduction in spending on domestically produced goods and services). Exports are added to investment, meanwhile, because they represent an additional 'injection' into the circular flow of income (that is, an increase in spending on domestically produced goods and services).

Now suppose that imports depend on the level of income:

$$M = mY \tag{10.10}$$

where m is the propensity to import. This suggests that as our income rises, we will purchase more goods produced abroad.

If we retain the descriptions of saving and investment behaviour in equations (10.1) and (10.2), then substituting equations (10.1), (10.2) and (10.10) into equation (10.9) gives us the following equation:[8]

$$s_\pi \pi Y + mY = \beta Y + X$$

Solving this last expression for Y produces the following equation:

$$Y = \frac{X}{s_\pi \pi + m - \beta} \qquad (10.11)$$

It follows from equation (10.11) that the *change* in output over time – which we can once again associate with economic growth – can be described as follows:

$$\Delta Y = \frac{\Delta X}{s_\pi \pi + m - \beta} \qquad (10.12)$$

Equation (10.12) tells us that the expansion of export demand drives the expansion of aggregate demand and hence output. If we introduce Kaldor's assumption that the saving-to-income and investment-to-income ratios ($s_\pi \pi$ and β, respectively) are roughly equal,[9] equation (10.12) becomes:

$$\Delta Y = \frac{\Delta X}{m} \qquad (10.13)$$

Note that the focus on the right-hand side of equation (10.13) is exclusively on features of international trade (m and X) as determinants of the expansion of output. This is representative of Kaldorian 'balance of payments constrained growth theory', which is explored in detail in Chapter 13.

Summary

Table 10.2 summarizes the main features of each of the three strands of Keynesian growth theory – Harrodian, Kaleckian and Kaldorian – described in detail above.

Properties of Keynesian growth theory

The three models presented in the previous section all share important features. One of the key features of short-run Keynesian analysis is the 'paradox of thrift' – the proposition that an increase in the saving rate will depress aggregate demand and hence income and, in the process, leave total saving unchanged

Table 10.2 A summary of the main features of Keynesian growth theory

	Key equation	Main 'driver' of growth	Nature of growth outcomes
Harrodian model	Equation (10.5) $$\Delta Y = \left(\frac{\beta}{s_\pi \pi} - 1 \right) Y_{-1}$$	Investment	Unsteady (growth will vary from period to period, possibly producing cycles)
Kaleckian model	Equation (10.8) $$\Delta Y = \frac{\Delta \alpha}{(s_\pi - \gamma)\pi - \beta}$$	Investment	Steady (constant rate of growth)
Kaldorian model	Equation (10.13) $$\Delta Y = \frac{\Delta X}{m}$$	Exports	Steady (constant rate of growth)

(see Chapter 7). The analysis in the previous section reveals that, according to Keynesian growth theory, this result has a counterpart in the longer term, when an increase in the saving rate will depress demand formation and hence growth. To see this, notice that any increase in the saving rate, s_π, causes the terms on the right-hand sides of equations (10.5), (10.8) and (10.12) to become smaller. This, in turn, reduces the rates of expansion of income on the left-hand sides of these equations. The rationale for this result is that the higher saving rate reduces the increments in consumption spending that are associated with any autonomous demand stimulus (regardless of its source), which reduces the rate of expansion of income. What all this suggests is that, in and of itself, thrift is not a virtue if the objective of society is to raise the rate of economic growth. This has contemporary relevance, because some Keynesian economists believe that prior to the onset of the Great Recession, *falling* saving rates in the United States (which according to the paradox of thrift will increase the rate of economic growth) helped offset the negative growth effects associated with rising income inequality (discussed in detail below).[10] In other words, economic growth in the United States during the 1990s and 2000s was higher than it would otherwise have been, because of the effects of the paradox of thrift.

A second key feature of Keynesian growth theory is the interplay between distribution and economic growth. Our examination of the historical growth record has already revealed that, owing to the pattern of income divergence that results from 'forging ahead' and 'falling behind', the process of economic growth is accompanied by changes in the distribution of income, as (on an international scale) the 'rich get richer' both absolutely and relatively.

However, Keynesian growth theory goes one step further, suggesting that changes in the distribution of income can be a *cause* of variations in economic growth. A particular concern is that redistribution of income away from wages and towards profits, which broadly speaking correlates with redistribution from less affluent to better-off households[11] will retard the rate of growth. This concern is clearly reflected in the Keynesian growth theories presented in the previous section. Notice that any increase in the profit share, π, causes the terms on the right-hand sides of equations (10.5), (10.8) and (10.12) to become smaller. This, once again, will reduce the rates of expansion of income on the left-hand sides of these equations.

This result is analogous to that obtained in the short run, when falling wages depress aggregate demand and hence output and employment. The rationale for the result is that the rising profit share boosts profits and so deprives high-spending working households of income, which depresses total consumption. This adverse effect on demand formation more than outweighs any accompanying positive effect, such as the boost to investment spending caused by a rise in the profit share that is evident in equation (10.6) of the Kaleckian growth model. The net result is that the rate of economic growth declines. The effect of income redistribution on economic growth is a particularly prominent theme in Kaleckian growth theory. Its contemporary relevance is reflected in widespread concerns that in economies such as the United States the negative effects on economic growth of increasing income inequality were – at least prior to the Great Recession – offset by unsustainable increases in household borrowing. This draws attention to the links between economic growth, finance (see Chapter 15) and crisis (see Chapter 16). It also suggests that reduced inequality – which may be an end in itself – is also conducive to enhancing both the extent *and* the sustainability of economic growth.

A final important theme in Keynesian growth theory is technical progress. That economic growth is accompanied by technical progress is not in doubt – just think of the many improvements in technology that have accompanied the rapid expansion of real per capita income during the 'growth era' described earlier in this chapter. But Keynesian growth theory has always maintained that technical change does not merely *accompany* but is, instead, *induced* by economic growth – in other words, that technical change is endogenous to the growth process. In Keynesian growth theory this thinking has long found expression in the form of Verdoorn's Law, which can be stated as follows:

$$\Delta q = \delta \Delta Y_{-1} \qquad\qquad (10.14)$$

According to equation (10.14), the expansion of output causes a subsequent expansion of productivity (output per person employed), q. Various reasons have been advanced for this relationship. The first can be traced back to Adam Smith's dictum that the 'division of labour depends on the extent of the market'. In other words, the expansion of output is conducive to specialization by trade: different producers can become expert in the production of a single good or service once the market for that good or service becomes sufficiently large. A second explanation for Verdoorn's Law is that increased output permits profitable utilization of capital equipment that is more productive but also both expensive and 'lumpy' (that is, difficult to buy in small quantities). Think, for example, of how many vehicles a factory would need to produce in order to justify investment in integrated assembly-line technology of the sort used by the world's largest vehicle manufacturers. A final explanation concerns learning by doing – the simple principle that 'practice makes perfect'. The idea here is that increases in output increase the amount of 'doing' and, as a result, increase learning by doing and hence productivity.

One important feature of equation (10.14) is that it suggests that the demand-led expansion of actual output affects the productivity of the factors of production and hence the economy's potential output (which, as discussed earlier, depends on the availability and productivity of factors). Potential output is usually thought of as a supply-side variable. Equation (10.14), however, suggests that it is influenced by the process of aggregate demand formation that drives economic growth. This demonstrates that, from a Keynesian perspective, the demand and supply sides of the economy (represented here by actual and potential output) are dependent on one another in the process of economic growth.

According to Kaldorian growth theory, this last insight can be carried one step further. Suppose, then, that in addition to equation (10.14), we also observe:

$$\Delta X = \eta \Delta q \qquad (10.15)$$

According to equation (10.15), increased productivity increases export demand, by lowering the costs of production and hence the prices of exports, or by improving the quality of exported goods (or both). Notice that increased productivity now stimulates demand formation (in equation (10.15)) causing output to expand (in equation (10.13)). In other words, the expansion of potential output (as a result of Δq) now influences demand formation and hence the expansion of actual output (in equations (10.15) and (10.13)). Putting the pieces of the analysis together, this means that the expansion of demand stimulates the expansion of actual output (in equation (10.13)), which stimulates factor productivity (in equation (10.14)) and hence potential output, which further stimulates the expansion of demand (in equation (10.15)) and hence actual output (in equation (10.13)), and so on. We have now discovered the possibility of self-reinforcing virtuous and vicious circles of economic growth, which can be summarized by substituting equation (10.14) into equation (10.15) and then substituting the result into equation (10.13). This yields:

$$\Delta Y = \frac{\delta\eta}{m}\Delta Y_{-1} \qquad (10.16)$$

According to equation (10.16) an initially low rate of economic growth will propagate a subsequently low rate of growth (a vicious circle), whereas if an economy begins with a high rate of growth, its rate of growth will tend to remain high thereafter (a virtuous circle). These outcomes suggest that the growth process is historical in nature, or 'path dependent': the rate of growth today depends on the rate at which an economy has grown in the past. Notice the important relationship between this possibility and the observations made about income divergence due to 'forging ahead' and 'falling behind' at the start of the chapter. As previously noted, over the last two centuries the initially prosperous and rapidly expanding advanced economies have tended to maintain their rapid expansion, while less prosperous and slower-growing economies in the rest of the world have, in general, remained growth laggards.

As a result, the real per capita income of the advanced economies has increased both absolutely and relative to that of the rest of the world. The explanation for this phenomenon that emerges from Kaldorian growth theory is that the observed patterns of 'forging ahead' and 'falling behind' in the growth record reflect the historical or 'path dependent' nature of the growth process. Specifically, income divergence is explained by self-reinforcing vicious and virtuous circles of self-perpetuating slow and fast growth, from which it is difficult (although as examples such as South Korea demonstrate, not altogether impossible) to escape.

The preceding discussion demonstrates that in Keynesian growth theory 'demand matters' but 'demand is not all that matters'. The interaction of supply and demand emerges as an important theme in the determination of long-run growth outcomes – one that may even be crucial to understanding the single most prominent 'stylized fact' about economic growth: the divergence of incomes globally due to 'forging ahead' and 'falling behind'. This prompts one final observation about the growth process. An obvious extension of the ideas developed and discussed in this chapter is to think about supply-side *limits to growth* that may arise from the finite nature of the planet and the historical dependence of economic growth on the extraction of exhaustible resources. These themes are explored further in Chapter 17.

NOTES

* The author would like to thank the Dana Foundation for financial support that facilitated work on this chapter. Thanks also to Jesper Jespersen for his invaluable comments on an earlier draft.
1 This may not be the only or even the best measure of economic well-being, however. Hence while real per capita income is the basic metric of economic growth, alternative measures of well-being can be found in discussions of sustainable development (see Chapter 17).
2 Note the logarithmic scale in Figure 10.2. A change in the vertical distance between any two lines in Figure 10.2 therefore represents a change in the *relative* income of the groups of countries represented by these lines.
3 See, for example, Maddison (1991) and Cornwall and Cornwall (2001).
4 According to Stern (1991, p. 123, emphasis added), 'the study of growth. . .is about the accumulation of physical capital, the progress of skills, ideas and innovation, the growth of population, how factors are used, combined and managed and so on. *It is therefore, principally, about the supply side*'.
5 It may be tempting to regard actual and potential output as completely independent of one another in the Keynesian growth processes depicted in Figures 10.4 and 10.5. This would be a mistake, however, as will become clear later in this chapter.
6 See Cynamon et al. (2013, pp. 16–19) and Harvey (2014) for more extensive accounts of the US experience of demand formation since the early twentieth century.
7 Fundamental uncertainty exists when decision-makers lack information about possible future outcomes and/or the likelihood (probability) that these outcomes will occur. While activities like tossing a coin involve risk (possible outcomes and their likelihood are both known), in Keynesian macroeconomics, long-term economic decision-making involves fundamental uncertainty. See Davidson (1991) and Chapter 7.
8 Notice that the precise form of equation (10.1) used here is actually $I = \beta Y$. This mirrors the relationship between I and Y in Kaleckian growth theory (see the second term on the right-hand side of equation (10.6)).
9 See, for example, Palumbo (2009).
10 See, for example, Palley (2002).
11 See, for example, Atkinson (2009) and Glyn (2009).

REFERENCES

Atkinson, A.B. (2009), 'Factor shares: the principal problem of political economy?', *Oxford Review of Economic Policy*, **25** (1), 3–16.

Cornwall, J. and W. Cornwall (2001), *Capitalist Development in the Twentieth Century: An Evolutionary–Keynesian Analysis*, Cambridge, UK: Cambridge University Press.

Cynamon, B.Z., S.M. Fazzari and M. Setterfield (2013), 'Understanding the Great Recession', in B.Z. Cynamon, S.M. Fazzari and M. Setterfield (eds), *After the Great Recession: The Struggle for Economic Recovery and Growth*, New York: Cambridge University Press, pp. 3–30.

Davidson, P. (1991), 'Is probability theory relevant for uncertainty? A post Keynesian perspective', *Journal of Economic Perspectives*, **5** (1), 129–43.

Glyn, A. (2009), 'Functional distribution and inequality', in W. Salverda, B. Nolan and T.M. Smeeding (eds), *Oxford Handbook of Economic Inequality*, Oxford, UK: Oxford University Press, pp. 101–26.

Harvey, J.T. (2014), 'Using the *General Theory* to explain the U.S. business cycle, 1950–2009', *Journal of Post Keynesian Economics*, **36** (3), 391–414.

Kaldor, N. (1985), *Economics Without Equilibrium*, Cardiff, UK: University College of Cardiff Press.

Maddison, A. (1991), *Dynamic Forces in Capitalist Development*, Oxford, UK: Oxford University Press.

Maddison, A. (2008), 'Historical statistics of the world economy: 1–2008 AD' [tables], accessed 20 February 2016 at www.ggdc.net/maddison/Maddison.htm.

Palley, T.I. (2002), 'Economic contradictions coming home to roost? Does the US economy face a long-term aggregate demand generation problem?', *Journal of Post Keynesian Economics*, **25** (1), 9–32.

Palumbo, A. (2009), 'Adjusting theory to reality: the role of aggregate demand in Kaldor's late contributions on economic growth', *Review of Political Economy*, **21** (3), 341–68.

Stern, N. (1991), 'The determinants of growth', *Economic Journal*, **101** (404), 122–33.

Targetti, F. (2000), 'Nicholas Kaldor, 1908–1986', in P. Arestis and M. Sawyer (eds), *A Biographical Dictionary of Dissenting Economists, Second Edition*, Cheltenham, UK and Northampton, MA, USA: Edward Elgar Publishing, pp. 343–52.

A PORTRAIT OF NICHOLAS KALDOR (1908–86)

Nicholas Kaldor was born in Budapest and became a British citizen in 1934. He joined the faculty of the London School of Economics in 1932 (having previously been a student there) before moving to the University of Cambridge, UK in 1950. Kaldor was an early convert to Keynes's ideas and made numerous important contributions to Keynesian macroeconomic theory during a distinguished career. For example, he was a progenitor of the idea that the level of the interest rate is anchored to the central bank's policy rate (with the term structure determined by Keynes's theory of liquidity preference), an idea that is central to modern Keynesian monetary theory (see Chapter 3). He was also an active and much sought-after policy advisor on issues ranging from regional development to the design and reform of tax systems (Targetti, 2000).

At Cambridge University in the 1950s, Kaldor helped found post-Keynesian or Cambridge macroeconomics, a particular focus of which was the application of Keynes's principle of effective demand to the longer term. Kaldor's work as a member of the post-Keynesian school fell into two distinct phases. During the first (1956–62), he helped to fashion the post-Keynesian theory of economic growth and income distribution, showing how changes in income distribution could reconcile the equilibrium rate of growth with the potential rate of growth in a fully employed economy. This work also contributed to the post-Keynesian theory of the profit rate, a major theme in the so-called 'Cambridge capital controversies'. Kaldor also developed a technical progress function that showed how technical progress could be considered endogenous to the growth process.

During the second phase (1966–86), Kaldor's focus shifted from economic growth and distribution in one country to the determinants of differences in growth rates between countries. The key ideas that characterized his work during this second phase include: the importance of export demand as the key driver of aggregate demand formation; the induced effects of growth on technical progress (particularly in the manufacturing sector) via Verdoorn's Law; and the positive impact of productivity growth on export demand. These principles combine to produce vicious and virtuous circles of self-reinforcing slow or fast growth, which Kaldor used to explain persistent economic growth rate differences between nations and the widening gap between rich and poor.

The historical contingency of the growth process fed into one of the two major concerns of the final years of Kaldor's life: his critique of conventional equilibrium analysis. (The other major theme was his sustained attack on the monetarism of the Chicago School.) Kaldor deplored the stasis of equilibrium analysis, in which outcomes are determined by 'exogenous givens' that, for Kaldor, are *not* exogenous to the economic system and cannot, therefore, be taken as given. Ultimately, and in a statement worthy of his Cambridge colleague Joan Robinson, who also wrestled with the antagonism between history and equilibrium, Kaldor declared that 'the only truly exogenous factor is *whatever exists at a given moment of time*, as a heritage of the past' (Kaldor, 1985, p. 61, emphasis in original).

11

Wealth distribution

Omar Hamouda

 OVERVIEW

This chapter explains what wealth is and what is understood by wealth distribution:

- It points out the distinction between income distribution and income redistribution.

- It expands on the microeconomic approach of the neoclassical theory of income distribution based on marginal utilities and productivities.

- It argues that the macroeconomic perspective of the neoclassical Keynesian/monetarist model of aggregate demand and aggregate supply provides the justification for factor payments in terms of productivity.

- It provides some elementary statistical measures of wealth and income distribution, namely the Lorenz curve and the Gini coefficient.

- It applies the Lorenz curve and the Gini coefficient to two cases illustrating relative poverty, that is, the United States and the world.

- It presents traditional microeconomic theories of income distribution, notably the classical labour theory of value approach.

- It summarizes the contribution of John Maynard Keynes to the rise of macroeconomics and the post-World War II commitment to the welfare state.

- It explains Keynes's theory of employment and interest as absolutely essential to his theory of income distribution. The study of effective demand is the analysis in the aggregate of how to achieve balanced and equitable remuneration to the factors that create wealth.

KEYWORDS

- **Classical labour theory of value:** An exchange between two goods or services is made according to the amount of labour used to produce them.
- **Income distribution:** The distribution of the stream of income generated in the production of new wealth, from goods and services, among those factors that have participated in this production (labour, capital, and land).
- **Income redistribution:** The reallocation of wealth among members of a community, which might occur regardless of whether the contributors and/ or the recipients participate or not in the initial creation of that wealth.
- **Keynesian model:** Aggregate demand (AD) and aggregate supply (AS) correlate the aggregate product Y (or GDP) to the overall price level (P).
- **Liquidity preference (LP):** The choice between holding wealth in cash or lending it with interest; the higher the interest rate, the less is the preference for cash.
- **Marginal efficiency of capital (MEC):** The performance of the productive capital investment in terms of return; this is the concern of the entrepreneur.
- **Marginal propensity to consume (MPC):** The percentage of income received not saved but spent on consumption; this applies to income earners.
- **Neoclassical theory of value:** The desire or utility an individual has for 'things', which determines how goods and services are exchanged for each other and their relative prices.
- **Wealth:** This constitutes all things desired and valued by a community or an individual and held for direct enjoyment or trade. These things are considered assets, whether in the form of land, capital, supplies, works of art, monies, jewellery, skills, knowledge, information, and so on.

Why are these topics important?

While economists seem to have fewer issues with how resources should be used efficiently to create and increase wealth, they have extremely divergent views about how wealth should be shared. There is an abundance of literature with respect to wealth sharing and about who should decide who should have what. They range from the general to the more detailed, from one perspective to another, from empirically or logically analysed pieces to opinionated discussions. Wealth sharing is at the heart of economics; it is in fact its most important issue, of which its basic principles and ensuing analysis and policy prescriptions have profound implications for a society's type of socioeconomic organization. Whether it is a matter of what share of family inheritance, what factor remuneration in the work place, which subsidies and social assistance, the ramifications of how such questions are decided shape the basic fabric of any particular society.

Some introductory remarks

Why do police officers earn more than fire fighters? Why are two individuals of the same age, in similar circumstances, experience, competence, perhaps of different gender, paid differently? Why is the average annual personal income in Sweden more than US$40 000, while in Zimbabwe it is only US$400 a year? Why does a large segment of the Nigerian population live on less than US$2 a day, while 1 per cent of the population holds 40 per cent of the nation's wealth? Recently, King Albert of Belgium noted feeling impoverished, since his abdication from the throne, because his yearly state sinecure decreased from several million to a mere 900 000 euros. Are older people entitled to a pension whether or not they have contributed to savings?

All these questions have to do with wealth and the rationales for its acquisition and/or redistribution. Through time, thinkers and economists have tried to elucidate all aspects of wealth, and the debates continue. This chapter is interested in the distribution of wealth, and as such we must begin by clarifying what wealth is: is it given, created or both? If it is given, why and to whom? If created, how?

Issues related to wealth can be separated into two groups: (1) the distribution of income involves a discussion about its distribution among those involved in the creation of wealth, as well as a discussion about the processes that generate the stream or flow of income to those creating the added value, for their contribution, and (2) the *redistribution* of income, which is concerned with the allocation of a stock of wealth. Changes in the distribution of the stock of wealth existing at any point in time are handled through legislation, fiscal policy, donation, confiscation, and/or coercion. For example, governments may introduce inheritance taxes, tax deductions for gifts to charity, or liens on property. Other equally powerful groups may use extortion, sell contraband or stolen goods, exact bribes, and so on.

Not surprisingly, economic theory has had more to say about income distribution than about its redistribution, as the latter seems to entail a normative stand, in which there are often issues of relative power. Income redistribution requires a chapter on its own, as it is usually associated with fiscal policy (see Chapter 9).

The distribution of a stream or flow of income is traditionally studied under the heading of microeconomics, whose apparatus is used to explain how wages, profits and rents are determined, while redistribution of the stock of wealth is a component of macroeconomics, involving public finance, social welfare, income transfers, and so on. Since the 1990s there has also been the development of a new subfield of wealth distribution devoted principally to data analysis, touching all aspects of transfers and fiscal arrangements affecting education, pension plans, health, social assistance, gender, child poverty, and so on.

Mainstream economic theory of wealth distribution

For orthodox mainstream or neoclassical economists, the market economy is the best interactive economic organization, as it results in the most efficient allocation and use of all resources. Income distribution, in a society that consists of a collection of households, is an outcome of a balance of two forces: (1) the sum total of demands, which reflects consumers' expressing their needs, and (2) the sum total of supplies, emanating from firms' responding to those needs. The core of the model revolves around the households, which, in their choice of distributing their available time between leisure and work, determine how much effort (or employment) they are willing to offer to firms to produce output Y in exchange for a payment of wage w, of which some is used to acquire a share of consumer goods (consumption, $\frac{C}{Y} = cw$) and the rest is saved $\left(\frac{S}{Y} = (1 - c)w\right)$. c is the marginal propensity to consume.

The portion that is saved is returned to the firms as investment, a share of which, $\frac{I}{Y} = r$, will yield a return r for a future consumption. The income spent on the consumption goods $\left(\frac{C}{Y} = c\right)$ constitutes the returns to the firms to be used for the next period's wages. Since everything produced is either consumed or saved and what is produced is either consumption goods or investment goods, by definition saving is always equal to investment: $I = S$ (Figure 11.1).

For neoclassical economists, it is the desired needs of consumers that dictate the amount of employment offered, which translates into the employment realized, the production of goods, and finally the income for satisfying those needs. The income distribution among the factors contributing to the pro-

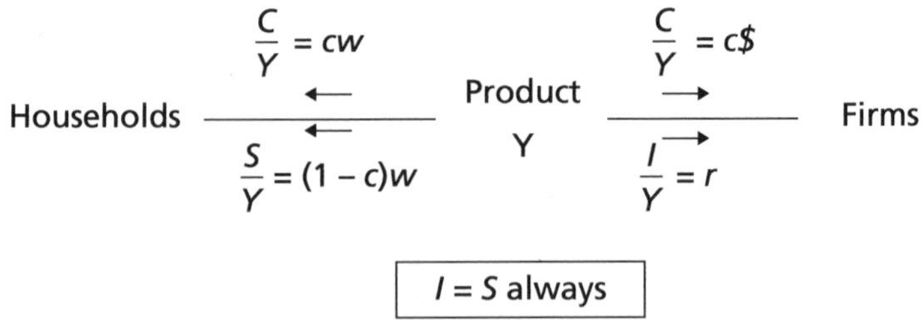

$$\frac{C}{Y} = cw \qquad\qquad \frac{C}{Y} = c\$$$

Households $\quad\xleftarrow{\qquad}\quad$ Product $\quad\xrightarrow{\qquad}\quad$ Firms

$$\xleftarrow{\qquad}\qquad Y \qquad \xrightarrow{\qquad}$$

$$\frac{S}{Y} = (1 - c)w \qquad\qquad \frac{I}{Y} = r$$

$$\boxed{I = S \text{ always}}$$

Figure 11.1 The neoclassical model

duction of the final output is determined unambiguously and uniquely by their marginal productivity. The total production of goods and services and the allocated shares of income from that given production are all determined simultaneously.

Hence, we can argue that there is equivalence between:

- what is produced and the income paid to produce goods and services;
- the income paid in the form of money and the total money in the economy;
- the total money and the expenditure of that money on goods and services;
- the expenditure of households and the total receipt of firms.

The circle is complete, illustrated by Figure 11.2.

Income distribution and marginal productivity: a microeconomics approach

Most of the foundational premises of neoclassical economics (the laws of supply and demand, diminishing marginal productivity, competition and the determination of factor payments, and market forces) are found in classical economics from Adam Smith to John Stuart Mill, including Ricardo and Marx. The contributions of Carl Menger, Léon Walras and Stanley Jevons shifted emphasis from the labour theory of value,

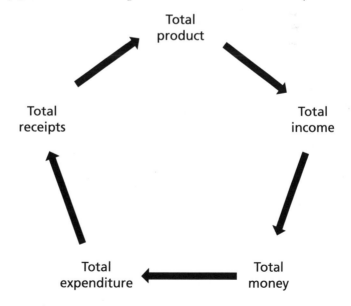

Figure 11.2 The circular flow

based on the labour cost of production, to the neoclassical theory of value. The market interaction between supply of and demand for goods and services, considered by the classics to be accidental and not of their concern, became central for neoclassical authors in determining their value theory.

Let us suppose two goods, 1 and 2, and their corresponding prices, P_1 and P_2. The ratio is established as:

$$\frac{P_1}{P_2} = \frac{MU_1}{MU_2},$$

which expresses the exchange rate between two goods in terms of their corresponding marginal utility (MU). That is to say, exchange between two goods or services is the result of one's desire to acquire something by relinquishing something else of equal utility. Furthermore, the factors of production (labour l and capital k) produce and generate the income used to buy the goods they produce. Individuals choose freely how to divide their available time, according to their desire to work for income or to enjoy unremunerated leisure. It is the offering of their work as service that constitutes the labour supply.

Near the turn of the twentieth century, John Bates Clark applied the law of diminishing marginal productivity to labour and capital to demonstrate that, in neoclassical theory, income distribution among factors of production is uniquely and unambiguously determined. Therefore, with the application of this notion to the inputs of production, the quantity of labour and capital used in production is determined by the corresponding marginal productivity of each factor (MP_l, MP_k). If P_k and P_l are the prices of factors k and l, then:

$$\frac{P_l}{P_k} = \frac{MP_l}{MP_k}$$

This ratio indicates that the amount of labour and capital used to produce a given level of output depends on their relative prices, 'wages' (w, the price of labour) and 'interest' (r, the price of capital):

$$\frac{w}{r} = \frac{MP_l}{MP_k}.$$

For a given amount of output produced with a given amount of labour and capital, both w and r are determined by their corresponding productivity. The determination of their prices is illustrated in Figure 11.3.

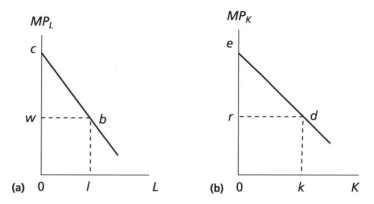

Figure 11.3 The neoclassical theory of income distribution

Whether successive units of labour are applied to a fixed amount of capital, as in Figure 11.3a, or successive amounts of capital are applied to a fixed level of labour, as in Figure 11.3b, Clark showed that the payment to labour, determined by MP_l, is given by area $0lbw$ (a), while the residual triangle wbc represents the payment to capital. When the exercise is repeated, the payment to capital, determined by MP_k, gives area $0kdr$ (b), and the residual triangle rde represents the payment to labour. The two exercises yield the same results: area $0lbw$ determined by MP_l is equivalent to residual area rde, and area $0kdr$ determined by MP_k is equivalent to residual area wbc.

It was also shown that when the marginal productivity approach is applied to determine factor payments, there is 'exhaustion' of the product. In other words, everything produced is distributed among the factors that contributed to the production of that output. In economics, this is referred to as Euler's theorem. Both Clark's contribution and Euler's application became the fundamental, powerful premises of factor payment determination in neoclassical microeconomics, found also in today's Keynesian macroeconomics textbooks.

Although Keynesian economics claims to be derived from John Maynard Keynes's (1936) *General Theory of Employment, Interest and Money*, and indeed uses Keynes's three fundamental concepts – the marginal efficiency of capital (MEC), the marginal propensity to consume (MPC), and liquidity preference (LP) – in its policy analysis it remains nonetheless a macroeconomics offspring of the neoclassical microeconomics model, which became known, as discussed in Chapter 1, as the neoclassical synthesis: a synthesis of some of Keynes's insights with neoclassical theory. As will be seen below, the Keynesian model and Keynes's own model are fundamentally different.

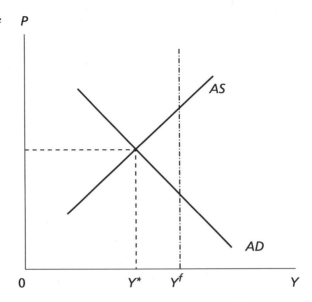

Figure 11.4 Aggregate demand and aggregate supply

Keynesians' and monetarists' aggregate demand: a macroeconomics approach

Since the 1960s, Keynesians and monetarists have shared the same neoclassical model in the dominant macroeconomics textbooks. There are slight variants reflecting the use of policy applications, and whether these are deemed effective (in the Keynesian perspective), or ineffective (in the monetarist perspective). The model is reduced to a simple relationship of aggregate demand (AD) and aggregate supply (AS) as shown in Figure 11.4.

Both curves are independent of each other. *AD* reflects the distribution of the national product in terms of aggregates – consumption, investment, government spending and net exports – while *AS* is derived from the level of employment, determined in the labour market, which in turn determines the corresponding level of production of goods and services (through the production function).

For monetarists, in a world of flexible prices and wages, the intersection of *AD* and *AS* yields output (Y^*) at full employment, Y^f. Keynesians, however, believe that wages, once set, cannot be revised downwards and are hence considered rigid or *sticky*. This rigidity, a so-called 'market imperfection', results in Y^*, which can be below full employment. To reduce discrepancy between Y^* and Y^f, Keynesians suggest government policies to maintain high employment or ways of shifting *AD* to the right.

Income distribution in the Keynesian/monetarist model is consistent with the neoclassical microeconomics approach; it does not add much to what is already known, except that the variables are now conceived in the aggregate. Wages are determined in the labour market through the interaction between demand for labour, reflecting the marginal productivity of labour, and supply of labour, expressed in the choice between work and leisure. Determination of the interest rate (in conjunction with liquidity preference, LP) and the rate of return from investment (in relation to MEC) are derived from the expenditure side, from which AD is built. The interest rate and the rate of return are indistinguishable. As well, in connection with MPC, which determines how much final product is consumed and how much is saved, is saving (S). Saving has a direct one-to-one relationship with investment (I): $S = I$ always.

The Keynesian macroeconomic theory has little to offer by way of answers to the questions of disparity posed at the beginning of this chapter. Keynesian policies, implemented to achieve certain political targets rather than others, as pursued since the 1960s, are at odds with rectifying income disparities, as the trend within and across most nations has been steadily increasing. In sum, successive governments in the industrial economies applying policies in the name of the welfare state ensuing from neoclassical, monetarist or Keynesian theories, have, since the 1960s, hardly been successful on the whole in keeping economies out of recession and in providing quality employment (few well-paid positions, with benefits and security, for example, government posts, as opposed to the large number of precarious, temporary and poorly paid jobs in, for example, the agriculture, retail, and tourism sectors). The labour opportunity dichotomy is to a large extent responsible for the increasing disparities. Keynes's own theory is suggested below, after an immediately ensuing discussion, as an alternative. First, however, it is to be noted that new interest in national accounting and the study of macroeconomic variables, such as national income, aggregate consumption, aggregate investment and government spending, has nonetheless led to the gathering of data and its analysis.

States of income distribution: a description

In the 1990s and 2000s, studies of all aspects of income distribution have flourished, many focused on the use of data to establish states of income distribution. There are numerous specialized journals that publish this type of study, for example, *Journal of Income Distribution*, *Review of Income and Wealth*, and *Journal of Income Inequality*. Although there are numerous

Figure 11.5 The
Lorenz curve

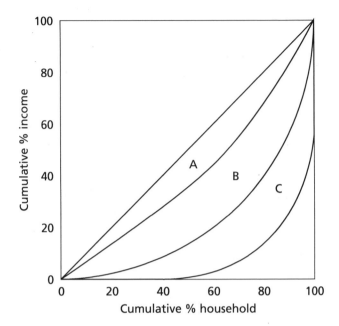

measurement tools to measure inequality, the simplest, primary ones are the
Lorenz curve and the Gini coefficient.

Lorenz curve

One way economists try to get an idea of how wealth is distributed is to clas-
sify the earnings of members of an entity (community, region or country),
from the lowest to the highest, by dividing the whole population into percentage groupings (quintiles, quartiles or deciles). They correlate each division with a corresponding income bracket. This is graphically represented in
the Lorenz curve (Figure 11.5), in which the vertical axis represents percentage income, while the horizontal axis represents population distribution in
percentages. A diagonal line serves to reflect equality: in an ideal world of
perfect income distribution, the same percentage of the population receives
the same percentage of income. The opposite situation, perfect inequality,
which would be when one member receives all the entity's income and the
rest none, is illustrated by the lower horizontal and the right vertical axes of
the Lorenz curve.

Curves A, B and C of Figure 11.5 are intermediary cases depicting various
degrees of inequality, such that the farther the curve from the diagonal, the
higher the degree of inequality.

Figure 11.6 The Gini coefficient

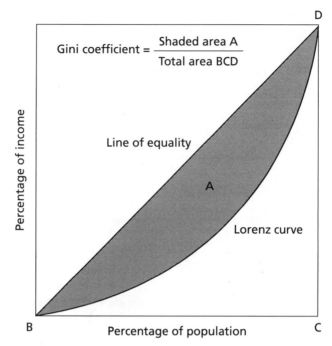

Gini coefficient = $\dfrac{\text{Shaded area A}}{\text{Total area BCD}}$

Gini coefficient

The Gini coefficient (or Gini index) is another measure of inequality (Figure 11.6). It reflects income distribution within a community, region, or country.

The curve BD describes a given distribution of income farther away or closer to the Lorenz curve diagonal (see Figure 11.5). The shaded area A, defined by the diagonal and curve BD, represents a given distribution. Area A becomes larger or smaller, as BD moves closer to the diagonal (perfect equality) or closer to triangle BCD (perfect inequality). The ratio of area A over the area of triangle BCD is defined as the Gini index and serves as a measure of income distribution. This ratio, the Gini coefficient, has a value between zero and one (0 per cent and 100 per cent): it is zero when curve BD is subsumed under the diagonal, and equal to one when it is fused with triangle BCD.

Just like the Lorenz curve, the Gini index can be used to describe income distribution within a single entity but can also compare disparities among entities. Figure 11.7 gives the Gini coefficient for a sample of countries.

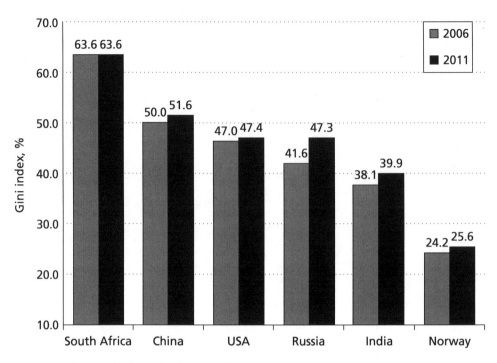

Figure 11.7 A sample of Gini coefficients

Norway has the lowest coefficient, which means that it has a more egalitarian income distribution. South Africa, on the other hand, has a higher number, reflecting a rather less egalitarian distribution. Gini coefficients are calculated for a given period. Figure 11.7 compares coefficients for two distinct periods, 2006 and 2011, showing deterioration in the disparity of income in almost every country noted, save South Africa, whose numbers did not change. In different periods in recent history, one can find country cases where there has been either deterioration followed by improvement or the reverse.

As an illustration of income disparity using the Lorenz curve, Figure 11.8 shows the data for a particular country, the United States. Income levels in the United States are depicted on the vertical axis; on the horizontal axis are the usual population groupings.

If one takes the national income (GNI) in 2011, which has been generated by that year's total US production of goods and services (GDP), and divides the GNI by the total population, one obtains the average per capita (per person) revenue in the United States. Figure 11.8 shows that average earnings (the 50 per cent mark) were about US$42 000 in 2011. It is obvious that this average earning is just an indicator, as is the Gini index for the United States

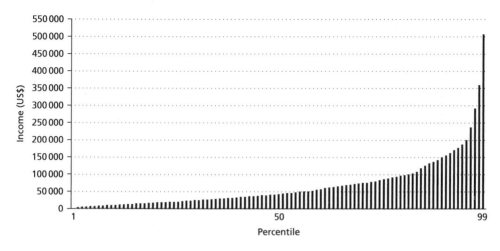

Source: Tax Policy Center (the dataset refers to May 2011), available online at http://taxpolicycenter.org/numbers/displayatab.
cfm?DocID=2970; last accessed 15 February 2016.

Figure 11.8 The Lorenz curve for the United States

(at about 47 per cent; see Figure 11.7), both being ways of measuring income
disparity in a nation. A closer look at the data in Figure 11.8 reveals, however,
a more detailed understanding of the disparity in earnings among Americans
in 2011. The curve shows that 20 per cent of the poorest Americans earned
less than US$17 000 that year, while 10 per cent of the richest earned more
than US$160 000 in the same period.

A Lorenz curve can also be constructed for the distribution of world income.
In Figure 11.9 one can see that the income distribution curve for the world
as a whole is much more pronounced than for that of the United States and
describes even greater inequality.

It is interesting to notice that all those in the United States earning more than
US$10 000 and less than US$20 000, considered to be part of the lowest 30
per cent poor in Figure 11.8, find themselves to be part of the 10 per cent
richest group from the perspective of world income. More striking is that all
those earning more than US$40 000 in the United States (which is also about
the average income per capita in many developed countries) are among the
1 per cent richest people in the world, compared to 30 per cent of the world's
population (2.3 billion people), who live on less than US$2 a day. Being rich
or poor in different parts of the world does not have the same significance
worldwide. In just what way the Lorenz curve, the Gini coefficient, and other
broad indices, such as the Index of Human Development (IHD), describe
world income distribution (what it is, what it means, and how disparities

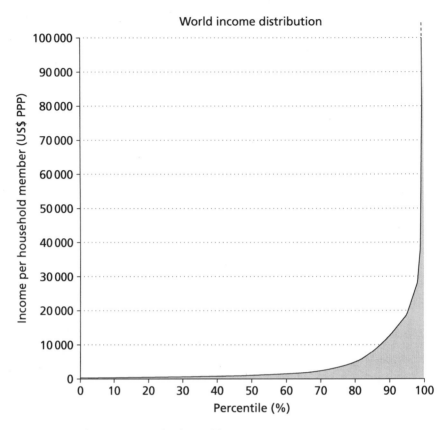

Figure 11.9 The Lorenz curve for the world

have come about) is the subject of continuing study and debate in many areas of economics, such as economic development, production and economic growth, and industrialization and productivity.

More in-depth empirical evidence shows that disparities in income and wealth distribution are diverse and changing through time in various directions. Theorizing these disparities requires models whose main variables reflect the interaction between income earners as contributors to the creation of wealth and as recipients of a share of that wealth. Understanding such models begins here with the return to classical economics, whose primary concern was the discovery of the laws governing factor payments.

Heterodox perspectives

Despite the existence of several alternative heterodox theories of wealth distribution, almost all use the basic framework and premises of the economics

Figure 11.10 The classical/Keynes model

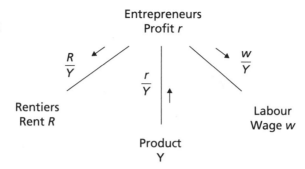

of either the classics or Keynes. The classical and Keynes models are constructed as a tripartite balance of forces of supply and demand for factors of production, based on the interactions among rentiers, entrepreneurs and workers. Rentiers provide land (in the classics) or financing (in Keynes) in exchange for a return (R), entrepreneurs lead and manage production and expect a profit (r), and workers offer labour for a payment of wage (w) for their productive effort. All three contribute to the creation of a certain level of product Y and receive a share $\frac{R}{Y}, \frac{r}{Y}$ and $\frac{w}{Y}$ of the total product, the share of rent, the share of profit and the share of wages, respectively; all shares add to 1 (Figure 11.10).

The classics studied income distribution from a microeconomics perspective. The ongoing production of goods and services generates a flow of income. At any specific period of time there is a given level of income specific to that level of production, which is divided among the factors of production that contributed to this outcome.

Classical economics and the law governing factor payment

While this was discussed in Chapter 2, it is worth repeating here for the purposes at hand. Assume a farmer who rents land and with the help of one labourer produces one bushel of grain valued at P, its price or its return. That value is shared between the worker, who provided his labour (L) (at wage, w), the land-owner or rentier, who supplied the land (for rent, R), and the farmer or entrepreneur, who invests capital (K) (at profit r); therefore:

$$P = w + r + R$$

What is the share of each party? For Adam Smith the use of land presents two characteristics: (1) not all lands have the same yield, thus two parcels of the

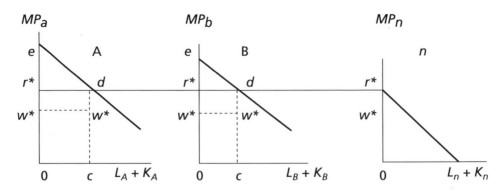

Figure 11.11 The classical distribution of income

same size may generate two different rents $(R_1$ and $R_2)$, and (2) following the law of decreasing marginal productivity, applying more and more amounts of labour and capital to the same parcel of land results in less and less marginal product. Figure 11.11 illustrates how the distribution of income to each factor is determined.

Classical economists made three important assumptions: (a) when labour is abundant, as it was in their time, wages tend to be at their minimum, (b) competition for work produces a uniform level of wages (w^*), which is tantamount to a horizontal labour supply (w^*w^*), and (c) since capital flows where the return is highest, competition for capital creates forces that tend to equalize profits (r^*). Suppose parcels of land of different yields, A, B, . . ., n, to which amounts of labour (L) and capital (K) are applied. As shown in Figure 11.11, wages (w^*) and profits (r^*) are the same from the use of land A, B, or n. In land A, if $L_A + K_A$ is utilized, land A will generate an amount of total product equal to area $ocde$. If ow^* is the wage rate, and w^*r^* is the profit rate, then area ocw^*w^* represents the wage bill, $w^*w^*dr^*$ is the total profit, and the residual area der^* is rent.

It is clear from Figure 11.11 that wealth, the sum of the total product for each parcel of land, is considered to be created from a given endowment (of labour, capital and finance), and that the product is distributed entirely among its three factors: workers, entrepreneurs (or capitalists), and rentiers (or financiers). The thick black line of each diagram, which is lower for land B than for land A, and for land n than for land B, represents the diminishing or marginal productivity (MP) of labour and capital in the utilization of each land. As for rent, it is higher for land A than for land B. In the case of the marginal land n, the first units of labour and capital produce just enough to pay for wages and profits, but they do not generate enough for rent. Thus, the owners of lands of type n would have to rent them for free or not at all.

From Figure 11.11, one also sees that if rent is considered residual, as the classical economists assumed it to be, then it is the marginal land that determines the marginal product of capital and labour. Hence:

$$P = w + r$$

or more appropriately, if it takes L labour and K capital to produce a certain amount of grain, then the expression can be rewritten as:

$$P = wL + rK$$

Classical economists proceeded to a simplification of this expression by assuming that capital K is produced with both labour and capital at time $t - 1$, and K_{t-1} is produced with labour and capital at time $t - 2$, and so on. They thereby reduced K to its labour content and called it indirect labour. Hence P can be written as:

$$P = wL^*$$

where L^* is the sum of direct and indirect labour (see Chapter 2).

Suppose two goods, 1 and 2, and their corresponding prices, P_1 and P_2. In the classical labour theory of value, the ratio

$$\frac{P_1}{P_2} = \frac{wL_1^*}{wL_2^*} = \frac{L_1^*}{L_2^*}$$

expresses the exchange rate of two goods in terms of the labour (direct and indirect) used to produce them.

For classical economists, from Adam Smith to John Stuart Mill, including Karl Marx, income distribution is tied to the study of production and the contribution of each class. The logical analysis entailed in the labour theory of value resulted in controversial debates about the source of the creation of wealth and the justification of the returns to each class. The controversy among schools of classical thought centred on numerous questions: Which among the three factors, labour, capital and land, is the creator of wealth? If the wage bill is fixed, can wage pressure be relieved only by satisfying the demands of one group of workers at the expense of another? And more generally, should private property be allowed? Violent, diverging views were held, which consequently had a profound influence on ideas about the merits of the market economy versus collectivism. For Marx, for example, for whom labour is the sole creator of value, the entire return from production ought to go to labour, and workers should have full control of the means of production.

Pre-World War II economics was polarized. On the one side, dominant neoclassical economics, in the tradition of its classical predecessor, relied mainly on market mechanisms to justify income distribution. On the other side was the Marxian perspective, which rejected the validity of deterministic market forces and its consequent distribution. The severity of the crisis of 1929 and the revealed inability of economic theory to help find ways of getting an economy out of depression led some economists, in particular Keynes, to think of alternative ideas.

A new macroeconomics approach: stock of wealth and social well-being

The publication of *The General Theory* by Keynes in 1936 radically changed the study of economics, both in its theory and its policy. Keynes provided a new approach based on macroeconomic variables and on social accounting. Rather than relying on individual supply and demand, as was the case in the previous study of economics, Keynes shifted the emphasis to aggregate supply and aggregate demand. Keynes's general idea, simple in its essence but difficult and cumbersome in its conception, created much confusion and a rift between his theory and the corrupted Keynesian interpretation.

Keynes called 'effective demand' the productive output brought about through the interactions among rentiers who provide financing, entrepreneurs who manage production, and workers who offer labour. In a monetary economy of production, employment and income depend mostly on entrepreneurs, who anticipate what they think are the needs of the rest of the community and then invest in the employment and the production from which wealth is created. The ensuing income may or may not satisfy all desired needs, and/or may satisfy the needs of some more than others. In Keynes's theory, labour costs and production precede income, while investments are made on the basis of expected future income. Entrepreneurs' decisions to produce or not and with how much labour depend mostly on anticipated profits. For Keynes, it is thus their assessment of the effective demand that determines employment and income distribution.

Keynes's aggregate demand and aggregate supply correlate a level of employment to expected proceeds or return on investment. Labour is passive in determining investment. Finance, however vital, is in constant flux, and the

Figure 11.12 Keynes's effective demand

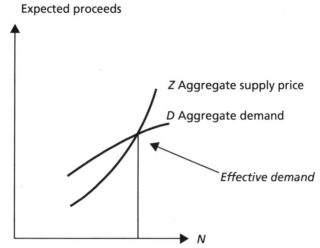

cause of instability in the economy is the volatility of investment. It is caused by the attitude toward liquidity determined by financial activity. Money, credit contraction and expansion, and financial speculation are the major variables affecting the determination of income distribution, but they also cause the redistribution of income among wages, profits and rents.

Keynes provided a theoretical mechanism that allows for the creation of employment and income in a monetary market economy. Employment requires investment, and incentives to invest depend on profits. Thus, for Keynes, aggregate profit, more as means than end, is his theoretical starting point.

In Figure 11.12, employment is correlated to 'expected proceeds', namely, the return on investment.

Keynes, in an original way, applied classical marginal productivity to investment, measured in money, for a given production and employment. The amount of investment determines returns on investment; wages are residual. Just as in the classical case with different lands (see above), here there are different production–employment processes to which a level of investment is applied.

Keynes constructed a prospective yield schedule or curve of the corresponding diminishing productivity of various investments in the aggregate (Figure 11.13). He contrasted that schedule to the supply price curve, which describes how returns are divided and paid back to the rentiers (and entrepreneurs) as

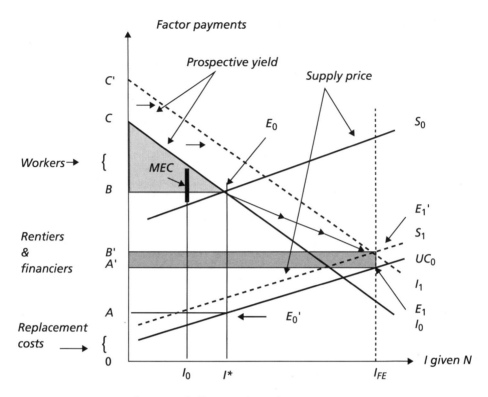

Figure 11.13 The marginal efficiency of capital

interest, dividends and costs related to the utilization of capital (replacement, amortization, administration, and so on).

In Figure 11.13, use of investment I^*, which corresponds to a given level of employment, generates production income area $0CI^*E_0$, which is divided between profits (area $B0I^*E_0$) and wages (area CBE_0). To increase the level of employment, investment must increase. One way is to shift the prospective yield curve to the right, which can be achieved with an increase in productivity or a change in prices or taxes. A second way would be as a result of shifts in the supply price curve to the right, as a consequence of a lower cost for borrowing funds or replacing equipment. Both these shifts permit movement of the intersection E_0 to E_1'. With more investment and more employment, the triangle CBE_0, the total wage bill, increases, while area $B0I^*E_0$, the payment to rentiers, becomes smaller. The second way to increase investment is through a policy of lowering the interest rate.

Keynes's most novel proposal was in the area of monetary policy. He felt that money, being legal tender ('state money'), should be made available at low interest rates to entrepreneurs to encourage investment, for them to be able to maintain a marginal efficiency of capital (MEC) or return on their investment high enough to stimulate more investment. An abundance of available money would counterbalance financial lenders, who would otherwise take advantage of tight money or liquidity preference (LP) to extract high interest. It is in this context that Keynes (1936) introduced his famous expression 'the euthanasia of the rentier', meaning that the monetary authorities would thereby keep the financial sector in check. Maintaining a high level of investment is a prerequisite to increasing employment and improving labour wages. As long as the economy is near (but not at) full employment, fiscal policy also directed toward the community's (marginal) propensity to consume (MPC) would keep inflation in check.

Central to Keynes's theory of income distribution are the concepts of MEC, LP, and MPC. They are built into his prospective yield schedule and supply price curve, as well as the interrelated aggregate demand and aggregate supply that constitute effective demand. They are conceived to impact firms' investment and employment. The MEC, LP, and MPC in the Keynesians' and the monetarists' models filter their impact through AD, which is independent of AS. As part of AD, they boost any expenditure forming GDP, of which consumption is the largest component.

In conclusion, it is obvious that the classical/Keynes model of a market balance of forces is more appropriate than that of the orthodox model to tackle the general aspects of income distribution among the three classes. The answers to the questions posed at the start cannot be found in economics alone but require taking the institutional setting into account, which defines the relative powers impacting the distribution and redistribution of income and wealth. In a monetary economy, the legal management of state money rests with financial institutions, which gives banks considerable privileges in the creation and channelling of credit, not always in the best interests of all. For his policy to be effective Keynes felt that the banking system must be separate and independent of the financial sector. Although private, it would remain nonetheless an arm of a nation's central bank; its unique role would, however, simply be to provide liquidity to the economy.

Without the legislation permitting limits on corporate liability and the amassing of huge capacity by financers, capital accumulation and takeovers would be difficult to constrain. Without conferring concession rights in the work place, unions would have a hard time protecting the interests of their particular members. Present situations, such as the emergence of powerful poles of decision-making, the relegating of the risk factor to government,

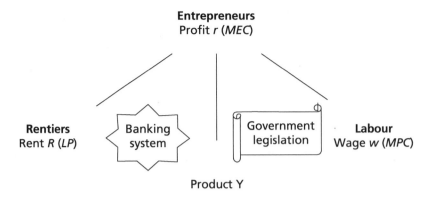

Figure 11.14 Relative economic power groups

the conferring of concessions, licences and benefits to particular groups, all contribute to hierarchies of relative power within a society, which explains the variety of disparities (Figure 11.14).

Some concluding remarks

The establishment of the welfare state in the 1950s and 1960s, with sustained economic growth and high levels of employment as its main economic goals, has meant a continuous commitment to specific Keynesian policies. Policy guidance from Keynesian economic theory in order to stimulate aggregate demand, consisting of adopting measures affecting distribution through MEC, MPC and LP, has resulted in increased government spending and the expansion of credit for mass consumption to be used as the engine of economic growth since the 1980s. Consumption, to the point of addiction, encouraged and developed by the rentiers, has shifted the distribution of income from both wage earners and entrepreneurs to their favour. There is growing evidence that Keynesian policies are increasing income disparity, even though they temporarily dampen the effects of recessions. Further, new practices of indebtedness, which consist in abetting consumption first, before the production and generation of income, with all the uncertainty this entails, have drastically changed attitudes toward effort and production, promoting short-term gain and the 'quick exit' rather than long-term stability.

Keynes's unorthodox theory offers an alternative: encouraging policy measures, affecting MEC, MPC and LP, in order to stimulate effective demand from the production perspective. That is to say, production, the necessary securing of employment, and the ensuing generation of income comes first, before consumption. State money made available to entrepreneurs and an interest rate held low, along with a profitable rate of MEC, are the conditions that encourage investment and in turn employment. They will occur only if the functions of the banking system are separate from those of speculative financial institutions and are under the strict control of the central bank to manage the legal tender for the good of society as a whole.

The well-being of a society, in terms of both economic and social stability, rests to a large extent on an equitable distribution of income, which in Keynes reflects balance between the various members of society (rentiers, entrepreneurs and workers), whose means and ends permit their participation in the creation of wealth. The key to reaching that goal was for Keynes neither speculation nor avid consumption, but employment, the exertion of effort in production.

 REFERENCES

Keynes, J.M (1936), *The General Theory of Employment, Interest and Money*, London: Macmillan.

Marx, K. (1867), *Das Kapital, Volume I*, Hamburg: O. Meissner.

Marx, K. (1885), *Das Kapital, Volume II*, Hamburg: O. Meissner.

Marx, K. (1894), *Das Kapital, Volume III*, Hamburg: O. Meissner.

Marx, K. and F. Engels (1848), *Manifest der Kommunistischen Partei*, London: J.E. Burghard.

A PORTRAIT OF KARL MARX (1818–83)

The life of Karl Marx, a German philosopher and economist, spanned the nineteenth century, from the rise of the Industrial Revolution to the apogee of free-market capitalism. Marx was appalled by the harsh impact of the progress of industrialization on the lives of ordinary people. Marx's ideas of worker exploitation, mass pauperization, and an increasing gap between the accumulated wealth of a few and the misery of the large number had a profound result for economics. Critical of individualism, private property and the laissez-faire of the then guiding classical economics, he advocated collectivism, cooperation in production, and communal ownership. Although most of his thinking was devoted to the criticism of capitalism, he dwelt little on theoretical alternatives.

Marxism, in Marx's name, became synonymous with class struggle and full control of the means of production as its ultimate goal. The rise of Marxism, antithetical to the liberal free-market ideas of Adam Smith and orthodox economics, created an irreconcilable clash between two visions of economic and political social organization to promote the betterment of human beings. In the twentieth century, attempts to apply Marxism began with the Russian Bolshevik Revolution in 1917, which led to the establishment of state socialism. The post-World War II polarization of the world and the subsequent Cold War dividing East from West were the direct consequences of the antagonistic visions.

Marx's contributions came in two waves. First, in an early phase, he believed in the possibility of changing the course of capitalism. With Fredrick Engels, he participated in drafting the famous *Manifesto of the Communist Party* (1848). As an editor, Marx used legal training and journalistic skill to promote his ideas. Active in organizing the working class to rise up and take control of their destiny, he fomented the 1848 revolution, which resulted in bloodshed and the repression that led to his exile from Germany. In a second phase, having retreated to London, Marx devoted himself to writing. He produced his *magnum opus*, the three-volume *Das Kapital*, a theoretical explanation and justification for the rejection of capitalism, which contains the 'seeds of its own destruction' (Marx, 1867, 1885, 1894).

Part IV

International economy

12

International trade and development

Robert A. Blecker

 OVERVIEW

This chapter covers the following topics:

- It explains that orthodox theories of comparative advantage imply that free trade benefits all countries, but only on the unrealistic assumptions of balanced trade and full employment; even then, trade creates losers as well as winners and may increase inequality within countries.

- It points out that in the heterodox view, because balanced trade and full employment are rarely observed in reality, trade usually follows absolute rather than comparative advantages. As a result, countries that achieve more rapid export growth and/or trade surpluses often benefit at the expense of others.

- It explains that changes in the terms of trade (international prices) redistribute the gains from trade between nations. Commodity price booms may benefit countries that are specialized in primary commodities, but can also result in what is called the 'Dutch disease' of currency appreciation, leading to deindustrialization.

- It observes that efforts to promote export-led economic growth are usually successful only in a limited number of countries at a time as a result of a 'fallacy of composition'. The only way that all countries in the global economy can grow faster together is by the adoption of more expansionary macroeconomic policies worldwide.

 KEYWORDS

- **Absolute competitive advantage:** A country having the lowest monetary cost of production of a good, as a result of some combination of low wages, a low currency value, or high productivity of labour; a key concept in the heterodox approach to trade.

- **Comparative advantage:** A country having the lowest relative (opportunity) cost of producing a good, meaning that it has to give up less of other goods to produce it than other countries; the cornerstone of the orthodox approach to trade.
- **Infant-industry protection:** Using trade barriers such as tariffs (taxes on imports) and quotas (quantitative limits on imports) to promote the development of new industries that can eventually become internationally competitive.
- **Terms of trade:** The relative proportion in which goods are exchanged internationally (how much imports a country can buy with its exports); especially important for exporters of primary commodities (agricultural and mineral products).
- **Trade balance:** The difference between the value of a country's exports and its imports; a positive balance is called a 'surplus' and a negative balance is a 'deficit'.
- **Trade liberalization:** Reducing trade barriers such as tariffs and quotas, either through multilateral negotiations or via regional/preferential trade agreements.

Why are these topics important?

International trade has been an important feature of the economic growth process since the dawn of modern capitalism. The colonial empires of the sixteenth through the early twentieth centuries were built on a very unequal form of trade, primarily involving the exchange of natural resources from the colonial areas for manufactured goods from the imperial powers. The countries that have grown most rapidly in recent decades, such as Japan, South Korea and China, have relied on exports of manufactures as a key part of their growth strategy. Supporters of the global trading system argue that unfettered trade leads countries to specialize in the products that they can produce most efficiently, resulting in higher productivity and increased consumption levels in all countries. Critics, however, charge that the global trading system often widens income gaps between more advanced and less developed nations, and can also exacerbate inequality in the distribution of income within countries.

The share of internationally traded goods and services in global GDP has increased dramatically over the past half-century, as shown in Figure 12.1. This tremendous expansion of trade has been driven by several factors, including deliberate efforts by governments to open up markets by negotiating reductions in trade barriers – a process known as 'trade liberalization' – as well as changes in technology that have revolutionized how products are made, how cheaply goods can be shipped, and how easily firms can

Source: World Bank (2014).

Figure 12.1 World trade in goods and services as a percentage of world GDP, 1960–2012

communicate with production facilities around the world. This chapter is concerned with theories that try to identify the relationship of international trade to long-run growth objectives and other core macroeconomic issues such as unemployment.

The orthodox approach: the theory of comparative advantage

The orthodox approach to international trade is known as the theory of comparative advantage. This section will explain this theory and some of its limitations, while later sections in this chapter will explore heterodox alternatives. The essential idea of comparative advantage is that every country should specialize in (and export) the goods that it can produce with the relatively lowest cost compared to other countries, while importing those goods that can be produced at a relatively lower cost abroad. The key question then is how to define the meaning of goods being relatively cheaper or more expensive. Based on the classical statement of the theory of comparative advantage

Table 12.1 Example of Ricardian comparative advantage

	Hours of labour required to produce:	
	Televisions (per unit)	Rice (per ton)
United States	2	4
East Asia	6	5

by David Ricardo ([1821] 1951), a simple and compelling way to define this concept is in terms of 'relative labour cost', that is, by comparing the cost in labour time of producing goods in each country, as in the following example.

An example of comparative advantage

To illustrate this theory, consider a simplified world economy consisting of two countries, the United States (USA) and East Asia (EA), that can produce two goods (televisions and rice) with the labour costs (person hours per unit of output) shown in Table 12.1. Given these (purely hypothetical) numbers, the relative cost of producing a television in the USA is only 2/4 = 0.5, which is the ratio of the hours of labour required to produce one television (two hours) to the hours required to produce one ton of rice (four hours). This ratio is very important, as it corresponds to the microeconomic concept of 'opportunity cost': the USA has to give up 0.5 tons of rice in order to produce each additional television.

In EA, however, the relative (opportunity) cost of a television is 6/5 = 1.2 tons of rice (because it takes six labour hours to produce a television and five labour hours to produce one ton of rice), so televisions are relatively more expensive to produce there (EA has to give up 1.2 tons of rice for each television it produces, compared with only 0.5 in the USA). Hence, we say that the USA has the comparative advantage in televisions. Because this is a purely relative comparison, the same logic implies that EA has the comparative advantage in rice. To see this, note that the opportunity cost of producing rice in the USA is 4/2 = 2.0 (the reciprocal of the US opportunity cost for televisions), while the opportunity cost of rice in EA is 5/6 = 0.83 (the reciprocal of the EA opportunity cost for televisions). Since 0.83 is less than 2.0, we can see that EA has the relatively lower opportunity cost for rice and hence will export it.

Note that, according to the theory of comparative advantage, a country does not need to have an absolute productivity advantage (that is, the lowest labour time per unit, or highest output per hour) in a good in order to export it. In our example, EA exports rice even though it has an absolute disadvantage in rice (it takes five hours of labour to grow a ton of rice in EA, compared with only four hours in the USA). Indeed, in our example the USA has the absolute advantage in both goods, but it only has a comparative advantage in televisions while EA has the comparative advantage in rice. Both countries can gain by trading according to their comparative advantages, provided that they exchange the goods in a proportion (called the 'terms of trade', or international relative price) that lies between their respective relative labour costs. Thus, in our present example, the terms of trade have to be greater than 0.5 and less than 1.2, measured in tons of rice per television.

In the highly simplified world of the comparative advantage model, free trade generally makes all workers better off compared to a situation in which each country tries to make both goods for itself (such self-reliance is referred to as 'autarky'). For example, if the international terms of trade are $3/4 = 0.75$ tons of rice per television, then a US worker can obtain more rice by spending two hours producing a television and selling it for 0.75 tons of rice, than by growing rice directly (given that the US worker would need four hours of labour to produce one ton of rice, he or she could only produce 0.5 tons of rice in two hours). Similarly, an EA worker can obtain more televisions by producing and exporting rice than by attempting to produce televisions at home. The increased quantities of the goods that consumers can afford when the goods are produced in the countries where they are relatively cheaper constitute what are called the 'gains from trade'. Of course, it may seem unrealistic that EA exports rice and imports televisions (and the USA does the opposite), and indeed it is; in a later section of this chapter, we will explain how and why EA will want to develop its television industry and reverse this pattern of trade (that is, export televisions and import rice).

Changes in the terms of trade

Even in the orthodox approach to international trade, there are some important caveats regarding the gains that countries receive if trade follows comparative advantage. One important qualification is that the gains from trade can be redistributed between countries if the terms of trade shift in favour of one country's exports and against the other's. In our example, if the terms of trade increase from 0.75 to one ton of rice per television, then – although both countries are still better off with trade compared with autarky – the television-exporting country (USA) gains relatively more and the television-importing country (EA) gains relatively less from the trade. Using our previous example, if a US worker who spends two hours producing a television can sell it for one ton of rice instead of 0.75 tons of rice, then clearly that worker will be able to consume more rice. However, an EA worker who spends five hours growing a ton of rice will be able to purchase less televisions if he or she only gets one television per ton of rice instead of $1.33 = 1/0.75$ (note that the terms of trade for rice are always the reciprocal of the terms of trade for televisions).

Going beyond this simple example, changes in the terms of trade can have a powerful impact on the income of countries that export various types of goods in the real world. One important case is the terms of trade for exports of 'primary commodities', namely, the agricultural and mineral products (including petroleum) that are the main exports of many countries in various regions of the world (for example, Australia, Brazil, Nigeria, and Russia). Figure 12.2 shows two key indexes of these international terms of trade, one for crude oil and one for non-energy primary commodities (agricultural and mineral goods). Both indexes were constructed by deflating the nominal price indexes (current price levels) for each type of commodity by a US

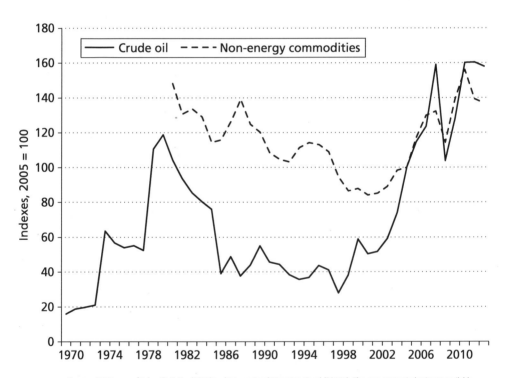

Sources: US Bureau of Labor Statistics (2014) and International Monetary Fund (2014a). The non-energy index is not available before 1981.

Figure 12.2 World terms of trade for crude oil and non-energy primary commodities, 1970–2013

producer price index, on the assumption that exporters of these goods spend their export revenue largely on imports of industrial products that are priced in US dollars in global markets. The data in Figure 12.2 illustrate how sharply the purchasing power of the exporters of oil or other commodities over industrial goods has varied over the past several decades. When the terms of trade for the primary commodity exporters rise (as in the 1970s or early 2000s), the real income of the exporting countries (for example, Mongolia or Saudi Arabia) rises, but there is a corresponding decrease in the ability of the countries that import these goods (for example, the USA or EU) to purchase them and hence a decline in their real income.

At various points in the twentieth century, many economists in developing countries feared that there would be a long-term decline in the terms of trade for primary commodity exports, which would reduce those countries' ability to import manufactured goods from industrialized countries. As Figure 12.2 shows, although these terms of trade did decline in the 1980s and 1990s, they were generally on a rising trend between 2000 and 2013, owing to a combination of strong global demand (especially from China) and speculative pressures in global commodity markets. However, at the time of writing (early 2016) the prices of many primary commodities (including oil) were falling rapidly as a result of weakening demand from producers of industrial goods (for example, the EU and China), so the future prospects for the commodity terms of trade are uncertain.

Although it may seem that it is always better for any country to have high terms of trade for its exports (whatever its exports may be), high terms of trade for primary commodity exports can be a mixed blessing. In fact, some have claimed that they can become a 'curse'. The reason is that high export prices for primary commodities give countries incentives to invest less in industry and manufacturing, which generally offer greater opportunities for improving technology and raising productivity and living standards in the long run than agriculture or mining. Thus, even if a country enjoys high per capita income as a result of high prices of primary commodity exports for some period of time, the resulting deindustrialization may inhibit the country's long-run development prospects.

This problem can be worsened if the increased export revenue leads to the appreciation of the country's currency, which makes its manufacturing industries less competitive in global markets. This phenomenon is often called 'Dutch disease', because it was observed in the Netherlands after the 1959 discovery of natural gas reserves there. Moreover, fluctuations in commodity prices and currency values are often driven by financial speculation, which can be destabilizing for commodity exporters and importers alike. A good example of this problem is found in the Canadian economy, where the boom in prices of oil and other primary commodities from about 2004 to 2014 led to an appreciation of the Canadian dollar that harmed manufacturing industries in industrial provinces like Ontario and Québec.

Distributional consequences of trade (winners and losers)

A second, very important set of qualifications within the orthodox approach concerns the fact that international trade can redistribute income among different groups within a country, that is, some people gain but others may lose as a result of an opening to trade. In reality, the citizens of a country are not all generic 'workers' as in the simple Ricardian model of comparative advantage discussed earlier,[1] and there are several dimensions along which the gains and losses from trade may be felt.

At the most basic level, we may distinguish between producers and consumers of any good. In general, consumers benefit if the goods they consume fall in price owing to greater competition from imports (think of cheap imported clothing from South Asia or Central America in the USA or EU), but domestic producers of these same goods in the importing countries lose (they get lower prices for what they sell, and workers in these industries may lose jobs). By the same logic, producers gain but domestic consumers lose when prices of exported goods rise because of high foreign demand for these goods.

However, we can also think of 'producers' as being divided into groups that own different productive inputs, like labour, land (natural resources) or capital. In this case, according to the neoclassical Heckscher–Ohlin model of trade, each country will have a comparative advantage in the goods that are relatively intensive in the use of the 'factors of production' (inputs) that are relatively 'abundant' in that country. For example, land-abundant countries like Australia, Brazil and Canada will export resource-intensive primary commodities, while labour-abundant countries like Bangladesh and China will export labour-intensive manufactures (or services, as in the case of India). An extension of this model called the Stolper–Samuelson theorem then tells us that owners of the inputs ('factors of production') that are relatively abundant in the country gain from free trade while owners of relatively scarce inputs lose, basically because the demand for the abundant factor rises when production of the exported good increases while the demand for the scarce factor falls as the country shifts resources out of the industry producing the imported good and into the export industry.[2] For example, low-skilled US workers would be expected to lose across the board from imports of labour-intensive goods like apparel or electronics, which would reduce demand for low-skilled labour in the USA, while high-skilled workers (scientists and engineers) would benefit from exports of high-technology goods like airplanes and computer software that increase demand for the services of such workers.

The Stolper–Samuelson theorem thus leads us to expect that trade would foster greater inequality between high- and low-skilled workers in advanced countries like the USA, but would reduce such inequality in developing countries like Mexico that export goods that are intensive in low-skilled labour. In reality, however, many studies have found that inequality between different groups of workers has increased as a result of trade not only in advanced countries like the USA, but also in developing countries like Mexico. This finding has led to the development of new theories that can explain how trade can foster greater inequality in all countries, not just in the more advanced ones where low-skilled labour is scarce.

One such new theory is the model of offshoring developed by Robert Feenstra and Gordon Hanson (1997). This model assumes that when jobs are outsourced from a rich country to a poorer country, the jobs that move (for example, jobs in automobile plants or autoparts factories that move from the USA to Mexico) are relatively low skilled in the richer country but relatively high skilled in the poorer country. As a result, the average composition of employment shifts toward relatively higher-skilled labour in both countries, so wages rise more for the high-skilled workers and wage inequality (the gap between the better-paid high-skill workers and the lower-paid low-skill workers) worsens in both countries.[3]

Nevertheless, it is important to recognize that trade does not always worsen inequality. In the countries that have been most successful at export-led growth, such as South Korea and China, real wages of workers eventually rise as the demand for labour begins to outstrip the supply, so the gains from trade become more widely shared. The reasons why this phenomenon is usually restricted to a relatively small number of countries will be discussed later in this chapter when we come to the 'fallacy of composition'.

The heterodox alternative: imbalanced trade, unemployment, and absolute competitive advantages[4]

The traditional theory of comparative advantage rests on the twin assumptions of balanced trade (the value of exports equals the value of imports) and full employment (which implies that everyone who loses a job as a result of imports gets a job in export production or another domestic industry). These assumptions are essential for the validity of the theory: together they ensure that trade only promotes efficiency in the allocation of resources and has no effect on the level of employment of these resources. In reality, however, most countries have imbalanced trade: either a surplus, meaning that the value of exports exceeds the value of imports, or a deficit, which indicates the opposite. In addition, there is typically some unemployment in most economies most of the time, and even if there is temporarily something close to full employment, this cannot be guaranteed to continue. Therefore, the heterodox approach examines the impact of trade in the real world where both imbalanced trade and unemployment are usually found.

If full employment is not guaranteed, then workers who lose jobs because of imports may not find jobs in the export sector or any other domestic activity, as is assumed (quite unrealistically) in the theory of comparative advantage. In the absence of full employment, workers who lose jobs because of imports and do not find employment elsewhere (or who get other jobs only at lower wages) will not share in the consumer gains from cheaper imports.[5] By the same token, if a country that has unemployed workers is successful in boosting its exports, it can create more jobs and need not sacrifice output of any other goods in order to produce more exports – so the issue of 'opportunity cost' becomes moot. Such a country can also reduce unemployment by protecting domestic industries from imports, for example through a tariff (tax on imports) or quota (quantitative restriction on imports).

As explained in Chapter 3, modern economies are best described as 'monetary economies of production', which means fundamentally that goods are exchanged for money and not bartered for other goods. The model of comparative advantage, in contrast, rests upon a barter vision of trade: one good (televisions) is exchanged directly for another good (rice), without any role for money. In the real world, however, goods are usually exchanged internationally for major or 'hard' currencies (for example, dollars, pounds or euros), which in turn can be converted into other financial assets (such as Treasury bills). As a result, some countries can build up trade surpluses by selling more in exports than they buy in imports, thereby acquiring net financial assets from other countries in exchange for their excess exports, while other countries have trade deficits, in which case they must be selling financial assets (or acquiring international debts) to cover the excess of their imports over their exports. For example, when China sells more goods to the USA than it imports from the USA, China uses the excess dollar earnings to increase its holdings of US financial assets such as stocks, bonds and treasury bills; this in turn increases the US net international debt to China.

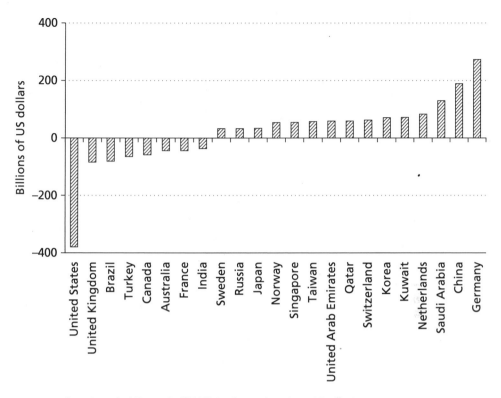

Source: International Monetary Fund (2014b). Data for several countries are IMF staff estimates.

Figure 12.3 Countries with current account surpluses and deficits in excess of US$30 billion, 2013

Global trade imbalances

Figure 12.3 shows the countries that had the largest trade imbalances (surpluses or deficits in excess of US$30 billion) as of 2013. As this figure shows, the USA has by far the world's largest deficit, while the largest surpluses are found in manufacturing exporters like China and Germany and also in resource exporters such as Saudi Arabia.

One of the factors that affects trade balances, especially for countries that export manufactured goods, is a country's unit labour costs (wage costs per unit of output) compared to other countries' unit labour costs, measured at the prevailing exchange rate (price of one currency in terms of another).[6] A country with lower unit labour costs, converted to a foreign currency (like the US dollar), will be likely to export more and import less, thereby tending to give it a bigger trade surplus. For example, countries like China and Mexico have taken advantage of relatively low wages combined with rising productivity in their export industries to achieve competitive advantages in many manufactured products, such as electronics and autoparts. In addition, in the late 1990s and early 2000s, China also maintained an artificially low value of its currency, the renminbi (also called the yuan), thereby making its exports even cheaper in dollar terms than they would have been otherwise. Indeed, as the renminbi has appreciated (risen in value) and Chinese wages have increased since around 2005, China's trade surplus has decreased and some labour-intensive industries (for example, apparel) have left China for countries that have even lower wages. In the euro area, where there is no internal exchange rate (because all countries use the same currency), a country like Germany can still obtain competitive advantages over other users of the same currency (for example, Italy or France) by keeping its wages low relative to the productivity of its workers (or, equivalently, having productivity grow faster than wages).

Whenever some countries have large trade surpluses and others have large deficits, much of global trade is following absolute competitive advantages (that is, the lowest monetary cost of production at prevailing exchange rates) rather than comparative advantages.[7] In this situation, international trade is not generally fulfilling its supposed mission of making sure that goods are always exported by the countries that can produce them most efficiently; some countries are exporting goods that they would not export if trade were balanced, while other countries are importing those goods instead of producing them for themselves.

Trade and unemployment

The issue of imbalanced trade is also linked to the problem of unemployment. In Europe, for example, surplus countries like Germany and the Netherlands have maintained lower rates of unemployment than deficit countries like Spain and Greece. Similarly, China has taken jobs away from the USA: estimates of US job losses caused by trade with China range from 1.5 million (Autor et al., 2013) to 2.7 million (Scott, 2012).

Deficit countries do not, however, always have high rates of unemployment. Sometimes, a country can have both a trade deficit and low unemployment rates, but this usually occurs when the country is borrowing to sustain aggregate demand at home. In this case, a country's consumers can buy goods and services in excess of what their current income would otherwise permit, thereby boosting the country's demand for imports and lowering its trade balance (as in the USA or Spain in the early 2000s, when both countries were experiencing debt-driven real estate booms). In such situations, the borrowing country can temporarily sustain low unemployment along with a trade deficit, but such a debt-led boom usually ends in a financial crisis and recession as occurred in the USA in 2008–09 and in Greece, Spain and other euro area deficit countries starting in 2009–10. After a financial crisis, deficit countries that had enjoyed temporary booms based on borrowing are usually compelled to make painful adjustments through higher unemployment and reduced incomes that in turn depress their purchases of imports, thereby 'improving' their trade balances. Hence, the deficit shown for the USA in Figure 12.3 for 2013 was about half of the US deficit at its peak in 2006 (approximately US$400 versus US$800 billion). Greece and Spain do not appear in Figure 12.3 because by 2013 they had eliminated their previously large trade deficits from before the euro area crisis, but in the process their unemployment rates soared to around 20–25 per cent.

Long-run development and infant-industry protection

Even if we abstract from the difficulties of unemployment and imbalanced trade, the traditional theory of comparative advantage suffers from another defect. The traditional theory is static, which means that it only investigates what is the best option for a country at a given moment in time, based on its current resources and technology. However, in the long run, countries must improve their technology in order to grow and raise their living standards, and in the process they may need to develop the capability to produce goods in which they do not have a pre-existing comparative advantage.

In the example shown in Table 12.1, adopting free trade and specializing in rice production for export was the best option for EA only because EA's technology for producing televisions was so poor. If EA could improve its technology, it could potentially become a manufacturing region that would export goods like televisions to the USA, instead of the other way around. To see this possibility, consider the example shown in Table 12.2, where EA has lowered its labour cost to two hours per television, the same as in the USA – presumably, by importing or imitating US television technology. Now, the

Table 12.2 Dynamic comparative advantage: technological improvement in East Asia

	Hours of labour required to produce:	
	Televisions (per unit)	Rice (per ton)
United States	2	4
East Asia	2	5

relative labour cost of a television is lower in EA than in the USA ($2/5$ = 0.4 versus $2/4$ = 0.5), so EA switches to having a comparative advantage in televisions. Henceforth, EA will export televisions in exchange for rice imported from the USA. This can be called 'dynamic comparative advantage', because over time the less developed country acquires the technical know-how required to produce a more advanced product and changes the direction of its trade.

But, how could the EA television industry ever get off the ground? If EA allows free trade under the conditions shown in Table 12.1, it would remain permanently specialized in rice and its manufacturing industries would remain underdeveloped; any potential television producers could not compete with relatively cheaper US imports. Therefore, EA may need to use tariffs or quotas to protect local producers of televisions from imports until those producers become efficient enough to compete on their own, a policy that is known as 'infant-industry protection'. Such protection is designed to enable a domestic industry to acquire improved technology and lower its costs to the point at which, eventually, the industry can survive without protection (and may possibly start to export).

There are some important qualifications to the case for infant-industry protection. First, in addition to (or instead of) trade policies, a government may choose to utilize other types of industrial policies. For example, the government could subsidize an industry through various means, such as by offering low interest rates on loans or providing necessary infrastructure and training. Thus, the promotion of infant industries need not be done exclusively through trade protection. Second, if trade protection is used, the tariffs and quotas should not be too restrictive or permanent, otherwise the protected industry might not have incentives to become more efficient and might never be able to export. There are many cases of countries that have protected and subsidized 'infant' industries that, in effect, never grew up to become efficient and competitive exporters. This is why many developing countries, including Mexico, South Korea and India, have at various points in time reduced formerly high levels of protection and sought to expose their producers to greater global competition. Protecting domestic industries via tariffs or quotas raises the costs of the products for domestic consumers, so it is important that the long-term gains from increased efficiency and eventual exports should outweigh the short-term costs of the protection.

Third, governments seeking to promote new industries face a choice of welcoming foreign multinational corporations (MNCs) to produce the more advanced goods, or else favouring domestic companies that could potentially produce them instead. The former path is in many ways easier, because foreign MNCs already have the necessary technology and know-how, but the MNCs may not want to share the technology and know-how with the 'host' country. Therefore, even though it is more difficult, it may be more beneficial in the long run to try to promote national firms in order to enhance domestic technological learning. But if the latter route is too difficult or is blocked by trade agreements (discussed below) that prohibit policies favouring national firms, then it may be possible to negotiate with foreign MNCs to ensure that they share their technology (for example, by encouraging them to train domestic workers in advanced technology or to form partnerships with local firms). Most major countries that have successfully developed (including, for example, the USA, Germany and Japan) have used infant-industry protection and other industrial policies at critical points in their history, and the few countries that have made the leap from developing to industrialized (most recently Korea) have done so by enabling their own national companies to become global innovators and technological leaders (the Korean multinational Samsung is a good example) (see Chang, 2002; Lee, 2013).

Trade liberalization and trade agreements

As noted above, it is sometimes necessary or helpful for countries to use restrictive trade policies strategically to help develop their economies. In addition, many countries adopt protectionist policies with the intention of boosting domestic employment, or simply to help domestic interest groups that would be unfavourably affected if trade were liberalized. Nevertheless, all of these policies – regardless of the motivation – are likely to have adverse consequences for other nations. The protection of an industry in one country can mean a loss of exports and jobs for another country. Similarly, a subsidy used to promote exports in one country can result in artificially cheap imports that displace domestic producers and reduce employment in another. To use our previous example, if EA protects or subsidizes its television industry, this will cause job losses for US television workers – who are unlikely to become rice farmers, and at best are likely to be re-employed at lower wages in the service sector.

For these reasons, a long line of economists going back to Adam Smith has referred to protectionism as a 'beggar-my-neighbour' policy: even if it enriches the protecting nation, it may impoverish others. Moreover, the fact that one country's trade and industrial policies can adversely affect other countries' industries and employment may lead to retaliation: a country may impose tariffs or other protectionist measures in response to a foreign country's interventions. If a large number of countries adopt retaliatory trade barriers at the same time, the effect is to shrink global trade and lessen the gains that any country can derive from participation in the world market.

This problem became most acute during the Great Depression in the 1930s. Although high tariffs and frequent retaliation did not cause the depression, as some have claimed, they certainly did not help the global economy to recover. Therefore, after World War II the victorious allies began a process of multilateral trade liberalization by engaging in broad-ranging negotiations over reciprocal reductions in tariffs and other trade barriers. This process started with the General Agreement on Tariffs and Trade (GATT), originally launched at a Geneva conference in 1947, and continued through the formation of the World Trade Organization (WTO) in 1995. As of November 2015, the WTO had 162 member countries.

In addition, smaller groups of countries have formed what are variously known as bilateral, regional or preferential trade agreements, leading to economic integration of the member countries. Some prominent examples include the European Union (EU) and North American Free Trade Agreement (NAFTA). The simplest type of trade agreement is a free trade area, in which trade barriers among the member countries are reduced or eliminated. More ambitious efforts at economic integration include a customs union (in which the member countries also adopt common external tariffs), a common market (in which the members allow free flows of labour and capital as well as goods and services), and an economic union (in which, in addition to all of the above, the countries seek to harmonize other aspects of their economic policies). However, one should be cautious in assessing actual trade agreements because they do not necessarily live up to their names. For example, Mercosur is supposed to be the 'common market of the South', but the member countries (Argentina, Brazil, Paraguay, Uruguay and most recently Venezuela) have never fully eliminated tariffs on each other's goods or negotiated a common external tariff, so it is not even really a free trade area or customs union.

The traditional analysis of trade agreements emphasizes the issue of trade creation versus trade diversion: do the gains from increasing trade among the member countries outweigh the possible losses from trading less with outside nations, which might be able to supply imports at lower costs? However, trade agreements have often been formed for many reasons that go beyond standard calculations of net gains from trade creation and diversion. Other economic reasons for trade agreements include: wanting preferential access for goods exported to a major trading partner; taking advantage of scale economies by producing for a larger market area; and trying to attract MNCs to invest in a country because it is a member of a larger trading bloc. These have been major motivations for smaller or less developed countries that have joined integration schemes with larger or more advanced countries, such as Mexico in NAFTA and Ireland in the EU. Sometimes the motivation is political, as when the countries in a region or alliance want to foster greater integration of their societies and be more unified in response to perceived external threats; this was an important reason for the efforts at European integration that led to the formation of the EU in 1992 and its subsequent expansion (see Chapter 14).

Regional or preferential trade agreements have gained a new impetus as a result of the breakdown of multilateral trade negotiations since 2001. A new WTO 'round' was launched at Doha in 2001, but as of 2016 there were no prospects of its successful conclusion. The major players such as the USA, EU, and leading emerging market nations (Brazil, China, India, and so on) cannot agree on various outstanding issues, including US demands for strengthened intellectual property rights and many countries' unwillingness to further liberalize their agricultural sectors.

As the multilateral process is stuck, many countries have gone ahead and formed more limited trade agreements with varying numbers of partners. In particular, the USA has used its leverage over smaller countries that want access to its market to win provisions that it cannot get in the WTO process, such as strengthened intellectual property rights (patents, copyrights, and so on) and investor–state dispute resolution procedures that favour multinational corporations.

As of 2016, two very broad trade initiatives were being proposed: a Trans-Pacific Partnership (TPP) that would include the USA, Japan and ten other countries around the Pacific Rim; and a Transatlantic Trade and Investment Partnership (TTIP) between the EU and the USA. Ironically, these negotiations have been fraught with difficulties because they are confronting the same big issues that have hampered the Doha Round of the WTO, and the USA does not have the same leverage with Japan or the EU that it has with the smaller countries with which it has negotiated bilateral trade deals (for example, Morocco or Peru). At the time this book went to press (early 2016), a TPP agreement had been negotiated but not yet ratified by the prospective member countries, including the United States, where significant opposition had emerged; the prospects for TTIP also remained uncertain at that time.

Manufactured exports and the fallacy of composition

In spite of the controversy over trade liberalization and trade policies, there can be no doubt that countries that have been successful at exporting manufactured goods have generally (with some exceptions, discussed below) had rapid economic growth that has significantly increased their income levels. Why are exports of manufactured goods usually so beneficial for promoting economic development? One key reason is economies of scale: by producing for a larger market, exporting firms can reduce their average costs by spreading out the fixed costs (for example, machinery and equipment, or research and development) over a greater quantity of output – and this is more likely to occur in manufacturing than agriculture or services. A second reason is that manufacturing activities engender greater technological learning within firms and more spillovers of knowledge between different firms and industries.

Third, manufacturing industries have generally been the main locus of technological innovation – the development of new and improved products and production processes – which is a key factor in driving long-run increases in productivity and incomes. In the twenty-first century, technological innovation has also spread to some service sectors (for example, software development) and other industries (including energy, agriculture and mining). Nevertheless, manufacturing remains key for one additional reason: it is the sector that produces the capital goods (machines and equipment) that are required to lower the costs of production and to make the newly developed or improved products in any sector of the economy.

In spite of these attractions of a development strategy focused on manufactured exports, only a relatively small number of developing countries (mostly in East Asia) have succeeded in using manufactured exports to leverage rapid, sustained growth in recent decades. For those countries that are abundant in natural resources (for example, in the Middle East, South America and Africa), the strong pull of comparative advantage has led them to continue to be specialized in primary commodity exports. Sometimes countries fail to adopt policies that would be conducive to success in manufactured exports, for example by allowing their currencies to become overvalued, not promoting or protecting infant industries, or not investing in the education and infrastructure required for success in the more advanced industries.

But among those countries that have attempted to pursue manufacturing export-led growth, the number of success stories has been limited by the 'fallacy of composition', or adding-up constraint (Blecker and Razmi, 2010). That is, not all countries can simultaneously increase their exports of manufactured goods at the very high rates seen in the most successful cases (for example, Korea and Taiwan in the 1980s, or China in the 2000s). The markets in the rich, industrialized countries are only so big and grow more slowly than world trade (recall that trade has grown much faster than GDP globally, as shown in Figure 12.1). Once the domestic producers in a given industry in an industrialized country (for example, local manufacturers of textiles and apparel) have been displaced, then the developing countries that want to enter these markets must compete very intensively for export opportunities in those markets.

Only the countries with the lowest monetary costs of production, the most competitive exchange rates and other favourable conditions can succeed, while the others are likely to fall behind and fail to achieve the desired export-led growth. Some countries may escape from this trap by moving 'up the industrial ladder' to more high-technology products, and may even become technological innovators themselves – Korea is a case in point, and China is moving rapidly in this direction. But even the markets for more advanced products can become saturated, and while it is possible to develop certain industrial 'clusters' or niches, there are limits to how many different niches the various exporting countries can find to exploit. The bottom line is that not all countries can succeed in enjoying rapid export-led growth at the same time. The very success of some countries creates challenges if not defeats for others. For example, Mexico displaced Japan, Korea and Taiwan in many segments of the US market after liberalizing its trade and joining NAFTA in the late 1980s and 1990s, but subsequently China displaced Mexico after the former joined the WTO in 2001 (Blecker and Esquivel, 2013).

The Mexican case suggests another cautionary note: although the total value of its exports of manufactures has grown enormously, a large portion of these exports consists of goods that are merely assembled in the country using imported parts and components. As a result, the 'value added' (the difference between total value and input costs) is only a small portion of the total value of many Mexican exports, and therefore the gains in domestic job creation have been disappointing. Furthermore, Mexico's manufactured exports are largely produced by (or under contract with) foreign MNCs that generally keep their most innovative and high value-added operations elsewhere. These elements of Mexico's export strategy have limited the overall growth gains that the country has received from its exports (Blecker and Ibarra, 2013).

Indeed, production processes are now spread out over many different countries, with different stages of production taking place in (and inputs supplied from) numerous different countries. Thus, an increasing portion of global trade today consists in intermediate and semi-finished products, as opposed to the more traditional raw materials and finished goods. This new pattern of trade is sometimes referred to as 'vertical specialization', because countries specialize in different stages of production rather than particular final goods, and it is also related to the concept of global supply (or value) chains. Countries need to participate in global supply chains in order to be competitive in today's world economy, but emerging nations also need to be careful that they eventually move up into the more innovative and higher value-added links in these chains rather than remaining permanently limited to labour-intensive assembly operations.

Conclusions

Finding the most beneficial trade strategy for a country today is more complicated than the old (and increasingly sterile) debate about 'free trade' versus 'protectionism'. The countries that have grown most successfully in the long run are those that have strategically deployed prudent means of promoting nascent domestic industries and encouraging exports, especially of manufactures. But each country needs to find its own best strategy, given its economic structure and external constraints.

Paradoxically, the policies that may be most important for making the global trading system work more to the benefit of all nations may not be trade policies or trade agreements at all. Especially, reforming the international monetary system to prevent some countries from achieving trade surpluses based on undervalued currencies could help to restore more balanced and mutually beneficial trade. In addition, competition over global trade and investment opportunities is exacerbated by the chronic lack of aggregate demand throughout much of the world economy, a problem that has been aggravated by recent financial crises and the austerity policies adopted (rather misguidedly) in their wake. By adopting the types of macroeconomic policies recommended in other parts of this book – especially by targeting monetary and fiscal policies on the achievement of full employment – the global trading system could operate more to the benefit of all countries and with less conflict than it does at present.

NOTES

1 Ricardo's original model of international trade had three classes of economic agents: workers, capitalists and landowners (see Maneschi, 1992); what was presented here is the so-called 'Ricardian' trade model as presented in standard textbooks. Recall the discussion in Chapter 2.
2 The Heckscher–Ohlin model is named for early twentieth-century Swedish economists Eli Heckscher and Bertil Ohlin, while the Stolper–Samuelson theorem is named for US economists Wolfgang Stolper and Paul Samuelson, who published it in 1941. Both the Heckscher–Ohlin model and the Stolper–Samuelson theorem assume that the factors of production are 'mobile' between industries, in the sense that any given

unit of labour, land or capital could possibly be employed in producing any of the traded goods. See Bivens (2008) for an in-depth discussion of this theorem and relevant empirical evidence. Reinert (2012) offers an introductory textbook-level presentation.

3 Another type of new theory that can explain why trade tends to worsen inequality in many different countries is found in models of trade with 'heterogeneous firms', that is, where some firms are more efficient or productive than others. In such models, only the most productive firms can be successful in exporting while less productive firms may be driven out of the market by trade, with the result that average profit margins of the remaining firms may rise and (because the more productive firms tend to use relatively more high-skilled labour) high-skilled workers may benefit more than low-skilled workers when trade opens up. See, for example, Amiti and Davis (2012), De Loecker and Warzynscki (2012) and Egger and Kreickemeier (2012).

4 See also Chapter 10 on the role of exports in long-run growth and Chapter 13 on the concept of a balance-of-payments constraint on growth.

5 Workers who do not find jobs may remain unemployed in advanced countries like the USA or the UK, where there are social insurance mechanisms to sustain them at least temporarily. In less developed countries, however, such welfare mechanisms often do not exist, and workers who do not find jobs in the modern sector cannot survive long without some sort of work. Thus, such workers tend to end up in the informal sector, for example by becoming street vendors or working in small shops where they have very low productivity and incomes. In these cases, we say that the workers are 'underemployed' instead of unemployed.

6 Note that, by definition, unit labour cost equals WL/PY, where W is the wage rate (per hour), L is hours of labour, P is the price of the goods, and Y is the quantity of output. Since this ratio can also be written as $(W/P)/(Y/L)$, we can see that unit labour cost also equals the ratio of the real wage to the productivity of labour (quantity of output per hour). Thus, unit labour costs can be reduced either by suppressing wages or, alternatively, by increasing productivity. All this is in domestic currency; unit labour costs then get translated into a foreign currency by multiplying by the exchange rate measured as the foreign currency value of the home currency (for example, dollars per pound in the UK).

7 Note that absolute *competitive* advantage, in the sense of lowest monetary cost, is not the same as absolute *productivity* advantage, in the sense of lowest labour time or highest labour productivity. The heterodox theory emphasizes the former, not the latter.

 REFERENCES

Amiti, M. and D.R. Davis (2012), 'Trade, firms, and wages: theory and evidence', *Review of Economic Studies*, **79** (1), 1–36.

Autor, D., D. Dorn and G.H. Hanson (2013), 'The China syndrome: local labour market effects of import competition in the United States', *American Economic Review*, **103** (6), 2121–68.

Bivens, J. (2008), *Everybody Wins Except for Most of Us: What Economics Teaches about Globalization*, Washington, DC: Economic Policy Institute.

Blecker, R.A. and G. Esquivel (2013), 'Trade and the development gap', in A. Selee and P. Smith (eds), *Mexico and the United States: The Politics of Partnership*, Boulder, CO: Lynne Rienner, pp. 83–110.

Blecker, R.A. and C. Ibarra (2013), 'Trade liberalization and the balance of payments constraint with intermediate imports: the case of Mexico revisited', *Structural Change and Economic Dynamics*, **25** (1), 33–47.

Blecker, R.A. and A. Razmi (2010), 'Export-led growth, real exchange rates and the fallacy of composition', in M. Setterfield (ed.), *Handbook of Alternative Theories of Economic Growth*, Cheltenham, UK and Northampton, MA, USA: Edward Elgar Publishing, pp. 379–96.

Bureau of Labor Statistics (2014), 'Producer price indices', accessed 4 June 2014 at www.bls.gov/data.

Chang, H.J. (2002), *Kicking Away the Ladder: Development Strategy in Historical Perspective*, London: Anthem.

De Loecker, J. and F. Warzynski (2012), 'Markups and firm-level export status', *American Economic Review*, **102** (6), 2437–71.

Egger, H. and U. Kreickemeier (2012), 'Fairness, trade, and inequality', *Journal of International Economics*, **86** (2), 184–96.

Feenstra, R.C. and G.H. Hanson (1997), 'Foreign direct investment and relative wages: evidence from Mexico's maquiladoras', *Journal of International Economics*, **42** (3–4), 371–94.

International Monetary Fund (2014a), 'International financial statistics', accessed 4 June 2014 at www.elibrary-data.imf.org.

International Monetary Fund (2014b), *World Economic Outlook Database*, accessed 4 June 2014 at www.imf.org/external/pubs/ft/weo/2014/01/weodata/index.aspx.

Keynes, J.M. (1936), *The General Theory of Employment, Interest and Money*, London: Macmillan.

Lee, K. (2013), *Schumpeterian Analysis of Economic Catch-Up: Knowledge, Path-Creation and the Middle Income Trap*, New York: Cambridge University Press.

Maneschi, A. (1992), 'Ricardo's international trade theory: beyond the comparative cost example', *Cambridge Journal of Economics*, **16** (4), 421–37.

Reinert, K.A. (2012), *An Introduction to International Economics: New Perspectives on the World Economy*, New York: Cambridge University Press.

Ricardo, D. ([1821] 1951), *Principles of Political Economy and Taxation*, Cambridge, UK: Cambridge University Press, third edition (reprinted).

Robinson, J. (1937), *Essays in the Theory of Employment*, London: Macmillan.

Robinson, J. (1956), *The Accumulation of Capital*, London: Macmillan.

Robinson, J. (1962), *Essays in the Theory of Economic Growth*, London: Macmillan.

Scott, R.E. (2012), 'The China toll: growing U.S. trade deficit with China cost more than 2.7 million jobs between 2001 and 2011, with job losses in every state', *Economic Policy Institute Briefing Paper, No. 345*.

World Bank (2014), 'World development indicators', accessed 4 June 2014 at http://databank.worldbank.org/data/home.aspx.

A PORTRAIT OF JOAN ROBINSON (1903–83)

Joan Robinson was a colleague of John Maynard Keynes at the University of Cambridge and a key member of his intellectual circle in the 1930s, when he was writing *The General Theory* (Keynes, 1936). She helped to bring the ideas of Karl Marx and Michał Kalecki into the somewhat insular world of Cambridge, and was also influenced by her discussions and debates with fellow Cantabrigians (especially Piero Sraffa and Nicholas Kaldor). She made contributions to economics in a wide range of areas including imperfect competition, endogenous money and economic development. However, she is best known for her work on economic growth and income distribution, especially in her *Accumulation of Capital* (1956) and *Essays in the Theory of Economic Growth* (1962). She was a major protagonist in the Cambridge controversies on capital theory from the 1950s through the 1970s.

Robinson's contributions to international economics began with her *Essays on the Theory of Employment* (1937), in which she criticized the use of 'beggar-my-neighbour' remedies for unemployment including tariffs, subsidies, wage suppression and competitive devaluations. She was also a trenchant critic of theories of automatic balance-of-payments adjustment and trade models that assumed balanced trade with full employment. In her later years, she denounced the 'new mercantilism' in which the more advanced countries sought to maintain their advantages over less developed countries, often by advocating 'free trade' for the latter while keeping their own markets closed. She was especially critical of the static nature of traditional models of comparative advantage, and called for a shift in economic theory generally from the use of equilibrium methods to analyses based on irreversible processes occurring in 'historical time'.

13

Balance-of-payments-constrained growth

John McCombie and Nat Tharnpanich

 OVERVIEW

This chapter covers the following topics:

- It explains why, for many countries, their long-run growth rate is constrained by their balance of payments to below their growth of productive potential. As such, it presents an alternative explanation to neoclassical growth theory.

- It explains that the 'balance-of-payments equilibrium growth rate' is derived as $y_{BP} = x/\pi = \varepsilon z/\pi$, where x and z are the growth of exports and world markets, ε is the world income elasticity of demand for the country's exports and π is the domestic income elasticity of demand for imports. This relationship, known as Thirlwall's Law, gives a good prediction for the growth rates of a large number of countries.

- It shows that non-price competitiveness (as reflected in international disparities in the values of both the income elasticities of demand, namely, ε and π) is more important than price competitiveness in international trade.

- It points out that, unlike the neoclassical approach to the balance of payments, relative prices do not change sufficiently to relax the balance-of-payments constraint. It is the growth of output that has to adjust.

- It shows how a decline in the growth rate of one group of countries (or trading bloc) can limit the growth of another.

 KEYWORDS

- **Balance-of-payments equilibrium growth rate:** The growth rate consistent with the balance of payments being in equilibrium.

- **Dynamic Harrod foreign trade multiplier:** This determines by how much the overall growth rate directly increases owing to an increase in the growth of exports.
- **Hicks supermultiplier:** The combined effect of the foreign trade multiplier and the effect of the further increase in the growth of domestic expenditure owing to the initial relaxation of the balance-of-payments constraint.
- **Non-price competitiveness:** This is reflected in the relative size of both the world income elasticity for a country's exports (ε) and the domestic income elasticity of imports (π).

Why are these topics important?

Neoclassical growth theory is essentially a supply-side explanation of the rate of change of output and productivity, and is generally confined to a closed economy. In the Solow (1956) model, economic growth is modelled using the aggregate production function and the assumptions of constant returns to scale and perfect competition. It is further postulated that savings determine investment. All factors are fully employed and there is no independent role for the growth of demand. Technical progress is assumed to be exogenous. While this last assumption is relaxed in neo-Schumpeterian and AK or 'linear-in-capital' models, they are still closed economy full employment models (see, for example, Valdés, 1999). However, in reality, most resources are not fixed. The quality and quantity of the labour input (including that from migration, disguised unemployment and the intersectoral reallocation of labour), the rate of capital accumulation, together with productivity growth (the last due to both increasing returns to scale and induced technical progress), are endogenous to the economic system, being largely determined by the growth of output (León-Ledesma and Thirlwall, 2002; McCombie et al., 2002; Thirlwall, 2002).

The neoclassical assumption is that the demand for imports and exports is highly price elastic so that relatively small changes in the relative prices of imports and exports rapidly bring the balance of payments (current account)[1] into equilibrium at the full employment of resources. But this is not supported empirically (see McCombie and Thirlwall, 1994, 2004). This means that a major constraint that limits economic growth in many countries is provided by the balance of payments, as a country cannot run an ever-increasing current account deficit indefinitely. Output growth has to adjust to bring the balance of payments back into equilibrium and this 'balance-of-payments equilibrium growth rate' is often below the growth of productive potential, or the natural rate of growth.

As a consequence, the growth rates of groups of countries, or major trading blocs, are inextricably interlinked. A recession in one country is transmitted through trade flows to its trading partners and should not be examined in isolation. See, for example, the early work on Project LINK (Hickman and Klein, 1979).

The purpose of this chapter is to outline this alternative Keynesian approach to economic growth. This approach has its origins in a short paper by Thirlwall (1979) and has been subsequently theoretically extended and subjected to empirical testing in a large number of articles (see, for example, McCombie and Thirlwall, 1994, 2004 and Thirlwall, 2011, Table 2, p. 343).

The determination of the balance-of-payments equilibrium growth rate

In the Keynesian tradition, economic growth is ultimately demand determined. To derive the balance-of-payments-constrained growth model, we start by considering the case where there is an initial disequilibrium in the current account. This may be expressed in terms of the balance-of-payments identity as follows:

$$P_d X + F \equiv P_f E M \tag{13.1}$$

where P_d, P_f and E are the domestic price of exports, the foreign price of imports, and the exchange rate (measured as the domestic price of foreign currency). X and M are the volumes of exports and imports and F is the value of nominal capital flows measured in terms of the domestic currency. F (> 0) measures capital inflows. Expressing equation (13.1) in terms of growth rates gives:

$$\theta(p_d + x) + (1 - \theta)f \equiv p_f + m + e \tag{13.2}$$

where the lower case letters denote growth rates and θ is the share of export earnings in total overseas receipts.

The export demand function may be expressed in terms of growth rates as follows:

$$x = \eta(p_d - e - p_f) + \varepsilon z \tag{13.3}$$

where z is the growth of world income,[2] and η (< 0) and ε are the price and world income elasticities of export demand, respectively. The import demand function also expressed in growth rates is given by:

$$m = \psi(p_f + e - p_d) + \pi y \qquad (13.4)$$

where m is the growth rate of imports, $\psi(< 0)$ and π are the price and domestic income elasticities of imports respectively.

Substituting equations (13.3) and (13.4) into (13.2) gives an equation for the growth of income as:

$$y = \frac{\theta \varepsilon z + (1 - \theta)(f - p_d) + (1 + \theta \eta + \psi)(p_d - e - p_f)}{\pi} \qquad (13.5)$$

We shall show below that, with one or two exceptions, it is unlikely that a country can run a substantial current account deficit for any length of time. Consequently, if we assume that the level, and growth, of net international financial flows are negligible in the long run (in other words, both $(1 - \theta)$ and $(f - p_d)$ equal 0), then equation (13.5) may be expressed as:

$$y = \frac{\varepsilon z + (1 + \eta + \psi)(p_d - e - p_f)}{\pi} \qquad (13.6)$$

Equation (13.6) expresses some familiar propositions.

First, if the sum of the absolute value of the price elasticities is greater than unity, that is, $|\eta + \psi| > 1$, so that the Marshall–Lerner conditions hold, then a faster rate of inflation at home than abroad, *ceteris paribus*, will reduce the growth rate, but only to a small extent if the value does not greatly exceed unity. The demand for imports and exports is likely to have low price elasticities where exports and imports are product differentiated and non-price competition is important. (If the Marshall–Lerner conditions sum to unity, then the change in the terms of trade will have no effect on the balance of payments.) Second, a *continuous* devaluation or depreciation of the exchange rate $(e > 0)$ will likewise increase the growth rate, provided that once again the Marshall–Lerner conditions hold. But it should be noted that to raise the growth rate (as opposed to improving the current account at any given growth rate) requires a sustained depreciation. Finally, a faster growth of world income, z, will raise the country's growth rate, but by how much depends crucially upon the size of the relative income elasticities of demand for exports and imports, namely, the ratio ε/π.

If relative prices expressed in a common currency do not change very much in the long run or the price elasticities of demand are small, then their contribution to the growth rate is likely to be negligible. If we assume that there is no effect, then what may be termed the balance-of-payments equilibrium growth rate is given by:

$$y_{BP} = x/\pi \tag{13.7}$$

or

$$y_{BP} = \varepsilon z/\pi \tag{13.8}$$

Equations (13.7) and (13.8) are alternative versions of what have become known as Thirlwall's Law (Thirlwall, 1979). It can be seen that differences in the balance-of-payments equilibrium growth rate are determined by disparities in the income elasticities ε (or the growth of exports, x) and π. These reflect differences in all aspects of non-price competitiveness, including quality, reliability, after-sales provision, and so on (McCombie and Thirlwall, 1994, Ch. 4). Hausmann et al. (2007) provide a similar emphasis on the importance of the sophistication of a country's exports for its economic growth.

For example, over the period 1951–73, the estimates of π for the United Kingdom and West Germany (as it then was) were 1.51 and 1.89. Given that their rate of export growth was 4.1 and 10.8 per cent per annum, from equation (13.7), y_{BP} is 2.7 and 5.7 per cent per annum respectively. These figures are virtually identical to the actual growth rates of output experienced by the two countries (McCombie and Thirlwall, 1994, Table 3.2, p. 241). West Germany's exports were growing faster than those of the United Kingdom, because the world income elasticity of demand for its exports was double that of the United Kingdom. This reflected the greater non-price competiveness of West Germany's exports compared with the United Kingdom.

The Harrod foreign trade multiplier and the Hicks supermultiplier

Thirlwall's Law can be interpreted in one of two ways (McCombie, 2004). The first, and simplest, is that it is a dynamic analogue of the Harrod foreign trade multiplier (Harrod, 1933). The second, and more general, interpretation is that it reflects the workings of the Hicks supermultiplier (Hicks, 1950).

Turning first to the Harrod foreign trade multiplier, this was originally derived on the assumptions of no savings and investment and no government spending and taxation (Harrod, 1933). Income consists of domestically produced consumption goods (C) and exports (X), and all income is spent on either home consumption goods or imports (M). Under these assumptions, trade is always balanced and income adjusts to preserve equilibrium on the current account. Let the import demand function be given by the linear specification:

$$M = M_0 + \mu Y \tag{13.9}$$

where M_0 denotes autonomous imports and μ is the marginal propensity to import.

As $X = M$, this may be written as:

$$Y = (1/\mu)(M - M_0) = (1/\mu)(X - M_0) \tag{13.10}$$

where $dY/dX = (1/\mu)$ is the static foreign trade multiplier that brings exports and imports back into equilibrium. It follows that as $X = M$ and $dX = dM$:

$$\frac{dY}{dX}\frac{X}{Y} = \frac{dY}{dM}\frac{M}{Y} \tag{13.11}$$

or

$$\frac{dY}{Y} = \frac{dX}{X}\left(\frac{dY}{dM}\frac{M}{Y}\right) = \frac{1}{\pi}\frac{dX}{X} \tag{13.12}$$

This may be expressed in the alternative notation as $y_{BP} = x/\pi$, which is one version of Thirlwall's Law, namely, equation (13.7).

Second, a more general approach is to view the foundations of the law as reflecting the workings of the Hicks supermultiplier. To see this, consider the specification of a Keynesian model expressed as:

$$Y = (X + A)/k \tag{13.13}$$

where A is autonomous domestic expenditure and $1/k$ is the standard Keynesian multiplier, which includes the marginal propensity to import. Expressing equation (13.13) in growth rates gives:

$$y = (w_x x + w_A g_A)/k \tag{13.14}$$

where w_x and w_A are the shares of exports and other autonomous expenditures in income, and g_A is the growth of other autonomous expenditures. If the growth of autonomous expenditures initially consists only of export growth, then the growth of income is given by:

$$y = (\omega_x x)/k \tag{13.15}$$

However, the balance-of-payments equilibrium growth rate, starting from initial balance of payments equilibrium $(X = M)$ may be expressed as:

$$y_{BP} = x/\pi = (\omega_x x)/\mu \tag{13.16}$$

as $\omega_x = X/Y = M/Y$ and $\mu = dM/dY$.

As $k > \mu$, by comparing equations (13.15) and (13.16) it can be seen that the balance-of-payments equilibrium growth rate exceeds the growth rate of income determined solely by the growth of exports. Consequently, the growth of exports not only has a direct effect through the foreign trade multiplier, it also has a secondary role in that by relaxing the balance-of-payments constraint, it allows the other components of autonomous expenditures to grow faster without the economy initially encountering balance-of-payments problems. The faster, and maximum, growth of other autonomous expenditures $(g_{A,\,BP})$ enabled by the initial relaxing of the balance of payments constraint is given by:

$$g_{A,BP} = k(1/\mu - 1/k)(\omega_x/\omega_A)x \tag{13.17}$$

The combined two effects represent the workings of the Hicks supermultiplier. The balance-of-payments-constrained growth rate may consequently be expressed as follows:

$$y_{BP} = (\omega_x x + \omega_A g_{A,BP})/k = x/\pi \tag{13.18}$$

Price and non-price competitiveness in international trade

A key assumption of the balance-of-payments-constrained growth model is that the rate of change of relative prices has a small impact on the growth of imports and exports and, hence, on the balance-of-payments equilibrium growth rate. The contribution to the growth of output from the rate of change of relative prices in relaxing the balance-of-payments constraint, if the current account is in equilibrium, is, from equation (13.6), given by the expression:

$$(1 + \eta + \psi)(p_d - e - p_f)/\pi \tag{13.19}$$

The first point to note is that the model does not depend upon the rate of change of the real exchange rate having no effect on the balance-of-payments equilibrium growth rate, just that the growth of output given by equation (13.19) is not large enough to raise y_{BP} to the natural rate of growth.

The first reason why the rate of change of relative prices has little effect on the balance-of-payments equilibrium growth rate concerns the size of price elasticities. The neoclassical model assumes that the country can sell as much as it wants to in foreign markets, so that the value of $(1 + \eta + \psi)$ is infinite or, at the very least, very large. Hence, all that is needed is a very small rate of change of the real exchange rate. However, for manufactured goods, which constitute the bulk of international trade, production tends to be oligopolistic or monopolistic with substantial product differentiation. Thus, the price elasticity of demand is very inelastic and it is non-price competitiveness that matters, as reflected in the magnitudes of ε and π (McCombie and Thirlwall, 1994, Ch. 4). If the sum of the price elasticities is −1, then the rate of change of relative prices will have no effect on the balance-of-payments equilibrium growth rate.

On the one hand, the success of a country in world markets is due to product innovation, namely, developing new products for which world demand will rapidly grow, or concentrating on already fast-growing markets. Price competition, on the other hand, might not only be ineffective, it can also have an adverse impact by worsening the non-price competitiveness of a country's exports. Brech and Stout (1981), for example, found that over the period 1970 to 1980 a depreciation of the British pound was associated with the substitution of low for high unit value goods, thus, worsening the quality of British exports.

The second reason for the unimportance of price competition stems from the fact that $(p_d - e - p_f) \approx 0$. Let us suppose that there is a small increase in the rate of depreciation of the nominal exchange rate, and so, initially, the rate of growth of exports and, hence, output increases. This may be offset in one of two ways.

The first concerns pricing to market. With a continuous currency depreciation it follows that, other things being equal, import prices in terms of the domestic currency will steadily increase. However, with pricing to market, the foreign firms attempt to preserve their export market share by cutting their export prices in terms of their domestic currency. In other words, the growth of the price of imports in terms of the foreign currency is not now affected by the rate of depreciation of the exchange rate. This involves, in effect, cross-subsidizing exports with some of the profits from the foreign firm's sales in its own domestic market. The recent literature on pricing to market emphasizes the negative relationship between the price elasticity of demand and the level of productivity of exporters. High-productivity firms, generally facing a lower price elasticity of demand, have a higher mark-up and more room to absorb changes in the exchange rate in order to maintain their market share than low-productivity firms (Martin and Rodriguez, 2004; Atkeson and Burstein, 2008; Melitz and Ottaviano, 2008; Berman et al., 2012). Because aggregate exports are often produced by the higher-productivity firms, the impact of exchange rate changes on prices and, hence, the balance of payments tends to be weak.

The second mechanism is real wage resistance and import price pass-through. To the extent that pricing to market does not occur, the domestic retail price index will increase because of the higher price of imports of consumer goods in terms of the domestic currency. The higher domestic cost of intermediate imported goods is also likely to pass directly into higher domestic consumer prices. These two effects may lead to an increase in the rate of growth of domestic prices that completely offsets the initial benefits of the nominal depreciation for the growth of the home country's exports. This will occur if labour succeeds, through wage bargaining, in increasing its nominal wages to offset the increase in the retail price level resulting from higher import prices (Wilson, 1976). Furthermore, as noted above, to increase the rate of growth, the real exchange rate must decline continuously, in which case it may well lead to a series of J-curve[3] effects, worsening the current account in the longer run.

It should be noted that the greater the effect of pricing to market, the less will be the need for the effect of wage resistance to offset the nominal exchange rate depreciation.

The role of the growth of capital flows

Over recent years there has been increasing liberalization of international financial flows and so the question arises as to what extent this has relaxed the balance-of-payments constraint. The answer is: not to any great extent. International financial markets become increasingly nervous if the net-foreign-debt-to-GDP ratio approaches a certain critical threshold, generally about 50 per cent. Moreover, the speed of the increase of net foreign liabilities, which is determined by the size of the current account deficit, is also an important factor (Catão and Milesi-Ferretti, 2013, p. 27).

Following McCombie and Roberts (2002), let the critical threshold of the net-foreign-debt-to-GDP ratio be $(D/Y)^*$, where D and Y are the stock of net foreign debt and the level of GDP respectively. Differentiating (D/Y) with respect to time gives:

$$\frac{d\left(\frac{D}{Y}\right)}{dt} = \frac{CA}{Y} - \frac{D}{Y}y \tag{13.20}$$

where CA/Y is the current-account-deficit-to-GDP ratio. For the net-external-debt-to-GDP ratio to be stable, $d(D/Y)/dt = 0$. Consequently, the critical threshold for the current account deficit (CA) is given by:

$$\left(\frac{CA}{Y}\right)^* = \left(\frac{D}{Y}\right)^* y \tag{13.21}$$

Thus, for any given growth rate, the critical net-debt-to-GDP threshold implies that there is a corresponding current account deficit critical threshold and vice versa. For example, if we assume that the critical threshold of the net-debt-to-GDP ratio is 50 per cent, then the maximum sustainable current account deficit is 0.5 per cent of GDP with a growth rate of 1 per cent per annum, rising to 3 per cent when the growth rate is 6 per cent per annum.

Nevertheless, the growth of financial flows is likely to make a negligible contribution to relaxing the balance-of-payments constraint. Let us again assume that the current-account-to-GDP ratio is constant. This implies that the growth of capital flows equals that of the growth of income (or $f - p_d = y$). With the usual assumption that the change in relative prices has no effect, the balance-of-payments equilibrium growth rate in equation (13.5) can be reduced to:

$$y_{BP} = \frac{\theta x}{(\pi - 1 + \theta)} \tag{13.22}$$

For illustrative purposes, consider an economy where exports are 30 per cent of income and π equals 1.5. If the critical current-account-deficit-to-income ratio is 2 per cent (so that $\theta = 30/32$), it follows that the balance-of-payments equilibrium growth rate is given by $y_B = 0.65x$, whereas if there is no growth in capital flows and the current account is in equilibrium $(\theta = 1)$, $y_B = 0.67x$. (This result proves relatively insensitive to the exact share of exports in GDP. If the figure is 10 per cent, the balance-of-payments equilibrium growth rate is $0.63x$ and if it is 50 per cent, the corresponding figure is $0.66x$.)

This approach may be extended to include explicitly the growth of net real interest rate payments on the overseas debt (Moreno-Brid, 2003).

Resource-constrained, policy-constrained and balance-of-payments-constrained growth

One consequence of the existence of the balance-of-payments constraint means that one group of countries (or a trading bloc) can constrain the growth of another group, even though with, say, just two trading blocs, the world economy as a whole is a closed economy. All that is required is for one group to be either resource (or capacity) constrained or policy constrained. A country is termed resource constrained if its rate of growth is so rapid that its growth is limited by the rate of expansion of its capacity. For example, capital accumulation may be at its maximum rate or there may be labour shortages, even with immigration and the intersectoral transfer of labour from declining to expanding sectors of the economy. Japan over the period 1950–1973, when the growth of the economy reached 10 per cent per annum, is a good example of this, and ran substantial trade surpluses. However, it should be emphasized that we are not in a neoclassical world, where the rate of growth is *exogenously* determined by the supply side. The rapid growth of Japan's exports was still a key factor in its spectacular economic performance. A country is policy constrained when, for example, because of inflationary concerns, deflationary policies are introduced that reduce the growth of income, such as occurred in many advanced countries in the 1970s.

We may illustrate this interaction between the two groups of countries using a simple numerical example (Table 13.1).

Group 1 are those countries that are balance-of-payments constrained and the countries of Group 2 are either policy or capacity (resource) constrained. Let us assume the latter are capacity constrained, so that they are growing at their natural rate, or the growth of their productive potential. Assuming that the rate of change of relative prices has no effect on the growth of exports or imports, the growth of the imports of Group 2 are given by the multiplicative import demand function, expressed in growth rates as $m_2 = \pi_2 y_2$. By definition, the income elasticity of demand for Groups 2's imports is identical to the income elasticity of demand for Group 1's exports, or $\pi_2 = \varepsilon_1$, and these are assumed to take a value of unity. It likewise follows that the income elasticity of demand for imports by Group 1 and the income elasticity of Group 2's exports are equal $(\pi_1 = \varepsilon_2)$ and are assumed to take a value of 2.

To begin with, let us assume that both groups are growing at their natural or productive potential rate of growth and this is initially 5 per cent per

Table 13.1 Balance-of-payments-constrained growth: the case of two groups of countries

	y_P	y_{BP}	π	ε	m	x
Initial growth rates						
Group 1	5	n.a.	2	1	10	5
Group 2	5	n.a.	1	2	5	10
Growth rates when Group 1 is balance-of-payments constrained						
Group 1	5	2.5	2	1	5	5
Group 2	5	n.a	1	2	5	5

Note: y_p is the growth of productive potential; y_{BP} is the balance-of-payments-constrained growth rate; n.a. means not applicable.

annum for each country. However, this is unsustainable. The reason is that the values of the income elasticities of demand for imports and exports of Group 1 mean that its imports and exports are growing at 10 and 5 per cent per annum respectively, as may be seen from Table 13.1.

This cannot continue in the long run, because Group 1 is running a persistent and increasing balance-of-payments deficit and, consequently, its net-overseas-debt-to-GDP ratio is increasing indefinitely. The only way that the balance of payments can be brought into equilibrium is for the growth rate of Group 1 to be curtailed to a growth rate of 2.5 per cent per annum by (say) domestic policy measures. At this growth rate, both its imports and exports are growing at 5 per cent per annum. The cost is that the growth of Group 1's output is half the growth of its productive potential (see Table 13.1). Group 2 is still growing at its natural rate of growth of 5 per cent per annum.

If we assume, however, that Group 2 is policy constrained, then increasing its growth rate would also have the effect of increasing the growth rate of Group 1, although the growth disparities would remain. If Group 2 now grows at, say, 7 per cent, then Group 1 can grow at 3.5 per cent, without running into balance-of-payments problems.

The problem is that there is an asymmetry in the international adjustment process, namely, the so-called 'deflationary bias'. There is much greater pressure on a deficit country to take deflationary measures to bring its balance of payments into equilibrium rather for than for the surplus country to reduce its current account surplus. See McCombie (1993) for a more detailed formal model of the two-country case.

Structural change and the multi-sectoral Thirlwall's Law

Following the multi-sector growth framework of Pasinetti (1981, 1993), which emphasizes export growth but does not contain a balance-of-payments constraint, Araujo and Lima (2007) were the first to incorporate structural change into the balance-of-payments growth model, which they termed the 'multi-sectoral Thirlwall's Law'. The aggregate income elasticities of demand for exports (and imports) are, by definition, equal to the weighted elasticities of the respective individual sectors. However, these weights are likely to change with structural change. Araujo and Lima (2007) show that even though the individual sectoral income elasticities of demand for imports and exports are constant, the balance-of-payments-constrained growth rate can increase if over time a country specializes more in those sectors where the individual export income elasticities of demand are the highest. This will also occur if the import-competing sectors where the income import elasticity of demand is also greatest, increase their relative share of domestic output.

The multi-sectoral Thirlwall's Law suggests that, even if the world income growth remains constant, a country's growth can still be enhanced by structural change that favourably affects the sectoral composition of exports and imports or there is an improvement in non-price competitiveness that alters the sectoral income elasticities, increasing ε_i and reducing π_i (where the subscript i is the sector), or both. Gouvea and Lima (2010) test this multi-sectoral model for four Latin American countries (Argentina, Brazil, Colombia and Mexico) and four Asian countries (South Korea, Malaysia, Philippines and Singapore) over the period 1962–2006. They found that, on balance, technology-intensive sectors have a higher income elasticity of demand for exports, but for imports there is little variation between sectors. For some countries, the multi-sectoral model has a higher predicted error than the aggregate model, but for both groups of countries the mean absolute error is lower for the multi-sectoral model. More importantly, they found that, for Latin America, the ratio of the sectorally weighted income elasticities of demand for exports and imports has hardly changed over the long period, but for East Asia the ratio has risen. This indicates the favourable impact of structural change in relaxing the balance-of-payments constraint.

Tests of the model and empirical evidence

Since the publication of Thirlwall's (1979) seminal paper, there have been numerous studies that test the balance-of-payments growth model. The results generally show support for the model for the data from both developed and developing countries alike. See Thirlwall (2011, Table 2, p. 343) for a summary of the empirical literature.

In essence, the test of the model is to see how closely y_{BP} predicts the actual growth rate (y_A) of countries (McCombie and Thirlwall, 1994). The most basic test is to use Spearman's rank correlation coefficient to test this correspondence for a pooled sample of countries (Thirlwall, 1979; Perraton, 2003). The rank correlation is typically over 0.7 and is statistically significant. This is not a parametric test, however, and can be criticized on the grounds that it does not show the quantitative relationship between y_A and y_{BP}.

The second test, which overcomes the latter objection, is to take the average deviation of the actual growth rate from the predicted rate, ignoring the sign. When this is done, the average deviation in most studies turns out to be less than one percentage point. However persuasive this test may be, it is not a parametric test either.

To overcome this drawback, two tests using regression analysis were developed to determine the predictive ability of the model. First, estimates of ε and π are determined by estimating the export and import demand functions for a particular country using appropriate regression techniques. These include tests for integration and co-integration using, for example, error correction models. It is often found that the Marshall–Lerner condition is barely met and the estimates of the price elasticities of demand for imports and exports are often not statistically significant.

From these estimates of the elasticities it is possible to calculate the values of $y_{BP} = x/\pi$ and $y_{BP} = \varepsilon z/\pi$. y_{BP}, x and z are usually the average growth rates calculated over periods of several years to avoid short-term fluctuations.

The first test is to regress y_{BP} on y_A using cross-county data and to test whether the constant is significantly different from zero and the regression coefficient is significantly different from unity. While this test overcomes previous criticisms, it has two drawbacks. First, there may be a bias if an incomplete sample of countries is taken, where the combined balance of payments do not balance. It would, however, be legitimate to take all the countries of the world, so that the sum of the surpluses equals the sum of the deficits. Second, the inclusion of an outlier such as a country that has run substantial balance-of-payments surpluses for many years may lead to the erroneous conclusion that, for all countries, their growth rate is not balance-of-payments constrained. An example is Japan in the early postwar years.

The second test that avoids all these difficulties, originally suggested by McCombie (1989), is to take each country separately and to estimate the hypothetical income elasticity of demand for imports that would make $y_A = y_{BP}$ (namely, π^*), where y_{BP} is given by equation (13.7). The statistical estimate of π used in calculating y_{BP} is obtained by estimating an import demand function that includes a relative price term. The null hypothesis is that π^* does not significantly differ from the statistical estimate of π. If this is the case, it would not refute the hypothesis that $y_A = y_{BP}$ and suggests that the role of the growth of capital flows and relative prices are quantitatively unimportant (or coincidently offsetting) in the model. A number of subsequent studies have relied on McCombie's (1989) test and have found good support for the model.

It is important to re-emphasize that for some countries to be balance-of-payments constrained requires some countries not to be. (As noted above, they may be capacity or policy constrained.) Consequently, the finding that a number of individual countries are not balance-of-payments constrained does not refute the relevance of the balance-of-payments growth model.

The validity of the model has been strengthened by more recent studies that apply various techniques that have recently been developed in time-series analysis. For surveys of the empirical studies, see McCombie and Thirlwall (1994, 2004) and Thirlwall (2011). See Felipe et al. (2010) and Tharnpanich and McCombie (2013) for regression studies showing that Pakistan and Thailand, respectively, were balance-of-payments constrained.

NOTES

1　The terms *balance-of-payments equilibrium* and *current account equilibrium* are used interchangeably.
2　This is often used as a proxy for the weighted growth of the overseas export markets of the country under consideration.
3　A J-curve is a curve whose initial segment is downward sloping and which then has a steep positive slope.

REFERENCES

Araujo, R.A. and G.T. Lima (2007), 'A structural economic dynamic approach to balance-of-payments-constrained growth', *Cambridge Journal of Economics*, **31** (5), 755–74.

Atkeson, A. and A. Burstein (2008), 'Pricing-to-market, trade costs, and international relative prices', *American Economic Review*, **98** (5), 1998–2031.

Berman, N., P. Martin and T. Mayer (2012), 'How do different exporters react to exchange rate changes?', *Quarterly Journal of Economics*, **127** (1), 437–92.

Brech, M.J. and D.K. Stout (1981), 'The rate of exchange and non-price competitiveness: a provisional study within UK manufactured exports', *Oxford Economic Papers*, **33** (Supplement), 268–81.

Catão, L.A.V. and G.M. Milesi-Ferretti (2013), 'External liabilities and crisis risk', *International Monetary Fund Working Paper, No. 13/113*.

Davidson, P. (1972), *Money and the Real World*, London: Macmillan (second edition 1978).

Davidson, P. (1982), *International Money and the Real World*, London: Macmillan.

Davidson, P. (1990–91), 'A post Keynesian positive contribution to "theory"', *Journal of Post Keynesian Economics*, **13** (2), 298–303.

Davidson, P. (2009), *The Keynes Solution: The Path to Global Prosperity*, Basingstoke, UK and New York: Palgrave Macmillan.

Felipe, J., J.S.L. McCombie and K. Naqvi (2010), 'Is Pakistan's growth rate balance-of-payments constrained? Policies and implications for development and growth', *Oxford Development Studies*, **38** (4), 477–96.

Gouvea, R.R. and G.T. Lima (2010), 'Structural change, balance-of-payments constraint, and economic growth: evidence from the multisectoral Thirlwall's Law', *Journal of Post Keynesian Economics*, **33** (1), 169–204.

Harrod, R.F. (1933), *International Economics*, Cambridge, UK: Cambridge University Press.

Hausmann, R., J. Hwang and D. Rodrik (2007), 'What you export matters', *Journal of Economic Growth*, **12** (1), 1–25.

Hickman, B.G. and L.R. Klein (1979), 'A decade of research by Project LINK', *Social Science Research Council Items*, **33** (3–4), 49–56.

Hicks, J.R. (1950), *The Trade Cycle*, Oxford, UK: Clarendon Press.

León-Ledesma, M.A. and A.P. Thirlwall (2002), 'The endogeneity of the natural rate of growth', *Cambridge Journal of Economics*, **26** (4), 441–59.

Martin, L.M. and D.R. Rodriguez (2004), 'Pricing to market at firm level', *Review of World Economics*, **140** (2), 302–20.

McCombie, J.S.L. (1989), '"Thirlwall's Law" and balance of payments constrained growth – a comment on the debate', *Applied Economics*, **21** (5), 611–29.

McCombie, J.S.L. (1993), 'Economic growth, trade interlinkages, and the balance-of-payments constraint', *Journal of Post Keynesian Economics*, **15** (4), 471–505.

McCombie, J.S.L. (2004), 'Economic growth, the Harrod foreign trade multiplier and the Hicks super-multiplier', in J.S.L McCombie and A.P. Thirlwall (eds) (2004), *Essays on Balance of Payments Constrained Growth: Theory and Evidence*, London and New York, Routledge, pp. 44–57.

McCombie, J.S.L. and M. Roberts (2002), 'The role of balance of payments in economic growth', in M. Setterfield (ed.), *The Economics of Demand-Led Growth*, Cheltenham, UK and Northampton, MA, USA: Edward Elgar Publishing, pp. 87–114.

McCombie, J.S.L. and A.P. Thirlwall (1994), *Economic Growth and the Balance-of-Payments Constraint*, Basingstoke, UK: Macmillan.

McCombie, J.S.L. and A.P. Thirlwall (eds) (2004), *Essays on Balance of Payments Constrained Growth: Theory and Evidence*, London and New York: Routledge.

McCombie, J.S.L., M. Pugno and B. Soro (eds) (2002), *Productivity Growth and Economic Performance: Essays on Verdoorn's Law*, Basingstoke, UK and New York: Palgrave Macmillan.

Melitz, M.J. and G.I.P. Ottaviano (2008), 'Market size, trade, and productivity', *Review of Economic Studies*, **75** (1), 295–316.

Moreno-Brid, J.C. (2003), 'Capital flows, interest payments and the balance-of-payments constrained growth model: a theoretical and empirical analysis', *Metroeconomica*, **54** (2–3), 346–65.

Pasinetti, L.L. (1981), *Structural Change and Economic Growth*, Cambridge, UK: Cambridge University Press.

Pasinetti, L.L. (1993), *Structural Economic Dynamics*, Cambridge, UK: Cambridge University Press.

Perraton, J. (2003), 'Balance of payments constrained growth and developing countries: an examination of Thirlwall's hypothesis', *International Review of Applied Economics*, **17** (1), 1–22.

Solow, R.M. (1956), 'A contribution to the theory of economic growth', *Quarterly Journal of Economics*, **70** (1), 65–94.

Tharnpanich, N. and J.S.L. McCombie (2013), 'Balance-of-payments constrained growth, structural change, and the Thai economy', *Journal of Post Keynesian Economics*, **35** (4), 569–98.

Thirlwall, A.P. (1979), 'The balance of payments constraint as an explanation of international growth rate differences', *Banca Nazionale del Lavoro Quarterly Review*, **128** (1), 45–53.

Thirlwall, A.P. (2002), *The Nature of Economic Growth: An Alternative Framework for Understanding the Performance of Nations*, Cheltenham, UK and Northampton, MA, USA: Edward Elgar Publishing.

Thirlwall, A.P. (2011), 'Balance of payments constrained growth models: history and overview', *PSL Quarterly Review*, **64** (259), 307–51.

Valdés, B. (1999), *Economic Growth: Theory, Empirics and Policy*, Cheltenham, UK and Northampton, MA, USA: Edward Elgar Publishing.

Wilson, T. (1976), 'Effective devaluation and inflation', *Oxford Economic Papers*, **28** (1), 1–24.

A PORTRAIT OF PAUL DAVIDSON (1930–)

Paul Davidson is one of the founding fathers of post-Keynesian economics in the United States, establishing in 1978, with Sidney Weintraub, the influential *Journal of Post Keynesian Economics*. However, he began his academic career studying for his PhD as a biochemist. He was awarded his PhD in 1959 at the University of Pennsylvania, where he came under the influence of Weintraub and developed his life-long interest in Keynes. His early academic publications were on Keynes, money and finance, and his arguments were brought together in his classic *Money and the Real World* (1972), written in 1970–71 while he was visiting the University of Cambridge, United Kingdom. This was followed up some ten years later with *International Money and the Real World* (1982), which, as its title suggests, was concerned with financial relationships among open economies. He sees the move from a fixed to a floating exchange rate regime as a major problem because of the destabilizing speculation it induces and also because of the deflationary bias. It is here that his approach overlaps with the balance-of-payments-constrained growth model. Davidson (1990–91, p. 303) summarized Thirlwall's Law as a significant contribution to post-Keynesian economic theory in its demonstration that 'international payments imbalances can have severe real growth consequences, i.e., money is not neutral in an open economy'.

Davidson's work since the 1980s also included an important series of papers showing the limitations to the rational expectations revolution. He explained that economic systems are non-ergodic (that is, where the economy displays path dependence and history matters), or subject to uncertainty rather than risk, a distinction emphasized by Knight and Keynes. Risk can be modelled as a probability distribution, whereas uncertainty cannot be. The subprime crisis and the failure of neoclassical economics to predict this demonstrate the importance of Davidson's work in this field. The causes, consequences and policy implications of the 2007–08 global financial crisis have been set out in his book, *The Keynes Solution* (2009).

14

European monetary union

Sergio Rossi

 OVERVIEW

This chapter:

- presents the history of the European monetary union, starting with the Werner Plans discussed in 1970 and then focusing on the Delors Plan (1989), which led to both the Maastricht Treaty signed in 1992 and the adoption of the euro, that is, a single European currency in 1999;

- explains the institution and workings of the European Central Bank, including its governance and lack of accountability with regard to its single monetary policy goal;

- focuses on the euro-area crisis, to explain its monetary and structural factors, thus showing the fundamental flaws of the European single-currency area as well as of its anti-crisis policies at both national and European levels;

- proposes an alternative path to European monetary integration, in the spirit of John Maynard Keynes's International Clearing Union based on a supranational currency unit, which can be issued without the need for member countries to dispose of their monetary sovereignty and thereby preserves national interest rate policies as a relevant instrument to steer economic performance at the euro-area level;

- points out the critiques raised by Robert Triffin against a single-currency area for Europe and discusses his own alternative proposal in that regard.

Readers will thereby understand the structural and institutional origins of the ongoing euro-area crisis.

⌐●⌐ KEYWORDS

- **Euro-area crisis:** Erupting near the end of 2009, mainstream economists consider it to be a 'sovereign debt crisis', while many heterodox economists argue it is a 'balance-of-payments crisis'.
- **European Payments Union:** From 1950 to 1958 a number of European countries experienced a multilateral payment system based on an international standard that they used to calculate their net (debtor or creditor) position once per month.
- **Fiscal consolidation:** A series of austerity measures designed to cut public spending in crisis-hit countries across the euro area, so as to induce economic growth by an increase in financial flows from capital markets.
- **Maastricht criteria:** A series of criteria enshrined in the Maastricht Treaty, in order for would-be euro-area member countries to converge nominally in economic terms, so as to be able to adopt the euro in a sustainable way.

Why are these topics important?

This chapter aims to assess the historical and theoretical origins of European monetary union as well as to grasp the structural and institutional factors of the euro-area crisis that erupted near the end of 2009, as soon as the then newly elected Greek government discovered and disclosed its actual public debt and deficit figures (much higher than previously announced). The analysis presented in this chapter is relevant to understanding the ideological framework supporting the economic policies adopted by euro-area member countries against the crisis and why these policies are not working as expected within that framework. The chapter also explains the monetary policy of the European Central Bank, both before and after the euro-area crisis erupted, thereby providing further important insights into understanding that a radically different series of economic policies is required in order to solve the crisis for good. On these grounds, the chapter also illustrates the workings of a supranational currency in the spirit of Keynes's 'bancor', which should be used by central banks only, to retrieve national monetary sovereignty and thus contribute via interest rate policy to steer the domestic economy. The portrait of Robert Triffin included in this chapter presents his views on European monetary union.

The mainstream perspective

Monetary union is considered as the achievement of fixing the exchange rates of the relevant national currencies, and replacing them with a single currency for psychological reasons that would make it too costly to abandon in order to re-establish the previous situation. In this perspective there would thus be no essential distinction on economic grounds between a fixed exchange rate regime and a single-currency area, both basically forms of monetary union.

In the mainstream perspective, there are two approaches to monetary union. The first (so-called 'monetarist') approach considers that by gradually reducing (close) to zero the fluctuation band within which foreign exchange rates may vary over time, the relevant countries can fix these exchange rates definitively and then replace their own currencies with a single currency. Exchange rate fixity would oblige the domestic economy of any country to converge – at least in nominal terms – with regard to the macroeconomic magnitudes of the so-called 'best-performing' country within the single-currency area. In the contrary case, the diverging economies would suffer a loss of competitiveness, hence a likely reduction of economic growth and an increase in unemployment levels. The second (so-called 'economist') approach, by contrast, considers that the reduction (to zero) of exchange rate volatility must occur only after the relevant countries have already converged in nominal terms to the level set by the best-performing economic system among them. Otherwise, the pressure to enlarge or to abandon the fluctuation band for the exchange rates of those countries that are having difficulty in abiding by with the convergence process would exacerbate tensions within the fixed exchange rate system, thereby putting the sustainability of the whole monetary union at stake.

Both approaches have been in the air during the discussions that led to the first and second so-called 'Werner Plans', presented in 1970 in order to monetarily integrate the (then six) member countries of the European Communities. At that time, the so-called 'economist' approach (mostly favoured by Germany) was considered better than the so-called 'monetarist' approach (proposed by France, Italy and Belgium).

In spite of this, the European monetary union project was put aside in the 1970s, as a result of the demise of the fixed exchange rate system decided at the Bretton Woods conference (July 1944). In fact, in 1971, the then US President, Richard Nixon, announced that the gold convertibility of the US dollar (US$35 for an ounce of gold) was suspended. This led to the abandonment of the Bretton Woods system in 1973, when the international monetary system became in fact a floating exchange rate regime. It was only towards the end of the 1980s that the European monetary union project was resumed, in order to dispose of the asymmetric workings (favouring Germany and the German mark) of the European Monetary System (EMS) set up in 1979, when the European Monetary Cooperation Fund was charged with issuing the European Currency Unit (ECU) in exchange for a share of gold reserves and US dollar deposits provided by the national central banks of those countries that were members of the European Communities at that time.

In 1988, the then President of the European Commission, Jacques Delors, chaired the Delors Committee, whose mandate was 'to study and propose concrete stages leading towards economic and monetary union' (Committee for the Study of Economic and Monetary Union, 1989, p. 1). As the Werner Plans already pointed out, the implementation of a monetary union according to the Delors Committee (p. 15) was to imply three major points:

- total and irreversible convertibility of all national currencies of member countries;
- complete liberalization of capital movements across member countries' borders as well as full integration of their banking systems;
- elimination of fluctuation margins and the irrevocable locking of exchange rates for national currencies of member countries.

These steps were to be accomplished while setting up a European monetary authority, first in the provisional form of a European Monetary Institute (1994–98), then in the form of a European Central Bank (ECB), which was set up on 1 June 1998, and then became the monetary authority of the whole euro area when the latter was established, on 1 January 1999. The ECB was prohibited from financing government spending across the single-currency area, which means that it is not allowed to buy government bonds on the primary market (where governments issue and sell their bonds to finance their spending beyond tax receipts). This institutional set-up was accompanied by a series of so-called convergence criteria that would-be euro-area member countries had to respect in order to join the single-currency area. Among these criteria, one finds the two most stringent rules for would-be euro-area countries, namely, the upper limit of 3 per cent for the ratio between public deficits and GDP and the upper limit of 60 per cent for the ratio between public debts and GDP (see Dafflon and Rossi, 1999). Other criteria included:

- an inflation rate that does not exceed by more than 1.5 percentage points the unweighted average of the inflation rates of the three countries where these rates are lowest across the whole European Union (EU);
- a nominal long-term rate of interest (usually on ten-year government bonds) that does not exceed by more than two percentage points the unweighted average of similar interest rates in the three EU countries where the rate of inflation is lowest;
- exchange rate stability, defined as a two-year period during which the

exchange rate of the currency concerned should not have been deval-
ued with respect to the euro, and the issuing country should have been
participating in the Exchange Rate Mechanism of the EMS without any
'severe tensions'.

A number of would-be euro-area countries met these criteria only owing to
a variety of accounting fiddles (see Dafflon and Rossi, 1999). Further, once
in the euro area, several countries did not respect the two fiscal criteria (as
regards public debts and deficits with respect to the country's GDP), but
were not sanctioned as expected, because the sanction procedure requires a
decision by the Ecofin Council, which is composed of the finance ministers
of the EU member countries. This procedure implies thereby that those in
charge of sanctioning a country's government might decide not to do this in
order for them to avoid their own countries' governments being sanctioned if
they do not respect the Maastricht fiscal criteria.

Other issues also negatively affect the economic governance of the euro area.
In particular, the statute of the ECB does not allow the latter to purchase
government bonds on the primary market. This 'no bailout' clause is meant
to avoid monetary policy supporting government spending, as it could lead
to some inflationary pressures that the ECB must avoid. The ECB mandate
is indeed to provide, first and foremost, price stability, which the ECB inter-
prets as making sure that the inflation rate in the euro area remains 'close to,
but below, 2 per cent' on a yearly basis. This has led Eurostat (the statistical
office of the EU) to set up a Harmonized Index of Consumer Prices (HICP),
which should allow the measurement of rates of inflation across the euro area
with the same methodology, because national indices of consumer prices
differ to a large extent and are therefore largely incomparable (see Rossi,
2001, Ch. 1).

In fact, as the first ECB president explained at the Monetary Dialogue of
17 February 2003, the ECB monetary policy strategy 'basically implies that,
in practice, we are more inclined to act when inflation *falls below* 1% and we
are also inclined to act when inflation *threatens to exceed* 2% in the medium
term' (Duisenberg, 2003, p. 10, emphasis added). There is thus an asymmetric behaviour of monetary policy-makers at the ECB, because they are
reluctant to reduce their policy rates of interest until measured inflation has
fallen below 1 per cent per annum, while they are willing to increase their
interest rates as soon as expected inflation (a virtual magnitude) is close to
or above 2 per cent, even though actual measured inflation might be lower.
This is owing to the importance given by so-called 'new consensus macroeconomics' to the control of inflation expectations by firms as well as individ-

uals (see Arestis, 2007). The ECB fears indeed that, if inflation expectations are higher than 2 per cent, its own monetary policy decisions become more difficult to implement successfully and/or could induce a much higher 'sacrifice ratio' – that is, 'the cumulative increase in the yearly rate of unemployment that is due to the disinflation effort divided by the total decrease in the rate of inflation' (Cukierman, 2002, p. 1).

The mainstream view about central bank independence, as a way to avoid government intervention in the decision-making process of monetary policy – thereby providing an institutional framework that should make sure price stability prevails – has made the ECB the most independent monetary authority all over the world. Central bank independence, however, does not necessarily mean that the central bank abstains from purchasing government bonds on primary markets, if these purchases can support the general economic objectives of public policies. In fact, Article 2 of the Statute of the ECB states that:

> [w]ithout prejudice to the objective of price stability, it shall support the general economic policies in the [European] Union with a view to contributing to the achievement of the objectives of the Union as laid down in Article 3 of the Treaty on European Union. (European Central Bank, 2012)

Notably, the latter article states that the European Union:

> shall work for the sustainable development of Europe based on balanced economic growth and price stability, a highly competitive social market economy, aiming at full employment and social progress, and a high level of protection and improvement of the quality of the environment. . . It shall promote economic, social and territorial cohesion, and solidarity among Member States. (Ibid.)

Now, both before and after the euro-area crisis erupted, the ECB has done close to nothing to contribute to the achievement of these objectives. As a matter of fact, in the first decade of the EMU, the ECB policy stance has been characterized by an anti-growth bias: it has been raising interest rates when inflation expectations threatened to be above 2 per cent, and has been reluctant to cut these rates when measured inflation was below 2 per cent. This attitude also affected the first two years of the euro-area crisis, since the ECB initially increased its policy rates of interest twice (in April and July 2011) and then decided to reduce them too late (starting in November 2011) and too slowly, with regard to both the dramatic development of the euro-area crisis and the sharp and prompt cut in interest rates decided by the US Federal Reserve since early 2008.

Further, the ECB has been a major actor in imposing so-called 'fiscal consoli-dation' (that is, austerity) policies to a variety of euro-area countries, with a view to them rebalancing their public accounts and thereby disposing of the alleged 'sovereign debt crisis' affecting the euro area negatively. These policies stem from the view that the euro-area crisis is the result of fiscal profligacy, which has led a number of countries 'to live beyond their means', so that – also to avoid moral hazard behaviour – these countries' governments should reduce their spending to rebalance their budgets in a growth-promoting way (see Mastromatteo and Rossi, 2015). The adjustment process in the public sector of these countries should also concern their private sector, so that 'unit labour costs' (the mainstream measure to assess a country's competitiveness) are reduced by a strong downward pressure on wages, which would allow prices to be reduced on the market for produced goods and services. The reference model is thus a neo-mercantilist regime for economic growth – as implemented by Germany since the early 2000s – that focuses on the export sector as the major, if not unique, engine of economic growth.

This mainstream view of both the euro-area crisis and the most appropriate policies to dispose of it is, however, flawed on both theoretical and empirical grounds. This crisis is not due to fiscal profligacy and therefore cannot be solved with austerity policies. A radically different perspective is required in order to both understand and eradicate the factors that instigated the euro-area crisis much earlier than 2009. Let us address them in the next section.

The heterodox perspective

The roots of the euro-area crisis are monetary and structural rather than behavioural. In other words, it was not the behaviour of economic agents in either the public or the private sector that originated such a systemic crisis. In fact, both the institutional setting and the monetary–structural framework of the European single-currency area are deeply flawed. A number of hetero-dox economists have been pointing this out in different ways since the euro area was designed in the 1990s (see Rossi and Dafflon, 2012). In particular, the 'original sin' of the euro is to be 'a currency without a state' (Padoa-Schioppa, 2004, p. 35). Indeed, Kenen (1969, pp. 45–6) pointed out long ago that '[f]iscal and monetary policies must go hand in hand', which means that both of them must be decided at the same institutional level and in a cooperative way between the government and the relevant central bank. This is not what occurs in the euro area. The ECB is in charge of monetary policy and, in light of its broad independence, does not consider coordinating its policy stance with national fiscal policies across the euro area. The latter polices, moreover, are much constrained by the Stability and Growth Pact signed in 1997 and by the so-called 'Six-Pack' – measures for economic and fiscal surveillance adopted in 2011 – which amount to balancing the public sector's budget without any leeway to carry out a countercyclical policy aimed at supporting economic growth and thereby contributing to achieving the general objectives of the European Union (see above).

Further, the implications of financialization, that is, a regime where financial markets and financial institutions become prominent with respect to economic activity and the needs of the population, affected the euro area negatively: they originated debt-led booms in Spain and Ireland and supported export-led growth in Germany to levels that were problematic for financial stability (Rossi, 2013). Owing to the ECB single monetary policy, whose 'one-size-fits-all' stance has been a much neglected factor of financial instability across the euro area, trade as well as financial imbalances in that area have been increasing during the first ten years of European monetary union, in both its 'core' countries (like Germany) and its 'periphery' (the so-called PIIGS, an acronym standing for Portugal, Ireland, Italy, Greece and Spain). As a result, debtor as well as creditor countries within the euro area have been initially profiting from an expanding credit bubble – as regards notably private sector agents, namely, firms and households – that burst once the consequences of the US subprime crisis crossed the Atlantic and negatively affected a number of European financial institutions (particularly French and German banks).

As Rossi (2007a, 2013) argues, financialization and free mobility of financial capital across the euro area have increased economic divergence between the 'core' and the 'periphery' of that area. Financial capital has been moving from 'core' countries like Germany (whose current account surpluses since the early 2000s have been providing a huge amount of savings that local financial institutions lent happily) to 'peripheral' countries, such as Spain and Ireland, in which they inflated a nationwide real estate bubble that burst in late 2008 as a result of the global financial crisis induced by the bankruptcy of Lehman Brothers in the United States. The growing unsustainability of these imbalances across the euro area remained unnoticed as long as residents (mainly financial institutions) in creditor countries were willing to lend to private and public sector agents in deficit countries the amounts the latter needed to finance their debts. Indeed, as Draghi (2014) pointed out, a monetary union implies a transfer mechanism between rich and poor member countries or regions: a viable monetary union includes a fiscal equalization mechanism in order to mitigate the financial differences between these countries or regions, thereby enhancing social cohesion and avoiding secessions. Since the euro area lacks such a mechanism, its existence during the first ten years has been made possible through private credit flows from the 'core' to its 'periphery' but at a non-negligible cost: while fiscal equalization implies unidirectional flows that are not remunerated, private credit flows must be reimbursed and are remunerated with an interest rate decided by the creditor (influenced by credit rating agencies), which for the debtor may be or become unsustainable over the long run.

This financial issue has been further aggravated by a monetary problem that remained unnoticed until the euro-area crisis erupted near the end of 2009: euro-area payments are not final payments for the countries concerned due to the workings of the TARGET2 system, despite the fact that they are final for the relevant residents (see Rossi, 2013). This is because the TARGET2 system does not involve the ECB as a settlement institution for national central banks thereby involved. Generally speaking, in fact, a central bank acts as the settlement institution for those banks that participate in the domestic payment system because of the book-entry nature of bank money and the fact that none can finally pay by issuing one's own acknowledgement of debt, which is only a promise of payment (see Rossi, 2007b). A central bank must therefore issue its own means of payment in order for banks to settle their debts finally. This is not what, to date, the ECB has been doing, since it abstains from 'monetizing' the TARGET2 system, which is therefore a clearing system through which national central banks never pay (are never paid) their net debtor (net creditor) position finally.

As a result, TARGET2 balances increased noticeably since the outbreak of the crisis at the end of 2009, mirroring the persistence of trade imbalances between 'core' and 'peripheral' countries in the euro area. Before the crisis broke out, the savings formed in surplus countries were lent to deficit countries, which therefore issued a number of private or public securities in order for them to borrow these savings. As a result, the TARGET2 balances were kept to a minimum. Since the crisis erupted in 2009, residents in creditor countries have stopped buying these securities, as credit rating agencies downgraded them. This induced a dramatic increase in balances within the TARGET2 system, because the savings formed in surplus countries have no longer been lent to deficit countries in the euro area.

Now, the various interventions elicited by the euro-area crisis, since the first bailout plan for Greece in 2010, have only been trying to address some of the consequences rather than the causes of that crisis, which is actually a balance-of-payments crisis rather than a sovereign debt crisis (see above). In fact, there is no problem *per se* in a trade deficit, as long the country concerned finally pays this deficit. The problem occurs when trade deficits are

Figure 14.1 The emission of money as a flow

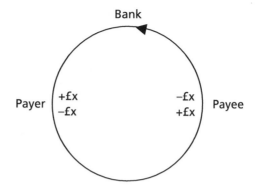

not paid finally, as this gives rise to payment deficits, which are a monetary–structural disorder, because surplus countries maintain a financial claim over deficit countries, as testified by their unsettled positions within the TARGET2 system and whose balances therefore accumulate over time (see Rossi, 2012a).

The solution to this problem needs monetary–structural reform. An orderly working payment system requires a settlement institution for each transaction between any two parties. The characteristic of such an institution is to issue the means of final payment, which is an operation involving three 'poles': the payer, the payee, and a go-between playing the role of settlement institution between the two agents involved (Figure 14.1).

Indeed, a final payment happens when 'a seller of a good, or service, or another asset, receives something of equal value from the purchaser, which leaves the seller with no further claim on the buyer' (Goodhart, 1989, p. 26). In order for this to occur, a bank must issue the number of money units needed to carry out the payment, as a result of which the payer disposes of a purchasing power (in the form of a bank deposit) that is transferred, via the bank or the banking system as a whole, to the payee. The result of this payment is a stock magnitude and is recorded by the bank as shown in Table 14.1.

Starting from a blank slate, to avoid the temptation of assuming the existence of a bank deposit before the relevant payment occurs, one notices that a bank's credit is needed in order for the payer to finally settle his or her debt against the payee. Something similar is required at the euro-area level for those payments that affect the position of national central banks within the TARGET2 system. As Keynes (1980, p. 168) noticed in his own 'plan' presented at the Bretton Woods conference:

Table 14.1 Loans and deposits resulting from the opening of a domestic credit line

Bank	
Assets	Liabilities
Loan to the payer	Deposit of the payee
+£x	+£x

> [w]e need an instrument of international currency. . .used by each nation in its transactions with other nations, operating through whatever national organ, such as a Treasury or a central bank, is most appropriate, private individuals, businesses and banks other than central banks, each continuing to use their own national currency as heretofore.

In this passage, the author provides an excellent synthesis between the monetary–structural need to set up an international settlement institution issuing a means of final payment between those countries (each represented by its own central bank) participating in this international payment system, and the importance of maintaining national currencies in place, as they allow a country to retain its monetary sovereignty and thereby to steer its own interest rates as an important tool to achieve the country's economic policy goals. As Keynes (1980, p. 234) explained, in reforming the international monetary architecture '[t]here should be the least possible interference with internal national policies, and the plan should not wander from the international terrain'. This implies that:

> [i]t is the policy of an autonomous rate of interest, unimpeded by international preoccupations. . .which is twice blessed in the sense that it helps ourselves and our neighbours at the same time. And it is the simultaneous pursuit of these policies by all countries together which is capable of restoring economic health and strength internationally, whether we measure it by the level of domestic employment or by the volume of international trade. (Keynes, 1936, p. 349)

Although the Keynes plan was not adopted at the Bretton Woods conference back in 1944, it inspired the setting up of the European Payments Union (EPU) in 1950, as a result of a proposal for a European Clearing Union put forward by Robert Triffin (see Triffin, 1985). As Triffin (1978, p. 15) put it, '[t]he EPU agreement was a remarkably clean and simple document, embodying sweeping and precise commitments of a revolutionary nature, which overnight drastically shifted the whole structure of intra-European payments from a bilateral to a multilateral basis'. This multilateral basis was provided by the Bank for International Settlements (BIS), which indeed operated as a settlement agent for EPU member countries, each represented by its own central bank. Once per month, the latter sent its bilateral payment orders, which the BIS cleared in order to establish a net multilateral (debtor or creditor) position for each of the participating central banks. This position was to be settled in gold or US dollars, if the debtor central bank had already exhausted the initial credit that each country received when the EPU was set up in 1950. This is the weak point of the EPU architecture: the lack of an international settlement institution, issuing its own means of final payment for the participating central banks. The BIS should have been operating not simply as a settlement agent (recording the bilateral and multilateral balances resulting from the EPU operations), but as a settlement institution, whose means of payment is required in order to settle all debts within the EPU.

Indeed, the monetary–structural flaw of the EPU (which was terminated in 1958) was to be reproduced in the TARGET system set up in 1999 to carry out large-value cross-border payments within the EMU. As a matter of fact, these payments 'are processed via the national RTGS [real-time gross-settlement] systems and exchanged directly on a bilateral basis between NCBs [national central banks]' (European Central Bank, 2007, p. 34). This means that the ECB does not intervene as a settlement institution. In fact, the ECB is just a participating central bank among others in the TARGET2 system, which means that it does not issue central bank money for the settlement of national central banks' (net) positions within that system (see Rossi, 2012a). Hence, these positions remain on the TARGET2 books as long as the underlying flows are not reversed, which means that a net importing (exporting) country should become a net exporting (importing) country in order for these positions to be settled eventually in real terms.

Now, as a result of the euro-area crisis, the rebalancing mechanism introduced by the so-called 'troika' (made up of the ECB, the European Commission and the International Monetary Fund) puts the onus of adjustment on debtor countries only, preserving the creditor countries, in particular Germany, from contributing to this adjustment via an increase in their imports from debtor countries (mostly in the 'periphery' of the euro area). However, as the latter countries suffer from 'fiscal consolidation' policies that reduce the size of their economies, they will not be able to increase their exports very much and will also reduce their imports from creditor countries, as a result of reduced available income, thereby aggravating the situation across the whole EMU rather than contributing to re-launching the euro-area economy over the long run. This is why the monetary–structural architecture of the EMU should be reformed in the spirit of Keynes's plan and considering the

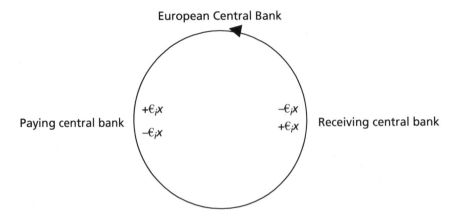

Figure 14.2 The emission of central bank money as a flow

shortcomings of the EPU as explained above. An international settlement institution for euro-area member countries should therefore be set up, with the task of issuing the means of final payment for national central banks – within the TARGET2 system – with the possibility to abandon the single currency, to reintroduce national currencies particularly in those countries where the single interest rate policy of the ECB causes more harm than good.

Let us explore the workings of an international settlement institution for those national central banks that participate in the TARGET2 system. For the sake of simplicity, the ECB should undertake this task and therefore issue the means of final payment between all central banks involved thereby.

Figure 14.2 shows the flow of central bank money that the ECB issues whenever there is a payment order involving two national central banks within the TARGET2 system.

Let us call 'international euro' ($€_i$) the international means of final payment issued by the ECB in this perspective. As Figure 14.2 shows, the number of (x) money units issued thereby are credited/debited to the paying as well as the receiving central bank, through an instantaneous circular flow whose result is a stock magnitude entered in Table 14.2.

The double entry in Table 14.2 testifies that the paid central bank has no further claim on the payer central bank, which is the hallmark of a final payment between them. Yet, it should be noted that the credit obtained by the paying central bank should be repaid as soon as the latter bank is credited for a commercial or financial export by the residents in its country. This may

Table 14.2 Loans and deposits resulting from the opening of an international credit line

European Central Bank

Assets	Liabilities
Loan to the paying central bank	Deposit of the receiving central bank
+€𝑥	+€𝑥

be facilitated by the fact that central bank deposits at the ECB are not remunerated: in this case, the paid central bank, acting on behalf of its country, will be induced to spend this deposit as soon as it is made, to purchase any financial assets that provide a return or to pay for some commercial imports. In both cases, this can allow deficit countries to finance their trade deficits with a sale of financial assets and to increase their own commercial exports, thus reducing trade imbalances through a symmetric rebalancing mechanism. This would actually be an expansionary process for the whole euro area, whose economic system would thus benefit from it, instead of suffering from the recessionary consequences that 'fiscal consolidation' measures are exerting on euro-area debtor countries at the time of writing. It would be a means of replacing austerity and recession with economic growth and solidarity across the euro area (see Rossi, 2012b).

 REFERENCES

Arestis, P. (ed.) (2007), *Is There a New Consensus in Macroeconomics?*, Basingstoke, UK and New York: Palgrave Macmillan.

Committee for the Study of Economic and Monetary Union (1989), *Report on Economic and Monetary Union in the European Community* [Delors Report], Luxembourg: Office for the Official Publications of the European Community.

Cukierman, A. (2002), 'Does a higher sacrifice ratio mean that central bank independence is excessive?', *Annals of Economics and Finance*, **3** (1), 1–25.

Dafflon, B. and S. Rossi (1999), 'Public accounting fudges towards EMU: a first empirical survey and some public choice considerations', *Public Choice*, **101** (1–2), 59–84.

Draghi, M. (2014), 'Stability and prosperity in monetary union', speech at the University of Helsinki, Finland, 27 November, accessed 16 February 2016 at www.ecb.europa.eu/press/key/date/2014/html/sp141127_1.en.html.

Duisenberg, W.F. (2003), 'Monetary dialogue with Wim Duisenberg, President of the ECB', EU Economic and Monetary Committee, Brussels, 17 February, accessed 21 October 2015 at http://www.europarl.europa.eu/RegData/seance_pleniere/compte_rendu/traduit/2003/02-17/P5_CRE%282003%2902-17_DEF_EN.pdf.

European Central Bank (2007), *Payment and Securities Settlement Systems in the European Union, Volume 1: Euro Area Countries*, Frankfurt: European Central Bank.

European Central Bank (2012), 'On the Statute of the European System of Central Banks and of the European Central Bank', *Official Journal of the European Union*, C326/230, accessed 21 October 2015 at https://www.ecb.europa.eu/ecb/legal/pdf/c_32620121026en_protocol_4.pdf.

European Union (2012), 'Consolidated version of the Treaty on European Union', *Official Journal of the European Union*, C326/13, accessed 21 October 2015 at http://eur-lex.europa.eu/legal-content/EN/TXT/PDF/?uri=CELEX:12012M/TXT&from=EN.

Goodhart, C.A.E. (1989), *Money, Information and Uncertainty*, second edition, London and Basingstoke, UK: Macmillan (first published 1975).

Kenen, P.B. (1969), 'The theory of optimum currency areas: an eclectic view', in R.A. Mundell and A.K. Swoboda (eds), *Monetary Problems of the International Economy*, Chicago, IL: University of Chicago Press, pp. 41–60.

Keynes, J.M. (1936), *The General Theory of Employment, Interest and Money*, London: Macmillan.

Keynes, J.M. (1980), *The Collected Writings of John Maynard Keynes, Volume XXV: Activities 1940–1944. Shaping the Post-War World: The Clearing Union*, ed. D.E. Moggridge, London and New York: Macmillan and Cambridge University Press.

Mastromatteo, G. and S. Rossi (2015), 'The economics of deflation in the euro area: a critique of fiscal austerity', *Review of Keynesian Economics*, **3** (3), 336–50.

Padoa-Schioppa, T. (2004), *The Euro and Its Central Bank: Getting United after the Union*, Cambridge, MA: MIT Press.

Rossi, S. (2001), *Money and Inflation: A New Macroeconomic Analysis*, Cheltenham, UK and Northampton, MA, USA: Edward Elgar Publishing.

Rossi, S. (2007a), 'International capital flows within the European Monetary Union: increasing economic divergence between the centre and the periphery', *European Journal of Economics and Economic Policies: Intervention*, **4** (2), 309–29.

Rossi, S. (2007b), *Money and Payments in Theory and Practice*, London and New York: Routledge.

Rossi, S. (2012a), 'The monetary–structural origin of TARGET2 imbalances across Euroland', in C. Gnos and S. Rossi (eds), *Modern Monetary Macroeconomics: A New Paradigm for Economic Policy*, Cheltenham, UK and Northampton, MA, USA: Edward Elgar Publishing, pp. 221–38.

Rossi, S. (2012b), 'Replacing recession and austerity with growth and solidarity across Euroland', in M. Méaulle (ed.), *Austerity Is Not the Solution! Contributions to European Economic Policy*, Brussels: Foundation for European Progressive Studies, pp. 33–40.

Rossi, S. (2013), 'Financialization and monetary union in Europe: the monetary–structural causes of the euro-area crisis', *Cambridge Journal of Regions, Economy and Society*, **6** (3), 381–400.

Rossi, S. and B. Dafflon (2012), 'Repairing the original sin of the European Monetary Union', *International Journal of Monetary Economics and Finance*, **5** (2), 102–23.

Triffin, R. (1960), *Gold and the Dollar Crisis: The Future of Convertibility*, New Haven, CT: Yale University Press.

Triffin, R. (1978), 'Gold and the dollar crisis: yesterday and tomorrow', *Princeton University Essays in International Finance*, No. 132.

Triffin, R. (1985), 'Une tardive autopsie du plan Keynes de 1943: mérites et carences' [A belated autopsy of the Keynes plan: merits and deficiencies], in A. Barrère (ed.), *Keynes aujourd'hui: théories et politiques*, Paris: Economica, pp. 513–21.

A PORTRAIT OF ROBERT TRIFFIN (1911–93)

Robert Triffin was born in Flobecq, Belgium, on 5 October 1911, and died in Ostend, Belgium, on 23 February 1993. In 1938 he obtained his doctoral degree from Harvard University, where he remained lecturing from 1939 to 1942. He was then appointed to the US Federal Reserve (1942–46), the International Monetary Fund (1946–48), and to the Organisation for European Economic Co-operation (1948–51). In 1951, he became a Professor of Economics at Yale University, where he remained until 1977, when he returned to Belgium and contributed to the debate on European economic integration until his death.

Triffin is best known for his critique on the Bretton Woods system. He notably pointed out a paradox in 1960 (since then known as the 'Triffin dilemma') within that system: the US dollar is an international reserve asset and the United States must therefore run a permanent trade deficit in its current accounts, but this reduces confidence in the US dollar across the world economy, since its exchange rate is weakened as a result of the permanent trade deficit in the US balance of payments (see Triffin, 1960).

Triffin was convinced that the international monetary system must be reformed along the lines of Keynes's plan, and tried to make the latter more palatable in order to get it realized (Triffin, 1960, p. 71). He repeatedly pointed out that the essential flaw of the Bretton Woods system consists in using national currencies as international reserves (p. 10). He thus proposed a radical reform of international payments, consisting of issuing an international means of payment to be used by national central banks only. This would allow the substitution of national currencies (mainly US dollars and pounds sterling) with a truly international reserve asset in any countries' official reserves (p. 102).

Triffin tried to implement the architecture of Keynes's plan within the framework of the European Payments Union (1950–58), which failed because of the lack of a proper international means of payment as suggested by Keynes.

Part V

Recent trends

15

Financialization

Gerald A. Epstein

 OVERVIEW

This chapter discusses the concept of financialization and its relevance to understanding the nature and dynamics of our modern capitalist economy:

- It also explains that financialization has many definitions but the most commonly used refers to the increasing role of financial motives, financial markets, financial actors and financial institutions in the operation of the domestic and international economies.

- It points out the indicators of financialization in contemporary capitalism, notably the increased size of the financial sector in many countries relative to the overall size of their economies, the increased share of total national income going to people engaged in financial activities, the increased orientation of managers of industrial and other 'non-financial' businesses toward 'financial activities' rather than 'production' activities and continuing or even increased incidence of bouts of financial instability and financial crises like the global financial crisis that erupted in 2007–08.

- It argues that mainstream economics, at least until recently, has tended to underplay the role of financialization in the macroeconomy, while a growing number of heterodox economists are exploring the nature and macroeconomic implications of financialization, including its impacts on income distribution, financial instability and long-term productivity growth.

- It summarizes the big debate about the age and meaning of financialization: is it hundreds or even thousands of years old or is it a relatively new phenomenon, 150 years or less? Relatedly, does it represent a whole new mode of organization for capitalism, or is it simply one among a number of key institutions and dynamics, along with globalization, digitalization and neoliberalism, that drive our economies today?

[🔑 KEYWORDS]

- **Financialization:** The increasing role of financial motives, financial markets, financial actors and financial institutions in the operation of domestic and international economies.
- **Neoliberalism:** The resurgence of nineteenth-century ideas associated with laissez-faire economic liberalism, which holds that markets should dominate the economy and the government should play a relatively small role within the economic system.
- **Rentiers:** Individuals, businesses or households that get a large share of their income from the ownership of financial assets.
- **Short-termism:** This occurs when economic actors are willing to sacrifice longer-term value for values in the present or very short-term future.

Why are these topics important?

For anyone who did not know it already, the global financial crisis that erupted in 2007–08 made it completely obvious that finance has become a powerful force in our economy. Unfortunately, most of the mainstream macroeconomics profession as well as many regulators and practitioners operating in the financial market itself were largely in the dark on the eve of the crisis. This is because the thrust of the mainstream analysis in the post-war period was designed to demonstrate that financial markets were either irrelevant to macroeconomic outcomes, or, by facilitating the efficient allocation of resources, a potent force for efficiency and growth (see Chapter 5). The idea that finance could cause the virtual meltdown of the global economy was foreign to their theories and far from their minds.

For heterodox economists, by contrast, at least since the work of the late Hyman Minsky, this fact had been well known (see again Chapter 5). 'Financialization' is the latest and probably most widely term used by analysts trying to 'name' and understand this contemporary rise of finance and its powerful role. The term was developed long before the crisis of 2007–08 but, understandably, since the crisis hit, it has become more popular and widely used.

What is financialization?

As discussed by British economist Malcolm Sawyer (2013), the term 'financialization' goes back at least to the 1990s and probably was originated by the US Republican political operative and iconoclastic writer Kevin Phillips, who defined financialization as 'a prolonged split between the divergent real and financial economies' (Sawyer, 2013, pp. 5–6).

Scholars have adopted the term, but have proposed numerous other definitions. Sociologist Greta Krippner gives an excellent discussion of the history of the term and the pros and cons of its various definitions (see Krippner, 2005). As she summarizes the discussion, some writers use the term 'financialization' to mean the ascendancy of 'shareholder value', that is, the dominance of stock values as a mode of corporate governance. Some use it to refer to the growing dominance of capital market financial systems where stocks and bond markets are key, as in the United States, over financial systems where banks are more important, as in continental Europe. Some follow the late nineteenth-century/early twentieth-century Austrian Marxist economist Rudolf Hilferding's lead and use the term financialization to refer to the increasing political and economic power of the rentier class and banks. For others, financialization represents the explosion of financial trading with a myriad of new financial instruments. Finally, for Krippner herself, the term refers to a 'pattern of accumulation (that is, saving and investment) in which profit making occurs increasingly through financial channels rather than through trade and commodity production' (Krippner, 2005, p. 14).[1]

What all these definitions have in common is the idea that finance has become more important and that it has become a more powerful driver of the economy now than in the past.

In order to cast a wide net and incorporate the key ideas in these diverse definitions, it is useful to define the term quite broadly and generally as 'the increasing role of financial motives, financial markets, financial actors and financial institutions in the operation of the domestic and international economies' (Epstein, 2005, p. 3). This definition focuses on financialization as a process, and is quite agnostic on the issue of whether it constitutes a new mode of capitalist organization or an entirely new phase of capitalism, or whether it is simply one important trend of capitalism along with several other important ones including globalization, digitalization and neoliberalism. Broad definitions like mine have the advantage of incorporating many features, but have the disadvantage, perhaps, of lacking specificity. Other analysts have used variations on the term 'financialization' to refer to more or less the same set of phenomena. For instance, Palley (2014, p. 8) uses the term 'neoliberal financialization' to emphasize the importance of neoliberalism as part and parcel of the rise of financialization. Some have not referred to financialization but to 'finance-dominated capitalism' (Hein, 2012).

How old is financialization?

Another important debate is on the periodization of 'financialization'. Is it only a recent phenomenon, say, important since the 1980s, or does it go back at least 5000 years, as Sawyer (2013, p. 6) has suggested? If it goes back a long time, does it come in waves, perhaps linked with broader waves of production, commerce and technology, or is it a relatively independent process driven by government policy such as the degree of financial regulation or liberalization (see Orhangazi, 2008a, 2008b)? Arrighi (1994) famously argued that over the course of capitalist history, financialization tends to become a dominant force when the productive economy is in decline, and when the dominant global power (or 'hegemon') is in retreat. A good example of this can be found in the early twentieth century, when Great Britain was losing power relative to Germany and the United States, and the UK economy was stagnating. This period was also characterized by a great increase in financial speculation and instability.

This raises the question of whether the current period of financialization is due to the reduced role of the United States in the world economy and the rise of China and India. The connection may seem distant, but some argue that the rise of both China and India means that US and European non-financial capitalists cannot compete as well as before, and therefore are turning to 'financial speculation' because they cannot compete in 'productive investment'.

Dimensions of financialization

If one takes a broad perspective on financialization, one can identify many dimensions of it. One is the sheer size and scale of financial markets and can be seen quite clearly in the large growth in the size of the financial sector relative to the rest of the economy over the last several decades. This growth in finance has been a general phenomenon in many parts of the world. For the most part we will focus in this chapter on data from the United States (see Epstein and Crotty, 2013).

The growth of finance relative to the size of the economy since 1980 has been nothing short of spectacular. A few pieces of data illustrate this point well. Let us start with profits of financial institutions. In the United States, financial profits as a share of GDP were around 10 per cent in the 1950s. By the early 2000s, financial profits constituted about 40 per cent of total profits in the United States, a historical high. After a sharp decline during the global financial crisis that erupted in 2007–08, financial profits have recovered to above 30 per cent of total profits, well above the average for the post-war period.

Naturally, with profits having grown so significantly, the size of the financial sector is likely to have been growing as well. Financial sector assets relative to GDP were less than 200 per cent from 1950 to 1985. By 2008, they had more than doubled to well over four times the size of the economy. After a short dip following the global financial crisis, financial sector assets had grown to almost 500 per cent of GDP by 2015.

Also, trends in the United Kingdom are similar to those in the United States, as regards both the size and profitability of the financial sector. Its profitability had been growing substantially in the post-war period until the global financial crisis erupted, and resumed its growth since that time. Indeed, since the crisis, growth of financial assets in the United Kingdom has outpaced those in the United States, Germany and Japan relative to GDP (Lapavitsas, 2013, pp. 205–11). More generally, the size of the financial sector and financial profits relative to the size of the economy have grown substantially in most European countries over this period.

Another dimension that characterizes financialization in many countries has been an increase in the financial activities and financial orientation of non-financial corporations: De Souza and Epstein (2014) present data on the financial activities of non-financial corporations in six financial centres, namely the United States, the United Kingdom, France, the Netherlands, Germany and Switzerland. They show that in all these six countries – with the possible exception of France – non-financial corporations significantly reduced their dependence on external borrowing for capital investment. Indeed, in three of these countries – the United Kingdom, Germany and Switzerland – non-financial corporations became net lenders, rather than net borrowers, indicating an increasing role for financial lending as a profit centre for non-financial corporations in these countries. Lapavitsas (2013) showed similar trends for the United States, the United Kingdom, Germany and Japan.

A key aspect of financialization that analysts consider as being particularly pernicious has been the vast increase of debt levels in many countries and many sectors (Taylor, 2014). In many countries, this debt is taken on by the financial sector itself, and by the real estate sector. Debt, or leverage, is an accelerator that enables the financial system to generate a credit bubble, thereby allowing some actors (such as private equity and hedge funds) to extract wealth from companies, and that can quicken the pace of economic activity more generally. It is the accelerator on the way down after the bubble bursts, leading to distress, deflation and bankruptcy. On the way up, debt helps to magnify the rate of return on your investment: if you put in $1 of your own investment and borrow $9, and you make a 10 per cent return on the $10 investment, then the dollar you earn is really a 100 per cent return on the dollar you put into the pot! But if this investment loses 10 per cent ($1) you will have lost 100 per cent of the dollar of your own money you put in. So debt (or leverage) magnifies your gains and losses.

Playing a key role in the development of financialization is the role of financial innovation, the change in financial products, instruments and techniques. To be sure, financial innovation has played a key role in the development of recent financial practices that contributed significantly to the massive growth in financial activities and that ultimately contributed to the financial crisis (Wolfson and Epstein, 2013). Among these key financial innovations have been securitization and structured financial products such as asset-backed securities (ABSs), collateralized debt obligations (CDOs), the growth of credit derivatives, such as credit default swaps (CDSs) that both facilitated and then became embedded in these structured products themselves, and innovations in wholesale funding of banks in global short-term markets. These financial innovations have implications that are global in scope. For instance, the Bank for International Settlements in Basel, Switzerland reports that the global use and level of trading in these instruments have grown spectacularly over the last several decades (Bank for International Settlements, 2013). This process of financial innovation has clearly helped to drive financialization, both within countries and globally.

Financialization and non-financial corporations

There are other important dimensions of the increased financial activities related to non-financial corporations. Among the most important is the increased role of financial activities as a determinant of the pay packages of top management of non-financial corporations, including, most importantly, the corporate CEO. Perhaps most important are stock options and other stock-related pay for non-financial corporate management. Stock options allow corporate executives to buy shares of the stock of the company, often at a great discount. The CEO thereby becomes a shareholder and this gives the executives an incentive to pump up the stock price in the short term, buy the stocks with their options, leaving them unconcerned about what happens to the price of the stock (or the value of the company) in the longer term. In the United States, where this is especially prevalent, CEOs on average receive

72 per cent of their compensation in the form of stock options and other stock-related pay (Lazonick, 2014).

This focus on stock prices leads the managers of non-financial corporations to use their revenue to buy back their company's stocks in order to raise stock prices and increase their own compensation. Lazonick refers to this pressure as leading to management policies of 'downsize and distribute'. This represents a dramatic shift with respect to the earlier strategy of 'retain and reinvest', by which management would retain profits and re-invest them into the human and technological capital of the firm. The numbers in the case of the United States are staggering. Using a sample of 248 companies that have been listed on the S&P 500 since 1981, Lazonick reports that, in 1981, firms used 2 per cent of net income for stock buybacks; between 1984 and 1993, such purchases averaged 25 per cent of net income, from 1994 to 2003, 37 per cent, while in the 2004–13 period they used a full 47 per cent of net income for stock buybacks (Lazonick, 2014). Large, well-known corporations used an even higher percentage of their income for buybacks.

This focus on stock prices is often seen as a prime example of 'shareholder value' ideology, a perspective considered by some as the very essence of 'financialization'. Shareholder value ideology, promoted in the mainstream of the economics profession by Michael Jensen, among others, argues that since shareholders own the corporations, the goal of the corporation management should be to maximize the corporate value for shareholders. Since, they argue, shareholders bear all the risk in the corporation, then this maximization is the most efficient corporate outcome. However, Lazonick (2014) shows that other stakeholders, like workers and taxpayers, bear as much if not more risk than shareholders. Also, Stout (2012) shows that shareholders do not really own the corporations, nor do they all share the same values as embodied in the Jensen ideal. Hence, 'maximizing shareholder value' does not mean maximizing share prices. But it does often lead to short-term, destructive orientation by the company's management.

This is one of the most discussed examples of the role of modern financial markets in creating more 'short-termism' as a major component of 'financialization'. 'Short-termism' means a short time horizon by economic leaders in making production, investment and financing decisions. This short-termism might lead to underinvestment in long gestation but highly productive and profitable (in the long-run) investments, underinvestment in labour development, underinvestment in research and development activities, and overinvestment in activities that generate short-run profits but that might generate long-run risks and/or losses (Haldane and Davies, 2011). The same kinds of pressures face portfolio managers for pension funds and other institutional investors, leading to a similar focus on short-term returns, sometimes at the risk of longer-term investments.

Evidence of short-termism includes the reduced holding period of equities in financial markets, survey evidence that managers will cut profitable long-term investments to reach short-term profit goals, and that investors have higher rates of required returns for longer-term investments than is necessary (see Haldane and Davies, 2011).

This short-term-oriented behaviour is alleged to affect non-financial corporation management not simply because of the direct incentives facing corporate CEOs, but also because of the pressure from outside investors and financial institutions. These include pension funds and related institutional investors (Parenteau, 2005) and also private equity firms (Appelbaum and Batt, 2015) and hedge funds (Dallas, 2011). These financial institutions use access to debt and financial engineering to extract value in the short run from non-financial corporations, possibly at the expense of investment, taxpayers and wage earners.

To summarize, this strand of literature suggests that financialization not only affects behaviour in the financial sector itself, but also has profound effects on non-financial corporations as well.

Financialization and households

Let us now turn our attention to the impact of financialization on the household sector.

As the global financial crisis that erupted in 2007–08 clearly showed, the process of financialization has not only caught financial and non-financial institutions in its orbit, but households as well (see Taub, 2014). After all, the epicentre of the financial crisis in the United States was in the home mortgage market and to some extent one segment of that market, the so-called 'subprime mortgage market'. Lapavitsas (2013) and others have argued that the process of financial incorporation of households led to the 'financial expropriation' of these households by financial businesses, and this expropriation was most clearly and obviously expressed by the massive loss in housing wealth experienced by poor people and minorities in the United States as a result of the crisis.

The incorporation of households into the 'circuits' of financialization goes beyond the intensive use of mortgage loans to buy homes, sometimes, as we noticed in 2007, with catastrophic consequences. The use of credit cards and other forms of consumer credit, and the widespread indebtedness of students through student loans, also comprise the webs of connections that households have come to have with financial markets. In the United States, for example, students have taken on more than US$1 trillion in student loans. This has happened during a period in which young people's employment prospects are still weak, even more so five years after the financial crisis erupted.

All in all, financialization has numerous dimensions, and has moved in some countries way beyond the 'financial sector' itself. Financial returns, financial motives, widespread use of debt and short-termism, among other aspects, have become crucial, if not dominant, for financial firms, non-financial firms and households. This growth in finance, which accelerated around 1980 in a number of countries, has taken on significant global dimensions as well.

The question naturally arises, what is the impact of financialization on the economy and on society?

Impacts of financialization

Much of the macroeconomic literature on financialization concerns, of course, the impact of financialization on crucial macroeconomic outcomes such as economic growth, investment, productivity growth, employment and income distribution. The massive literature on the global financial crisis has made it pretty clear that aspects of financialization, including the huge increase in private debt, the use of securitization and complex financial products, the widespread use of complex over-the-counter (OTC) derivatives, and the pernicious fraud and corruption, all contributed to the financial crisis and therefore, quite obviously, undermined financial and economic stability.

But the impacts of financialization on other macroeconomic outcomes are less obvious, and less studied. Before discussing particular impacts, it will be helpful to present some broad frameworks that have been proposed to understand the impact of financialization on macroeconomics (see Hein, 2012; Palley, 2014).

Macroeconomic models and financialization

Owing to space constraints we cannot provide a thorough overview of the rapidly expanding heterodox literature on models of financialization. Hence let us very briefly discuss one framework only, that of German economist

Eckhard Hein. Hein (2012) utilizes a Kaleckian model in which aggregate demand plays a key role in determining both investment and output and where income distribution between profits, wages, and 'rentier' or 'financial incomes' has a big impact on aggregate demand. Hein, for example, identifies three key channels through which financialization can affect macroeconomic variables and outcomes:

- the objectives of firms and the restrictions that finance places on firms' behaviour;
- new opportunities for households' wealth-based and debt-financed consumption; and
- the distribution of income and wealth between capital and labour on the one hand, and between management and workers on the other.

With his colleague Till van Treeck, Hein shows that within a Kaleckian framework expansive effects may arise under certain conditions, in particular when there are strong wealth effects in firms' investment decisions and in households' consumption decisions. However, they show that even an expansive finance-led economy may build up major financial imbalances, that is, increasing debt–capital or debt–income ratios, which make such economies prone to financial instability.

Financialization and investment

Engelbert Stockhammer (2004) pioneered the theoretical analysis of the impact of financialized managers' motives on investment. He showed that finance-oriented management might choose to undertake lower investment levels than managers with less financialized orientations. The key reason explaining this difference is that managers with financialized orientations have a more short-term orientation than other managers. Stockhammer (2004) presented macro-level econometric investment equations that have been consistent with this impact in several OECD countries.

Özgur Orhangazi (2008b) uses firm-level data to study the impact of financialization on real capital accumulation (investment) in the United States. He uses data from a sample of non-financial corporations from 1973 to 2003, and finds a negative relationship between real investment and financialization. Orhangazi explains these results by exploring two channels of influence of financialization on real investment. First, increased financial investment and increased financial profit opportunities may have crowded out real investment by changing the incentives of firm managers and directing funds away from real investment. Second, increased payments to financial markets may have impeded real investment by decreasing available internal funds, shortening the planning horizons of the firm management and increasing uncertainty.

Davis (2013) provides further evidence of the negative impact of financialization on real investment. She also studies a sample of non-financial firms, showing a significant difference between large and smaller firms in the degree to which they receive financial income as a share of total income. Larger firms appear to be more financialized in this sense. Using a firm-level panel, she investigates econometrically the relationship between financialization and investment, focusing on the implications of changes in financing behaviour, increasingly entrenched shareholder value norms, and rising firm-level demand volatility for investment by non-financial corporations in the United States between 1971 and 2011. Importantly, Davis (2013) finds that shareholder value norms have been associated with lower investment, though this relationship tends be true primarily of larger firms.

These results are consistent with the concerns expressed by heterodox analysts and others that financialization tends to reduce real investment.

Employment, human capital, research and development, and wages

An increasing chorus of analysts among heterodox economists including Appelbaum and Batt (2014), Lazonick (2014), as well as the Bank of England economists Haldane and Davies (2011), have expressed concerns that 'short-termism' associated with financialization may be coming at the expense of investments in human capital, research and development, employment, and productivity growth, which could have long-lasting negative impacts on the economy. There is some empirical work that is supportive of these fears. For instance, in a set of surveys of corporate managers, it has been shown that many chief financial officers are willing to sacrifice longer-term investments in research and development and hold on to value employees in order to meet short-term earnings per share targets. In a panel econometric study, other economists similarly find using firm-level data that managers are willing to trade-off investments and employment for stock repurchases that allow them to meet earnings per share forecasts. Appelbaum and Batt (2014) in a survey of econometric studies of private equity firms find that, in particular, large firms that use financial engineering to extract value from target companies have a negative impact on investment, employment, and research and development in these companies. In short, there is significant empirical evidence that 'short-termism' and other aspects of financial orientation have negative impacts on workers' well-being, productivity and longer-term economic growth.

Also, as many of these studies emphasize, these activities do not maximize shareholder value, but often increase incomes for some managers and shareholders, partly at the expense of other shareholders of the firms, not to mention their stakeholders, such as workers and taxpayers.

Income distribution

The analysis presented so far raises the issue of the overall impact of financialization on income distribution. A key issue in this area concerns the origin of financial profits (see Pollin, 1996). Are they the result of a provision of services by finance to the rest of the economy, as is asserted by most mainstream economic theory? Or does much of these profits come in this era of financialization from the extraction of income and wealth by finance from workers, taxpayers, debtors and other creditors? Levina (2014) proposes that much of financial income comes from access to capital gains in financialized markets and therefore does not necessarily reflect a zero-sum game, as is implied by those who argue that financial returns are extracted rather than result from increased wealth. This issue of the source of financial income is extremely difficult to sort out theoretically and there is no consensus on this topic (see Lapavitsas, 2013).

There has been some empirical work to look at the impact of financialization on income and wealth distribution. Descriptive analysis about the United States indicates that the top earners (the 1 per cent or even the 0.01 per cent of the income distribution) get the bulk of their incomes from CEO pay or from finance. Econometric work looking at the relationship between financialization and inequality is also growing. Tomaskovic-Devey and Lin (2011) present an econometric model indicating that since the 1970s, between US$5.8 and 6.6 trillion were transferred to the financial sector from other sectors in the economy, including wage earners and taxpayers.

Lin and Tomaskovic-Devey (2013), using a sectoral econometric analysis for the United States, find that in time-series cross-sectional data at the industry level, an increasing dependence on financial income, in the long run, is associated with reducing labour's share of income, increasing top executives' share of compensation, and increasing earnings dispersion among workers. They carry out a counterfactual analysis that suggests that financialization could account for more than half of the decline in labour's share of income, 9.6 per cent of the growth in officers' share of compensation, and 10.2 per cent of the growth in earnings dispersion between 1970 and 2008.

Dünhaupt (2013) finds a negative relationship between financialization and the labour share of national income in a larger set of OECD countries from 1986 to 2007.

Financialization and economic growth

As the massive recession stemming from the global financial crisis that erupted in 2007–08 makes clear, there is no linear relationship between the size and complexity of financial markets and economic growth. Several econometric studies have suggested an inverted U-shaped relationship between the size of the financial sector and economic growth. A larger financial sector raises the rate of economic growth up to a point, but when the financial sector gets too large relative to the size of the economy, economic growth begins to decline (see, for example, Cecchetti and Kharoubi, 2012). To the extent that this relationship is true, economists are still searching for an explanation. One argument is that as the financial sector increases in size, because of its relatively high pay levels, it pulls talented and highly educated employees away from other sectors that might contribute more to economic growth and productivity. As a university professor teaching economics since the 1980s, I can testify that many of my undergraduate students dreamed of going to work on Wall Street. Perhaps some of them could have contributed more elsewhere.

Conclusion

There is little doubt that the size and reach of financial activities, markets, motives and institutions has grown enormously in the last 30 years, relative to other aspects of the economy. There is a great deal of historical and empirical evidence that, at least to some extent, this growth has contributed to economic instability, an increase in inequality, and perhaps to a decline in productive investment and employment relative to what might have occurred otherwise. There is less consensus on whether this constitutes a new epoch, phase, or mode of accumulation or what exactly is causing this shift: is it underlying problems in the 'productive core' of the economy, a reaction to broader shifts in the global economy associated with globalization, technological changes associated with digitization, or primarily due to financial deregulation as being part and parcel of neoliberalism?

To some extent, public policies or programmes aimed at reducing the deleterious consequences of financialization depend on the underlying causes of the negative aspects of financialization. If the problem primarily stems from issues of financial regulation, then adopting strict financial regulations as suggested by many imposing a financial transactions tax to reduce short-term trading, prohibiting destructive stock buybacks, breaking up large banks, changing corporate governance so that corporations take into account the preferences of stakeholders, and a host of other reforms could well go a long way to taming financialization.

If the problems stem largely from the vast and growing inequality of income and wealth distribution and the political power that this inequality buys, then deeper reforms of taxation, wages and ownership as well as money in politics must be implemented.

If the problem goes deeper to the underlying capitalist dynamics that lead to financialization, then one must look at even more fundamental reforms.

NOTE

1   See also Lapavitsas (2013) and Orhangazi (2008a, 2008b) for important contributions in this regard.

REFERENCES

Appelbaum, E. and R. Batt (2014), *Private Equity at Work: When Wall Street Manages Main Street*, New York: Russell Sage Foundation.

Arrighi, G. (1994), *The Long Twentieth Century: Money, Power and the Origins of Our Times*, London and New York: Verso Books.

Bank for International Settlements (2013), *Triennial Central Bank Survey of Foreign Exchange and Derivatives Market Activity*, Basel: Bank for International Settlements.

Cecchetti, S. and E. Kharoubi (2012), 'Reassessing the impact of finance on growth', *Bank for International Settlements Working Paper, No. 381*.

Dallas, L.L. (2011), 'Short-termism, the financial crisis and corporate governance', *Journal of Corporation Law*, **37** (2), 264.

Davis, L. (2013), 'Financialization and the non-financial corporation: an investigation of firm-level investment behavior in the U.S., 1971–2011', *University of Massachusetts Department of Economics Working Paper, No. 2013-08*.

De Souza, J.P.A. and G. Epstein (2014), 'Sectoral net lending in six financial centers', *Political Economy Research Institute Working Paper, No. 346*.

Dünhaupt, P. (2013), 'The effect of financialization on labor's share of income', *Institute for International Political Economy Berlin Working Paper, No. 17/2013*.

Epstein, G.A. (2005), 'Introduction', in G.A. Epstein (ed.), *Financialization and the World Economy*, Cheltenham, UK and Northampton, MA, USA: Edward Elgar Publishing, pp. 3–16.

Epstein, G.A. and J. Crotty (2013), 'How big is too big? On the social efficiency of the financial sector in the United States', in J. Wicks-Lim and R. Pollin (eds), *Capitalism on Trial: Explorations in the Tradition of Thomas E. Weisskopf*, Cheltenham, UK and Northampton, MA, USA: Edward Elgar Publishing, pp. 293–310.

Haldane, A.G. and R. Davies (2011), 'The short long', speech at the 29th Société Européenne Universitaire de Recherches Financières Colloquium on 'New Paradigms in Money and

Finance?', accessed 22 October 2015 at www.bankofengland.co.uk/archive/Documents/historicpubs/speeches/2011/speech495.pdf.

Hein, E. (2012), *The Macroeconomics of Finance-Dominated Capitalism – and its Crisis*, Cheltenham, UK and Northampton, MA, USA: Edward Elgar Publishing.

Krippner, G. (2005), 'The financialization of the American economy', *Socio-Economic Review*, **3** (2), 173–208.

Lapavitsas, C. (2013), *Profiting Without Producing: How Finance Exploits Us All*, London and New York: Verso Books.

Lazonick, W. (2014), 'Profits without prosperity', *Harvard Business Review*, September, 1–11.

Levina, I.A. (2014), 'A puzzling rise in financial profits and the role of capital gain-like revenue', *Political Economy Research Institute Working Paper, No. 347*.

Lin, K. and D. Tomaskovic-Devey (2013), 'Financialization and US income inequality: 1970–2008', *American Journal of Sociology*, **118** (5), 1284–329.

Orhangazi, Ö. (2008a), *Financialization and the US Economy*, Cheltenham, UK and Northampton, MA, USA: Edward Elgar Publishing.

Orhangazi, Ö. (2008b), 'Financialisation and capital accumulation in the non-financial corporate sector', *Cambridge Journal of Economics*, **32** (6), 863–86.

Palley, T.I. (2014), *Financialization: The Economics of Finance Capital Domination*, Basingstoke, UK and New York: Palgrave Macmillan.

Parenteau, R.W. (2005), 'The late 1990s' US bubble: financialization in the extreme', in G.A. Epstein (ed.), *Financialization and the World Economy*, Cheltenham, UK and Northampton, MA, USA: Edward Elgar Publishing, pp. 111–48.

Polanyi, K. (1944), *The Great Transformation*, New York: Farrar & Rinehart.

Pollin, R. (1996), 'Contemporary economic stagnation in world historical perspective', *New Left Review*, **219** (1), 109–18.

Sawyer, M.C. (2013), 'What is financialization?', *International Journal of Political Economy*, **42** (4), 5–18.

Stockhammer, E. (2004), 'Financialisation and the slowdown of accumulation', *Cambridge Journal of Economics*, **28** (5), 719–41.

Stout, L. (2012), *The Shareholder Value Myth: How Putting Shareholders First Harms Investors, Corporations and the Public*, San Francisco, CA: Berrett-Koehler Publishers.

Taub, J. (2014), *Other People's Houses: How Decades of Bailouts, Captive Regulators, and Toxic Bankers Made Home Mortgages a Thrilling Business*, New Haven, CT: Yale University Press.

Taylor, A. (2014), 'The great leveraging', in V.V. Acharya, T. Beck and D.D. Evanoff et al. (eds), *The Social Value of the Financial Sector: Too Big to Fail or Just Too Big?*, Hackensack, NJ: World Scientific Publishing, pp. 33–65.

Tomaskovic-Devey, D. and K. Lin (2011), 'Income dynamics, economic rents, and the financialization of the US economy', *American Sociological Review*, **76** (4), 538–59.

Wolfson, M.H. and G.A. Epstein (eds) (2013), *The Handbook of the Political Economy of Financial Crises*, Oxford, UK: Oxford University Press.

A PORTRAIT OF KARL PAUL POLANYI (1886–1964)

Karl Paul Polanyi was a Hungarian–American economic historian, economic anthropologist, political economist, historical sociologist and social philosopher. He is best known for his opposition to traditional economic thought and for his book titled *The Great Transformation* (Polanyi, 1944). Polanyi is also remembered today as the originator of substantivism, a cultural approach to economics that emphasizes the way economies are embedded in society and culture. Polanyi's masterpiece, *The Great Transformation*, became a model for historical sociology and, in recent years, has been revisited to explore the impacts and likely trajectory of phenomena such as financial liberalization.

Polanyi was born into a Jewish family in Vienna in 1886, at the time the capital of the Austro–Hungarian Empire. Polanyi graduated from Budapest University in 1912 with a doctorate in Law. From 1924 to 1933 he was employed as a senior editor of the prestigious magazine *The Austrian Economist*. It was at this time that he first began criticizing the Austrian School of economists, who he felt created abstract models that lost sight of the organic, interrelated reality of economic processes. After the accession of Hitler to office in January 1933 accompanied by a rising tide of fascism in Austria, he left for London in 1933, where he earned a living as a journalist and tutor and obtained a position as a lecturer for the Workers' Educational Association in 1936. His lecture notes contained the research for what later became his greatest work, *The Great Transformation*. However, he would not start writing this work until 1940, when he moved to Vermont to take up a position at

Bennington College, where he completed and published his book to great acclaim in 1944. In the 1950s and 1960s, Polanyi lived in Canada in Pickering Ontario, where he died in 1964.

The Great Transformation deals with the social and political upheavals that took place in the United Kingdom during the rise of the market economy and relates these crucially to the rise of fascism in Europe and the causes of World War II. Polanyi contends that the modern market economy and the modern nation-state should be understood not as separate elements but as the single human invention that he calls the 'market society'. This creation of the market society is the 'great transformation' that features in his book's title. The great transformation was begun by the powerful modern state, which was needed to push changes in social structure and human nature that allowed for a capitalist economy. For Polanyi, these changes implied the destruction of the basic social order that had reigned throughout earlier history. Central to the change was that social factors of production like land and labour would now be sold on the market at market-determined prices instead of allocated according to tradition, redistribution, or reciprocity. He referred to this commodification of land and labour as the creation of 'fictitious commodities', because to sell these on a market was not only such a dramatic change from how they were treated for thousands of years, but also because they are so essential to human life. In fact, they cannot really be treated as commodities without generating dire consequences.

The other key fictitious commodity of a capitalist economy, according to Polanyi, is

➡

←

'money'. This attempt to treat labour, land and money as if they could be entirely governed by the market, rather than embedded in and regulated by the broader social order, results in massive social dislocation and spontaneous moves by society to protect itself. In effect, Polanyi argues that once the free market attempts to separate itself from the fabric of society, social protectionism is society's natural response, which he calls the 'double movement'. Polanyi thus attempted to turn the tables on the orthodox liberal account of the rise of capitalism by arguing that 'laissez-faire was planned', whereas social protectionism was a spontaneous reaction to the social dislocation imposed by an unrestrained free market. The Great Depression was the crisis of the market economy based on these fictitious commodities. And both fascism and World War II were partly created by society through the double movement, where society tried to reassert itself to try to protect itself from the ravages of the market. Polanyi argued that, ultimately. a form of socialism would be a far better way for society to embed and regulate the market forces for social stability and health.

Polanyi's ideas have had a resurgence in response to the rise of 'neoliberalism' and associated 'free market' thinking. Some scholars have argued that Polanyi's analysis helps to explain why the resurgence of free market ideas have resulted in such manifest failures as persistent unemployment, widening inequality, and the severe financial crises that have stressed Western economies over the past 40 years. They suggest that the ideology that free markets can replace governments is utopian and dangerous.

Nobel Prize winning economist Joseph Stiglitz favours Polanyi's account of market liberalization, arguing that the failures of 'shock therapy' in Russia and the failures of IMF reform packages echo Polanyi's arguments. Polanyi's arguments about the double movement have suggested that more control over the market economy by society is necessary to sustain healthy social outcomes.

16

Imbalances and crises

Robert Guttmann

OVERVIEW

This chapter:

- points out the prevalence of imbalances and crises;

- explains the mainstream view of equilibrium and exogenous shocks;

- discusses Marx's overproduction versus Keynes's underconsumption;

- presents Kalecki's cyclical dynamics of growth and distribution;

- focuses on business cycles and credit cycles (Hayek versus Minsky);

- explains external imbalances and adjustment options.

KEYWORDS

- **Cyclical growth pattern:** Rather than moving along a steady-state balanced growth path as claimed by mainstream economists, our economy's growth pattern is inherently subject to cyclical fluctuations. In that context downturns known as 'recession' can be seen as rebalancing processes by which the market mechanism imposes its discipline.
- **Excess supplies:** The innate tendency of a capitalist economy to end up driving total supply (and the underlying production capacity) beyond total demand, be it because of overproduction conditions (Marx) or underconsumption limits (Keynes).
- **External adjustment:** In a globalized economy nations are not just facing internal imbalances to cope with, but, more than ever, are also exposed to shocks from abroad. More generally, they have to keep their economic and financial interactions with the rest of the world more or less in balance, lest they become vulnerable to painful (external) adjustment via currency price fluctuations, economic policy changes, or crisis-mediated restoration of balance.

• **Financial instability:** The cyclical growth dynamics of profit-driven market economies is reinforced by a parallel credit cycle in the course of which excessive levels of indebtedness taken on during the euphoric boom phase end up leaving overextended debtors vulnerable to any disruption of income and credit supplies. When this disruption arises, as is inevitable in the course of the cyclical growth dynamics of our economy, financial crises will typically arise and trigger a recessionary adjustment.

Why are these topics important?

Capitalism has a long record of instability. Market imbalances, whereby demand and supply do not match, build up and then explode into crises when generalized enough or enduring for sufficiently long periods. As a matter of fact, it is often through crises that the economic system ultimately corrects its imbalances when no other (market-driven or policy-induced) adjustment mechanism has been allowed to work. In this sense, imbalances are inherent to our system. This reality, one of gradually unfolding imbalances triggering crisis-induced adjustments, is generally outside the purview of mainstream economists who see markets as self-adjusting, hence imbalances cannot be built in. Luckily we have a great body of heterodox thinking in that direction, and one has to draw from these thinkers to explain one of the central characteristics of the capitalist system – its propensity towards imbalances and crises.

The mainstream view of a self-adjusting economy

Mainstream economists have always marvelled at the market mechanism organizing the interaction between supply and demand. Emphasis in economics on the market's self-balancing abilities was already evident from the very beginning, when Adam Smith (1759, 1776) coined the expression 'invisible hand' to describe how markets regulated themselves to the benefit of all. A century later, in the Marginalist Revolution (Jevons, 1871; Menger, [1871] 1950; Walras, [1873] 1954), this self-regulation capacity of a market economy came to be anchored in the notion of 'equilibrium', given its primary expression in the famous demand-and-supply 'scissors' or 'cross' diagram by Alfred Marshall (1890).[1] His elegant depiction of the market's balancing process assumed that competition among buyers as well as sellers, coupled with the innate desire on both sides to come to terms, would yield a mutually agreed price that clears the market and leaves every participant in it satisfied.

The mathematical models and/or graphical diagrams, which the standard neoclassical approach has used ever since Alfred Marshall, basically assume away all the forces that may prevent such automatic self-balancing. They treat time as logical time $(t - n, \ldots, t; t + 1, \ldots, t + n)$ able to move in both directions, presume rational actors in pursuit of maximizing their benefits, or describe markets as 'perfectly competitive' and hence fully flexible. From that perspective it is easy to arrive at 'equilibrium' and see any 'disequilibrium' (that is, an imbalance) as a temporary aberration caused by exogenous forces disrupting the self-regulating market mechanism (such as unions interfering with the labour market and government regulation restraining product markets).

In reality, however, time is historic and as such only moves forward; human beings are not rational thinking machines but make decisions with cognitive biases, and markets are often 'imperfectly competitive' inasmuch as some market participants exercise more market power than others. Under these conditions, 'equilibrium' is a far less assured thing. It might then also be true that, rather than being caused by exogenous factors bent on disrupting the market, imbalances are endemic to how the economic system operates in reality, away from its textbook depiction.

If we were to take such an alternative view, we would concede, for instance, that economic theory ought to explain why economies periodically go through brutal downturns known as recessions. But the mainstream approach, so wedded to the market's power of quasi-instantaneous self-balancing, would rather insist – as yet another expression of its fundamental belief in equilibrium – on a balanced or steady-state growth path.[2]

More recently, neoclassical economists have gone a bit further in accepting the possibility that there may be periods where exogenous shocks, whether positive or negative, and affecting either the supply side or the demand side, may move the economy temporarily off its equilibrium path. They recognize that such periods may be of more than just passing length, after which the economy tries to find its way back to a steady state of growth. But this approach, so-called 'real business cycle' theory (Kydland and Prescott, 1982; Long and Plesser, 1983), makes cyclical fluctuations an exception rather than the rule. And it focuses exclusively on the 'real' economy of physical production, ignoring the possibility of disturbances from the monetary and financial side.

Overproduction versus underconsumption

All the while orthodox economists have insisted on a balanced growth path, the economy has instead performed by moving along in a distinct up-and-down pattern. And this discrepancy between theory and empirical reality has in turn always left space for alternative ways to look at how a capitalist market economy performs over time. The history of economic thought has in that regard been profoundly shaped by the contributions of two great economists and visionaries, one dying the year the other was born (1883) – Karl Marx and John Maynard Keynes respectively. Both men put forth coherent alternatives to the orthodoxy's vision of an automatically self-balancing economy moving along a balanced growth path to emphasize instead that system's innate propensity to move in terms of cycles. Marx identified a systemic propensity for overproduction ('excess supplies') as the main culprit for such recurrent up-and-down fluctuations. Keynes, on the other hand, stressed the inability of the system to generate sufficiently high levels of total spending ('aggregate demand') for full employment to be attained, pointing instead to capitalism's underconsumption tendency.

Marx's challenge

As the great classical political economists, notably Adam Smith and David Ricardo, had done before him, Karl Marx believed that the profit rate had a tendency to decline in the long run. But unlike his predecessors putting the blame on the growing plentifulness of capital depressing its price, Marx ([1867] 1992, [1894] 1959) provided a more complex, two-pronged explanation.

Marx's argument about tendentially declining profitability is rooted in competition forcing producers to adopt increasingly automated and capital-intensive production methods, as a prerequisite for the productivity gains needed to stay competitive and to lower their unit costs. Once this position is attained, firms can then either lower the sales price of their products (and still maintain their profit margin) or obtain higher profit margins (at the same sales price). But that drive eventually undermines itself to the extent that such automation of production methods shrinks the source of profit: the unpaid labour time extracted from the workforce ('surplus value') relative to the ever-growing capital base. The result is declining profit rates, because the numerator in the profit rate ratio (that is, profits) cannot keep up with its denominator (capital).

It should be noted here that Marx also identified counter-tendencies capable of slowing or even reversing the profit rate decline.[3] To increase the profit rate, capitalists could revert to any or all of these important counter-tendencies: (1) increasing the rate of exploitation of workers, (2) decreasing the wage, (3) cheapening the plant and equipment used in production ('constant capital'), (4) relative overpopulation, and (5) foreign trade. During an economic crisis, all these counter-tendencies are more likely to be used by entrepreneurs, thereby reaffirming the role played by crises as a clearing-out mechanism with which to restore balance.

Marx then pointed to a second, parallel source of intrinsic imbalance that rendered capitalist economies inherently cyclical: the dual and contradictory nature of the wage. On the one hand, the wage is the principal source of income for consumption expenditures by households, and the largest part by far of total demand in the economy. But the wage is also a private cost for businesses, often their largest production cost item. Each capitalist wants the wages of his or her own workers to be as low as possible while at the same time wanting the wages of all other workers (serving as potential consumers) to be as high as possible.

Barring the social wage component provided for by the government (for example, a pension fund and health insurance) and collective bargaining agreements with unions, the wage is mostly determined in the labour market as a private cost and hence kept as low as possible, too low in fact to absorb the rising output capacity of firms pursuing increasingly automated production methods in competition with each other. Marx saw overproduction conditions therefore as inevitable and the primary trigger of crises. By eliminating the weakest firms and forcing surviving producers to slash production volumes, crises would in turn serve to eliminate such conditions of overproduction.

Keynes's insight

Keynes had a different starting point for his discussion of capitalism's propensity for crisis, which ultimately looked at the economy as a whole and ended up giving us a new macroeconomic level of analysis. Writing during the Great Depression of the 1930s, Keynes (1936) understood that Marshall's then dominant market equilibrium framework could not explain this phenomenon. How was it possible to have a sustained decline in economic activity with mass unemployment for so many years? What had happened to the Marshallian argument in favour of the markets' self-balancing capacity to get us out of the crisis and restore full employment?

Keynes understood correctly that most markets had ceased to function like 'perfectly competitive' markets. More and more, product markets had moved from having many small sellers to a structure dominated by fewer larger-sized firms with the market power to set prices. Firms in such imperfectly competitive market structures typically set prices as a function of their unit costs (under normal production conditions) to which they would then add a target profit margin.[4] These producers would respond to any shortfall in demand for their products with cutbacks in output rather than engage in self-defeating price wars. One reason for their resistance to lower prices in the face of excess supplies was rigid labour costs as more and more workers came to be covered by collective bargaining agreements negotiated on their behalf by trade unions.

In other words, institutional changes in the *modus operandi* of our economy – more highly concentrated market structures with fewer and larger producers capable of administering their prices, wages set in advance by multi-year contracts – had rendered prices much less likely to fall. But that growing downward rigidity of prices also implied that the clearing of markets in the face of excess supplies, via lower prices encouraging more buying, had ceased to function properly.

In analysing the Great Depression of the 1930s, Keynes recognized the prevalence of such downwardly rigid price behaviour, extending in particular also to labour markets. But Keynes went a step further to figure out why the economy would not recover even after prices had finally come down considerably.[5] And here he pointed to a crucial fallacy of composition, where what is good and therefore seems logical for individual actors is not so for the system as a whole. On the contrary, it may actually be disastrous for the whole system. Specifically, individual firms with some degree of price-setting power in 'imperfectly competitive' markets would try to stave off price wars and instead be inclined to reduce their output and employment levels whenever their inventories built up amidst slowing sales volumes. While this response makes sense for any firm trying to preserve profits by cutting costs, it has a negative impact on other actors tied to the firm. Both the workers laid off by the firm as well as its suppliers, who now are selling less to the firm, will lose income. And such income losses will cause these actors to cut back their spending, affecting yet another group of sellers adversely. The negative multiplier effect of spending cutbacks translating into income losses, which trigger further cuts in spending, can overpower the economy as a whole and paralyse it even in the face of falling prices, as happened during the 1930s.

The Keynesian revolution

The Keynesian revolution in the aftermath of the Great Depression in the 1930s provided a macroeconomic dimension to economic analysis, rooted in the realization that what makes sense for individuals alone may prove disastrous for all of them together, so that the economy must be understood as more than just the amalgam of markets grouping together individual buyers and sellers. Keynes took this insight to argue in favour of an extra-market agent, who is neither bound by the profit motive nor by the typical budget constraints, stepping in to pull the economy out of its doldrums by injecting doses of spending. This agent was the government, capable of deficit spending whenever needed to boost total demand. His policy prescription of aiming for greater budget deficits to boost the economy found immediate followers among politicians desperate enough to try something new – as in Roosevelt's New Deal in the United States.

Marx and Keynes pointed to the same contradiction embodied in the dual nature of the wage as largest source of total demand and dominant item of production costs. Keynes argued consistently that the private (profit-motivated) sector was incapable of generating adequate levels of total demand to assure high levels of employment. While such spending additions as more business investment or greater net exports could compensate, the sheer size of household consumption (as a percentage of total spending) and its inherent ceiling by restrictions on wage income tend to make total demand inadequate (relative to full employment output) unless boosted by larger budget deficits by the public sector.

To summarize, both Marx and Keynes pointed to the market economy's inability to sustain a balanced growth path on its own. While Marx stressed the system's propensity for overproduction and Keynes highlighted instead its underconsumption tendency, both disputed the mainstream's emphasis on the market's self-balancing powers to maintain continuous equilibrium.

Growth and distribution

If the dual nature of the wage as the largest source of aggregate demand and private business costs lies behind the inherent supply–demand imbalance identified by both Marx and Keynes, then it stands to reason that there should be a link between income distribution and the growth dynamics of capitalist economies. We are talking here in particular about functional income distribution, notably the wage share relative to other slices of the income pie going to capital (profit share, interest share).[6]

Polish economist Michał Kalecki (1937, 1938, 1942, 1971) tried to reconcile this link by tracing the dynamic relationship between wage shares and profit shares over the growth cycle while also seeking to identify their principal determinants. For Kalecki the interaction between these two strategic income shares played a major role in the (ultimately cyclical) growth dynamics. This Kaleckian link between growth and distribution integrates micro-level actions, notably an investment function and mark-up pricing by firms operating in imperfectly competitive market structures, with the macro-level determinants of wage and profit shares to yield a more profound insight into capitalism's inherently complex balancing act between total demand and total supply.[7]

Wage rates and productivity growth

Kalecki's attempt to link growth and distribution points to a crucial relationship highlighted by all three heterodox masters – Marx, Keynes and Kalecki. This is the evolution of the wage rate relative to that of productivity. As crystallized in Keynes's important discussion of the so-called 'efficiency wage', the balanced growth of our economy depends on both of these variables growing pretty much at the same rate over time.

If productivity growth outpaces that of wages over a sustained period of time, then sooner or later productivity-driven supply will shoot beyond wage-dependent total demand. This is exactly what happened in the United States during much of the 1920s and also 2000s, resulting both times in the spread of overproduction conditions that set the stage for a major crisis first in October 1929 and then again in 2007.

If, on the other hand, nominal wages grow faster than productivity for several years, then you are more likely to see unit labour costs getting pushed up. This may very well result in (cost-push) inflation. To the extent that firms cannot fully pass on higher unit costs onto higher prices, their profits get squeezed and this will hamper their long-term growth potential. We saw such stagflation conditions take root in the United States during the 1970s, when productivity growth suddenly came to a halt for nearly a decade while nominal wages still rose (albeit less than inflation, thus causing a fall in 'real' wages for much of that troubled period). It is better then to have both wages and productivity grow at pretty much the same rate. When that happens, total supply and demand can expand in balanced fashion at that rate too. And at the same time wage and profit shares are thereby also kept relatively stable.

Cyclical growth dynamics

Kalecki argued the strategic significance of income distribution, in particular the importance of profits in their dynamic interaction with investment, in terms of a cyclical growth pattern. In other words, the feedback effects between profits and investment spending driving business behaviour played out in terms of a cyclical pattern of ups and downs. In such a cycle, growth accelerates at first to reach a peak, at which point the economy turns down until that decline bottoms out and recovery resumes – only for the same cyclical pattern to be repeated again.

Business cycles

When looking at how and why our economy grows in such a recurrently cyclical fashion, we see, as both Marx and Keynes did, that recoveries tend to turn into euphoric booms during the course of which demand cannot keep up with supply and the system eventually overshoots. In this context the crisis may then be viewed as a process whereby imbalances, which may have accumulated over time, are forcibly counteracted by actors (producers and consumers) making the necessary adjustments in the face of untenable situations. Businesses may react to a build up of unsold inventories by cutting back production, even at times prices, to rid themselves of those excess stocks. Consumers may at that point also cut back and so further depress total demand. But the key to this crisis-driven adjustment process is for supply to fall faster than demand.

Credit

While one can argue, with Marx or Keynes, that capitalist economies have an inherently cyclical growth pattern, empirical evidence suggests that these cycles are reinforced by the typically pro-cyclical behaviour of credit. When looking at the historic record of any advanced capitalist economy, one can see that most economic downturns were preceded by sudden outbursts of financial instability negatively affecting funding conditions in our credit system, and so forcing cutbacks in the face of squeezed credit. This is especially true for depressions, a deeper and longer downturn than the regularly recurrent recessions that are part and parcel of the normal business cycle fluctuations. A depression starts typically with a spectacularly violent financial crisis, such as the worldwide banking turmoil of 1873, the crash of October 1929, or the subprime crisis after August 2007.[8]

Inclusion of financial instability in our discussion of business cycles necessitates consideration of credit as a significant macroeconomic force in the growth process. Our market economy can achieve higher growth rates (and even temporarily stave off acute overproduction conditions that would have triggered a recession on their own) by making credit easily available at reasonable interest rates. Such credit allows borrowers to spend beyond their current income level and so relaxes their budget constraint.

Endogenous credit money

Credit-funded spending boosts used to depend on savings by private agents (households, firms) and their transformation into loanable funds by financial intermediaries ('banks') offering surplus-savings units ('savers') deposits for their savings and then using these funds to make loans to deficit-spending units ('borrowers').

Thanks to Roosevelt's monetary reforms in 1933–35, following the collapse of the gold standard in September 1931, our banking system has been capable of going beyond the simple financial intermediation exercise of mobilizing savings and turning them into loanable funds. These reforms – in particular the Glass–Steagall Act of 1933 and the Bank Act of 1935 – established a more expansive credit system for which these measures provided endogenous creation of an elastic currency (so-called 'credit money') within the banking system that has facilitated continuous debt financing of excess spending.[9]

This fact too has escaped mainstream economists. Their monetary theories (see Friedman, 1956, 1968) presume somehow that we still live in a world of an exogenously fixed money stock under the strict control of the central bank; in other words a vertically sloped money supply curve.

Financial instability

While we have institutionalized endogenous money creation in the banking system tied to credit extension of banks ('credit money') to provide our economy with an elastic currency, this improvement has come at the expense of another major source of imbalances, namely, incidences of financial instability. Our system of credit money has made affordable credit much more accessible for the great majority of economic actors. But this improved access to debt has caused a greater danger of financial instability. That kind of situation may arise at any time when debtors find themselves having taken on too much debt relative to their income creation capacity that they end up unable to service their debts. Or there may be a sharp decline in the price of financial assets, such as when there is a stock market crash.

But these incidences are often no more than isolated moments of trouble for some, passing events without major repercussions for the overall performance of the economic system as a whole. For them to have a bigger impact on the overall economy, they have to reach a scale large enough to disrupt credit supplies from the banking system feeding the economy.

Yet we know from observation that almost every cyclical turning point in our economic system has involved a financial crisis pushing the economy into recession. We have to account for this undeniable empirical fact with an appropriate theoretical framework that acknowledges the recurrent pattern of financial instability at or near the peak as a trigger of recessionary adjustment. We have, in the end, two good theories that fit the bill – the Austrian School and Hyman Minsky's financial instability hypothesis.

The Austrians

The Austrian School (Von Mises, [1912] 1953, 1949; Von Hayek, 1931) emphasized a credit cycle in the course of which an irresponsibly lax central bank permits a build up of debt and overspending in the wake of excessively low interest rates. Being spoiled with ample supplies of cheap loans, businesses end up making too many bad investment decisions (so-called 'malinvestment') and hence find themselves in a crisis.

When looking at the US Federal Reserve's recent record of responding to any recession, even a shallow and short one, by pushing for much lower interest rates and maintaining those long into recovery (as in 1982–87, 1991–94 and 2000–04), there is something to be said for that line of argument. The Austrians have therefore in recent years found more followers. A more important reason for their recent success, however, is ideological. Theirs is a deeply conservative approach that emphasizes the danger of letting the government interfere with the market mechanism in a discretionary fashion. They blame credit overextension on mistaken central bank policy rather than viewing it as an inherent part of the business cycle dynamics typifying capitalist economies. While pro-cyclical monetary policy feeding credit overextension at first and then tightening near the peak amidst signs of overheating has been a clear feature of many business cycles in both the United States and elsewhere, that key argument of the Austrians rests confined to a 'policy mistake' that justifies their overall conclusion to keep the role of government (in this case the central bank) in our economy minimal. This ideological preference – and the Austrians are consistently libertarian in their policy conclusions – fails to give sufficient weight to the more profound idea that advanced capitalist economies with highly developed financial systems are inherently subject to credit cycles from which follow a propensity to financial instability.

Minsky's financial instability hypothesis

If we truly want to understand financial crises as a phenomenon endemic to our capitalist system, we must turn to post-Keynesian economists. They are the followers of the 'true' Keynes, in sharp contradistinction to various neoclassical reinterpretations that squeezed this original, at times even subversive, thinker back into the general equilibrium box.[10] Among post-Keynesians exploring the ties between credit, money and economic activity, Hyman Minsky (1982, 1986, 1992) in particular came to stress the importance of financial instability at the cyclical peak as trigger of downturns. After the events of 2007–08 his focus on financial instability as an endogenous feature of capitalist economies with correspondingly cyclical growth patterns has regained the attention it deserves.

Business cycle dynamics *à la* Kalecki or Keynes are reinforced in both upswing and downswing phases by a parallel credit cycle whose sharp turning point at the cyclical peak arises when acute explosions of financial instability of sufficient force push the economic system into recessionary adjustment. For Minsky this is likely to happen when a growing number of debtors reach excessive levels of indebtedness during the upswing phase to render them highly vulnerable to any slowdown of income generation.

Minsky's argument rests on distinguishing between three different financing positions, each one comparing current income generation with given levels of debt servicing charges (that is, regular interest payments and timely repayment of principal):

- In the *hedge finance* position, agents (households, businesses) earn enough income to pay off all of their debts; they face no risk from their indebtedness.
- In the *speculative finance* position, borrowers have enough income to service their debts. But they no longer can pay these debts off all at once. This is obviously a somewhat riskier position to find oneself in.
- Finally, in the *Ponzi finance* position, agents have to take on new debt just to service their old debts. The Ponzi position is very dangerous and can get easily out of hand. Once fallen into such a downward spiral of having to borrow more and more, debtors will typically be obliged to take on increasingly short-term debt becoming due that much faster. Whereas any disruption of income creation can easily move a debtor from a speculative position to a Ponzi position, even slight declines in income can have a devastating impact on the debt-servicing capacity of Ponzi debtors. Minsky aptly described such a position as one of 'financial fragility'.

Incidences of financial instability can happen anytime when excessively indebted actors default on their debts and impose losses on their lenders.

Such incidences become a financial crisis when there are a lot of overextended Ponzi debtors rendering the entire system fragile. Minsky argued that increased financial fragility of the entire system is built into the cyclical dynamics of capitalist economies.

During upswing phases, when the economy grows rapidly and incomes rise tangibly, that favourable position breeds optimism. Widespread belief in a good future drives many actors to borrow more and their lenders to extend credit quite willingly. As investment bets materialize successfully, borrowers and their creditors are willing to take on a bit more risk in pursuit of still higher returns. Here financial innovations take on an important role to the extent that they make it easier to get more debt and live with higher levels of leverage. As recoveries turn into (debt-fuelled and innovation-driven) booms, widely shared euphoria induces systematic underestimation of risks.

This careless pursuit of quick riches turns many actors eventually into Ponzi debtors, often recognized as such only ex post, when hitherto rapid income growth has peaked or even started to decline while previously low interest rates have risen. Near the cyclical peak, rising debt servicing costs clash with sharply decelerating income growth, as falling profit rates and spreading overproduction begin to manifest themselves while demand for credit spikes and/or monetary policy tightens in the face of accelerating inflation rates. This squeeze on overextended debtors yields then an incidence of financial instability that, by demonstrating unmistakably the degree to which the entire system has become fragile, shifts the mood swiftly from euphoria to fear, even panic. In the wake of the subprime crisis, Wall Street has come to call this brutal turning point a 'Minsky moment'. There is considerable disagreement among post-Keynesians as to whether or not this crisis of 2007–08 was a Minsky crisis, not least because it emerged from excessive household debt, whereas Minsky himself focused primarily on corporate debt. But the very prominence Wall Street gave to his work by calling the panic following Lehman Brothers's bankruptcy in September 2008 a 'Minsky moment' showed the need for integrating financial crises into our macroeconomic framework of analysis.

Financial crisis as a rebalancing adjustment mechanism

When a 'Minsky moment' occurs, credit just freezes up. Lack of access to credit prompts desperate debtors to dump their assets into declining markets in a mad scramble for cash to survive. Creditors suffer major losses to the point where they too may fail. Simultaneous pull-backs by borrowers and lenders trigger recessionary adjustment, which inevitably follows such a 'credit crunch'. In that process overextended producers slash their output levels and production costs. While these reactions lower total supply, they also depress total demand especially when they cause lay-offs and lower wage income.

Stabilization requires total supply to fall faster than total demand for excess inventories to be eliminated. Recessionary adjustment also requires deleveraging across the board, either by writing off bad debts or getting rid of old debts while abstaining from taking on new debt commitments. Eventually these crisis-induced adjustments will have corrected the underlying imbalances sufficiently to make recovery possible.

Such conditions of restabilization will arrive earlier and more surely with the help of what Minsky termed 'Big Bank' (that is, a strong central bank serving as effective lender of last resort) and 'Big Government' (that is, an adequately sized government capable of larger deficit spending). Minsky considered these two institutions of economic policy particularly indispensable in stopping a possibly self-feeding spiral of forced asset sales, debt liquidations, losses and cutbacks, which may easily get out of control and throw the economy into depression – the famous debt deflation spiral identified by Fisher (1933) as the primary mechanism underlying the Great Depression of the 1930s.

External imbalances and adjustments

So far our discussion has been confined to imbalances and crises on a national scale. But since the early 1980s we have gone through an intense globalization process, which has made a large number of countries more interdependent. What happens in one corner of the world has immediate and direct repercussions for other regions.

International crisis dynamics

We have seen this process also in terms of contagion, where a crisis spreads from the country of origin to neighbours and beyond – the so-called 'LDC debt' crisis of 1982–89 (a debt crisis affecting over 50 lesser developed countries), the crisis of the European Monetary System in 1992–93, the 'Asian' crisis of 1997–98 ultimately spreading within a year to Russia, Brazil and Argentina as well, and finally the Great Recession of 2008–09 reaching a truly worldwide dimension after its initial manifestation as a bursting US housing bubble.

In each of these four crises the transmission mechanisms driving contagion from one country to the next were financial in nature, whether in the form of speculative attacks on currencies deemed hopelessly overvalued, capital flight by panic-stricken investors, or worried lenders cutting back their credit facilities. This is not really surprising in light of the fact that finance is today easily the most globalized aspect of economic activity.[11]

Underlying those internationally transmitted financial crises that we have witnessed recurrently since the 1980s are the so-called 'external imbalances'. Those mostly took the form of chronically large trade deficits and/or excessive borrowing from abroad ('capital imports') both of which led to unsustainable balance-of-payments disequilibria that undermined available foreign exchange reserves. In each instance the crisis, whether a currency crisis or a debt crisis or a combination of both, would hit countries suffering excessive balance-of-payments deficits.

The balance of payments

Any national economy's connection to the rest of the world occurs through its so-called 'balance of payments', which accounts for all the transactions between that country and the others. Trade in goods and services, investment income, and unilateral transfers (like remittances, which are funds immigrant workers send back to relatives back in their home countries), are all grouped together in the so-called 'current account'. Capital transfers, including those of financial capital (like portfolio investments comprising loans or trades in securities), all show up in the so-called 'capital account'. Each of these transactions can be a credit item, as when a country sells (either goods, services, or assets) to another country and gets paid by them, or a debit item, which arises when a country buys from another country and therefore has to pay the latter country. An external deficit (with regard to other countries) arises in whatever transaction category when debit items exceed credit items there, amounting to a net outflow of funds.

The balance of payment should always be balanced. Hence, if a country runs a current account deficit, it will have to finance it by running a capital account surplus, meaning that it will have to be a net seller of assets to investors abroad. This is just another way of saying that, in most instances, it will have to borrow funds (in other words, take loans or sell securities) abroad. Whenever its capital account surplus is not large enough to cover its current account deficit, the deficit country has to use its reserves.[12] Crises occur when the debtor nation has accumulated too high a level of external debts owed abroad in the wake of chronic or excessive current account deficits and/or has depleted its reserves.

Currency depreciation

Normally countries should not let it get to that point, since such crises – the kinds caused by excessively large external imbalances – tend to have an especially dramatic impact on very large numbers of actors within the domestic economy now forced to go through a wrenching readjustment process as rapidly as possible. We therefore have to explore ways in which countries running large and/or chronic current account deficits can bring them under control and, possibly, even revert back to surpluses for build up of depleted reserves. There are several possible scenarios for such 'adjustments', to use the jargon of economists.

The most obvious one is an appropriate change in the exchange rate. Any country running balance-of-payments deficits will have more money flowing to the rest of the world than coming in from abroad. The outflows represent supply of its currency whereas inflows constitute demand for its currency. Such excess supplies of its currency in the wake of balance-of-payments deficits will drive down the exchange rate of its currency. As the deficit country's currency depreciates, foreign goods, services and assets all become more expensive, since the same foreign currency amount now requires a bigger amount of the domestic currency to pay for it. The opposite is true for the actors abroad, with domestic items having been rendered cheaper for them as they now have to put up only a smaller amount of their strengthened currency for a given domestic price.

In theory this currency depreciation should then eliminate the underlying external deficit, as domestic actors cut back purchases of now costlier products from other countries while actors abroad get attracted to now cheaper domestic items. In practice, however, this may not work out as smoothly, as these quantity changes in the right direction may be (at least temporarily) outweighed by the cost effects of higher prices on foreign goods, services, and assets.[13]

Changes in policy mix

Another adjustment path may arise for deficit countries through internal changes that rebalance the domestic economy to the benefit of its external balance. Let us start with the Keynesian equation:

$$Y\,(\text{GDP}) = C\,(\text{Consumption}) + I\,(\text{Investment}) + G\,(\text{Government expenditures}) + NX\,(\text{Net exports, meaning Exports }X \text{ minus Imports } M)$$

Then take the other side of the same coin:

$$Y \text{ (National income)} = C + S \text{ (Savings)} + T \text{ (Tax revenues)}$$

Since these two equations express Y in different ways, one measured in terms of output produced and the other measured in terms of the income created by such production, we can put the two together. After some rearranging, we then obtain:

$$X - M = NX = (S - I) + (T - G)$$

From that accounting identity it is easy to discern that the external current account (im)balance NX depends on the positioning of the two internal (im)balances between savings and investments in the private sector and the budget balance in the public sector. Changing these two balances impacts directly on the current account balance.

If you want the latter to go down, you can use monetary policy to impact on the private sector balance: higher interest rates, for instance, would probably boost S and weigh down I. Or you can try to change the public sector balance with a change in fiscal policy, consisting in this case of deficit-reducing efforts to raise more taxes T and/or slow government spending G. So you can tighten monetary policy or fiscal policy, or pursue a combination of both. But such austerity measures are a hard sell politically, since they slow economic growth, create more unemployment, and make income less likely to grow, if at all.

Crisis-induced adjustments

So governments refrain from making these necessary, but politically difficult, changes in their policy mix until it is too late, at which point external deficits, left unattended for too long, trigger a crisis of confidence among investors living abroad. Once your country gets thrown into the hurl of such a crisis, it goes through a fairly radical adjustment induced by precisely that crisis on its own. Typically, firms and consumers scramble to hoard cash for precautionary purposes as they cut back sharply on their spending, making S shoot up, while business investment falls sharply (lowering I).

Such sudden private sector reversal to surplus, imposing massive spending reductions amidst recession, may be somewhat mitigated by an opposite movement towards greater deficits in the public sector, much of which is automatic in light of fiscal stabilizers kicking in during a recession to lower

T (as tax revenues decline automatically with shrinking economic activity) and raise G (as some income maintenance programmes shoot up during the downturn, such as unemployment benefits).

To the extent, however, that the private sector adjustment dominates the public sector reaction in the opposite direction, the external sector will find its current account balance (NX) improving. This makes sense also in real life, since a downturn at home would lower imports while at the same pushing domestic producers harder to export in compensation for the slowing sales at home. Once again it is through crisis that we get adjustments that should have happened earlier less painfully, but did not.

Symmetric adjustments

Much of this adjustment among deficit countries, difficult as it is, would be rendered a whole lot easier if surplus countries would do their bit and adjust at the same time in the opposite direction. If a chronic surplus country, like Germany, lowers its current account surplus by, say, half, there would be that much less of an adjustment to do by the deficit countries in, say, the rest of Europe. So the ideal situation would be to have simultaneous reductions of external imbalances among both sets of countries, the deficit countries as well as the surplus countries (see Chapter 14).

But this is not likely to be the case, since there is a fundamental asymmetry between them. Deficit countries are eventually obliged to bring their external deficits under control, when they have accumulated too much external debt or run out of reserves. Surplus countries, on the other hand, do not have any such structural limitation. They are in a position to accumulate reserves basically forever, as illustrated by China's US$4 trillion in reserves built up since the 1990s. And why would they voluntarily make themselves 'weaker', rendering wilfully less effective those comparative and competitive advantages that yielded the chronic external surpluses in the first place? So, in reality, the adjustment burden is usually not distributed even-handedly between deficit countries and surplus countries, placing the burden more on the former than the latter.

The international monetary system

The precise distribution of adjustment burdens depends ultimately on the prevailing international monetary system (IMS) in place to guide the monetary flows and financial transactions between countries. The IMS typically comprises the choice of internationally accepted media of exchange, determination of exchange rates, and the modalities of adjustment in the face of external imbalances.

At times we have had IMS arrangements that explicitly provided for a symmetry in adjustment burdens, as was the case during the gold standard (1879–1931) whose so-called 'specie-flow adjustment mechanism' subjected deficit countries to deflationary shocks in the wake of gold outflows while at the same time imposing inflationary shocks on surplus countries owing to gold inflows. Another example for such symmetry was the European Monetary System (1979–99), which provided explicitly for simultaneous currency devaluations by deficit countries and currency revaluations by surplus countries.

Today's market-regulated multi-currency IMS does not have such symmetry, however. On the contrary, it contains one added bias of asymmetry, making life harder for the weaker deficit countries. Still based on the US dollar as the primary form of world money, that system affords the United States an 'exorbitant privilege' as issuer of the world's principal international medium of exchange. Having to supply dollars created inside the US banking system to other countries, the United States has to run external deficits that assure net outflows of dollars to the rest of the world. In that sense it is fair to say that all the other countries automatically finance US balance-of-payments deficits whenever they use these dollars to pay each other or as reserves. This amounts to saying that the United States has the advantage of being able to cover its external deficits by borrowing from the rest of the world in its own currency indefinitely, at very low interest rates, and without strict repayment schedule. Whenever some of its foreign debt comes due, the United States just 'rolls' over that debt by replacing one bundle of paper becoming due with another bundle of paper.[14]

In this kind of arrangement, in which the United States is freed from any external constraint and can thus pile up external deficits for quite some time, other non-privileged debtor nations are pushed aside by the world's creditors automatically financing US deficits and so providing less funding support for the other deficit nations. The latter do not therefore have as much space for their deficits to get covered as they would have had without the creditors' preferential treatment of the United States.

Concluding remarks

As should have become obvious from the discussion in this chapter, our capitalist market economy is subject to a variety of built-in imbalances, which play themselves out in typically cyclical fashion. Supply may outpace demand to the point of overproduction (or underconsumption) after which excess capacities have to be cut back. Tenuous links between income distribution and the economic growth process further reinforce the dynamics of cyclical up-and-down fluctuations. Business cycles tend to be reinforced by parallel credit cycles, which feed the overproduction tendency on the upswing and the cutback dynamics following financial crises. As our national economies become increasingly integrated amidst accelerating globalization, the international dimension of imbalances and crisis gains strategic significance. Here we have to figure out how, amidst growing balance-of-payments disequilibria, needed adjustments often end up only getting triggered in the course of currency crises and crisis-induced changes in the policy mix.

NOTES

1 The Marginalist Revolution of the early 1870s aimed successfully at the classical political economy's labour theory of value, which at the time had taken a provocative direction in the hands of Karl Marx ([1867] 1992).

2 The classic model depicting such a non-cyclical, steady-state growth pattern as capitalism's more or less automatic tendency is the so-called Solow–Swan model, after Robert Solow (1956) and Trevor Swan (1956).

3 See Chapter 14 of Volume III of *Capital* (Marx [1894] 1959).

4 This pricing formula is at the heart of heterodox thinking about the modern firm, as so well captured by Michał Kalecki (1942) or Alfred Eichner (1976).

5 In the end, the demand shortfall of the Great Depression was so overwhelming and enduring that prices finally did come down significantly, falling in the United States alone by nearly a quarter from pre-crisis levels over a four-year period.

6 Functional income distribution refers to the relative sizes of the national income shares going to wages, profits, or financial capital income (such as interest and dividends), as opposed to personal income distribution measuring what percentage of the total income pie goes to the top 20 per cent as opposed to, say, the lowest 20 per cent, the next lowest 20 per cent, and so forth.

7 Kalecki's ability to integrate micro-level and macro-level aspects set the stage for later efforts in that direction among post-Keynesian economists, notably Eichner (1976) or more recently the so-called agent-based models (see, for instance, Setterfield and Budd, 2011).

8 A recession occurs when the economy experiences two consecutive quarters of negative GDP growth, meaning that the economy has shrunk during six consecutive months. A depression, on the other hand, would typically last a minimum of two years and push the rate of unemployment above 10 per cent.

9 Elsewhere (see Guttmann, 1994) I have analysed the radical implications of Roosevelt's monetary reforms giving us a supply-elastic credit money, as opposed to supply-inelastic commodity money prevailing under the gold standard. Such elastic currency helped transform our economy in terms of permitting chronic budget deficits, business funding of large-scale investments in mass production technology, consumer debt, and coverage of external (balance-of-payments) deficits.

10 Early relevant examples of US post-Keynesian economists are Davidson (1972), Eichner and Kregel (1975) and Weintraub (1978). A good discussion of the mainstream view of money (as exogenous stock) versus the post-Keynesian view of credit-money (as endogenous flow) is Moore (1988).

11 Elsewhere, in Guttmann (2009), I have analysed this phenomenon of global finance as a crucial new force tying countries more closely to each other but also exposing them together to greater volatility.

12 These reserves usually consist of gold, key currencies (like US dollars, euros), or so-called special drawing rights (SDRs) issued by the International Monetary Fund (IMF) for official settlements between

governments of debtor and creditor nations. If not earned from previous surpluses, reserves can also be borrowed in international money and bond markets or, as a last resort, from the IMF.

13 This delayed impact of currency depreciation on the external balance of a country, thanks to price effects dominating volume adjustments in the face of relatively inelastic trade patterns, is known as the Marshall–Lerner condition, named after Alfred Marshall ([1879] 1930) and Abba Lerner (1952). Price inelasticities pertaining to foreign trade may be so strong in the short run, that the external deficit actually gets worse in the immediate aftermath of depreciation before gradually improving – the so-called 'J-curve' effect first identified as such by Magee (1973).

14 For a discussion of the 'exorbitant privilege' of the United States thanks to the world money status of its currency, see Bergsten (1996) and Eichengreen (2007).

 REFERENCES

Bergsten, C.F. (1996), *The Dilemmas of the Dollar: Economics and Politics of United States International Monetary Policy*, Armonk, NY: M.E. Sharpe.

Davidson, P. (1972), *Money and the Real World*, New York: John Wiley and Sons.

Eichengreen, B. (2007), *Global Imbalances and the Lessons of Bretton Woods*, Cambridge, MA: MIT Press.

Eichner, A. (1976), *The Megacorp and Oligopoly: Micro Foundations of Macro Dynamics*, Cambridge, UK: Cambridge University Press.

Eichner, A. and J. Kregel (1975), 'An essay on post-Keynesian theory: a new paradigm in economics', *Journal of Economic Literature*, **13** (4), 1293–314.

Fisher, I. (1933), 'The debt-deflation theory of great depressions', *Econometrica*, **1** (4), 337–57.

Friedman, M. (1956), *Studies in the Quantity Theory of Money*, Chicago, IL: University of Chicago Press.

Friedman, M. (1968), 'The role of monetary policy', *American Economic Review*, **58** (1), 1–17.

Guttmann, R. (1994), *How Credit-Money Shapes Our Economy: The United States in a Global System*, Armonk, NY: M.E. Sharpe.

Guttmann, R. (2009), 'Asset bubbles, debt deflation, and global imbalances', *International Journal of Political Economy*, **38** (2), 46–69.

Jevons, S. (1871), *The Theory of Political Economy*, London: Macmillan.

Kalecki, M. (1937), 'A theory of the business cycle', *Review of Economic Studies*, **4** (2), 77–97.

Kalecki, M. (1938), 'The determinants of distribution of national income', *Econometrica*, **6** (2), 97–112.

Kalecki, M. (1942), 'A theory of profits', *Economic Journal*, **52** (206/207), 258–67.

Kalecki, M. (1971), *Selected Essays on the Dynamics of the Capitalist Economy, 1933–1970*, Cambridge, UK: Cambridge University Press.

Keynes, J.M. (1936), *The General Theory of Employment, Interest and Money*, London: Macmillan.

Kydland, F. and E. Prescott (1982), 'Time to build and aggregate fluctuations', *Econometrica*, **50** (6), 1345–70.

Lerner, A. (1952), 'Factor prices and international trade', *Economica*, **19** (73), 1–15.

Long, J. and C. Plesser (1983), 'Real business cycles', *Journal of Political Economy*, **91** (1), 39–69.

Magee, S. (1973), 'Currency contracts, pass-through, and devaluation', *Brookings Papers on Economic Activity, No. 1*, pp. 303–25.

Marshall, A. ([1879] 1930), *The Pure Theory of Foreign Trade, The Pure Theory of Domestic Values*, London: London School of Economics and Political Science.

Marshall, A. (1890), *Principles of Economics*, London: Macmillan.

Marx, K. ([1867] 1992), *Capital, Volume I*, London: Penguin Classics.

Marx, K. ([1894] 1959), *Capital, Volume III*, New York: International Publishers.

Menger, C. ([1871] 1950), *Principles of Economics*, New York: Free Press.

Minsky, H.P. (1982), *Can 'It' Happen Again? Essays on Instability and Finance*, Armonk, NY: M.E. Sharpe.

Minsky, H.P. (1986), *Stabilizing an Unstable Economy*, New Haven, CT: Yale University Press.

Minsky, H.P. (1992), 'The financial instability hypothesis', *Levy Economics Institute of Bard College Working Paper, No. 74*, accessed 22 October 2015 at www.levyinstitute.org/pubs/wp74.pdf.

Moore, B.J. (1988), *Horizontalists and Verticalists: The Macroeconomics of Credit Money*, Cambridge, UK: Cambridge University Press.

Setterfield, M. and A. Budd (2011), 'A Keynes–Kalecki model of cyclical growth with agent-based features', in P. Arestis (ed.), *Microeconomics, Macroeconomics, and Economic Policy*, London and Basingstoke, UK: Palgrave Macmillan, pp. 228–50.

Smith, A. (1759), *A Theory of Moral Sentiments*, Edinburgh: Kinkaid & Bell.

Smith, A. (1776), *The Wealth of Nations*, London: Strahan & Cadell.

Solow, R. (1956), 'A contribution to the theory of economic growth', *Quarterly Journal of Economics*, **70** (1), 65–94.

Swan, T. (1956), 'Economic growth and capital accumulation', *Economic Record*, **32** (2), 334–61.

Tugan-Baranovsky, M.I. (1894), *Industrial Crises in Contemporary England: Their Causes and Influences on the Life of the People*, St. Petersburg: Skorokhodov.

Tugan-Baranovsky, M.I. (1898), *The Russian Factory in Past and Present*, St. Petersburg: Panteleev.

Von Hayek, F.A. (1931), *Prices and Production*, London: Routledge.

Von Mises, L. ([1912] 1953), *The Theory of Money and Credit*, New Haven, CT: Yale University Press.

Von Mises, L. (1949), *Human Action: A Treatise on Economics*, New Haven, CT: Yale University Press.

Walras, L. ([1873] 1954), *Elements of Pure Political Economy*, Homewood, IL: Irwin.

Weintraub, S. (1978), *Capitalism's Inflation and Unemployment Crisis: Beyond Monetarism and Keynesianism*, Reading, MA: Addison-Wesley.

A PORTRAIT OF MIKHAIL TUGAN-BARANOVSKY (1865–1919)

Mikhail Tugan-Baranovsky was a leading economist and political figure in pre-revolutionary Russia. Of Ukrainian origin, Tugan-Baranovsky early on became a proponent of legal Marxism, a uniquely Russian interpretation of Marxism that used Marx's notion of revolutions occurring in the most advanced capitalist nations to argue in favour of capitalist development as a necessary condition for later revolution. This set the legal Marxists apart from other anti-Tsarist movements such as the Russian socialists known as *narodniks* emphasizing the vanguard role of the peasantry or the communists grouped around Lenin stressing the leadership role of industrial urban working-class elites to justify immediate uprisings.

The political tensions among these three brands of opposition to the ruling order shaped Tugan-Baranovsky's entire adult life, culminating in his ill-fated and aborted experience as Secretary of Finance of the Ukrainian People's Republic during the October Revolution.

More rewarding was his academic career, which left us with a remarkable record of publications in a short period of time. From the very start Tugan-Baranovsky stood out as an original critic of Marxist labour theory of value, established himself as one of pre-revolutionary Russia's leading historians of economic thought, and contributed in important fashion to our understanding of the link between distribution and capitalism's cyclical growth dynamics. Later on, when he turned away from Marxism, Tugan-Baranovsky focused on the cooperative movement. He was the teacher of leading Soviet economist Nikolai Kondratiev, who gave us the notion of long waves.

Among Tugan-Baranovsky's most important contributions are *Industrial Crises in Contemporary England* (1894) and *The Russian Factory in Past and Present* (1898).

17

Sustainable development

Richard P.F. Holt

  OVERVIEW

This chapter:

- presents an overview of why we cannot equate economic growth with development in order to achieve sustainable development;

- provides a new definition of economic development that incorporates not just growth, but also quality of life and sustainability;

- proposes a very different method for development from neoclassical economics by looking at the roles of *all* capital stocks for sustainable development, which include not just manufacturing capital but also public, human, environmental and social capitals;

- explains that to achieve sustainable development we must go beyond a weak definition of sustainability to a strong definition where the focus is on a new measurement of the standard of living – a definition that captures a broadly-based measurement of social welfare represented by economists like Amartya Sen.

  KEYWORDS

- **Broadly-based standard of living:** An overall well-being that goes beyond the assumption that economic growth by itself will bring improvement in quality of life.
- **Capital stocks for sustainable development:** Valuing all capital stocks used in producing income, quality of life, and sustainability, which include manufacturing, human, environmental, public and social capitals.
- **Sustainable development:** A broadly-based and sustainable increase in the overall standard of living for individuals within a community.
- **Sustainable indicators:** Comprehensive indicators to track changes in the different capital stocks and quality of life factors to achieve sustainable development and improve quality of life.

Why are these topics important?

The impact of economic growth on the environment has recently become an important public policy issue. Concerns about global warming, depletion of natural resources, and worldwide population size have heightened the public awareness that certain growth patterns might be unsustainable both for society and the environment (Holt, 2005, 2009; Stern, 2007; Holt et al., 2009). However, the issues associated with economic growth are much broader than just whether we have adequate natural resources for long-term growth. The assumption that more economic growth automatically brings a higher quality of life that is sustainable is also being questioned. Keynes ([1931] 1963) raised this concern in his essay 'Economic possibilities for our grandchildren' by implicitly asking if continuous economic growth does improve our well-being. John Kenneth Galbraith ([1958] 1969, 1971) posed a similar question by asking whether growth automatically gives us a higher quality of life in an affluent society. Kenneth E. Boulding (1966) in his famous article 'The economics of the coming Spaceship Earth' challenged the goals and values of economic growth and asked: is it desirable? These questions force us to rethink the linkage between economic growth, quality of life and sustainability. They also require us to re-evaluate the relationship between economic growth and economic development, and ask whether they are the same.

Neoclassical economics has traditionally equated economic growth with economic development with the implicit assumption that benefits of economic growth will 'trickle down' to improve quality of life and provide sustainability (see Solow, 1956; Lucas, 1988; Maddison, 1991; Friedman, 2005). There is also the assumption of a trade-off between equality and economic growth, because economic incentives are needed for economic growth (see Panizza, 2002; Partridge, 2005, 2006).

This chapter questions these assumptions by arguing that our standard of living encompasses much more than just increases in total output and income. For example, if per capita income increases but there is more air pollution, less economic opportunity, and traffic congestion in a community, then the standard of living may have fallen. Sustainable development is different from economic growth in that it covers not just growth, but also quality of life and sustainability (Greenwood and Holt, 2010b). That is, all three are on equal footing instead of having quality of life and sustainability 'trickle down' from economic growth, as assumed in mainstream economics. Sustainable development means addressing all three jointly and recognizing the inherent linkages and possible trade-offs among them. It also calls for us to acknowledge the necessity and role of *all types* of capital for sustainability, instead of just the focus on manufacturing capital as we find in neoclassical economics.

This leads us to a very different way of measuring and defining the standard of living. If the standard of living is defined as a measurement of *overall* well-being, where economic growth can actually take away from one's standard of living, then we need to detach growth from development and look for a broader definition of well-being.

The structure of this chapter is the following. First, there is an overall discussion of why we need to make a distinction between economic growth and development in pursuing policies for improving quality of life and sustainability. Then we lay the foundation for a new approach to economic development, which incorporates quality of life, sustainability *and* economic growth. This method is very different from neoclassical economics, which focuses on private manufacturing capital for development. Instead, we will look at the roles of all types of capital stocks for sustainable development and recognize their interdependence and linkages. The different capital stocks include manufacturing, public, human, environmental and social capital. We then give a new definition of the standard of living – a definition that truly captures a broadly-based measurement of social welfare represented by economists like Amartya Sen (1987). We start by looking at the neoclassical model for economic development.

The neoclassical model of economic growth and development

Traditionally, neoclassical economics focused on short-run price theory instead of dynamic growth models to explain development. In the 1940s that started to change with the post-Keynesian Harrod–Domar model that incorporated 'growth' through levels of saving and productivity of capital (Harrod, 1939; Domar, 1946). Harrod recognized that growth and cycles in the economy are not separate as many neoclassical economists at that time assumed. By developing a simple single-sector model that was driven by a savings function depended upon the level of change of output and investment driven by the rate of change of output, he was able to formulate an economic growth model where the level of investment could exceed or be below its desired level, thereby causing cyclical fluctuations.

Though not dealing directly with the Harrod–Domar model's concern with economic fluctuations, Robert Solow and Trevor Swan independently developed an economic growth model that dealt with many of its shortcomings. It was a simple model where economic growth follows a steady-state path. The production function has constant returns to scale, diminishing marginal productivity of capital and labour determined by the growth rates of labour and technology. These are determined exogenously (Solow, 1956; Swan, 1956). A limitation of the Solow–Swan model is having exogenous technological development. In response, endogenous growth theory models were developed where economic growth is the result of endogenous and not external forces (Romer, 1986, 1994; Pack, 1994). Endogenous growth theory allows an increasing variety of quality of machinery and external economies from investment in new capital, which can eliminate diminishing returns (Greenwood and Holt, 2010a, p. 161).

What is evident in all these models, for those who are concerned with sustainable development, is the absence of natural resources as a unique limiting factor. The focus is always on capital, labour and technology. There is the overall view that natural resources and sustainability issues can be dealt with by technological change (Nordhaus and Tobin, 1972); the use of market pricing (Coase, 1960), and allocation of non-renewable resources over time by the right discount rate (Hartwick, 1977, 1989). Solow (1974, p. 11) made it very clear that he did not see limitations of natural resources as an issue for economic growth, when he stated in his 1974 Richard Ely Lecture to the American Economic Association that 'the world, can, in effect, get along without natural resources'. In sum, the neoclassical growth model deals with sustainability by technology, substitution effects and market allocation of natural resources over time with a discount rate. This has led to a debate about what is meant by 'sustainability' between mainstream and heterodox economists.

The debate over 'strong' and 'weak' sustainability

Most mainstream economists recognize that there are external costs associated with pollution and that non-renewable resources need to be managed. Solow (1992, 1994), for example, has argued that any depletion of natural resources needs to be matched with increases in manufactured capital. The idea that human-made capital can be substituted for natural capital has led to a heated debate between neoclassical and ecological economists of what is the meaning of sustainable development, which has given us two very different definitions of 'sustainability' (Holt, 2009). The first, championed by neoclassical thinking, has been called the 'weak' definition, where losses of non-renewable natural capital can be substituted for human-made capital. The second comes from ecological economists. They believe natural capital needs to be sustained for its unique quality, giving us a 'strong' definition (Holt, 2005, p. 176). A working definition of the 'strong' view comes from the United Nations Brundtland Commission: 'Sustainable development is development which meets the needs of the present without compromising the ability of future generations to meet their own needs' (Brundtland, 1987, p. 7).

This fits nicely with a heterodox approach to sustainable development, which includes eradicating social evils like unemployment and poverty today along with saving natural resources for future generations. This is a challenging agenda where present needs to end poverty, for example, are eradicated without compromising the well-being of future generations by degenerating our natural resources. Ecological economists believe sustainable development cannot be achieved through endless economic growth, but instead changes with our consumption, production and energy use to protect all types of accumulated capital, particularly social and natural.

The neoclassical approach is very different, where increased economic growth provides needed income for investments in new manufacturing capital and technology that can be used for present and future development. This is represented in the 'weak' definition of sustainability. At the heart of this definition is the assumption that there will be adequate substitutes of human-made capital for natural capital. This has become known as the 'Hartwick–Solow' rule (see Hartwick, 1977, 1989; Solow, 1974, 1986). While they admit that there might be some exceptions to the rule, overall it will hold and allow for sustainable development even if natural resources are depleted. In regard to external costs associated with pollution or global warming, we can turn to taxes (Pigou, 1929) and defined property rights (Coase, 1960) to capture these social costs. Over time the need for new manufactured capital and the use of taxes and property rights will give incentives to entrepreneurs to develop new capital substitutes and resource-saving technologies. And with a carbon tax or tradable pollution permits we will be able to deal with the external costs associated with environmental problems like global warming.

Ecological economists have responded by arguing the environment is not simply an input to the economy. More importantly, the economy exists *within* society and the environment (see Daly, 1996; Daly and Farley, 2004). A sustainable development approach takes the effects of economic decisions and policies on all capital stocks into consideration, and acknowledges the *unique role* natural capital plays. Unlike other types of capital, there are aspects of certain types of natural capital that cannot be reproduced or protected by private ownership or government actions. The environmental saying 'think globally, but act locally' reflects both the global and individual mien of natural capital and its importance for sustainability. Recognizing that there are different types of natural capital is important, some are renewable and others not. Forests and fish are renewable, if well managed. But other forms like the air we breathe, the water we drink and the waste absorption of the atmosphere and oceans are limited and provide life-giving services that cannot be replaced by any other form of capital.

There is also the question of whether efficiency should be the only or even the primary goal with sustainable development, as we find with the traditional economic growth model. Instead broader and more encompassing social and environmental goals might be needed (Greenwood and Holt, 2010a). Should efficiency be looked at as a means or an end in itself, as we find with neoclassical economics when considering sustainable development? Contrary to the neoclassical view, post-Keynesians have argued that efficiency has meaning only in a framework of social goals such as full employment or, in this case, sustainable development (Holt, 2007). They also point out that the neoclassical 'weak' definition of sustainability is void of economic and political power, which can affect how natural resources are used and distributed. If one group can control or limit the use of natural resources and shift environmental and health costs onto another, this can cause unjust harm to poor and powerless groups, besides not allocating resources in the most efficient way (see Galbraith, [1958] 1969; Holt et al., 2009).

DeGregori (1974, pp. 759–70) points out that with corporate power, as an example, we might accept economic outcomes that we would not in other areas of our lives. He quotes the institutionalist Ayres (1962), 'poisoning one's wife is a mortal sin, whereas poisoning thousands of people by selling adulterated food or drugs is a mere business misadventure'. This follows the concerns of those who hold a 'strong' definition of sustainable development, where the people being 'poisoned' are future generations that have no power to influence the decisions of the present generation (Greenwood and Holt, 2010a, p. 163).

For heterodox economists the lack of realism about the real world and how power impacts markets, is one of the problems with the 'weak' definition of sustainability. The mainstream view has competitive firms as price-takers, which limit their economic power. But industries associated with energy use and natural resources are likely to be concentrated, which allow for price discrimination. This means that efforts to use a carbon tax or tradable permits as a way to adjust for social costs associated with pollution becomes difficult, since there are so many structural and institutional factors that can lead to price discrimination in these markets (like financial markets that can speculate on the value of future tradable permits, which makes their prices volatile). Yet, those who advocate the use of market auction permits to deal with global warming assume competition in these markets. The distribution of wealth and power is not central to the neoclassical world-view of environmental policies. For heterodox economists it is, as they realize the role of inequality and power in economic decisions. Individual and firm decisions can be influenced by social and political factors such as conventions, habits, emulation, market structures, and even fraud (Galbraith, [1958] 1969, 1974, 1996). This can lead to aggregate suboptimal outcomes that do not protect environmental goods and natural capital. There are also inefficiencies associated with prisoner's dilemma, dictator and ultimatum games. Markets by themselves cannot resolve these dilemmas (Kahneman et al., 1986a, 1986b). Given the uniqueness and life-giving importance of natural capital for sustainable development, we cannot leave the protection of these resources in the hands of 'free' markets alone and need a 'strong' definition of sustainability to protect these resources.

Growth versus development

Related to the debate over a 'strong' or 'weak' definition of sustainability is whether we should equate economic growth with economic development. In mainstream economics, growth and development are generally used interchangeably (Brinkman, 1995), with the assumption that economic growth will bring better quality of life and increase the standard of living (Friedman, 2005). If one looks carefully at neoclassical growth models, private manufacturing capital does all the heavy lifting, along with technology. Since economic growth is equated with economic development, public policies for economic development are associated with the expansion of private capital, that is, low capital gains taxes and less environmental regulation on private capital. Private capital is 'the goose that lays the golden egg' for development. Public spending is there to build infrastructure to support private capital, and investments in human capital are evaluated by the quality they add to it. The composition and distribution of economic growth are to be resolved through the market or political process (Greenwood and Holt, 2010a).

The problem with this view is the assumption that economic growth from private manufacturing capital will give us sustainable development (Earl, 1995). Private manufacturing capital bears the primary responsibility in neoclassical economics for growth, but we should remember that it is derived from natural and human capital (Greenwood and Holt, 2010b, pp. 5–7).

Sustainable development requires not relying on one type of capital over another. This means understanding how we can sustain *all* capital stocks that contribute to our economy, society and environment (Zolatas, 1981; Norgaard, 1994; Daly, 1996; Greenwood and Holt, 2010b; Holt and Greenwood, 2014). For example, by expanding private manufacturing onto areas that destroy wetlands, this could lead to flooding due to lack of water absorption. If one recognizes that sustainable development means having an awareness of the interrelationships between various capital stocks, we might be able to develop public policies that avoid this type of problem.

Many non-market aspects that we would want as part of our standard of living like health, public safety and climate stability, do not necessarily move in tandem with total output and income. Growth in average GDP over the last decades in the United States has not 'trickled down' to provide more well-being for all (Zacharias et al., 2014). Also, economic growth can be volatile and temporary, possibly setting the economy on a path that is economically, environmentally and socially unsustainable (Holt, 2005, 2009). Finally, development should provide improvements in the standard of living that are broadly-based. When the benefits of development are skewed toward a particular group or when the costs of growth are borne by certain groups over others, we have not achieved sustainable development. When growth leaves too many people behind, it does not improve the overall quality of life. For at least the last 30 years, such inequality has been noticed in the United States with steady economic growth that has benefitted particular groups over others (see Jones and Weinberg, 2000; Piketty and Saez, 2003; Holt and Greenwood, 2014).

This does not mean that those who hold to sustainable development are anti-growth. Economic growth brings income and consumer spending that truly can increase our standard of living. But growth can also take away from our standard of living by creating more congestion, urban sprawl, pollution, inequality, changes in our social and private lives that make civic and personal engagements more difficult, which can possibly lead to a 'negative' trickle-down effect (Greenwood and Holt, 2012). The consequence is that economic growth can either add or take away from our standard of living and not be sustainable.

Sustainable development differs from neoclassical growth theory in three important ways:

- Instead of having a trickle-down effect, we should have a 'percolating up' model that takes into consideration economic opportunity, environmental and quality of life issues for future development. This recognizes that economic growth alone with not solve all the problems associated with sustainable development and there can be trade-offs between economic growth and economic development.

- There is an appreciation and understanding of the roles of all capital stocks and their contributions to sustainable development.
- We need to go beyond ideology and be pragmatic in our approach to development. When market forces work, we should use them, but some forms of capital require more public investments and protection than others. An ideology against public investment will not allow us to achieve the level of sustainable development that we need.

Let us now look at the role that heterodox economics has played with helping to define true economic development that benefits the economy, society and environment.

Heterodox economics and true economic development

Institutionalists were the first to make the distinction between economic growth and development, as they saw growth as necessary, but not sufficient for economic development (Galbraith, [1958] 1969, 1996; Ayres, 1962; Myrdal, 1973). While the neoclassical approach focuses on allocation, institutionalists focus on improving value with development. They look at economic development as an evolutionary process pushed, for example, by technology. Once established in a community or society, the overall standard of living should improve for a broad spectrum of the population. Klein (1974, p. 801), representing the institutionalist approach, states about development that 'the traditional emphasis. . .is on allocation rather than valuation. Progress involves valuation through time, while growth involves simply an increase in whatever it is the economy happens to be doing'. Myrdal (1973, p. 190) expressed the same view in a different way: 'the upward movement of the whole social system. . .not only production, distribution of the produce, and modes of production are involved but also levels of livings, institutions, attitudes, and policies'. Veblen captured the qualitative changes that occur in development as compared to growth measured by total output when he stated that true development requires fundamental changes in institutions, how we do things and think (Veblen, [1914] 1922, [1919] 1961; Greenwood and Holt, 2010a, p. 164).

John Kenneth Galbraith brought 'power' into the picture by showing how large corporations and economic interests in an affluent society can set the agenda for economic growth over development: 'Growth, being a paramount purpose of the society, nothing naturally enough is allowed to stand in its way. That includes its. . .diverse effect, on the environment, on air, water, the tranquillity of urban life, the beauty of the countryside' (Galbraith, 1974, p. 286). He emphasized the same issue in *The Affluent Society* ([1958] 1969) when he wrote about 'private wealth and public squalor'. But one of his major contributions to development, which is often overlooked, is that he laid the foundation for a theory of human capabilities, which was later developed by Amartya Sen (1993).

Galbraith was also one of the first economists to show problems with using traditional economic measures of growth as a way of estimating social well-being (see Galbraith, [1958] 1969). He questioned early on the relation between economic growth and quality of life, and explained why we need a new measurement for economic development that includes not just growth, but also quality of life and sustainability (see Galbraith, [1958] 1969, 1971, 1996). His pioneer work has led to more recent scholarship in quality of life, sustainable economic development, and human capabilities (see Allardt, 1993; Power, 1996; Sen, 1999). This has helped us to redefine social welfare and provide critiques of traditional welfare economics (Sen, 1987; Norgaard, 1994; Power, 1996).

Besides the institutionalists, another important heterodox school to influence the meaning of sustainable development is ecological economics. Following the work of Georgescu-Roegen, Boulding and Daly, ecological economists have done significant work showing that natural resources are not 'free gifts from nature', but are resources that can be depleted (see Holt et al., 2009). They have also made it clear that natural capital is more than just an input in the production process, for it includes life-giving elements of the biosphere that have no substitutes (ibid.). Overall, they questioned the feasibility of economic growth over the long run and economic development policy needed for fundamental reform. Some of the primary concerns of ecological economists with undifferentiated economic growth would be the following:

- the size and growth of populations and their impact on economic, social and environmental systems;
- the need to go beyond substitution effects of capital and recognize the role of different capital stocks;
- endless economic growth is simply unsustainable both for society and the environment;
- the neoclassical assumption that 'more is better' needs to be questioned both for its quantitative and qualitative meaning;

- compared to neoclassical economics, we need a dynamic and complex model instead of one that is static.

This leads us to post-Keynesian economists and their work with radical uncertainty.

While ecological economists have explained the importance of preserving certain types of natural capital that are non-replaceable and life-giving, post-Keynesians have pointed out that the future is unpredictable based on the relation between physical, biological and institutional factors in the development process. The future is uncertain rather than known or known with some probability distribution (see Keynes, 1936, 1937). Davidson (1982–83, 1988, 1991, 1996) has brought this point home by arguing that uncertainty is part of a non-ergodic world, as compared to the ergodic world of neoclassical economics. Systems are ergodic if both their key parameters and structure are stable over time, which means that we can extrapolate from the past to the future. Non-ergodic systems experience structural change or parameter changes over time, which means that consumers and firms cannot figure out what the future will be like.

Since the consequence of future environmental damage cannot be known, we cannot perform controlled experiments with the Earth and a parallel Earth to see how pollution affects one but not the other. When we deal with economic development that can have significant impact on the environment, post-Keynesians have argued that we need to recognize the radical uncertainty or non-ergodic world we live in (Holt, 2005, 2009). Yet, we need economic development. Instead of assuming a world where we can calculate and, at some level, predict levels of environmental risk as in neoclassical environmental management models, the prudent post-Keynesian approach of using complex non-linear dynamic models and applying precautionary principles to derive policies makes more sense. For example, Lavoie (2005) has developed a post-Keynesian theory of consumer choice based on precautionary principles like procedural rationality, satiable needs, separability, growth and subordination of needs and non-independence and heredity.

Following the work of Lavoie, the second characteristic of post-Keynesian economics that is helpful for understanding the dynamics of sustainable development is that individual decision-making is dependent on social factors, such as human relations, conventions, habits and emulation rather than individual rational choice. This means that sustainable development requires us to look at social rationality (as compared to just individual rationality) and at the consequences of these social decisions in development, which can lead us to suboptimal outcomes in markets. The 'prisoner's dilemma' is an example. Such dilemmas, post-Keynesians argue, are common in everyday life, and environmental policy decisions need to take them into consideration. Like the prisoner who confesses, the free rider in society does not pay to support community needs for clean air and water, because he or she believes everyone else will contribute to the common good. Of course, if everyone followed this logic, then the aggregate outcomes create serious sustainable problems that affect not just present, but also future generations.

The third insight post-Keynesians provide for sustainable development is that economic analysis involves an examination of economies moving and evolving through historical time rather than economies that logically adjust from one equilibrium position to the next. Joan Robinson (1974) criticized neoclassical economics for its preoccupation with equilibrium analysis and the use of logical time. She suggested that economists should focus more on how economies *evolve* over time, like the institutionalists, instead of how they move to some timeless point. Post-Keynesians, like Robinson (1974) and Kaldor (1985), believed that economic systems do not have a point of rest and it is better to look at economic development as moving through historical time, where the past and the present matter. By ignoring historical time, neoclassical economists disregard the path dependency of economic systems and their impact on consumers, firms, society, and the environment. For example, if we move from one equilibrium point that stresses economic growth and we later become concerned about environmental degradation caused by earlier behaviour, moving to a new equilibrium does not erase that degradation.

The heterodox approach gives us a pluralistic approach to sustainable development. As mentioned, institutionalists were the first to stress the difference between economic growth and development. Ecological economists expressed concerns of the uniqueness of natural capital. Post-Keynesians have shown us the effects of uncertainty, social rationality and path dependency in dealing with sustainable development. We should also mention feminist economics and their focus on 'provisioning' rather than choice as the central problem of economic decision making, which fits with a sustainable development. As Julie Nelson (1993, p. 296) writes, '[o]ne can think of economics as the study of humans in interaction with the world which supports us – of economics as the study of organization of the processes which provision life'. The heterodox approach gives us a more realistic and richer method to deal with sustainable development by focusing on historical time, radical uncertainty, and the uniqueness of natural capital. The heterodox method also does a better job of dealing with power and culture in understanding individual choices and public decisions. As we will now discuss, a pluralistic approach recognizes the interdependence of all capital forms for economic growth rather than attributing almost everything to private manufacturing capital. Finally, and maybe more importantly, heterodox economists recognize the importance of justice, equality and opportunity as part of any true sustainable development model. So what would a sustainable development model look like? How can we develop policies that support and improve sustainable development?

Investments for sustainable development

The primary driving force behind sustainable development is the valuing of all capital stocks used for producing income, quality of life and sustainability. Besides private capital that yields a profit, there are other types of capital that play roles for economic growth, which include natural, public, social and human capital. All of these are needed for sustainable development. It is important to appreciate the interconnection between these different capital stocks. Instead of looking at private capital as the muscle behind economic development, we now see the interconnection of all forms of capital, with natural capital having unique life-giving qualities that cannot be substituted. This allows us to understand the unintended consequences of the use of one capital stock on another.

For example, as we expand the infrastructure of a town, this might destroy the natural capital of surrounding wetlands. This might create significant flooding due to lack of water absorption, which means building and spending *more* on infrastructure to solve the flooding problem that was caused by destroying the natural capital. Sustainable development forces us to think about the complex interrelationships between various capital stocks and the costs associated with the development and use of one type of capital over another. Investments in all these capital stocks are there to serve people, reflecting the values and goals of our economy, society and environment. Some of these stocks are owned privately and others publicly, showing the social complexity of their relationship.

Though it might seem odd to think of the environment as an equal partner with private manufacturing capital in development, the following figures might help us appreciate this relationship. In the first figure we have the economy, society and environment as separate entities with some overlap (Figure 17.1).

The economy is the largest sphere. In this model, manufacturing capital is the foundational force for economic growth and well-being. Other forms of

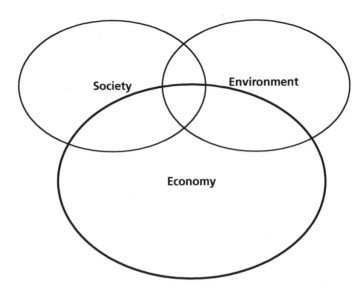

Figure 17.1 The traditional view of economy, environment and society

capital such as natural or human capital are secondary, and have value in their ability to support private capital. Natural capital gives us oil, water and land for the production process. Human capital and society are there for quality improvements of private manufacturing capital – to accommodate the needs of private capital for economic growth and to create jobs. Benefits from economic growth are then expected to 'trickle down' to the other kinds of capital (human, natural, social and infrastructure) to sustain them.

Many heterodox economists are working hard to move away from the traditional view of Figure 17.1 to a new paradigm that shows the dynamic relationship between the environment, society and the economy, and the use of different capital stocks (Daly, 1996; Holt et al., 2009; Greenwood and Holt, 2010b). This is represented in Figure 17.2, which gives us a very different story from the traditional view.

The economy is now a subset of society and the environment. This allows us to see the synergies between all the capital stocks. It also allows us to see more clearly what are the trade-offs with the use of the different capital stocks. In this model, private capital does not play the major role as in the earlier model for economic development.

A model of sustainable development differs in three important ways from the more traditional model represented in Figure 17.1. First, sustainable development does not accept as accurate the 'trickle-down effect', where economic growth based on investment in private capital will sustain all capital stocks

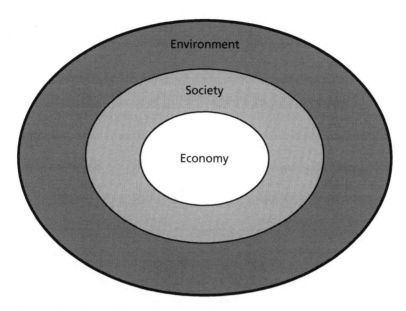

Figure 17.2 Sustainable development: economy, environment and society

needed for the economy, society and nature. Second, all capital stocks need to be protected for their intrinsic value, independent of market values. True development requires investments in all of them, and no capital stock is more important than another. Third, economic growth is not the same as sustainable development measured by output of goods and services. Instead, the goal is improving a broader definition of the standard of living that includes quality of life and sustainability. This gives us a true measurement of economic development that tells us the *full cost* of development. In the past, the impact of economic growth on the quality of life and the environment has only been acknowledged *later* in the process of growth. For heterodox economists, these factors need to be recognized up front, so we can see the consequences of economic growth on sustainable development.

A sustainable development approach goes beyond our present fixation on private capital. We need to make a distinction between resources that are renewable and those that are not. We need to appreciate where technology/ human knowledge can be a substitute for natural capital and where it cannot. Social capital needs to be explored more to understand its positive aspects (see Bowles and Gintis, 2002). Finally, the impact of institutions on development needs to be understood (see Ayres, 1962; Greenwood and Holt, 2008). By recognizing the role of all capital stocks and the unique position that natural capital plays, we are able to have economic development that is based on and around people, respects our natural resources and the values and goals of social communities. We turn now to creating a better working measurement of economic development.

Measuring a new standard of living for sustainable development

With a new and exciting way to look at development, we need a new measurement. As mentioned, concerns about quality of life, the environment, inequality and future generations have led to widespread dissatisfaction with economic growth as a unilateral goal. This has resulted in efforts to come up with an alternative measurement to gross domestic product (GDP). A problem with GDP as a measurement is its inability to differentiate between goods that have a positive effect on sustainability and those that take away from it. The GDP measures only production of goods and services that involve a market transaction, which misses much of the social provisioning that takes place in one's family life and community. For example, a parent staying home to raise children or helping elderly people in one's community can actually lower GDP though providing very valuable services. States and cities do not have a GDP measure and usually use personal income to measure well-being, but again it only measures economic activity. Providing alternative indicators to at least supplement per capita income or GDP is crucial for us to know what types of policies to put into place for sustainable development and to make sure those policies are accountable to the public.

An example of an alternative measurement used for sustainable development has been the genuine progress indicator (GPI). The index subtracts some of the costs of growth from GDP while adding an estimated value for non-market activities like household and volunteer work. It is a variant of the Index of Sustainable Economic Welfare (ISEW) first proposed by Daly and Cobb (1994). Developed in 1994, the GPI gives us a better measurement of economic well-being. The measurement particularly addresses depletion of non-renewable resources and the costs of pollution, commuting, crime and other external factors that might affect quality of life and sustainability. Another example of an alternative measurement comes from the work of Amartya Sen.

Traditional welfare economics argues that lowering a person's income will make them worse off while more income increases well-being. But as Sen points out, an increased level of consumption of meaningless goods and more production by menial labour (both registered as positive outcomes in traditional measurements of economic growth) can have a negative impact on people's quality of life. It can also fail to provide them with more freedoms and in fact limit their choices (Sen, 1999). Sen's pioneering work has shown that one can be in a community with lower per capita income as compared to another and be personally much better off if that community provides larger options for personal growth like nourishment, education, health care, and a safe environment – all of which greatly increase the person's welfare more than just a change in their income (see Sen, 1987, 1993, 1999). Sen's writings go beyond economic growth and extend to the goals of sustainable development by incorporating human capabilities.

Sen's work on welfare as capabilities has led to a variety of new applications in public policy in improving lives in developing countries. Besides criticizing traditional welfare economics, Sen has developed new measurements for indexing quality of life by looking at poverty, inequality and gender. All of these indexes move beyond income as a way to measure well-being – pushing the notion that we must take things other than income into consideration. Probably the most influential one is the Human Development Index (HDI). Created for the United Nations, the HDI takes into consideration not just per capita income, but also life expectancy, adult literacy and health. The HDI became part of the United Nations' (1990) first annual *Human Development Report*, when Sen was working there as a consultant. The index is a weighted average of income that is adjusted for distribution and purchasing power and other factors that weigh in human capabilities. The index is classified by the deprivation of what is potentially achievable. The value of HDI ranges from 1 to 0, with 1 being the highest. This measure has encouraged developing countries to look beyond economic growth as a sole judge of policy to income distribution, education, health care, life expectancy and safety as important components of social welfare (Greenwood and Holt, 2010a, p. 171).

Public attention to and interest in these alternative measurements are starting to attract the attention of different cities and states throughout the world. The popularity of these new indicators demonstrates two aspects of our changing world. First, higher income and economic growth do not capture many of the social and environmental amenities of quality of life important for development. Second, new indicators register increased costs associated with economic growth such as degradation of our environment. To understand what new policies to put in place to support the demand for a better quality of life and to lower costs associated with economic growth, these new indicators will play a vital role in providing new data on issues surrounding sustainable development.

Conclusion

As we face a new future with new global challenges, the old neoclassical model of economic growth is not up to the job. It is time for heterodox economists, who have been doing exciting new work in the area of sustainable development, to move forward. Galbraith's ([1958] 1969) point that he made 50 years ago is still meaningful today – we face a problem of social imbalance between private affluence and public squalor. Now the social imbalance can best be described as one between all the capital stocks for sustainable development. By making a distinction between economic growth and economic development, and appreciating the role of all capital stocks is a step in the right direction to overcome this imbalance. This chapter provides an alternative paradigm that puts the economy, society and environment on an equal footing, creating a new model for development. As populations increase and there is more concern with quality of life and environmental issues like global warming, a new way of looking at sustainable development becomes ever more urgent.

 REFERENCES

Allardt, E. (1993), 'Having, loving, and being: an alternative to the Swedish model of welfare research', in M. Nussbaum and A. Sen (eds), *The Quality of Life*, Oxford, UK: Oxford University, pp. 88–94.

Ayres, C.E. (1962), *The Theory of Economic Progress: A Study of the Fundamental of Economic Development and Cultural Change*, second edition, New York: Schocken Books.

Boulding, K. (1966), 'The economics of the coming Spaceship Earth', in H. Jarrett (ed.), *Environment Quality in a Growing Economy*, Baltimore, MD: John Hopkins University Press, pp. 3–14.

Bowles, S. and H. Gintis (2002), 'Social capital and community governance', *Economic Journal*, **112** (483), F419–F436.

Brinkman, R. (1995), 'Economic growth vs. economic development: toward a conception clarification', *Journal of Economic Issues*, **29** (4), 1171–88.

Brundtland, G. (1987), *Our Common Future: Report of the World Commission on Environment and Development*, Oxford, UK: Oxford University Press.

Coase, R. (1960), 'The problem of social cost', *Journal of Law and Economics*, **3** (1), 1–44.

Daly, H.E. (1996), *Beyond Growth: The Economics of Sustainable Development*, Boston, MA: Beacon Press.

Daly, H.E. and J.B. Cobb, Jr. (1994), *For the Common Good: Redirecting the Economy toward Community, the Environment, and a Sustainable Future*, second edition, Boston, MA: Beacon Press.

Daly, H.E. and J. Farley (2004), *Ecological Economics: Principles and Applications*, Washington, DC: Island Press.

Davidson, P. (1982–83), 'Rational expectations: a fallacious foundation for studying crucial decision-making processes', *Journal of Post Keynesian Economics*, **5** (2), 182–98.

Davidson, P. (1988), 'A technical definition of uncertainty and the long-run non-neutrality of money', *Cambridge Journal of Economics*, **12** (3), 329–37.

Davidson, P. (1991), 'Is probability theory relevant for uncertainty? A post Keynesian perspective', *Journal of Economic Perspectives*, **5** (1), 129–43.

Davidson, P. (1996), 'Reality and economic theory', *Journal of Post Keynesian Economics*, **18** (4), 479–508.

DeGregori, T. (1974), 'Power and illusion in the marketplace: institutions and technology', *Journal of Economic Issues*, **8** (4), 759–70.

Domar, E. (1946), 'Capital expansion, rate of growth, and employment', *Econometrica*, **14** (2), 137–47.

Earl, P. (1995), *Microeconomics for Business and Marketing*, Cheltenham, UK and Northampton, MA, USA: Edward Elgar Publishing.

Friedman, B.M. (2005), *The Moral Consequences of Economic Growth*, New York: Vintage Books.

Galbraith, J.K. ([1958] 1969), *The Affluent Society*, second edition, Boston, MA: Houghton Mifflin.

Galbraith, J.K. (1971), 'Economics and the quality of life', in *Economics, Peace and Laughter*, Boston, MA: Houghton Mifflin, pp. 3–25.

Galbraith, J.K. (1974), *Economics and the Public Purpose*, Boston, MA: Houghton Mifflin.

Galbraith, J.K. (1996), *The Good Society: The Humane Agenda*, Boston, MA: Houghton Mifflin.

Greenwood, D.T. and R.P.F. Holt (2008), 'Institutional and ecological economics: the role of technology and institutions in economic development', *Journal of Economic Issues*, **42** (2), 445–52.

Greenwood, D.T. and R.P.F. Holt (2010a), 'Growth, development and quality of life', in R. Garnett, E.K. Olsen and M. Starr (eds), *Economic Pluralism*, London: Routledge, pp. 160–75.

Greenwood, D.T. and R.P.F. Holt. (2010b), *Local Economic Development in the 21st Century: Quality of Life and Sustainability*, Armonk, NY: M.E. Sharpe.

Greenwood, D.T. and R.P.F. Holt (2012), 'Negative trickle-down and the financial crisis of 2008', *Journal of Economic Issues*, **46** (2), 363–70.

Harrod, R.F. (1939), 'An essay in dynamic theory', *Economic Journal*, **49** (193), 14–33.

Hartwick, J.M. (1977), 'Intergenerational equity and the investing of rents from exhaustible resources', *American Economic Review*, **67** (5), 972–4.

Hartwick, J.M. (1989), *Non-Renewable Resources Extraction Programs and Markets*, Chur, Switzerland: Harwood.

Holt, R.P.F. (2005), 'Post Keynesian economics and sustainable development', *International Journal of Environment, Workplace, and Employment*, **1** (2), 174–86.

Holt, R.P.F. (2007), 'What is post Keynesian economics?', in M. Forstater, G. Mongiovi and S. Pressman (eds), *Post Keynesian Macroeconomics*, London and New York: Routledge, pp. 89–107.

Holt, R.P.F. (2009), 'The relevance of post-Keynesian economics to sustainable development', in P. Lawn (ed.), *Environment and Employment: A Reconciliation*, London and New York: Routledge, pp. 146–60.

Holt, R.P.F. and D.T. Greenwood (eds) (2014), *A Brighter Future: Improving the Standard of Living Now and for the Next Generation*, Armonk, NY: M.E. Sharpe.

Holt, R.P.F., S. Pressman and C.L. Spash (eds) (2009), *Post Keynesian and Ecological Economics: Confronting Environmental Issues*, Cheltenham, UK and Northampton, MA, USA: Edward Elgar Publishing.

Jones, A.F. and D.H. Weinberg (2000), *The Changing Shape of the Nation's Income Distribution: 1947–1998*, US Census Bureau Current Population Reports No. P60-204, June.

Kahneman, D., J.L. Knetsch and R.H. Thaler (1986a), 'Fairness as a constant on profit seeking: entitlements in the market', *American Economic Review*, **76** (4), 728–41.

Kahneman, D., J.L. Knetsch and R.H. Thaler (1986b), 'Fairness and the assumption of economics', *Journal of Business*, **59** (4), 285–300.

Kaldor, N. (1985), *Economics without Equilibrium*, Armonk, NY: M.E. Sharpe.

Keynes, J.M. ([1931] 1963), 'Economic possibilities for our grandchildren', *Essays in Persuasion*, New York: W.W. Norton, pp. 358–73.

Keynes, J.M. (1936), *The General Theory of Employment, Interest and Money*, London: Macmillan.

Keynes, J.M. (1937), 'The general theory of employment', *Quarterly Journal of Economics*, **51** (2), 209–23.

Klein, P.A. (1974), 'Economics: allocation or valuation?', *Journal of Economic Issues*, **8** (4), 785–813.

Lavoie, M. (2005), 'Post-Keynesian consumer choice theory for the economics of sustainable forest management', in S. Kant and R.A. Berry (eds), *Economics, Natural Resources and Sustainability: Economics of Sustainable Forest Management*, Dordrecht: Kluwer, pp. 67–90.

Lucas, R.E. (1988), 'On the mechanics of economic development', *Journal of Monetary Economics*, **22** (1), 3–42.

Maddison, A. (1991), *Dynamic Forces in Capitalist Development*, Oxford, UK: Oxford University Press.

Myrdal, G. (1973), '"Growth" and "development"', in *Against the Stream: Critical Essays in Economics*, New York: Pantheon Books, pp. 182–96.

Nelson, J. (1993), 'Gender and economic ideologies', *Review of Social Economy*, **51** (3), 287–301.

Nordhaus, W.D. and J. Tobin (1972), 'Is growth obsolete?', in *Economic Research: Retrospect and Prospect, Volume 5: Economic Growth*, Cambridge, MA: National Bureau of Economic Research, pp. 1–80.

Norgaard, R. (1994), *Development Betrayed: The End of Progress and a Coevolutionary Revisioning of the Future*, London and New York: Routledge.

Pack, H. (1994), 'Endogenous growth theory: intellectual appeal and empirical shortcomings', *Journal of Economic Perspectives*, **8** (1), 55–72.

Panizza, U. (2002), 'Income inequality and economic growth: evidence from American data', *Journal of Economic Growth*, **7** (1), 25–41.

Partridge, M. (2005), 'Does income distribution affect U.S. state economic growth?', *Journal of Regional Science*, **45** (2), 363–94.

Partridge, M. (2006), 'The relationship between inequality and labor market performance: evidence from U.S. States', *Journal of Labor Research*, **27** (1), 1–20.

Pigou, A.C. (1929), *Economics of Welfare*, London: Macmillan.

Piketty, T. and E. Saez (2003), 'Income inequality in the United States, 1913–1998', *Quarterly Journal of Economics*, **158** (1), 1–39.

Power, T. (1996), *Environmental Protection and Economic Well-Being: The Economic Pursuit of Quality*, second edition, Armonk, NY: M.E. Sharpe.

Robinson, J. (1974), *History versus Equilibrium*, London: Thames Polytechnic.

Romer, P. (1986), 'Increasing returns and long-run growth', *Journal of Political Economy*, **94** (5), 1002–37.

Romer, P. (1994), 'The origins of endogenous growth', *Journal of Economic Perspectives*, **8** (1), 3–22.

Sen, A. (1970), *Collective Choice and Social Welfare*, London: North Holland.

Sen, A. (1981), *Poverty and Famines: An Essay on Entitlement and Deprivation*, Oxford, UK: Oxford University Press.

Sen, A. (1987), *On Ethics and Economics*, Oxford, UK: Basil Blackwell.

Sen, A. (1993), 'Capability and well-being', in M. Nussbaum and A. Sen (eds), *The Quality of Life*, Oxford, UK: Oxford University Press, pp. 30–53.

Sen, A. (1999), *Development as Freedom*, New York: Knopf.

Solow, R. (1956), 'A contribution to the theory of economic growth', *Quarterly Journal of Economics*, **70** (1), 65–94.

Solow, R. (1974), 'The economics of resources or the resources of economics', *American Economic Review*, **64** (2), 1–14.

Solow, R. (1986), 'On the intergenerational allocation of natural resources', *Scandinavian Journal of Economics*, **88** (1), 141–9.

Solow, R. (1992), *An Almost Practical Step Toward Sustainability*, Wallingford, UK and New York: Resources for the Future.

Solow, R. (1994), 'Perspectives on growth theory', *Journal of Economic Perspectives*, **8** (1), 45–54.

Stern, N. (2007), *The Economics of Climate Change: The Stern Review*, Cambridge, UK: Cambridge University Press.

Swan, T.W. (1956), 'Economic growth and capital accumulation', *Economic Record*, **32** (2), 334–61.

United Nations Development Programme (1990), *Human Development Report*, New York and Oxford, UK: Oxford University Press.

Veblen, T. ([1914] 1922), *The Instinct of Workmanship and the State of the Industrial Arts*, New York: B.W. Huebsch.

Veblen, T. ([1919] 1961), 'On the nature of capital', in *The Place of Science in Modern Civilization*, New York: Russell and Russell, pp. 324–86.

Zacharias, A., E.N. Wolff and T. Masterson et al. (2014), 'Economic well-being in the United States: a historical and comparative perspective', in R.P.F. Holt and D.T. Greenwood (eds), *A Brighter Future: Improving the Standard of Living Now and for the Next Generation*, Armonk, NY: M.E. Sharpe, pp. 23–50.

Zolatas, X. (1981), *Economic Growth and Declining Social Welfare*, New York: New York University Press.

A PORTRAIT OF AMARTYA SEN (1933–)

Amartya Sen was born in Maniganj, Bangladesh on 3 November 1933 to a Bengali family. He was educated at Presidency College in Kolkata, where he received his first BA in economics. Later he went to Trinity College, Cambridge, and received his second BA in 1955, and PhD in 1959. Over his long career, he has taught at a number of universities including the Universities of Jadavpur and Delhi, the London School of Economics, the University of London, and Oxford. In 1988 he moved to Harvard University and taught there for ten years. In 1998 he was appointed master of Trinity College, Cambridge, a position he held until 2004, when he returned to Harvard as Lamont University Professor. He won the Nobel Prize in Economics in 1998 for his work in welfare economics.

Sen is best known for his groundbreaking work in welfare economics and the affects of economic polices on well-being. In 1970, he published his most influential book, *Collective Choice and Social Welfare*, where he addressed issues surrounding individual rights and majority rule. Extending this work, he focused on issues of basic welfare and new measurement and definitions of welfare and poverty that are not captured by traditional neoclassical methods of measurement or definitions.

Personally experiencing the Bengal famine of 1943, Sen wrote another significant book, *Poverty and Famines: An Essay on Entitlement and Deprivation* (1981). He argued that in the case of the Bengal famine in 1943, the problem was not having an adequate food supply, but the distribution of the food to particular groups. This showed that in many cases of famine the cause is not shortage of foodstuff but social and economic factors. Both these books show Sen's lifetime interest in distributional issues and concern for impoverished members of society.

Conclusion: do we need microfoundations for macroeconomics?

John King

OVERVIEW

This chapter:

- explains that the microfoundations dogma threatens the existence of macroeconomics as a separate subdiscipline. It has damaging implications for macroeconomic policy, since it implies support for fiscal austerity, wage cuts, and deflation;

- points out that the microfoundations dogma emerged in the 1970s in the context of the 'great stagflation';

- shows that the mainstream arguments in favour of microfoundations are not strong; the two most important criticisms involve downward causation and the fallacy of composition;

- points out that the fallacy of composition is involved in some important macroeconomic 'paradoxes';

- suggests some alternative metaphors for the relations between microeconomics and macroeconomics;

- draws some general lessons from the question of microfoundations.

KEYWORDS

- **Downward causation:** Cause–effect relations that run downwards, from macro to micro, for example from society to its individual members, or from the economy to the individual agents who operate in it.
- **Emergent properties:** Properties of a system that cannot be predicted, even if we have a complete understanding of all the basic features of that system.

- **Fallacy of composition:** The logical fallacy that may arise when we ignore the possibility that a statement that is true of any individual considered separately is false when applied to them all, taken together.
- **Metaphor:** The application of a name or descriptive phrase to an object or action to which it is not literally applicable, for example 'food for thought' or 'leaving no stone unturned'.
- **Methodology:** The view of reality adopted by practitioners of a scientific discipline and the mode of reasoning that they follow, based on their understanding of ontology and epistemology derived (consciously or not) from the philosophy of science.
- **Microfoundations:** A spatial or constructional metaphor used to justify a micro-reduction strategy, in which the neoclassical model of utility-maximizing individuals underpins the aggregate economy and permits the reduction of macroeconomic theory to microeconomics.
- **Micro-reduction:** A special case of inter-theoretic reduction – the attempt to explain one theory in terms of another theory from a different domain – in which macro-problems are solved by reference to micro-theory.

Why are these topics important?

The disappearance of macroeconomics

Since the publication of Keynes's (1936) *General Theory of Employment, Interest and Money*, macroeconomics has been regarded as a separate, semi-autonomous subdiscipline within economics, on a par with microeconomics and every bit as important. The dogma that we must provide microfoundations for macroeconomics, however, threatens to destroy this view, since it involves 'reducing' macroeconomics to microeconomics and doing away with what Keynes described as 'the theory of output and employment *as a whole*' (Keynes, 1936, p. 293, original emphasis).

If the microfoundations dogma is accepted, macroeconomics becomes nothing more than an application of microeconomic theory. There is no longer a case for teaching it as part of the core of an economics degree. It should instead be offered as an option, like industrial organization or environmental economics. This is what the anti-Keynesian, 'new classical' economist Robert Lucas looked forward to almost 40 years ago. Before the global financial crisis that erupted in 2007–08, this seemed to be happening.

Implications for policy

All this carries some very dangerous implications for macroeconomic policy. In particular, the microfoundations dogma has been used to justify fiscal austerity and wage cuts. The case for fiscal austerity comes from treating the government's finances in the same way as the finances of an individual or a household. In the German Chancellor Angela Merkel's famous words after the collapse of Lehman Brothers in 2008: 'We should simply have asked the Swabian housewife. . . She would have told us that you cannot live beyond your means' (Skidelsky, 2013). In other words, if households should not live beyond their means, then governments should not either.

The case for wage cuts to reduce unemployment also seems to be straightforward. In any individual market (for labour or for goods) the existence of excess supply proves that the price (or wage) is too high and needs to be reduced. So, when there is unemployment, real wages need to be reduced. For the same reason, deflation (a falling price level) seems clearly to be a good thing, since price cuts eliminate excess supply. Wage and price 'flexibility' (downwards) seems to be a good thing, while wage and price rigidity is bad.

However, previous chapters will have suggested to you that these policy conclusions are quite wrong. First, a government is not a household, and the rules that quite rightly apply to the finances of individuals cannot be applied to public finance without causing serious macroeconomic damage. For the government, the correct principle is 'functional finance', not 'sound finance' (see Chapter 9). Second, the level of employment as a whole is determined in the product market, not in the labour market. It depends on the level of effective demand, which is a macroeconomic variable – easily the most important macroeconomic variable, as shown in Chapter 7. Third, there are very good reasons for preventing deflation, as Keynes (1936) explained in Chapter 19 of *The General Theory*. His conclusions have been vindicated in recent history by the poor performance of the Japanese economy in the quarter of a century since 1990 (see Chapter 16).

The mainstream perspective

A textbook example

One recent graduate textbook, published in 2008 by the prestigious Princeton University Press, begins by distinguishing 'modern macroeconomics' from the old-fashioned Keynesian variety. In modern macroeconomics, the author explains:

> the economy is portrayed as a dynamic general equilibrium (DGE) system that reflects the collective decisions of rational individuals over a range of variables

that relate to both the present and the future. These individual decisions are then coordinated through markets to produce the macroeconomy. (Wickens, 2008, p. 1)

This, the author claims, is a great improvement on 'the traditional Keynesian approach to macroeconomics, which is based on ad hoc theorizing about the relations between macroeconomic aggregates' (ibid.).

This is a rather strange use of the expression 'ad hoc', which the *Concise Oxford Dictionary* defines as 'for this particular purpose, or special(ly)'. Wickens (2008) seems to mean something rather different: 'lacking any foundation in mainstream, neoclassical consumer theory'. This is a criticism often made against the Keynesian consumption function, which links aggregate consumption expenditure to current aggregate income, and is the basis of the income multiplier analysis that underpins the principle of effective demand. Keynesians maintain that these are two separate problems. It is neither necessary nor possible to reduce the macroeconomic issue of aggregate consumption to the microeconomic question of individual consumer behaviour (see Chapter 7). Why should anyone think otherwise?

The origins of the microfoundations dogma

We have to begin almost a century and a half ago, with the Marginalist Revolution in economics that replaced the classical economists' emphasis on social classes and aggregate economic outcomes with a focus on individual utility maximization. Adam Smith (in 1776) and David Ricardo (in 1815) had analysed the relationship between economic growth and the distribution of the national income between workers, capitalists and landlords. Writing in the 1870s, William Stanley Jevons, Carl Menger and Léon Walras were much more interested in individual decision-making and the coordination of their decisions in competitive markets (see Chapter 2).

This gave rise to the principle of methodological individualism, which was also advocated in the mid-twentieth century by some philosophers of science and social theorists (see Kincaid, 1998). Davis (2003, p. 36) describes it as 'the view that not only can one always in principle replace explanations of social entities by some individualist explanation, but one ought to do so whenever practically possible'. There was a vigorous debate on methodological individualism among sociologists, anthropologists and philosophers of science in the 1950s. It failed to win over most social scientists. The philosopher Steven Lukes (1968, p. 125) dismissed it as 'a futile linguistic purism'. 'Why should we be compelled to talk about the tribesman but not the tribe', he asked, 'the bank-teller but not the bank?' (ibid.).

For the most part, mainstream economists kept out of this debate. They would not have found it easy to justify reducing the analysis of the banking system to statements about the behaviour of bank tellers. But after 1936 there was always going to be a potential problem for economics in reconciling the new Keynesian macroeconomics, which claimed to provide a distinctive new 'theory of output and employment *as a whole*', with the old marginalist theory of *individual* outputs and levels of employment in particular product and labour markets. In particular, there was a potentially serious problem in reconciling the new theory of aggregate employment with the old microeconomics of individual labour markets, broken down by industry, region and level of skill.

In 1956, with the publication of Robert Solow's neoclassical growth model, a new problem was created. There was now an apparent inconsistency between the short-run Keynesian model, in which investment determined saving and both capital and labour could be in excess supply, and the long-run neoclassical model, in which saving determined investment and capital and labour were always fully employed. There were two ways out of this contradiction: either apply the principle of effective demand to the long-run model of economic growth, or eliminate it from the short-run model of income and employment. One led to the post-Keynesian analysis of demand-determined growth, the other to the 'real business cycle' models of the new classical economists (see Chapters 7, 10 and 16).

Things came to a head in the crisis years of the 1970s, the era of the 'great stagflation', when the Phillips curve became unstable and both inflation and unemployment increased rapidly. Macroeconomic theory seemed to have broken down, and Keynesian macroeconomics in particular was increasingly discredited (as shown in Chapter 7, however, it was only the neoclassical interpretation of Keynes that had failed). There was a particularly important question that no one seemed able to answer: what determined people's expectations of future inflation?

It was vital to have a convincing answer to this question, since inflationary expectations were (and are) an extremely important influence on the actual inflation rate (see Chapter 8). And there was a more general problem, as Lucas pointed out at the time. To predict the consequences of changes in macroeconomic policy, econometricians used forecasting models that relied on the stability of the macroeconomic equations governing the key variables – the consumption function, the investment function, the wage level, the price level. But the parameters of these equations might well be altered by the policy changes themselves, making the predictions unreliable.

Take the (important) example of inflationary expectations. If firms and households reacted to changes in monetary, fiscal or labour market policy by revising their expectations of future inflation – always in an upward direction, or so it seemed in the 1970s – the forecasting equations would yield the wrong estimates of inflation. Thus successful forecasting requires that the econometricians have some reliable information about how individuals and firms actually form their expectations of future inflation.

No one – least of all Keynes – would deny that knowledge of microeconomics can make a significant contribution to macroeconomics. But Lucas went much further, denying the need for a distinct, semi-autonomous subdiscipline of macroeconomics altogether. In his 'new classical' economics, the principles of individual maximization and market clearing equilibrium are applied directly to all questions of macroeconomic theory and policy: there are no specifically macroeconomic problems to be solved.

Not surprisingly, there was a political element in all of this. It was bound up with the rise of neoliberalism: the doctrine that all social problems have a market solution, and the application of this doctrine to all areas of social and economic policy. Neoliberal politics began with the governments of Margaret Thatcher and Ronald Reagan in the 1980s and is still going strong. Privatization and deregulation were only part of the neoliberal policy package. 'Sound finance' and price and wage 'flexibility' (downwards) were also called for, or so it seemed to neoliberal macroeconomists, who had rejected the principle of effective demand in the course of their critique of the 'traditional ad hoc Keynesian theorizing'.

The upshot was an insistence on the use of models with RARE microfoundations: that is to say, models that began by assuming the existence of *representative agents* with *rational expectations* (RARE). Both halves of this set of initials are problematic. The good reasons for objecting to rational expectations have already been set out in Chapter 6. The assumption of representative agents is even less plausible, since it entails that all individuals are identical. There is thus no reason for them to trade with each other, no reason why their decisions should be coordinated, and therefore no role for markets.

Some mainstream arguments in favour of microfoundations

Quite often, no explicit reason is offered for the insistence on providing RARE microfoundations for macroeconomics, or indeed any other sort: it is simply taken for granted. After all, who could possibly complain about a building having foundations? In fact, this is a good example of question-begging or persuasive language, like 'free market economics' (in Australian English, 'economic rationalism'). Who would want to be *un*free (or *ir*rational)? Again the political dimension is lurking, just below the surface. The philosopher George Lakoff (1996) has shown how the conservative right has succeeded in cornering the market in persuasive metaphors – 'moral strength', 'moral bounds', 'moral nurturance', 'the-nation-as-family' – leaving the liberal and social democratic left floundering. The 'microfoundations' metaphor has achieved something similar for neoliberal economics and thus (indirectly) for neoliberal politics.

Where mainstream economists do try to justify the microfoundations metaphor, they use arguments like the four that follow. First, microeconomics is more basic than macroeconomics, so that in order to be persuasive, sound, reliable and robust, macroeconomics must make explicit reference to microeconomics. Second, the economy is made up of individuals, who must therefore be the starting point for any analysis of the ways in which they interact. Third, microeconomic models have been used successfully to deal with all manner of social and political questions, like voting behaviour, crime, discrimination and the family, so they should be applied also to macroeconomics. Fourth, micro-reduction has succeeded in the natural sciences, most obviously in biology with the triumph of modern genetics, and the principle should therefore be extended to economics.

This final argument is worth pursuing. Richard Dawkins, best-selling author of *The Selfish Gene* (1976), advocates the general principle of hierarchical reduction. In another book, *The Blind Watchmaker* (1996), he uses a revealing example:

> The behaviour of a motor car is explained in terms of cylinders, carburettors and sparking plugs. It is true that each of these components is nested atop a pyramid of explanations at lower levels. But if you asked me how a motor car worked you would think me somewhat pompous if I answered in terms of Newton's laws and the laws of thermodynamics, and downright obscurantist if I answered in terms of fundamental particles. It is doubtless true that at bottom the behaviour of a motor car is to be explained in terms of interactions between fundamental particles. But it is much more useful to explain it in terms of interactions between pistons, cylinders and sparking plugs. (Dawkins, 1996, p. 12)

The hierarchical reductionist, Dawkins continues:

> explains a complex entity at any particular level in the hierarchy of organization, in terms of entities only one level down the hierarchy, entities which, themselves,

are likely to be complex enough to need further reducing to their own constituent parts, and so on. . .the hierarchical reductionist believes that carburettors are explained in terms of smaller units. . .which are explained in terms of smaller units. . .which are ultimately explained in terms of the smallest of fundamental particles. Reductionism, in this sense, is just another name for an honest desire to understand how things work. (Ibid., p. 13)

Perhaps the provision of microfoundations for macroeconomics is also simply the result of 'an honest desire to understand how things work'?

A heterodox critique

In fact, none of these arguments is very convincing – Dawkins's hierarchical reductionism least of all, as we shall see shortly. What of the other arguments for microfoundations? What can we learn from the statement that microeconomics is 'more basic' than macroeconomics? The *Concise Oxford Dictionary* offers two definitions of the word 'basic'. The first is 'fundamental', 'serving as the base or foundation'. This provides some synonyms for 'basic', but otherwise does not take us any further. It is just a different way of stating the same thing. The second definition is 'constituting a minimum', and an example is provided: Eleanor Roosevelt's (1961) description of a poor Asian country where 'the basic food of the people is rice for every meal'. Other examples given are 'basic English' (with a very limited vocabulary) or 'basic pay' (the lowest possible wage – in Australia the legal minimum wage was for many years known as the 'basic wage'). This does not seem to help the case for microfoundations, any more than the final example that the dictionary offers: 'basic industry', meaning 'an industry of great economic importance'.

What of the argument that, since 'the economy is made up of individuals', we have to start by analysing individual behaviour? This involves a rather elementary confusion between ontological reduction and explanatory reduction. To say that A (the economy) is made up of Bs (individual human beings) is to say something about ontology – what exists. It is rather obviously true. But it does not follow from this that A can and must be explained in terms of statements about Bs, and only in terms of statements about Bs. We have already encountered one example, with A as the banking system and Bs as the tellers (and other employees) who work for the banks.

Consider a more personal example. There is a sense in which you and I are made up of our body parts: head, toes, arms, legs, vital organs, naughty bits. But we would feel insulted if someone claimed to be able to explain our character, personality, thoughts, emotions and behaviour solely by reference to those body parts. Something – probably a great deal – would be missing from such an explanation.

The third argument relies on the apparent success of the 'economics imperialism' project. Mainstream microeconomic models and econometric techniques have – supposedly – been applied to problems that were previously the preserve of political scientists, sociologists, anthropologists and other lesser breeds, with such success that they have been forced to give up much of their intellectual territory to the economists. You wish! This is what leading economic imperialists like Gary Becker would have liked to happen, but there is not much evidence to show that they have succeeded. It is not a strong argument for the application of micro-reduction to macroeconomics.

Finally, there is the argument that hierarchical reduction has succeeded in the natural sciences, above all in biology, and should therefore be applied to economics. Many biologists agree with Dawkins, but many do not. In a famous critique, *Not in Our Genes* (1984), Richard Lewontin, Steven Rose and Leon Kamin emphasized the complexity of the relationship between an organism and its environment:

> Organisms do not simply adapt to previously existing, autonomous environments; they create, destroy, modify, and internally transform aspects of the external world by their own life activities to make this environment. Just as there is no organism without an environment, so there is no environment without an organism. Neither organism nor environment is a closed system; each is open to the other. (Lewontin et al., 1984, p. 273)

This points to two insuperable difficulties with Dawkins's argument: downward causation and the fallacy of composition.

Downward causation and the fallacy of composition

The difficulties posed for Dawkins by downward causation can be seen very clearly from his automotive example. Changes in the social, political, economic and cultural context in which cars are driven frequently affect not just the car as a whole machine, but also some or all of its parts. Thus causation runs downwards, from the larger to the smaller units, and not just upwards from the smaller to the larger, as Dawkins maintains. To understand the causes of changes in car components over time, we need more than knowledge of metallurgy, chemistry and particle physics, more even than complete knowledge of these things. We also need to know about society, politics, psychology, and the economy.

There are two well-known examples of downward causation from the mid-twentieth-century motor industry. One is provided by the fins and other ornamental embellishments, with no engineering advantages, that were added to cars in the 1950s on the insistence of marketing specialists who drew on studies of consumer psychology in order to suggest ways of increasing brand loyalty and therefore also profitability. The other was the belated introduction, in the 1960s and 1970s, of a range of safety features in the wake of an intense political controversy over the dangers involved in driving cars without them. In both cases causation ran downwards, from human society to the component parts of its machines – from larger units to smaller units, from macro to micro.

Neither is it possible to infer all the properties of the car from a complete knowledge of its parts. Cars are not just pieces of machinery. They have social, political, economic and cultural significance. They are studied by traffic engineers, by urban sociologists, by town planners and even by political economists who are interested in the demise of the so-called 'Fordist' stage of capitalist development. None of them could conceivably be satisfied with information about car components, not even if it was accompanied by knowledge of metallurgy, chemistry and particle physics. This is not to say that information about the parts might not be useful to them, in some circumstances, or that they should dismiss such information as trivial or misleading. But it would certainly not be sufficient, and would probably not be very enlightening for their particular purposes.

To deny this involves a fallacy of composition: a statement that is true of any individual considered separately may be false when applied to them all taken together. To take an example from everyday life: with the introduction of all-seater football stadiums in the United Kingdom after the 1989 Hillsborough disaster, any individual supporter who stands up to get a better view does indeed get one, but if they all stand up no one's view is improved.

The fallacy of composition is closely related to the concept of emergent properties, which are defined as properties of a system that are autonomous from the more basic phenomena that give rise to them. In other words:

> a state or other feature of a system is emergent if it is impossible to predict the existence of that feature on the basis of a complete theory of basic phenomena in the system. . . A closely related idea is that emergent properties cannot be explained given a complete understanding of more basic phenomena. (Bedau and Humphreys, 2008, p. 10)

Again, the use of the word 'basic' does nothing to advance the case for the microfoundations dogma.

To return to Dawkins's example: a complete theory of car components would not allow us to explain the social, political, economic and cultural significance of the motor car. These are emergent properties, which cannot be inferred from a theory of the parts and cannot be reduced to it. That is why we need traffic engineers, urban sociologists, town planners, and political economists, in addition to metallurgists and motor mechanics.

Some economic examples

In Keynesian macroeconomics there are several well-known cases in which a fallacy of composition can be identified. For some reason they are usually described as 'paradoxes'. First, and most obvious, is the 'paradox of thrift' (see Chapter 7). A decision by any individual to save a larger proportion of his or her income may lead to more saving by that individual. However, in the absence of increased investment this will not be true of an increase in everyone's savings propensity, which will simply reduce their incomes and leave the volume of aggregate saving unchanged. This proposition is at least 300 years old. As Keynes noted, it was popularized by Bernard Mandeville in his 1714 *Fable of the Bees*.

A realistic monetary theory must allow for the paradox of liquidity. This term is of quite recent origin, but the principle is long established in the literature on financial panics (see Chapters 5, 15 and 16). If any individual bank or other financial company wishes to increase its liquidity, it can always do so (at a price). But if all financial companies attempt to do so, the consequence will be a reduction in aggregate liquidity and (in the absence of government intervention) the real possibility that the whole system will collapse. The global financial crisis that began in 2007–08 provided a dramatic example of this principle.

The Kaleckian paradox of costs is rather similar. A wage rise is very bad news for any individual capitalist. But it may be good news for them all, taken together, if the consequent rise in consumption expenditure raises the level of economic activity and thereby increases aggregate profits. In practice, this may or may not be the outcome: it all depends on the values of the relevant parameters. But it cannot be ruled out in principle.

Kalecki's profit equation offers yet another example. In a closed economy with no government, and on the assumption that workers do not save, aggregate profits are equal to and determined by the sum of capitalist expenditure on consumption and investment. Thus 'capitalists get what they spend', but only as a class. Any capitalist who thinks that it applies to him or her as an individual will end up in jail (if they are caught).

These are all cases where individual behaviour is governed by macro-economic requirements. The logic of our macroeconomic analysis tells us that, in aggregate, saving cannot increase unless investment rises. The viability of the entire financial system may be threatened by individual firms' quest for increased liquidity. Under some circumstances increased wages may lead to higher profits, not lower profits, in aggregate. Total profits always depend on total spending. None of these results is immediately obvious, none could be inferred from knowledge of microeconomics alone, and every one of them also entails the existence of downward causation, from macro to micro.

Macrofoundations for microeconomics?

The potential significance of downward causation has led some heterodox economists to argue that we need macrofoundations for microeconomics. There are good reasons for taking this argument seriously, first because of the irreducibly macroeconomic nature of many important problems (as noted above), and second because what may be termed the prevailing macro-economic regime has profound implications for individual behaviour. To understand individual decisions, it is often necessary to know something about the macroeconomic context in which these microeconomic decisions are being made. The early Keynesians believed that a 'full employment economy' would be quite different from an 'unemployment economy', especially in the labour market, where – in Kalecki's famous phrase – full employment posed a potentially very serious threat to 'discipline in the factories'.

So the macroeconomic context is very important indeed. Whether it establishes a case for 'macrofoundations' is another matter. There is something perverse about the idea of 'foundations' that exist at a higher level than the edifice that they are supposed to be foundations of, whether the edifice is physical or intellectual in nature. For this reason, I think, the term 'macro-foundations' is best avoided.

A strong case can be made, however, that economists need to provide social and philosophical foundations for their theories, micro and macro (see Chapter 1). Both macroeconomists and microeconomists need to be aware that they are attempting to model capitalism, not peasant agriculture or hand-icraft production. There are (at least) two classes of agents, capitalists and workers, and it is the former who own the means of production and control the production and sale of commodities. Firms are not simply the agents of households. Production is motivated by profit, not – at least, not directly – by the utility functions of asocial, classless 'consumers'. Since profit is by definition the difference between revenue and costs, that is, the difference between two sums of money, it is pointless to model a capitalist economy in terms of barter (see Chapter 3).

These social foundations of any meaningful economic theory are inescapable, but they are routinely violated in the mainstream models that employ RARE microfoundations, as can be seen from the opening pages of Michael Wickens's textbook that I quoted at the beginning of this chapter.

As for the philosophical foundations of economics, a minimum requirement would be some form of scientific realism, including (but not restricted to) a substantial degree of 'realisticness' (see Chapter 1). As Keynes insisted, economic theory should have some bearing on 'the economic society in which we actually live'.

Some alternative metaphors

We have seen how important it is for economists to be careful with the language that they use, and especially with their metaphors. 'Microfoundations' is a good example of a very bad metaphor. But this does not mean that economists should avoid the use of metaphors altogether. Even if this were possible, it would be unwise. In macroeconomics, some hydraulic metaphors are legitimate and helpful: the 'circular flow' of income and expenditure is the most obvious example, along with the 'circulation' of money and the treatment of investment and saving as 'injections' and 'leakages' respectively (see Chapter 7).

Even spatial metaphors have their uses. The great Austrian-American economist Joseph Alois Schumpeter (1883–1950) is said to have described static and dynamic economic theory as being 'separate buildings' – though he did not state which was the Kindergarten and which the Institute of Advanced Study. Perhaps the relationship between microeconomics and macroeconomics should also be thought of as a horizontal rather than a vertical one?

I can offer another personal example, this time from my former employer. Many years (and several administrative restructurings) ago, La Trobe University had an Economics building and a Social Science building, side by side, each four stories high. At either end of the two buildings there was a bridge at the second level, making it easy to get from the one to the other without going right down to the ground floor. Each building had its own solid foundations but – rather obviously – neither building was the foundation of the other. Occasionally economists and social scientists moved from one building to the other to talk to each other (not often enough, I fear). Perhaps microeconomics and macroeconomics should be thought of in this way? They too are separate but close to each other, and there is a considerable volume of two-way traffic between them.

One problem with this metaphor is that we probably need more than two buildings, and the network of bridges between them might get very complicated. Between the individual human agent (the 'micro' building) and the global economy (the 'macro' building) there are several intermediate dimensions, including industries, sectors, regions and nations. Schumpeter's modern disciples often refer to the need for 'mesoeconomics' as a sort of middle level of theorizing, between macroeconomics and microeconomics, but even this does not seem adequate.

Just possibly a Russian doll analogy might be more helpful. There can in principle be any number of dolls. Each one is nested inside the larger one above it. They are similar, but not identical, since the amount of detail has to be reduced as we move from larger to ever-smaller dolls. The largest of the dolls is the most beautiful and the most interesting, but it is also the most complicated and most difficult to understand. The smallest doll is the plainest and least fascinating, but also the easiest to make sense of. There is no case for discarding the largest doll or for concentrating our attention on the smallest.

Of course, this metaphor also has its problems. A set of Russian dolls does not change much over time, give or take some fading or cracking of the paintwork. And they do not interact with each other in any meaningful way. No analogy is perfect, and it is a good idea to bear this in mind when you are thinking about the use of metaphors by economists. We cannot live without them, and it would be silly to try, but we do need to be careful with them.

Heterodox microfoundations for heterodox macroeconomics?

Unfortunately, some heterodox economists have disregarded this important lesson. It is undoubtedly true that heterodox microeconomics is very different from mainstream microeconomics (see the Introduction to this book). It emphasizes oligopoly rather than perfect competition, and mark-up pricing rather than Michael Wickens's Walrasian auctioneer. Preferences are viewed as socially determined or 'endogenous' to the economic system: this is another important example of downward causation.

These important differences have led some heterodox economists to claim that they too are providing microfoundations for macroeconomics. It is just that theirs are very different from, and much better than, the microfoundations supplied by the mainstream. This is an understandable reaction to a very difficult situation. It is hard enough these days for heterodox economists to be taken seriously by the mainstream, and a failure to provide microfoundations seems to make it even harder. But I think that it is still a serious mistake. No heterodox economist would defend the reduction of macroeconomics to microeconomics, or deny the importance of downward causation and the fallacy of composition. But by adopting the mainstream's misleading metaphor they are giving too much away; they are muddying these already murky waters.

Why it all matters

We need to remind ourselves again why this is all so important. It is not just a question of being careless with words. As noted at the beginning of the chapter, really important issues of economic policy are at stake. If all macroeconomic questions can be reduced to microeconomics, and there is no need to worry about the fallacy of composition, then austerity and wage cuts are easy to justify. The government, like the household, cannot live beyond its means, and must cut its spending to ensure that it does not. Mass unemployment means that the labour market has not cleared, and wages must be cut to make the quantity supplied equal to the quantity demanded.

All this is wrong, as earlier chapters have suggested. The government is not a household, and austerity often does much more harm than good. Across-the-board wage cuts reduce incomes and so lead to a decline in consumer demand. A falling price level would be very bad news. In macroeconomics *ceteris* are not *paribus* (all other things are *not* equal). The attempt to reduce macroeconomics to microeconomics is a very bad idea, and when applied to policy decisions it can have very bad consequences.

Once again, this does not deny the relevance of microeconomics to macroeconomics (or for that matter vice versa), simply that the two bodies of knowledge exist side by side, neither being the foundation of the other. Macroeconomics is relatively autonomous, and certainly not independent (compare Catalonia with Portugal, Wales with the Irish Republic,

Puerto Rico with Canada). And there is mutual causation between macro-economics and microeconomics, upwards and downwards.

There are some broader lessons for us all from the microfoundations delu-sion. First, we need to mind our language: we should think carefully about the metaphors we use, and make sure that they are helpful and not mislead-ing. Second, we should pay serious attention to the methodology of econom-ics: the philosophy of science is never going to be easy, but we neglect it at our peril. Third, we should be good neighbours: we should talk to political scientists, sociologists and anthropologists, and not talk down to them. They have dealt with the same issues of micro-reduction that confront us as econo-mists, and they may well have something to teach us. If you have friends who are studying in these other departments, why not ask them what they think about these issues?

 REFERENCES

Bedau, M. and P. Humphreys (eds) (2008), *Emergence: Contemporary Readings in Philosophy and Science*, Cambridge, MA: MIT Press.

Davis, J.B. (2003), *The Theory of the Individual in Economics: Identity and Value*, Abingdon, UK and New York: Routledge.

Dawkins, R. (1976), *The Selfish Gene*, Oxford, UK: Oxford University Press.

Dawkins, R. (1996), *The Blind Watchmaker*, Harmondsworth, UK: Penguin.

Keynes, J.M. (1936), *The General Theory of Employment, Interest and Money*, London: Macmillan.

Kincaid, H. (1998), 'Methodological individualism/atomism', in J.B. Davis, D.W Hands and U. Mäki (eds), *The Handbook of Economic Methodology*, Cheltenham, UK and Northampton, MA, USA: Edward Elgar Publishing, pp. 294–300.

King, J.E. (2012), *The Microfoundations Delusion: Metaphor and Dogma in the History of Macroeconomics*, Cheltenham, UK and Northampton, MA, USA: Edward Elgar Publishing.

Lakoff, G. (1996), *Moral Politics: What Conservatives Know that Liberals Don't*, Chicago, IL: Chicago University Press.

Lewontin, R.C., S. Rose and L.J. Kamin (1984), *Not in Our Genes: Biology, Ideology, and Human Nature*, Harmondsworth, UK: Penguin.

Lukes, S. (1968), 'Methodological individualism reconsidered', *British Journal of Sociology*, **19** (2), 119–29.

Mandeville, B. (1714), *The Fable of the Bees or Private Vices, Public Benefits*, London: J. Roberts.

Ricardo, D. (1815), *An Essay on the Influence of a Low Price of Corn on the Profits of Stock*, London: J. Murray.

Roosevelt, A.E. (1961), *The Autobiography of Eleanor Roosevelt*, New York: Harper & Brothers.

Skidelsky, R. (1967), *Politicians and the Slump: The Labour Government of 1929–31*, London: Macmillan.

Skidelsky, R. (1983), *John Maynard Keynes: Hopes Betrayed, 1883–1920, Volume I*, London: Macmillan.

Skidelsky, R. (1992), *John Maynard Keynes: The Economist as Savior, 1920–1937, Volume II*, London: Macmillan.

Skidelsky, R. (2000), *John Maynard Keynes: Fighting for Britain, 1937–1946, Volume III*, London: Macmillan.

Skidelsky, R. (2003), *John Maynard Keynes: 1883–1946: Economist, Philosopher, Statesman*, London: Penguin Books.

Skidelsky, R. (2009), *Keynes: The Return of the Master*, London: A. Lane.

Skidelsky, R. (2013), 'Post-crash economics: some common fallacies about austerity', *The Guardian*, 21 November, accessed 20 February 2016 at http://www.theguardian.com/business/2013/nov/21/post-crash-economics-austerity-common-fallacies.

Skidelsky, R. and E. Skidelsky (2012), *How Much is Enough? The Love of Money and the Case for the Good Life*, London: A. Lane.

Smith, A. (1776), *The Wealth of Nations*, London: Strahan & Cadell.

Solow, R. (1956), 'A contribution to the theory of economic growth', *Quarterly Journal of Economics*, **70** (1), 65–94.

Wickens, M. (2008), *Macroeconomic Theory: A Dynamic General Equilibrium Approach*, Princeton, NJ: Princeton University Press.

A PORTRAIT OF ROBERT SKIDELSKY (1939–)

Robert Skidelsky was born in China in 1939 to parents of Russian ancestry (part Jewish, part Christian). He read history at Jesus College, Oxford and then, from 1961 to 1969, was a research student and then research fellow at Nuffield College. In 1967 he published his first book, *Politicians and the Slump*, based on his PhD dissertation (Skidelsky, 1967). Three years later he became Associate Professor of History at Johns Hopkins University, but his early academic career was a chequered one. His 1975 biography of Oswald Mosley was felt by many to be too sympathetic with the British fascist leader, and he was refused tenure at Johns Hopkins, returning to the United Kingdom as Professor of History, Philosophy and European Studies at the much less prestigious Polytechnic of North London. In 1978 he was appointed Professor of International Studies at the University of Warwick, where he has remained ever since, in 1990 becoming professor of political economy in the economics department there.

Skidelsky is best known for his magisterial three-volume, 1700-page biography of Keynes (Skidelsky, 1983, 1992, 2000); a single condensed volume (a mere 1000 pages) was published in 2003 (Skidelsky, 2003). His short 2009 book, *Keynes: The Return of the Master*, provides an accessible introduction to Keynes's ideas and their application to the post-2007 Great Recession (Skidelsky, 2009). *How Much is Enough? The Love of Money and the Case for the Good Life*, co-authored with his philosopher son Edward, appeared in 2012 (Skidelsky and Skidelsky, 2012).

He lives in Keynes's former country home at Tilton in East Sussex, and in 1991 was created a life peer as Baron Skidelsky of Tilton. He has been a member of the Labour, Conservative and Social Democratic Parties, but is now unaffiliated. Skidelsky is a powerful critic of government austerity programmes in Britain and the European Union, and has made a convincing case against the micro-reduction project in mainstream macroeconomics, arguing that the teaching of macroeconomics should be taken out of the hands of microeconomists and incorporate ideas from politics, philosophy and history. Readers should subscribe to his website www.skidelskyr.com, which will supply them with thought-provoking material (every week or two) on current controversies in economics and economic policy.

Index

absolute competitive advantage 259, 279
accelerator effect 222
Accumulation of Capital 281
adding-up theorem 46
advanced economies 130, 148, 214–16, 217, 229, 344, 346
The Affluent Society 368
Africa 276
agents *see* economic agents
aggregate consumption 160, 241, 384
aggregate demand 151–69
  and aggregate supply
    J.M. Keynes on 250–53
    see also Keynesian model
  bank lending and expectations of 86
  definitions 151, 153
  demand management policies 168–9
  expected 166–8
  fiscal policy and 90, 131, 194
  forces shaping 220–22, 232
  government intervention 27
  income multiplier 164–6
  Kaleckian model 328
  Keynesian economics
    and growth 218, 222–4
    and output 159–64
  macroeconomic theories 155, 156
  neoclassical theory 156–9, 218
  subcomponents 153–4
aggregate investment 241
aggregate liquidity 391
aggregate profits 251, 391
aggregate supply
  aggregate demand and
    J.M. Keynes on 250–53
    see also Keynesian model
  expected 166–8
  neoclassical model 157–8
agriculture 29, 33, 55, 57, 58, 59, 217
alienation 189
allocation of resources 37, 49, 236, 268, 320, 362

'alternating movements of creation and cancellation of money' 87
amortization 161–2, 190
animal spirits 26, 35, 161, 200, 223, 224
anti-growth bias 145, 305
Appalled Economists 24
Appelbaum, E. 329
Araujo, R.A. 294
Argentina 121, 274, 294, 349
Arrighi, G. 322
Asian crisis (1997-98) 349
Asian economies 214, 215, 216, 294
asset-backed securities (ABSs) 324
assets 123, 124, 142, 143, 205, 323
assumptions
  balance-of-payments-constrained growth model 286–7, 288
  in modelling 30–31
  of self-adjusting economy 152
  theory of monetary circuit 82–3
asymmetric information 122
austerity policies 24, 200, 383, 395, 398
  see also fiscal consolidation
Australia 264, 266, 388
Austrian School 334, 346
automatic stabilizers 193, 200–201
autonomous demand 213, 221–2, 224, 226
autonomous factors, affecting bank reserves 113, 114
average propensity to save 198
average wage rate 52
Ayres, C.E. 364

bad economic models 31
bad loans 114
balance sheets 107–114, 117, 122–3, 130
balance-of-payments 350
  -constrained growth rate 225, 282–96, 299
    Harrod foreign trade multiplier 286–8
    Hicks supermultiplier 287–8
    price and non-price competitiveness in international trade 288–90

resource-constrained and policy-constrained
countries 292–3
role of growth of capital flows 290–91
structural change and multisectoral Thirwall's
Law 294
tests of model and empirical evidence 294–6
adjustment 281
crisis 301
deficits 293, 350, 351, 354
equilibrium growth rate 282, 283, 284–6, 288–9, 293
identity 284
balanced budget 202, 206
balanced trade 267, 281
bancor 301
Bank Act (1935) 345
Bank of England 103
Bank for International Settlements (BIS) 141, 311, 324
bank notes 103–4
Banking School 75, 116
bankruptcy 140, 324
banks/banking 385
asymmetric information and weak development
122
at heart of monetary production economy 83
deposits 101, 105, 108, 109, 121, 124, 125, 127, 142,
183
failures 104, 121
financial crisis and pessimism of 89
heterodox perspective 102–7
and modern payment system 107–114
importance in macroeconomic analysis 98
institutions 101, 103, 140
loans 83, 85, 89, 100, 101, 104, 114, 121, 124, 140,
142
see also credit
near collapse of international 121
need for independence 253
orthodox perspective 99–102, 116
uncertainty 85–6, 90–91
see also central banks; commercial banks/banking
Barker, W. 85
Barrère, A. 116
barter theory of money 76, 77–9, 99
barter vision of trade 268
Basel Accords 140–41
Batt, R. 329
beggar-my-neighbour policies 273, 281
Belgium 302
Bernanke, B. 31, 122

Big Bank 349
Big Government 349
Blecker, R.A. 276–7
The Blind Watchmaker 387
bonds 125, 127, 128, 130, 139, 199, 204, 205, 303,
304
borrowers 84, 86, 104, 121, 122, 140
Bortis, H. 46, 59–60, 64–5, 67, 70, 72–3
Boulding, K.E. 360, 368
bounded rationality 35
Brazil 23, 121, 212, 213, 214, 264, 266, 274, 275, 294,
349
Brech, M.J. 289
Bretton Woods conference/system 1, 93, 136, 302, 309,
315
broadly-based standard of living 359
Brundtland Commission (UN) 363
bubbles 134, 138–9, 140, 143, 144, 145, 307, 323–4
budget balance 202, 206
budget deficits 169, 193, 195, 198, 199, 200, 202–3,
205, 206, 209, 301, 342
budget surplus 200, 202, 209
Bundesbank 137
'bursts of optimism and pessimism' 27, 35, 76, 89, 90,
161
business cycles 53, 70–72, 122, 126, 129, 131, 133,
200–201, 202, 217, 223, 338, 344, 355, 385

Caballero, R. 72–3
Cambridge capital controversies 65–6, 232, 281
Cambridge Circus 171
Canada 24, 112, 266
capabilities 368, 375
capacity utilization 62, 63, 83, 88
capital see circulating capital; factors of production;
financial capital; fixed capital; marginal efficiency
of capital; monopoly capital
capital account surplus 350
capital accumulation 181, 190, 253, 283, 292, 328
capital expenditures 194
capital flows 290–91, 296
capital formation 187–90, 192
capital imports 350
capital stocks 359, 361, 366, 367, 371, 372–3, 376
see also human capital; manufactured capital; natural
capital; public capital; social capital
capital transfers 350
capital-theoretic debate 65–6, 72, 232, 281
capitalism 35, 126–7, 131, 256, 321, 337

capitalist economies 118, 210, 334, 344
  see also advanced economies; monetary economies
    of production
capitalist reproduction 129
capitalists 33, 34, 392–3
carbon tax 363, 364–5
cartels 53, 54, 128
catching up 213, 216, 217
cause-effect relations 381
Cencini, A. 183
central banks
  as government fiscal agents 113
  independence 144, 305
  as lenders of last resort 110, 142, 349
  monetary policy 134–47
    credibility 144–5
    of the ECB 304, 305
    heterodox perspective 141–7
    orthodox perspective 136–41, 143
  reserves 107–8, 111–12, 113, 114
  see also Bank of England; European Central Bank;
    Federal Reserve
ceteris paribus condition 28
change 28–9
  see also institutional change; structural change(s)
cheques 109
Chicago School 232
China 212, 244, 260, 267, 268, 269–70, 275, 277, 322,
  353
choice(s) 119, 369, 370
circular process of production see social and circular
  process of production
circulating capital 61, 104, 126
Clark, J.B. 238, 239
classical economics 33–4, 212, 237, 247–50
classical-Keynesian counter-revolution 62–4
classical-Keynesian political economy 59, 64–73
clearing balances 110, 112
closed economies 195, 283, 292, 391–2
cognitive dissonance 35
collateral 142
collateralized debt obligations (CDOs) 324
Collective Choice and Social Welfare 380
Colombia 294
colonialism 260
commercial banks/banking 98, 103, 107, 114, 115, 116
commodity money 99, 100, 101
common good 24, 147, 370
common markets 274

companies see firms/companies
comparative advantage 260, 261–7, 271, 272, 281
competition 63, 339
competitive advantage 259, 270
competitive markets 52
conflict, classical perspective 33–4
conflict theory of inflation 176
conservative bias 24–5
consumer choice 369
consumer credit 327
consumer demand 182–3, 395
consumer price index (CPI) 179
consumers 27, 266
consumption 63, 87
  income and 254, 384
  and inflation 175
  spending power and 43
  taxation and 199
  see also aggregate consumption; luxury consumption;
    marginal propensity to consume; private
    consumption; public consumption;
    underconsumption
contagion 349–50
convergence criteria (Maastricht) 301, 303, 304
corn model (Ricardo's) 59–61
corporate executives 324–5, 326, 330
corruption 327
cost(s)
  debt servicing 348
  of development 373
  impact of technological progress on 178–9
  of living, inflation and 179–80
  paradox of 391
  of production 50, 55, 63, 84, 129, 162, 164, 166, 185,
    228, 238, 276, 277
  see also external costs; financing costs; labour costs;
    marginal costs; opportunity costs
cost minimization 49, 99
cost-push inflation 176, 343
counterparty deposits 104
credit
  banks' decision to lend 85–6
  central role in production 104
  consumer 327
  and inflation 175
  and money creation see money, creation
  overextension 346
  as a policy instrument 168
  pro-cyclical behaviour 344–5

credit bubbles 138, 145, 307, 323–4
credit cards 327
credit crunch 72, 349
credit cycles 337, 346, 347, 355
credit default swaps (CDSs) 324
credit flows 308
credit rating agencies 308
credit standards 139
credit-debit relations 102
creditor countries (euro area) 307, 311
creditworthiness 84, 86, 104, 110
crisis-induced adjustments 337, 344, 348–9, 352–3
critical net-debt-to-GDP threshold 290–91
cross (Marshallian) 49, 337
crowding in 193, 198, 204
crowding out 159, 193, 198, 203–4, 328
culture 370
currency
    appreciation 265
    depreciation 168, 289, 351
    devaluations/revaluations 354
current account 350
    deficits 269, 283, 285, 290–91, 350, 351
    surpluses 269, 293, 307, 353
current expenditures 194
customs unions 274
cyclical growth pattern 336, 343–9
cyclical movements 53
    see also business cycles
cyclically adjusted budget 202

Daly, H.E. 368
Das Kapital 61, 129, 256
Davidson, P. 116, 299
Davies, R. 329
Davis, J.B. 384
Davis, L. 329
Dawkins, R. 387–8, 389, 391
De Souza, J.P.A. 323
debt 117
    and business cycles 133
    and financialization 323–4
    formation, production as a process of 84
    from national income 118
    long-term 130
    money as spontaneous acknowledgement of 183
    see also external debt; indebtedness; net debt; public
        debt
debt deflation spiral 349

debt service payments 133
debt servicing costs 348
debt structures 133
debt-led booms 270–71, 307, 348
debt-to-GDP ratio 206, 209, 303, 304
debtor countries (euro area) 307, 311, 313
debtors (Ponzi) 348
decision-making 35, 365, 369–70
deferred consumption 157
deficit-to-GDP ratio 291, 303, 304
deflation 140, 182, 190, 324, 383
deflationary bias 293, 299
deflationary shocks 354
DeGregori, T. 364
deindustrialization 212, 217, 265
Delors Committee 303
demand
    increasing 90
    investment as sensitive to 88
    modelling 30–31
    see also aggregate demand; consumer demand;
        effective demand; supply and demand; total
        demand
demand curve 49, 50, 53, 54, 66, 125, 166
demand management policies 151, 152, 159, 167,
    168–9
demand price 50
demand-led growth 211, 213, 385
depressions 140, 344
    see also Great Depression
deregulation 386
derivatives 324, 327
deviation of growth rate test 295
Diamond, D. 121
Dillard, D. 79
direct labour 43, 59, 60, 61, 67
disembodied firms 189
disequilibrium 53, 284, 338
disposable income 160, 163, 165, 166
distribution
    international trade and 266–7
    political economy 59, 61, 63
    Sen's concern for issues of 380
    see also income distribution; income redistribution
distributive justice 45, 61, 65
divergence 211, 214–16, 226, 229, 307
division of labour 228
Doha Round 275
dollar (US) 177, 354

dot.com bubble 138–9

'double coincidence of wants' 78, 79, 99

double movement 335

double-entry book-keeping 103, 104, 142, 178, 183, 188, 189, 192, 308

'downsize and distribute' policy 325

downward causation 381, 389–91

Draghi, M. 307

Dünhaupt, P. 331

Dutch disease 265

Dybvig, P. 121

East Asia 271, 272, 276, 294

Ecofin Council 304

ecological economics 362–3, 368–9, 370

econometric models/studies 328, 329, 330, 331, 385–6

economic activity

   budget deficits 200, 203

   influenced by external shocks 53

   investment and 210

   principle of effective demand 43

   as supply-determined 47, 63

economic agents

   behaviour 27, 46, 53, 99, 182

     see also individual behaviour; rational behaviour

   in commodity money economies 100

   purchasing power of money 178

   rational expectations 144

   and unemployment 182

   see also capitalists; consumers; firms/companies; government(s); household(s); intermediaries; rentiers; workers

The Economic Consequences of the Peace 93

economic crises 58

   (2007-) 23, 25, 36, 89, 119, 123, 135, 173, 299, 320

   contagion 349–50

   deficit countries 271

   failure of mainstream economics in predicting 31

   imbalances and 344

   monetary circuit theory 89

   monetary policy-making 145

   need for heterodox approach in analysis of 1

   overproduction as trigger for 340

   systemic 141

   see also crisis-induced adjustments; depressions; recessions

economic development 211–30

   economic growth equated with 360

   heterodox economics and true 367–71

orthodox economics 361–2

sustainable 222, 368

economic growth 23, 211–30

   central bank policies 145

   cyclical 336, 343–9

   defined 211

   demand-led 211, 213, 385

   equated with economic development 360

   export-led 267, 276–7, 307

   financialization and 331

   income distribution 34, 212, 226, 227, 232, 281, 342–3

   international trade and 260

   Keynesian economics 222–30

   linked to theory of money 81

   measurement 212

   neo-mercantilism 306

   orthodox economics 361–2

   power and 367–8

   as a public policy issue 360

   quantitative easing 116, 139

   savings, investment and 47

   secular stagnation as low permanent 24

   Solow model 283

   statistical record 213–18

   sustainable 222, 227

   trickle-down effect 366, 372

   versus sustainable development 365–7

   see also balance-of-payments, -constrained growth rate; long-run economic growth/development

economic illness 58

economic integration 118, 274, 355

economic policies 22, 23, 26, 34, 35

   see also fiscal policy(ies); monetary policy

economic possibilities for our grandchildren 360

economic power 254, 321, 364

economic theories 42–73

   belief in immutability of 29

   history of 46–54

   importance 44

   political economy 54–72

   two broad groups 44–6

economic unions 274

economics 21–39

   'as a science' argument 28–30

   definitions of 37–8

   ideology in 25–7, 35, 62, 346

   mathematics in 22, 31–3, 126, 337–8

   models in *see* models

as a moral science 33, 70
need for a heterodox approach 1
pre-World War II 250
and the social sciences 33–6
see also classical economics; heterodox economics; orthodox economics
economics approach 44–5
'economics imperialism' project 389
The Economics of the Short Period 171
economies of scale 165–6, 275, 276
economist approach, to monetary union 302
economists *see individual economists*; master-economists
effective demand 43, 45–6, 52, 53, 63–4, 65, 71, 166–8, 210, 232, 250, 383, 385
efficiency 364
efficiency wage 343
'efficient allocation of scare resources' 37, 236, 320
Egypt 214
Eichner, A.S. 24, 148
elaborated multiplier 165–6
embeddedness 36, 334
emergent properties 381, 390
employment
    effective demand and 52, 63, 166
    factors of production and 53
    financialization and 329
    income distribution 43
    inflation targeting and 145
    investment and 129
    levels 45–6, 54, 70, 144, 200, 341
    macroeconomic theories 155
    maximization 145, 147
    rentier savings and depression of 129–30
    trend output and 67–9, 70, 71, 73
    trends, advanced economies 217
    see also full employment; unemployment
empty money 184, 190
endogenous growth theory 362
endogenous money creation 75, 83, 115, 281, 345
Engels, F. 256
entrepreneurs 50, 52, 54, 70, 131, 247, 250, 254, 340, 363
environment 360, 372, 389
environmental damage 369
Epstein, G. 321–4
equality 360, 371
equation of exchange 136–8
equilibrium *see* macroeconomic equilibrium; market equilibrium

equilibrium analysis 49–51, 171, 232, 370
equilibrium price 49, 50, 53, 141
ergodic systems 369
An Essay on the Influence of a Low Price of Corn 75
Essays in the Theory of Economic Growth 281
Essays on the Theory of Employment 281
euro area 271
    crisis 112, 145, 301, 305, 306, 308
    financialization 307
    institutional structure 116
    Maastricht criteria 304
    payments 308
Europe 23, 24, 110, 119, 127, 168, 221, 270
    see also individual countries
European Central Bank (ECB) 112, 145, 303, 304–6, 311
European Clearing Union 310
European Currency Unit (ECU) 302
European Monetary Cooperation Fund 302–3
European Monetary Institute 303
European Monetary System (EMS) 354m 349
European Monetary Union (EMU) 300–313
    EMS crisis (1992-93) 349
    heterodox economics 306–313
    mainstream perspective 301–6
    Stability and Growth Pact 202, 306–7
European Payments Union (EPU) 301, 310–311
European Union (EU) 274, 275, 305
    see also individual countries
Eurostat 304
'euthanasia of the rentiers' 131, 253
ex nihilo money creation 104, 108, 114, 116
excess supplies 336, 339, 341, 351, 383, 385
exchange economy 45, 48, 49, 79–80
exchange rate(s) 302
    devaluation/depreciation 285, 290
    fixed 302
    flexible 168
    impact on balance-of-payments 290
    pass-through 138
    stability 303–4
exogenous givens 232
exogenous shocks 338
expansionary policies
    abandonment of 23
    demand management 167–8
    fiscal 24, 27, 36, 90, 158, 169, 199
    monetary 158
    see also quantitative easing

expenditure flows 105
export demand 211, 224, 225, 228, 232
export demand function 284, 295
export income elasticity of demand 283, 284, 285, 286, 292, 293, 294, 296
export price elasticity of demand 283, 285, 286, 289, 295
export-led growth 267, 276–7, 307
exports 154, 163, 164, 224
  see also international trade
expropriation 192, 326
external adjustment 336, 349–54
external costs 362, 363
external debt 192, 268, 350, 353, 354
external debt-to-GDP ratio 290, 293
external deficits 350, 353, 354
external shocks 53
extra-market agents 342

Fable of the Bees 391
factor income 153, 154, 157, 160
factor payments 239, 246, 247–50
factors of production 46, 47, 49, 65–6, 155, 219, 238, 266, 334
failure hypothesis 217
fallacies of composition 38–9, 276–8, 341, 382, 390–92, 395
falling behind 213, 216, 217, 226, 229
falling saving rates 226
fascism 334, 335
Federal Reserve 31, 138, 139, 144, 305, 346
Feenstra, R. 267
Felipe, J. 296
feminist economics 370
fictitious commodities 334–5
final finance 105, 106
final payment 135, 142, 309, 310
finance motive 84
finance-dominated capitalism 321
financial capital 128, 147, 307, 350
financial deepening 104, 105, 106
financial engineering 326, 329
financial fragility 140, 347, 348
financial innovation 127–8, 324, 348
financial instability 35, 121, 122, 126, 131, 133, 145, 251, 322, 331, 337, 344, 345–6
financial instability hypothesis 346–8
financial institutions
  balance sheets 122–3

profits 322–3
  see also banks/banking system; non-bank institutions
financial markets
  differences in interest rates 126
  and foreign-debt-to-GDP ratio 290
  international integration 118
  orthodox versus heterodox perspectives 320
  prominence in economic discussions 119
  and short-termism 325–6
financial regulations 107, 140–41, 332
financial restabilization 349
financial savings 87, 106, 157, 160
financial stability 133, 138, 327
financial stabilization 349
financial system 117–32
  consequences of long-term finance 127–30
  Keynes' analysis 130–32
  mainstream economics 119–23
    problem with 123–6
  needs of modern capitalism 126–7
financial wealth 117
financialization 118, 319–32
  defined 320–21
  dimensions 322–7
  euro area 307
  impacts 327–31
  periodization 322
  policies/programmes reducing 331–2
financing costs 127, 129–30
financing structures 133
fine tuning (fiscal) 200–201
firms/companies
  behaviour 26, 44
  Companies Acts 127
  financing 127
  government spending and increased revenue 90
  privately-owned 83
  savings 205
  value of 120
  see also disembodied firms; multinational corporations; non-financial corporations
Fiscal Compact 202
fiscal consolidation 1, 23, 199, 301, 306, 311, 313
fiscal contraction 24
fiscal equalization mechanism 307–8
fiscal policy(ies) 193–209
  and aggregate demand 90, 131
  defined 193
  expansionary 24, 27, 36, 90, 158, 169, 199

functional finance and post-Keynesian approach to 201–6
importance of 89
need for 194–7
role of automatic stabilizers 200–201
fiscal profligacy 202–3, 306
Fisher, I. 349
fixed capital 61, 62, 67
    formation 187–8, 192
    goods 62, 176
    investment 104
flexible exchange rate 168
flexible price system 120
flux 98, 105
forecasting 200–201, 386
forging ahead 213, 216, 217, 226, 229
fractional reserve banking 100, 107
France 24, 55–6, 81, 302, 323
Franco-Italian Circuit School 116
fraud 327
free market(s) 26, 27, 35, 41, 256, 335, 365, 387
free trade 263, 266, 271, 272, 281
free trade areas 274
French Keynesian economists 116
frictional unemployment 173, 180, 181
Friedman, M. 52, 158
'fringe of unsatisfied borrowers' 86
full employment 37, 45, 47, 52, 72, 196, 202, 203, 204, 210, 267–8, 281, 392
functional finance 201–6, 383
fundamental economic table 55–8, 59
fundamental prices 45, 47, 64–5
fundamental uncertainty 223
'funding of the deficit' 205

Galbraith, J.K. 360, 367, 368, 376
Garegnani, P. 66, 67
General Agreement on Tariffs and Trade (GATT) 274
general equilibrium 45, 49, 53, 72, 177
general price level 177
The General Theory of Employment, Interest and Money 25, 30, 32, 43, 52, 63, 64, 66, 77, 81, 82, 93, 130, 161, 239, 250
Geneva Conference (1947) 274
genuine progress indicator (GPI) 374
Germany 70, 269, 270, 273, 286, 302, 306, 307, 311, 322, 323, 353
Gertler, M. 122
Gini coefficient 243–6

Glass-Steagall Act (1933) 345
global power (dominant) 322
global supply chains 278
gold convertibility 302
gold standard (1879-1931) 354
golden rule 184, 186
goldsmith bankers 100
Gossen, H.H. 48
Gouvea, R.R. 294
government(s)
    as an obstacle to market equilibrium 25–6
    control over paper currency 104
    expenditure *see* public spending
    fiscal profligacy 202–3, 306
    interventions and market failures 38
    market stability 27
    responses to economic crises 23, 27, 36
    role in monetary circuit 90
government bonds 139, 199, 204, 205, 303, 304
government policy
    and external adjustment 351–2
    see also fiscal policy(ies)
Graziani, A. 81, 84
Great Crash 119, 344
Great Depression 23, 24, 36, 119, 152, 221, 274, 335, 341
Great Recession 23, 201, 202, 221, 226, 227, 349
The Great Transformation 35–6, 334
Greece 23, 270, 271, 307
gross domestic product (GDP) 54, 153, 154, 155, 161, 163, 200, 366, 374
    see also debt-to-GDP ratio; deficit-to-GDP ratio
Guide to Post-Keynesian Economics 148
Guttmann, R. 355

Hahn, F. 81, 171
Haldane, A.G. 329
Hanson, G. 267
Harcourt, G.C. 65, 72
Harmonized Index of Consumer Prices (HICP) 304
Harrod foreign trade multiplier 283, 286–7
Harrod, R. 32, 213, 221
Harrodian growth theory 222–3
Harrod–Domar model 361
Hartwick-Solow rule 363
Harvard University 24
Hausmann, R. 286
Hawtrey, R.G. 147
Heckscher–Ohlin model 266

hedge funds 124
hedging 118, 133, 347
Hein, E. 328
helicopter money 136, 142
heterodox economics 1, 27, 36, 37, 38
  banks and modern payment system 107–114
  causes of inflation 176
  central banks and monetary policy 141–7
  critique of microfoundations 388–9
  European Monetary Union 306–313
  financial market 320
  international trade 267–71
  microfoundations for heterodox macroeconomics 394–5
  monetary economies of production 79, 80–90
  money and banking 102–7
  sustainable development 363, 364
  true economic development 367–71
  unemployment 183–90
  wealth distribution 246–50
  Wealth of Nations 41
  see also post-Keynesian economics
heterogenous firms 279
Hicks supermultiplier 283, 287–8
hierarchical reduction 387–8, 389
The High Price of Bullion, a Proof of the Depreciation of Bank Notes 75
Hilferding, R. 128–9, 132, 321
historical growth record 213–18, 226
historical time 82, 281, 338, 370
history 22, 36, 46–54, 159
hoarded savings 76, 87, 89, 105, 183
hoarding 48, 58
Holt, R.P.F. 360, 362–9, 372–3, 375
household(s)
  as borrowers and lenders 121, 124, 127
  disposable income 160, 163, 165, 166
  and financialization 326–7
  saving(s) 105, 120, 121, 129, 130, 205, 222, 223, 224
  see also financial savings; hoarded savings
  utility-maximizing 44
How Much is Enough? The Love of Money and the Case for the Good Life 398
human capital 329, 365, 371, 372
Human Development Index (HDI) 245, 375
Human Development Report (1990) 375
human nature 35, 47
Hume, D. 41
Humphrey, C. 79

hydraulic metaphors 393
hypotheses 28

ideology 25–7, 35, 62, 346, 367
illiquidity 125
imagined state, barter as an 79
imbalances 336–56
  cyclical growth dynamics 343–9
  in the EU 307
  external adjustment 336, 349–54
  financialization and 328
  fiscal policy and correction of macroeconomic 169
  growth and distribution 342–3
  mainstream view of a self-adjusting economy 337–8
  overproduction versus underconsumption 338–42
  social 376
  see also economic crises; trade imbalances
immutable laws 23, 28
imperfect competition 54, 281, 338, 340–41
import demand function 284–5, 287, 292, 295, 296
import income elasticity of demand 283, 285, 292, 293, 294, 296
import price elasticity of demand 283, 285, 289, 295
import price pass-through 290
imports 70, 163, 164, 165–6, 224–5
  see also international trade
income 58
  and consumption 384
  full employment 196, 203
  middle classes 130
  money and 183–90
  and well-being 374
  see also disposable income; national income; net income; per capita income
income distribution 65, 67
  aggregate demand 328
  conflict over 34
  consumption 43, 254
  defined 234
  economic growth 34, 212, 226, 227, 232, 281, 342–3
  effective demand 53
  factors affecting 251
  financialization and 330–31
  and inflation 176
  interest rates and 126
  Keynes' theory 253
  Keynesian/monetarist model 241
  marginal productivity 237–40
  in market economy 236–7

monetary policy and 141, 143
output and employment 43, 70
societal well-being 255
states of 241–6
theoretical approaches 44, 45
and wealth 235
income elasticity of demand for imports and exports
    283, 284, 285, 286, 292, 293, 294, 296
income flows 101, 105, 124, 235
income inequality 34, 36, 226, 227, 242–6, 254, 260,
    267, 330, 331, 332
income multiplier 151–2, 164–6, 171, 384
income redistribution 227, 234, 235–6, 251, 266
increasing risk, principle of 210
indebtedness 121, 130, 133, 173, 186, 254, 327, 337,
    347
Index of Sustainable Economic Welfare (ISEW) 374
India 244, 272, 275, 322
indirect labour 43, 59, 60, 61, 67
indirect taxation 178
individual behaviour 23, 26, 38, 141, 156, 386, 388, 392
industrial capitalism 126, 131
industrial change, and unemployment 180
Industrial Crises in Contemporary England 358
inequality 365, 366
    see also income inequality
infant-industry protection 260, 271–3
inflation 52, 144, 343, 385
    causes 175–6
    criticisms of traditional analysis 176–80
    definitions 173, 174
    ECB monetary policy 304
    expectations 305
    heterodox economics 183–90
    measurement 174–5
Inflation, chômage et malformation du capital 192
inflation rate 303
inflation targeting 143–4, 145
inflationary expectations 386
initial finance 84, 104–5
*An Inquiry into the Nature and Causes of the Wealth of
    Nations* see *Wealth of Nations*
insolvency 123
instability *see* financial instability; market instability
institutional change 28–9, 341
institutionalists 367–8
institutionalized scarcity 116
institutions 23, 26, 35, 38, 46, 54, 373
insurance companies 124, 125

interbank market(s) 110, 111, 123, 140, 142
interest
    defined 117
    see also rate(s) of interest
interest payments, government debt 194, 199, 204, 291
interest rate channels 138, 140
interest rate rule 138
intermediaries/intermediation 100, 101, 102, 106, 116,
    118, 123, 124–5, 142, 184, 345
international banking system 121
international crisis dynamics 349–50
international monetary architecture 309–313, 315
International Monetary Fund (IMF) 335
international monetary system (IMS) 353–4
International Money and the Real World 299
international payments 192, 315
international settlement institution 312–13
international trade 259–79
    aggregate demand 163–4
    heterodox economics 267–71
    Kaldorian growth theory 224, 225
    liberalization and trade agreements 273–5
    long-run development and infant-industry
        protection 271–3
    manufactured exports and the fallacy of composition
        276–8
    orthodox economics 261–7
    price and non-price competitiveness 288–90
    see also exports; imports
investment(s)
    decisions 35, 88, 124, 197, 328, 346
    determination of output and employment 129
    expenditures 63, 100, 199
    financialization and 328–9
    intentions 198, 202, 203, 205
    planning of 88
    profits and 343–4
    rate(s) of return 131, 241
    requirements and preferences 126
    savings and 43, 47, 66, 125, 127
    for sustainable development 371–4
    see also aggregate investment; malinvestment;
        overinvestment; private investment; public
        investment; underinvestment
investment multiplier 43
investment-driven growth 222–4
invisible hand 41, 337–8
involuntary unemployment 43, 45–6, 53, 58, 63, 68, 70,
    156, 173, 181–2

Ireland 23, 275, 307
Italy 23, 81, 302, 307

J-curve effects 290
Japan 70, 213, 214, 260, 273, 275, 277, 292, 295, 323, 383
Jensen, M. 325
Jespersen, J. 159
Jevons, W.S. 49, 78, 237, 384
joint stock companies 127
Juglar cycle 217
justice 371

Kahn, R. 164, 169, 171
Kaldor, N. 213, 221, 232, 370
Kaldorian growth theory 224–5, 228–9
Kalecki, M. 81, 116, 129–30, 131, 201, 205, 210, 213, 221, 342–3, 391–2
Kaleckian growth theory 223–4
Kaleckian model 328
Kamin, L. 389
Kay, J. 31
Keynes: The Return of the Master 398
Keynes, J.M. 34, 35, 58, 116, 125, 145, 182, 343
    aggregate supply and demand 250–53
    alternative to self-balancing economy 340–41
    analysis of finance 130–32
    concerns about economic growth 360
    deflation prevention 383
    on economics as a moral science 33
    on economics as science 29
    on importance of economic theories 44
    income multiplier 171
    international payment system 309–10
    on master economists 21–2
    monetary economies of production 81, 82, 84, 86, 89
    monetary policy 139, 252–3
    portrait of 93
    on uncertainty 26
    see also classical-Keynesian counter-revolution; *The General Theory of Employment, Interest and Money*
The Keynes Solution 299
Keynesian economics 239
    aggregate demand *see* aggregate demand
    economic growth 218–19, 222–30
    see also new Keynesian economics; post-Keynesian economics
Keynesian model 64–5, 234, 239, 240–41

Keynesian Revolution 62–4, 70, 341–2
King, J. 382
Klein, P.A. 367
knowledge 22, 28, 131, 276, 373
Kondratiev cycle 70–71, 217, 223
Kondratiev, N. 358
Krippner, G. 321
Kuznets swings 217, 223

labour
    social process of production 58
    see also division of labour; factors of production
labour costs 61, 67, 250, 262, 271
    see also relative labour costs; unit labour costs
labour demand 166
labour market 37
labour market equilibrium 52, 53–4, 156, 157, 158
labour market rigidities 159, 182–3
labour opportunity dichotomy 241
labour productivity 67, 69, 144, 166
labour theory of value 59, 234, 237–8, 249, 358
labour value principle 43, 45, 64–5
Lafleur, L.-R. 85
lags, in economic forecasting 201
'laissez-faire' 25–6, 335
Lakoff, G. 387
land
    in classical economics 33
    see also agriculture; factor payments; factors of production
Lange, O. 133
Lapavitsas, C. 323, 326
Largentay, Jean de 116
Laspeyres price index 174–5, 178
Latin American economies 214, 215, 216, 294
Lavoie, M. 82, 88, 369
law of diminishing marginal productivity 238
law of diminishing marginal utility 48
law of equalization of the marginal utility-price ratios 48
Lazonick, W. 325, 329
LDC debt crisis (1982-89) 349
Le Bourva, J. 87
'learning by doing' 228
legal Marxism 358
legislation, an obstacle to market equilibrium 25–6
Lehman Brothers 119, 135, 140
lenders of last resort 110, 142, 349
Leontief quantity system 54, 59
Leontief, W. 64, 133

Lerner, A. 201, 202
Les Economistes Atterrés 24
Lesser Depression 23
Levina, I.A. 330
Lewontin, R. 389
liabilities 123, 124, 199
Lima, G.T. 294
limits to growth 230
Lin, K. 330
lines of credit 84, 139
liquidity 98, 124, 125, 251, 391, 392
liquidity preference (LP) 105, 140, 232, 234, 239, 241, 253, 254
loanable funds 101, 102, 106, 125, 197, 345
 see also banks/banking, loans
logical time 338
long-period Kondratiev cycle 70–71, 217
long-period or trend output and employment 67–9, 70, 71, 73
long-run aggregate supply curve 158
long-run economic growth/development 214
 forces shaping demand formation 220–22
 infant-industry protection 271–3
 supply versus demand in determination of 218–20
long-term finance 125, 127–30
long-term rates of interest 125, 130, 131, 168, 303
Lorenz curve 242, 243, 245
Lucas, R. 53, 382, 385, 386
Lukes, S. 384
Luxemburg, R. 129
luxury consumption 128

Maastricht criteria 301, 303, 304
McCloskey, D. 32
McCombie, J.S.L. 290, 293, 296
macro-groups 33, 82–3
macro-uncertainty 85, 86, 90
The Macrodynamics of Advanced Market Economies 148
macroeconomic equilibrium 43, 45, 66, 222, 224
macroeconomic theory 155
macroeconomics
 asymmetric information 122
 Cabellero on goal of 72–3
 distinguished from microeconomics 38–9
 heterodox microfoundations for heterodox 394–5
 microfoundations
  and disappearance of 382
  and implications for 382–3
 traditional Keynesian approach 384

 see also modern macroeconomics; new classical economics
macrofoundations, for microeconomics 392–3
mainstream economic *see* orthodox economics
malinvestment 346
Malthus, T.R. 212
management, finance-oriented 324–5, 328
Mandeville, B. 391
Mankiw, G. 24–5
manufactured capital 362, 363, 365, 371–2
manufactured exports 276–8
marginal analysis 48–9
marginal costs 43, 48, 49, 50, 51, 62
marginal efficiency of capital 234, 239, 241, 253, 254
marginal principle 43, 60
marginal productivity 43, 48–9, 237–40, 251, 362
marginal propensity to consume 160, 164, 165, 166, 234, 236, 239, 241, 253, 254
marginal propensity to import 165, 166, 225, 287
marginal propensity to save 160
marginal utility 43, 48, 238
Marginalist Revolution 43, 47, 49, 62, 337, 384
mark-up pricing 63, 67, 71, 84, 148, 290, 343, 394–5
market clearing 52–3, 156, 386
market economy 194–5, 236, 334
market equilibrium 25–6, 152, 337, 338, 340
 see also disequilibrium; general equilibrium; labour
  market equilibrium; partial equilibrium
market failures 37–8
market imbalances 337, 338
market imperfection 240
market instability 26–7
market liberalization 335
market power 156, 167, 210, 338, 340
market prices 47, 63
market society 334
market stability 27, 128
markets
 economics as a study of 23
 ideological approaches 25–6
 see also financial markets; free market(s); labour
  market
Marshall, A. 21, 44, 45, 49, 62, 337
Marshall–Lerner conditions 285, 295
Marx, K. 33, 58, 64, 81, 116, 129, 182, 212, 237, 249–50, 343
 alternative to self-balancing economy 339–40
 portrait of 256
 reactions against 61–2

Marxism 256, 358

mass unemployment 128, 340, 395

master-economists 21–2

mathematics 22, 31–3, 126, 337–8

maturity hypothesis 217

maturity transformation 125

'maximizing shareholder value' 325

Meade, J. 171

means of payment 38, 98, 102, 103, 106, 114, 141, 311, 315

The Means to Prosperity 93

Meek, R.L. 55

Menger, C. 49, 237, 384

merchant capitalists 126

Mercosur 274

Merkel, A. 383

mesoeconomics 394

metaphors 382, 387, 393–4, 396

methodological individualism 384

methodology 382, 396

Mexico 121, 212, 217, 267, 269–70, 272, 275, 277, 294

micro-reductionism 382, 387–8, 389, 396, 398

micro-uncertainty 85, 86, 89, 90

microeconomic models 387

microeconomics 44, 235

    distinguished from macroeconomics 38–9

    macrofoundations for 392–3

microfoundations 63, 120, 124

    definition 382

    disappearance of macroeconomics 382

    heterodox critique 388–9

    implications for macroeconomics 382–3

    mainstream arguments in favour of 386–8

    origins 384–6

middle classes 130

Middle East 276

middle-income economies 214, 215, 216

Mill, J.S. 237, 249

Miller, M. 120

Minsky, H.P. 132, 133, 320, 346–7

Minsky moment 348

models 29, 30–32, 116, 121, 122, 126, 266–7, 327–8, 330, 337–8, 361–2, 387

modern macroeconomics 383–4

Modigliani, F. 120

Modigliani–Miller theorem 120

monetarism 52–3, 144, 177, 232, 240–41, 302

monetary aggregate 135, 136, 137, 138

monetary base 205

monetary circuit 81–90, 98, 116

monetary economies of production 46, 54, 64, 67, 76–91, 181, 192, 268

    definition 76

    employment and income 250

    fixed capital formation 187

    heterodox perspective 80–90

    orthodox perspective 77–80

Monetary Economies of Production: Banking and Financial Circuits and the Role of the State 116

monetary flows 88, 100, 105, 106

monetary policy

    central banks and *see* central banks, monetary policy

    expansionary 158

        see also quantitative easing

    influence over investment 162

    instruments 168

    Keynes proposal 252–3

    price stability 176

    pro-cyclical 346

    to drive down interest rates 131

monetary relations 98

monetary targeting 135, 136–8

monetary-structural reform 309–313, 315

money

    creation 75, 83, 84–5, 104, 107, 108, 114, 115, 116, 142, 281, 345

    demand for 64

    in economics 39

    as exogenous 45

    as a fictitious commodity 335

    heterodox perspective 80–90, 102–7

    and income 183–90

    in models/modelling 31

    orthodox perspective 77–80, 98–9, 116

    political economy 46, 55

    process of production 65

    and rate of interest 125

    Say's law 48

    supply 52, 64, 101, 175, 176

    see also credit; purchasing power of money; quantity theory of money

Money and the Mechanisms of Exchange 78

money multiplier 101, 107, 135, 136, 142

Money and the Real World 299

money wage rate 47, 62–3, 66, 67

Monnaie et macroéconomie: théorie de la monnaie en déséquilibre 116

monopolies 54, 289

monopoly capital 128, 129
Moore, B. 116
moral hazard behaviour 306
moral science 33, 70
morality 41
Mosler, W. 116
motivations 35
multilateral trade liberalization 274
multinational corporations (MNCs) 272–3, 275, 277
multisectoral Thirlwall's Law 294
Myrdal, G. 367

narodniks 358
nation-state 334
national accounting 241
national accounting identity 154, 195
National Accounting System (NAS) 152–5, 161
national income 43, 58, 118, 198, 244, 331, 384
natural capital 362–3, 363–4, 365, 368, 370, 371, 372, 373
natural laws 23
natural prices 47
natural rate of interest 146, 196
natural rate of unemployment 157, 158
natural resources 360, 362, 364, 368
needs and wants 35
negative saving 124
Nelson, J. 370
neo-mercantilism 281, 306
neoclassical economics *see* orthodox economics
neoclassical synthesis 51–2
neoliberal financialization 321
neoliberalism 1, 320, 331, 335, 386
Netherlands 163, 265, 270, 323
network theory 122–3
new classical economics 52–3, 120–21, 386
new consensus macroeconomics 304
New Deal 342
new Keynesian economics 53–4, 64, 122
Nixon, R. 302
nominal long-term rate of interest 303
non-bank financial institutions 122, 140, 144
non-bank intermediaries 106
non-ergodic systems 299, 369
non-financial corporations 323, 324–6, 328, 329
non-performing loans 140
non-price competitiveness 283, 286, 288–90, 294
non-renewable resources 362, 364, 374

North American Free Trade Agreement (NAFTA) 274, 275, 277
Northern Rock 119
Norway 244

Occupy Wall Street 34
offshoring model 267
oligopoly(ies) 54, 289, 394
On the Principles of Political Economy and Taxation 60
open economies 138, 163, 299
open economy analysis 224
open-market operations 113, 168
opportunity 371
opportunity costs 262, 268
optimism 26, 27, 35, 76, 86, 89, 90, 159, 161, 348
optimization behaviour 156
organisms 389
Orhangazi, Ö. 328
orthodox economics 25, 27, 30, 31, 36, 37
    aggregate demand 156–9
    arguments in favour of microfoundations 386–8
    central banks and monetary policy 136–41, 143
    classical–Keynesian counter-revolution 62–3
    disastrous consequences of applying policies arising from 77, 91
    economic development 361–2
    economic growth 218, 360, 361–2
    European Monetary Union 301–6
    financial market 320
    financial system 119–23
        problems with 123–6
    growth theory 283
    history 49–52
    inflation 175–6, 177, 179
    international trade 261–7
    macroeconomics 38, 383–4
    market failures 37–8
    monetary economies of production 77–8
    money and banks/banking 98–102, 116
    need for fiscal policy 195–7
    self-adjusting economy 337–8
    supply and demand 43
    theory of value 62, 234, 238
    unemployment 182–3
    wealth distribution 236–41
output 58
    budget deficits and 200
    effective demand and 63
    factors of production and 53

income distribution and 70
inflation targeting and 145
investment and 129
Keynesian theory 159–64
linked to theory of money 81, 84
neoclassical growth model 157–9
and productivity 228, 229
stabilization 145, 147
over-the-counter (OTC) derivatives 327
overinvestment 325
overnight loans *see* interbank market
overproduction 43, 48, 63, 336, 343, 355
versus underconsumption 338–42
ownership 127, 128

Palley, T.I. 176, 321
paper currency 103–4
paradox of costs 391
paradox of liquidity 391
paradox of thrift 38, 46, 161, 225–6, 391
Paraguay 274
parallel credit cycles 337, 347, 355
Pareto optimum 44
Parguez, A. 81, 87, 116
partial equilibrium 49–51
Pasinetti, L. 64, 294
path dependence 229, 370
pattern of accumulation 321
payment deficits 309
payment and settlement systems 98, 107–114, 308,
       309–313
pension funds 125, 326
per capita income 212, 214, 215, 216, 217, 227, 229,
       245, 265, 360, 374, 375
percolating up 366–7
perfect competition 50, 156, 166, 283, 340
personal growth 375
pessimism 26–7, 76, 86, 89, 90, 159, 161
Phillips curve 169, 385
Phillips, K. 320
physics 30
Physiocrats 41
planning of investment 88
planning of production 83–4
pluralism 1, 22, 24, 370, 371
Poland 121
Polanyi, K.P. 36, 334–5
policy-constrained countries 292–3
political economy 45–6, 54–72

political science 22, 35
Ponzi finance 133, 347, 348
portfolio theory 119–20
Portugal 23, 307
post-classical economics *see* heterodox economics
post-Keynesian economics 36, 148, 168, 232
efficiency 364
financial instability 346–7
fiscal policy 197–200, 201–6
role of money and finance 80
sustainable development 369–70
pound (sterling) 177, 289
*Poverty and Famines: An Essay on Entitlement and
       Deprivation* 380
power 44, 365, 367, 370
see also economic power; global power; market
       power; social power; spending power
power relationships 35, 45
preferential trade agreements 274–5
'pretense-of-knowledge' syndrome 73, 145
price(s)
competitiveness in international trade 288–90
determination 45, 84, 148, 340–41
discrimination 364, 365
flexibility 240, 383, 386
formation of 66–7
level 52, 138, 139, 141, 143, 158
see also deflation; inflation
neoclassical economics 45, 47, 50, 51
of production 45, 55, 59, 62, 63, 64–5, 66
Quesnay model 55
rigidity 383
stability 135, 139, 143, 144, 145, 176, 304, 305
technological progress and 178–9
see also market prices; natural prices; relative prices;
       stock prices
price elasticity of demand for imports and exports 283,
       285, 286, 289, 290, 295
price-wage spiral 176
primary budget position 194, 206, 209
primary commodity exports 264–5, 266, 276
Principles of Economics 44, 51, 62
Principles of Political Economy and Taxation 44, 61, 75
prisoner's dilemma 370
private banking system 104
private consumption 152, 153–4, 157, 159, 160, 199
private credit flows 308
private equity 125, 326, 329
private investment 152, 153–4, 159, 161–2, 168

private sector savings 205
private sector transactions 108–112
privately-owned firms 83
privatization 386
pro-cyclical monetary policy 346
probability distribution, to risk 126, 299
producers 266
production
    macroeconomic theories 155
    new classical economics 120–21
    purchasing power of money 176–7
    rentier savings and depression of 129–30
    see also cost(s), of production; factors of production;
        monetary economies of production;
        overproduction; price(s), of production; social
        and circular process of production
Production of Commodities by Means of Commodities 62
production function 283, 362
production possibility frontier (PPF) 218, 219
productivity
    export demand 228
    financialization and 330, 331
    growth 232, 283, 329, 343
    output and 228, 229
    price elasticity of demand 290
    see also labour productivity; marginal productivity
profit(s)
    aggregate 251, 391
    capital formation 189, 190, 192
    financial institutions 322–3
    investment and 61, 129, 343–4
    normal business 166
    origin of 330
    rates 45, 61, 63, 66, 71, 232, 339–40
profit equation (Kalecki's) 391–2
profit-making 321
profit-maximization 44, 49, 50, 100, 101, 156, 166
profit-seeking goldsmiths 100
progressive tax systems 200, 201
Project LINK 284
proper principles 32
propriety 47
protectionism 259, 271–3, 274, 335
provisioning 370
prudent banking 104, 115
psychology 22, 35
public capital 371
public consumption 153–4, 169
public debt 144, 199, 202, 206, 301

public investment 153–4, 159
public sector transactions 112–14
public spending 195, 241
    avoidance of monetary policy supporting 304
    categories 194
    dramatic increase during wars 70
    on goods and services 162–3
    and inflation 175
    monetary circuit 90
    political economy 55, 56
    as a response to economic crises 23, 27
    to boost total demand 342
purchasing power of money 173, 176–7, 178, 192

quality of life 359, 360, 361, 365, 366, 368, 375
quantitative easing 1, 116, 135, 139–40, 168, 175
quantity theory of money 136, 138, 176, 178
quantum monetary theory 192
Queen of England 31
Quesnay, F. 41, 55–8, 59
quotas 268, 272

radical uncertainty 152, 369
RARE models 386, 393
rate(s) of interest 63–4, 86, 125–6
    charged by central banks 142
    currency depreciation and low 168
    determination of 241
    long-term 125, 130, 131, 168, 303
    monetary policy 138, 139, 140, 142–3, 144, 304, 305
    natural 146, 196
    private credit flows 308
    short-term 125, 168
rate(s) of return from investment 131, 241
rational behaviour 44–5, 49, 50, 55, 121
rational expectations 144, 299, 386
rational portfolio choice 119
rationality 35, 369, 370
Reagan, R. 386
real analysis 80
'real bills' doctrine 104, 115
'real business cycle' theory 338, 385
real economy 45
real estate bubbles 138, 140, 144, 307
real wage rate 60–61, 156, 157, 158, 166, 167
realistic maps 60
recessionary adjustment 349
recessions 27, 139, 140, 336, 338, 346
    see also Great Recession

reflux 76, 87, 98, 105, 106
reforms, regulatory 140–41
regional trade agreements 274, 275
regression analysis 295
relative labour costs 262, 263, 272
relative prices 45, 78, 174, 177, 238, 283, 285, 288, 289, 291, 292, 296
renewable resources 364
rent 60
rentiers 33, 34, 129–30, 131, 247, 250, 253, 320
research and development 329
reserve army of unemployed 37
reserves (central bank) 107–8, 111–12, 113, 114
resource-constrained countries 292–3
resources
  allocation 37, 49, 236, 268, 320, 362
  depletion 360, 362, 374
  misallocation of 26
  see also natural resources; non-renewable resources; renewable resources; scarce resources; unemployed resources
'retain and reinvest' policy 325
retaliatory trade policies 273–4
Rethinking Economics 24
Ricardian equivalence 199
Ricardo, D. 33, 43, 44, 48, 58, 59–64, 182, 212, 237, 262, 384
  portrait of 75
  reactions against 61–2
Richard Ely Lecture (1974) 362
risk 121, 126, 133, 210, 299, 325
Roberts, M. 290
Robertson, D. 192
Robinson, A. 171
Robinson, J. 32, 60, 81, 85, 116, 125, 171, 192, 232, 281, 370
Rochon, L.P. 83, 85, 116, 142
Roosevelt, E. 388
Roosevelt, F.D. 342, 345
Rose, S. 389
Rossi, S. 142, 175–6, 303–4, 306–9, 311, 313
Royal Bank of Scotland 119
RTGS system 311
Russia 118, 244, 264, 335, 349
'Russian doll' analogy 394

sacrifice ratio 144
Samuelson, P. 51

saving(s) 63, 124
  decisions 197
  falling rate, and negative growth 226
  fixed capital formation 187
  intentions 198, 202, 203, 205
  and investment 43, 47, 66, 125, 157
  private sector 205
    see also household, saving(s)
  rentiers 129–30
  as supply of new capital 66
    see also marginal propensity to save; paradox of thrift
savings function 197–8
savings and loans associations, failures 121
Sawyer, M. 88, 320, 322
Say, J.-B. 43, 48
Say's Law 43, 48, 63, 83, 155, 218
scarce resources 37, 51, 63
Schmitt, B. 81, 188, 189, 192
Schumpeter, J. 38, 45, 51, 70, 72, 80, 81, 131, 133, 393
science 27, 28–30, 192, 396
Seccareccia, M. 84, 89, 103, 116
secular stagnation 24
securitization 324, 327
self-adjusting economy 152, 168, 337–8, 339
self-interest 47
self-reinforcing cycle of growth 229, 232
Sen, A. 361, 368, 374–5, 380
Setterfield, M. 355
settlement balances 110
shadow banking 29, 123
shareholder value 321, 325, 329, 330
shares 125, 127, 128
shock therapy 335
short-run aggregate supply curve 158
short-term deposits 125
short-term finance 129
short-term lending 115
short-term markets 324
short-term rates of interest 125, 168
short-termism 320, 325–6, 329–30
simple income multiplier 164–5
Six-Pack 307
Skidelsky, R. 398
Smith, A. 33, 41, 46, 47, 59, 98, 182, 212, 228, 237, 247, 337–8, 384
Smithianism 61
social capital 371, 373
social and circular process of production 46, 54, 55, 56, 57, 58, 59, 62, 63, 64, 65

social classes 33, 35, 41, 67, 130
social factors, in decision-making 369–70
social imbalance 376
social income transfers (benefits) 163, 165, 169, 194, 200
social movements 34, 35
social optimum 44
social power 45, 61, 65, 67
social protectionism 335
social rationality 369, 370
social sciences 33–6
social stability 335
social surplus 43, 45, 54, 58, 67
social transformation 212
social wage 340
socialism 256, 335
society
    classical perspective 33–4
    economy as a subset of 372
    French (1750) 55–6
    in political economy 54–5
    well-being 250–54, 255, 330, 359, 360, 361, 368, 374
socio-ethical principle 47
socioeconomic system 46, 47, 54, 55, 59, 70
sociology 22, 35–6
Solow model 283, 385
Solow, R. 361–2
sophistication (mathematical) 33
South Africa 244
South America 276
South Korea 216, 217, 229, 260, 267, 272, 277, 294
sovereign debt crisis 192, 301, 306
Spain 23, 270, 271, 307
spatial metaphors 393–4
Spearman's rank correlation coefficient 295
specie-flow adjustment mechanism 354
speculation 58, 131, 133, 265–6, 322, 347
spending power 43, 53, 70, 204
Sraffa, P. 59, 62, 63, 64, 66, 171, 192
Stability and Growth Pact 202, 306–7
stagflation 343, 385
stagnation 24, 128
standard of living 173, 271, 359, 360, 361, 365, 366, 373, 374–5
state of confidence 162
state(s) see government(s)
statistical records 154–5, 213–18
Steindl, J. 129, 130, 132
Stiglitz, J. 27, 122, 335

stock 88, 100, 124
stock market 126
    booms 123, 128, 129, 133
    crashes 119, 121, 128, 344
    financiers 131
    prices 325
stock options 324–5
Stockhammer, E. 328
Stolper–Samuelson theorem 266–7
Stout, D.K. 289, 325
strong sustainability 363, 364, 365
structural budget 202
structural change(s)
    economic development 212
    multisectoral Thirwall's Law 294
    non-ergodic systems 369
    unbalanced growth and 216–17
    and unemployment 180
structured financial products 324
student debt 327
subprime mortgage market/crisis 138, 140, 299, 307, 326
subsidies, to promote exports 273
substantivism 334
supermultiplier 43, 59, 66, 67–70, 72
supply curve 49, 50, 53, 54, 62, 125, 158, 166, 345
supply and demand
    economic theories 43, 48, 49, 51, 53
    and full employment 45
    imbalances 337
    of labour 156
    long-run growth 218–20, 229
    of money, and rate of interest 125
supply price 50
supply-side limits to growth 230
supranational currency 301
surplus 33, 34, 57
surplus principle 43, 60, 61, 65
sustainable development 359–76
    debate over 'strong' and 'weak' sustainability 362–5
    defined 359
    economic growth versus 365–7
    EU objective 305
    heterodox economics 363, 369–71
    investments for 371–4
    role of capital in 361
sustainable economic development 222, 368
sustainable economic growth 222, 227
sustainable indicators 359, 374–5

sustainable public deficit 206
Sveriges Riksbank 103
Swan, T. 361–2
Switzerland 70, 81, 323, 324
symmetric adjustments 353
sympathy 41
system of national payments 192
systemic crises 141

tableau économique fondamental 55–8, 59
Taiwan 277
TARGET2 system 308, 309, 311, 312
tariffs 268, 272, 274
tax revenue(s) 165, 194, 195, 200, 201, 203, 206
tax systems, progressive 200, 201
taxation 163, 165, 178, 363, 364–5
Taylor rule 135, 146
technological innovation 276
technological learning 273, 276
technological progress 178–9, 181, 227–8, 232, 271, 272
technology 373
technology-intensive sectors 294
temporary unemployment 157
terms of trade 260, 263–6
Tharnpanich, N. 296
Thatcher, M. 23, 386
The Theory of Moral Sentiments 41
theory of the monetary circuit *see* monetary circuit
'there is no alternative' (TINA) 23
'think globally, but act locally' 364
Thirlwall, A.P. 284, 294, 295, 296
Thirlwall's Law 286, 287, 294, 299
thrift, paradox of 38, 46, 161, 225–6, 391
time 82, 202, 281, 338, 370
Tomaskovic-Devey, D. 330
'too big to fail' 140, 142
total demand 27, 128, 138, 139, 190, 336, 340, 342, 343, 344, 349
total saving 225
total supply 190, 336, 343, 349
total utility 48
tradable permits 363, 364–5
trade agreements 273–5
trade balance 260
trade deficits 268, 270, 271, 308–9, 313, 350
trade imbalances 164, 268, 269–70, 271, 278, 292, 307, 308–9, 313, 350
trade liberalization 260, 273–5

trade surpluses 164, 268, 269, 270, 278, 292
trade unions 26, 28, 30, 34, 37, 45, 54, 156, 167, 182
Traité d'économie politique 48
Trans-Pacific Partnership (TPP) 275
Transatlantic Trade and Investment Partnership (TTIP) 275
transformation problem 62
A Treatise on Money 171
trend output *see* long-period or trend output and employment
trickle-down effect, economic growth 366, 372
Triffin, R. 301, 310, 315
troika 311
trust 98, 110, 114
Tugan-Baranovsky, M. 358

unbalanced budget 202
unbalanced growth 216–17
uncertain expectations 159, 162
uncertainty 26–7, 64, 85–6, 89, 90–91, 123, 152, 223, 299, 369, 370
underconsumption 336, 355
    overproduction versus 338–42
underinvestment 325
unemployed resources 120
unemployment 54, 128, 168, 385
    asymmetric information and 122
    definitions 173, 180–82
    heterodox economics 183–90
    natural rate of 157, 158
    orthodox economics 182–3
    temporary 157
    trade and 268, 270–71
    wage cuts to reduce 383
    and wages 52, 62–3
    see also involuntary unemployment; mass unemployment; voluntary unemployment
unit labour costs 269, 279, 306, 343
United Kingdom 118, 121, 122, 127, 213, 214, 286, 322, 323
United Nations 152, 363, 375
United States 23
    central bank *see* Federal Reserve
    economic growth 24, 213, 214, 220–21, 226, 227
    financial sector/system 118, 121, 122, 127
    financialization 322–3, 324–5, 327, 328, 330
    income distribution 244–5
    inequality 366
    international trade 163, 267, 268, 270, 271, 273, 275

as issuer of international medium of exchange 354
monetary policy 139, 140, 144
overproduction 343
unemployment rate 168
unsteady growth 217, 223
Uruguay 274
utility maximization 44, 48, 156, 382, 384

valuation 367
value
of firms/companies 120
neoclassical theory of 62, 234, 238
see also labour theory of value; labour value principle;
shareholder value
value added 277
van Treeck, T. 328
Veblen, T. 128–9, 367
velocity of circulation 136, 137
Venezuela 274
Verdoorn's Law 227–8
vertical specialization 278
voluntary unemployment 53, 173, 180–81

wage(s)
consumption and profit realization 129
cuts 383, 395
determination 45, 60–61, 241, 340
dual nature of 342
flexibility 240, 383, 386
necessity for fairness in agricultural 58
resistance 290
rigidity 156, 240, 383
see also factor payments; social wage
wage rates
and productivity growth 343

see also average wage rate; money wage rate; real wage
rate
Wall Street 348
Walras, L. 49, 237, 384
Walrasian theory 45, 49, 50, 52, 72–3
weak sustainability 362, 363, 364
wealth 234
excessive accumulation 46
financial 117
societal well-being and stock of 250–54
wealth distribution 233–55
conflict over 34
financialization and 330
heterodox perspectives 246–50
introductory remarks 235–6
mainstream economic theory 236–41
monetary policy and 141, 143
new macroeconomic approach 250–54
wealth effects 128, 143, 328
Wealth of Nations 41, 75, 98
Weintraub, S. 299
Weiss, A. 122
welfare economics 368, 374–5, 380
welfare states 163, 165, 166, 221, 241, 254
well-being 250–54, 255, 330, 359, 360, 361, 368, 374
Werner Plans 302, 303
Wickens, M. 384, 395
Wicksell, K. 81, 125
workers 33, 34, 84, 85, 247, 250, 330
world income distribution 245–6
World Trade Organization (WTO) 274, 275, 277
World War II 70, 221, 274, 335
Wray, L.R. 116

zero rate of interest 140